THE
FOUR-CORNERED
FALCON

Creating the North American Landscape

Gregory Conniff

Bonnie Loyd

Edward K. Muller

David Schuyler

Consulting Editors

Published in cooperation with
the Center for American Places,
Harrisonburg, Virginia

⮌ The Four-Cornered Falcon

Essays on the Interior West and the Natural Scene

REG SANER

THE JOHNS HOPKINS UNIVERSITY PRESS

Baltimore and London

Grateful acknowledgment to the editors and the staff of the following publications in which, with the exception of the book's title essay, earlier versions of the essays first appeared: *American Voice*, *The Best American Essays, 1991*, *Georgia Review*, *Gettysburg Review*, *High Plains Literary Review*, *Michigan Quarterly Review*, *New England Review/Bread Loaf Quarterly*, *Ohio Review*, *Southwest Review*, and *Western Humanities Review*.

Endpaper photo: From dyptich-panorama titled "From Island in the Sky, Utah, 1991," © Charles Walters.

© 1993 Reg Saner
All rights reserved
Printed in the United States of America on acid-free paper

The Johns Hopkins University Press
2715 North Charles Street
Baltimore, Maryland 21218-4319
The Johns Hopkins Press Ltd., London

Library of Congress Cataloging-in-Publication Data
Saner, Reg.
    The four-cornered falcon : essays on the interior west and the natural scene / Reg Saner.
        p.   cm. — (Creating the North American landscape)
    ISBN 0-8018-4449-5
    1. West (U.S.) — Description and travel—1981–   2. Landscape—West (U.S.)   I. Title.   II. Series.
F595.3.S26   1993
917.8—dc20   92-14212

For Anne, who came with me
into the mountains

In the United States there are more places
where nobody is than where somebody is.
That is what makes America what it is.

—GERTRUDE STEIN

And what is Earth's eye, tongue, or heart else, where
Else, but in dear and dogged man?—Ah, the heir
To his own selfbent so bound, so tied to his turn,
To thriftless reave both our rich round world bare
And none reck of world after, this bids wear
Earth brows of such care, care and dear concern.

—GERARD MANLEY HOPKINS,
"RIBBLESDALE"

CONTENTS

PREFACE

This book began many thousands of years ago, epochs in fact, as does everything: with ice, for example, crashing down by the mega-ton over summits of granite. That such ice had no thought of me, or the mountain gorge its slow-motion apocalypse was creating, or anything we know of didn't prevent the following pages from beginning with a day spent just hiking and looking around in the enormous furrow it ploughed.

Images of my being there then found their way into a journal I've kept for years, so as to keep vestiges of such days alive. The journal was private, and yet—like all journals—it secretly hoped for a reader. Each time I leafed among entries in their bright red binder, on the other hand, most felt so laconic, so tersely focused on details of plants or animals or equipment—cross-country skis and waxing conditions, tent weight, snowshoes, terrain elevations, packs, food, insect repellent, rain gear—it was clear that what I'd valued in this or that outing was *there* all right, but encoded. Even if its clipped phrases opened, for me, on all manner of sights the actual words didn't say, they'd have meant little or nothing to others.

With an exception. The journal's latest entry, that one about the mountain gorge, was neither laconic nor technical. Instead, it had been written for an expatriate named Jim; crippled, housebound, and living—of all places—in a working-class suburb of Florence, Italy. Our acquaintance there had led to correspondence. My "day well-spent" had first been a letter to him, simply because it was such news as I had. Then, for my journal, I restored a lot of detail that my friend—a stroke victim and a dear, simple-hearted man—wouldn't have made much of. Yet because the original impulse had been to help a fellow American many thousands of miles away *experience* Colorado as I had on that especially radiant day, the journal's latest pages suddenly weren't matter-of-fact any more.

Having left the typescript of my latest journal installment where I leave a lot of things—lying around the house—I went off to work. That afternoon my office phone rang. The caller was my favorite voice. She had read the manuscript, and, though she'd never visited those scenes, had relished my account of them in terms taking me by surprise. Still, the writing didn't quite fit any category I knew of. Who but next of kin would care to read them?

The letter to Jim had been so enjoyable, however, that I found myself becoming a sort of double agent whose other allegiance was to a carbon copy. My journal now had a reader, an actual one, a shut-in far from the West I loved and wanted him to know; to know firsthand—as we both knew he never could. Cards or notes from his Italian wife and two Italian-American sons arrived now and then, emphasizing how much my letters meant to Jim, how he looked forward to them. My nagging sense of duplicity eased, yet didn't vanish. "After all," I rationalized, "they *are* my news, they *are* what I do and care about. What else would I write? Food prices? Politics?"

Though Jim and I continued swapping letters, they and this book soon diverged. What I mailed to the tiny apartment on Via Lorenzo Viani grew again appropriately chatty, newsy, haphazard—as was fitting—with only random comments on golden eagles or meadow mice. As for the book, an impetus of deeper concerns quickly took over. Pages accrued. Western terrain had long stirred in me a fairly passionate impulse to witness. There were also abiding curiosities that had wanted satisfying. That meant going to look. In turn, that meant taking time which—or so my conscience kept hinting—should've been spent on less grandiose enterprises than trying to see what I was part of. On the other hand, a lifetime has always seemed too rare, too surreal an opportunity to throw away on success.

So much for beginnings. As essays in this book neared completion, my favorite voice and I were invited to Villa Serbelloni, Italy, a cultural center run by the Rockefeller Foundation. Daily life overlooking Lake Como was, by unanimous agreement of the villa's lavishly pampered guests—whose countries varied as widely as Thailand and Estonia—an enchantment inside a dream. More to my purpose, looking at American space and the West from Europe lent the perspective I'd counted on in bringing the manuscript to completion.

Auspices continued good. While in Italy, I was invited to join a Utah search for peregrines, which led to the book's penultimate essay. To have begun with a mountain gorge and a marmot-mentioning Roman called Pliny (never thinking beyond his cameo appearance in a few early pages); then several years later to find myself enjoying Pliny's native shores, while actually completing what those pages began— well, that almost implies benign intervention by some portly Roman ghost.

Also, help came from some very generous mortals. The favorite voice, for example, who knew from the first—far better than I—that her man wasn't cut out for a desk job.

In another, less personal instance, women and men making up the University of Colorado's Council on Research and Creative Work granted travel money that fueled my 1978 Volvo wagon through many thousands of miles of American space. The same university's Graduate Committee on the Humanities generously provided airfare to Geneva and back. Then there were the editors of reviews and quarterlies, whose ongoing interest lent confidence; more than my self-doubtful side could ever have summoned. On the biblical principle that the last shall be first, there has been the editor of the Creating the North American Landscape series, George F. Thompson, whose vision rekindles trust in what is often called, warningly, the real world.

Other kindnesses included that of Jeff Mitton, a biologist at the University of Colorado, who knows conifers as only a professional can. I'm grateful for his perusing "The Mind of a Forest," by way of checking its scientific basis. Clayton White, another biologist, this time at Brigham Young University, read "The Four-Cornered Falcon" with the same purpose in view. Ted Walker, a geologist well-versed in eolian sand and sandstone formation, read "The Ideal Particle and the Great Unconformity." William Weber, foremost among Colorado taxonomists and, happily, himself a member of the Linnean Society of London, was kind enough to read "Naming Nature." Their gifts of time and expertise evoke in me a gratitude not merely formulaic. Any errors of fact that may have crept in are, of course, mine and only mine.

Efforts to save *Falco peregrinus* have by now spanned a generation. They were begun for the falcon's own sake, but its sudden, unprecedented decline was also recognized as a warning to *Homo sapiens*.

Hence the title essay of this book, written when the bird was still officially listed as endangered. Just as my manuscript was going to press, however, the Peregrine Fund recommended that *Falco peregrinus* of the Southwest be removed from the endangered category and listed as threatened. Ominous as "threatened" sounds, the change is auspicious. It signals that mating pairs of our four-cornered falcon have made a partial comeback to their former numbers. A peregrine's cry isn't very musical, really, but it's one whose brightening future I am delighted to end this foreword on.

THE
FOUR-CORNERED
FALCON

Pliny and the Mountain Mouse

∽

Dim though his brain may be, the marmot feels winter will come soon. And long. Longer than any of his previous twelve. From each of these, gaunt after seven or more months of hibernation in a rocky burrow, he has wakened; to at once waddle forth, to rummage spring snow for juicy alpine tundra plants, to mate, to sun, now and then to frolic with others in his chummy colony, and—properly fattened—to reenter the burrow: again to sleep away winter.

His "language" of gesture and squeaks is enormously older than words; but no European language names even the continent this particular marmot lives on. His region of high rocks hasn't yet been discovered by Old World tongues, though one day it will be called "colorado" by men speaking a version of Latin. That his home among granite chunks sits twelve thousand feet in the air, with superb mountain views on three sides, the marmot-brain translates to *always*, and *always* to *is*.

Even for this marmot, whose sense of history isn't wider than body fat and the sun's present height, today's rise and set of sky is numbered: August 24, A.D. 79.

You and I aren't here yet. At such altitude, nobody is. In A.D. 79, "nobody" is still only Indians. "Somebody" is only a marmot. Cool wind, blowing lightly out of late summer, licks his pelt. Opulent tufts of cinnamon fur lift along the plump back, slur a moment, subside. Because in the warmish afternoon, his ridgeline is only just dappled by the fast blue shadows of cloud-faces that mythologies copy, this marmot suns. He lies full-stretch on a rock slab. To stir himself overmuch would burn off precious fat his busy incisors have nibbled all the brief tundra summer to acquire, so he moves only his head, in those quick, darting glances small animals learn from their instructors the foxes, the coyotes, the eagles.

Close cousin to groundhogs and woodchucks, the high-country *Marmota flaviventris*, or yellow-bellied kind, often relies on talus-piles of granite to provide fortresslike burrows only a bear or wolverine could dilapidate. Such hideaways protect the numerous offspring, five or six to a litter, which by summer's end are full grown.

Does the marmot breed to defeat predators, or do they prey on his colony to defeat his fast breeding? The answer is part of that circle whose opposites create each other; the molecular keys in the blood, the living shapes taken by time. A ravenous hawk; a slightly ludicrous bag of fat fur. Appetites that have learned how to repeat themselves. To what end? None that any living creature—now or to come—ever will know. To be. Each to do its kind.

Seven thousand miles to the east, in the Roman resort town of Herculaneum, guests leaving a dinner party find their way home through moonlit, sultry, sea-level air; air that thickens to an indigo blur across the Neapolitan bay toward the naval base at Misenum. There, sweating out the dog days of August—even at night—sits Pliny the Elder, a science writer whose tireless goose quill nibbles away at the creamy blankness on a fresh vellum. Pliny is himself fat as butter, and sweats as if he were melting, but he is as usual hard at it well before dawn, an omnivore of other men's books, which—he frankly admits—his own writing feeds on, just as his compulsive quill-nib feeds on blank vellum like a tiny animal storing up fame.

Among stones of a continent Pliny never heard of, the marmot has eaten back his lost bulk hardly a day too soon, and has almost finished lining his burrow with tundra grasses gathered for stuffing into the sleeping chamber as insulation and nest. Food will be body fat, however much his summer's nibbling has managed to accrue. And high-country autumn comes early. He knows it not as a name but a time when his world begins entering more into shadow. *If* the oncoming winter is neither too deep nor too long, his body fat will suffice.

During hard winters, however, dormancy proves a risky survival device. One marmot in five either freezes outright or starves. Among the small mercies of nature, on this twenty-fourth day of Augustus, is this particular marmot's blindness to his future. Breeze tousling his glossy pelt doesn't tell what it hears: that the oncoming season is coming to kill him, turn him to stone. And to quench the others sharing the family burrow.

Heat haze of southern Italy, moon-silvered. Pliny sweats, dips his quill into an inkhorn, and shares the same ignorance.

Just now, however, his scientific compulsion spurs him to update earlier pages of his already voluminous *Natural History*. Pliny is inserting some new facts about marmots, which he calls Alpine mice: "Some people say they form a chain and let themselves down into their cave that way, male and female alternately holding the next creature's tail by the teeth. One, lying on its back, hugs a bundle of grass and is hauled in by the others. Consequently at this season their backs show marks of rubbing."

Pliny's view of human life is rather gloomy; mankind as he knows it staggers along from misery to fresh misery, ruin to ruin. But the natural world! As inexhaustible as fascinating. "Some people say" may sound, he is fully aware, hardly better than gossip; yet nature is so prodigal of oddities that one's wildest guess may prove too tame. Like the haymaking marmot his pen has just described, Pliny's habit of reaping truth from old books and storing it up in his own year-upon-year scribbling, book after book, rules his waking hours so compulsively he hardly spares time to bathe, much less to ask himself, "Why?" Nor will he ever.

He never will, because what neither Pliny-the-nature-writer nor his friends across the bay in Herculaneum and Stabiae foresee is, simply, "Nature": in a few hours the trim, vineyarded summit of Vesuvius will blow sky high. In a few hours, Pliny's concern for those friends and his scientific curiosity will combine to strangle him. Soon, on the undiscovered continent of which Pliny knows nothing, a particular "Alpine mouse" will waddle into his burrow, plug the entrance with small stones and hay, then begin a winter trance no summer can waken.

The same incurable yen that draws Pliny unaware toward his suffocation saves his nephew. Before setting sail across the Bay of Naples for his fatal lesson in vulcanology, the uncle invites Pliny the Younger—an eighteen-year-old—to come along if he wants. In aftertimes, by then an author himself, the nephew will recall, "To this invitation I answered that I'd rather continue studying. Besides, as it happened, my uncle had assigned me an essay to write." Writer's itch runs in the family.

At twelve thousand feet along an unknown continental divide, the night of twenty-fourth Augustus opens with snow crystals flying past; ice migrations of white flies that sting like salt. Meanwhile, along the Vesuvian shores it is finally morning. All night a hailstorm of pumice has scorched the roofs of Stabiae, piling up, drifting. A cinder snow that smokes. Roof beams crack and collapse, house walls totter.

By the seashore Pliny the Elder gulps at the air, supported between two slaves who lay him down on a scrap of sailcloth. He calls for cold water, drinks it, flops back. By now volcanic ash has begun its steady, floating fall. It descends soundlessly. Panicked Romans scatter the stuff as they run, stumble, collapse. Lightly, the ash begins to clothe each fallen body. In a few days it will smother the town. Years hence, in a reminiscent mood Pliny the Younger will sit—obese as his uncle— pushing a quill across vellum: "Three mornings later his body was found on the spot, intact . . . more like a man asleep than dead."

Three mornings later it is evening in another country, whose mountain sun has just set. Lofty ridgelines looking down into their own lakes see that sunset dismantled. Summer-plump, backside ruddied by alpenglow, the marmot stands hindlegged atop his rock, forepaws snugged against chest-fur, nose whiskers twitching, brown eyes staring east. He gives a reedy squeak. Answered by another . . . then another. A marmot "harem" and colony, a dozen in all, talking to themselves. They've harvested tundra plants, almost enough. How hard they've worked their worn pelts show: the narrow squeeze to and fro since mid-summer, carrying cut grasses past snug entrance rocks and deep into the burrow, has scraped their back-fur haggard.

A trained and patient ear, or a marmot's, could identify as many as six distinctive variants on the shrill calls that led ancient Alpine people to nickname these animals "whistlers": Calls of "Eaglehawk!" Calls of "My rock, not yours!" Calls of "Fox!" Calls of "Love *me*! Love *me*! Love *me*!" Calls of "Wingflown! Foxgone!" No wonder their silly, piping squeaks this evening are almost musical. After a gestation of about a month, the summer's young have reached full size of six to ten pounds in just weeks. Only the last of the haymaking remains. Abruptly the east-squinting marmot, boss male of the harem, falls silent. Up out of the distant, alluvial, proto-Coloradan plain floats a great fullness, a moon pale as winter; pale as a sun made of snow.

We can be here now. It's our turn . . . to be, and be curious. We know all about Pompeii, Stabiae; know Herculaneum too was buried.

Oh yes, volcanic detritus enclosed many of the dead so perfectly that—in modern times, once Pliny's contemporaries had, as it were, evaporated—plaster casts could be made of their living absences. Lime-white, like snowmen. Startlingly "us," therefore touching. Theoretically. Anyhow, we ourselves avoid erupting volcanoes.

And, yes, it is poignant—in theory—to think of a marmot family in its burrow, like a banked fire; each furry curl asleep, nose between hind paws, like so many embers ashed over. Winter sets in: the marmot body temperature dips to about ten degrees above freezing. From pulsing twice every second the hibernating heart slows to half that. Then slower. Finally, as much as a full quarter-minute or more goes by . . . between beats.

During hibernation marmots rouse, stir somewhat, then sleep again—unless their body fat runs out, or winter cold runs too long too deep, and the tiny heart ceases. As when a lit match, held upright, weakens till its shrunken flame seeps back into the matchhead; a glow, a red cinder—suddenly black.

But the small, distant deaths of animals common as wind don't sadden anyone. No more than we're saddened by all the once-upon-a-time crickets and dormice ashed over at Pompeii. Besides, those life-like but plaster agonies recovered from Pompeiian dailyness are of folks who would have died ages ago, even if Vesuvius's summit hadn't smithereened. Centuries *are* distance, aren't they?

Of his unswerving industry, how much did Pliny expect would survive? Apart from his considerable military service, he wrote a work twenty "books" long on Rome's wars with Germany, wrote an eight-book text on rhetoric, penned a lengthy chronicle of his own times in thirty-one books, and crowned his literary achievement with that eccentric museum, his *Natural History*, gleaned from authors and treatises innumerable. Time, which called Pliny out of the dust into sunlight, and which lent him his encyclopaedic curiosity, has ground nearly all that to powder. He knew well how "Nature" begets and devours us, just as Chronos ate his own children. Of Pliny's written mind, only the *Natural History* has made it all the way to now.

As for his year upon year of curious labor, might some lost remnants exist as an undetectable nuance in what the European mind has become? Surely so. However, such consolation feels cheerless as a cubic meter of interstellar medium: one or two floating atoms, the rest a black vacuum.

Which makes Pliny's compulsive curiosity, despite his patchwork and pack-rat science, all the more touching. Laborious days and nights belied his own glum estimate of the human situation. We survive by not believing what we know. Is that because our unconscious knows something truer than fact? Maybe it knows that what we most admire can't die, including the best of ourselves—which we don't invent, merely inherit or borrow. And which, like the world, is nobody's possession. Is wavelengths, passing through us.

And passing through those wilderness creatures that cold will freeze solid this winter? A gnat is the weight of astonishing centuries, surely as a finch wing has been shaped by however old the sky is. But our emotions require of objects a certain size to help bridge the gap between them and ourselves. Where's the line to be drawn? At bugs on a windshield? By no means even then. So says reason. Reason says the line must be a circle wide as our minds.

So when it comes to the spark in all animal hardihood—meaning ours—I often see an outcrop on Colorado's continental divide. To think mountains "majestic" we mustn't inhale overlong their bone-barren summits and crazed smash-ups of rock. A few hours, or days; then clear out. Nothing has been here since the beginning, but great crags pretend they have. They pretend we living things aren't here at all; or if so, mere passing fancies of the sun. Even in midsummer their petrified light can chill, so winter near their summits can be—in the root sense of the word—terrific. To look at ice cliffs long, and in storm, and alone . . . kills the heart. Nonetheless, atop one uppermost slab near the Corona trail suns a lone marmot; sluggish, dim-witted, inconsiderable, heroic.

Straight overhead the sky is an ultraviolet blue so intense it verges on purple. Late August sun drills down. Light breeze pours over the divide, ruffling the marmot's pelt, glossy as a chestnut. Moment to moment his head winks north, winks west in quick, circumspicuous caution. The sunning torso, plump as a loaf, doesn't stir. He sees me, and sees me keeping my distance. He has no idea.

He knows nothing, really, of the success of his own species, doesn't know that his ancestors reached North America from Asia, across the land bridge spanning what is now the Bering Strait, and were at home here, just like this, when Pliny the Elder wrote and Vesuvius erupted. Now found all over the globe, he has gone where not even the map can go, hearing rivers that had never been heard. He has been snared, trapped, poisoned, and shot: for his fur in Mongolia, for his oil in lands diverse as Switzerland and Siberia. Under the guise of woodchuck he is thought a mere varmint and thus—in much of the United States—an appropriate focus for gunsights. His avatars waddled about and snoozed beneath Pleistocene skies of the Ice Age. He is content to live where little else can. He endures.

How could he know that I, the biped who under a backpack leans slightly forward and stares, admire his stamina entirely? How could either of us foresee that his serio-comic, jawless profile, his buck teeth, twitchy nose whiskers and sluff of a tail, his wide-eyed blinkings and lookouts for predators will combine with the twelve thousand foot altitude to make his silly bump of a figure not only wholeheartedly dear to me but—long as I live—half immortal?

When did humans first find the marmot amusing? Pliny's account seems to have been written with a smile. Certainly the mountain mouse—as the French tongue still names him—once delighted Europeans visiting the fairs and markets where animal trainers entertained; among the camels and tame bears, spectators could see many a humble marmot "dancing" to flute notes played by its keeper, often a child from the Tyrol.

Amusement, however, did not prevent Alpine dwellers in modern times from hunting the slow creature almost to extinction, both for its fat—reputed to cure rheumatism, among other ills—and for its pelt. As late as 1944 an estimated sixteen thousand marmots were killed in Switzerland alone, till naturalists persuaded pharmaceutical dealers that marmot-annihilation would benefit no one. Though belief in the curative powers of marmot fat still persists among folk of the European Alps, the animals have dodged the threat of extinction. In contrast, Mongolia's Bobac marmot breeds so fast no such threat exists—despite the millions of furs annually harvested there, and the many hundreds of tons of marmot fat. And despite the fact that Mongolian marmots often carry plague.

As for me, before and since, I've seen marmots by the hundreds, seen their low profiles flow over or peer out of rock piles from here to the end of the world. In Alaska's Brooks Range I made my first acquaintance with his species by way of a raided food cache the critters gnawed into. In Switzerland's sole national park I've watched marmot youngsters wrestle each other repeatedly, as we did when kids, for the sheer fun of it, toppling, flopping, grappling each other and rolling together downhill. That Swiss pair didn't behave *like* human kids. Their play-wrestling seemed *identical*.

On a frosty mid-July night high in Colorado's Gore Range the weird roar that woke me was marmot incisors munching a hole in my empty Nalgene waterbottle. One twilight evening just below the 14,200-foot summit of Longs Peak, bright marmot-whistles seemed to match the first few stars like question and answer. A mile from the crest of Arapahoe Pass there's a particularly untimid marmot who, as I approach, rises hindlegged to his full height of some eighteen inches and, in exactly the same spot, tries to stare me down. Amid that shattered labyrinth of stone chaos, his world and home, what a bold fellow he is! Since marmots live but a dozen years or thereabouts, his annual defiance feels huge. We gaze at each other. In our silence much seems possible, though nothing much happens: two creatures, looking a little farther than themselves.

But that *other* marmot surviving miles away on the Corona Trail—why should he, a dozen years after my glimpse of him, continue to seem so special? There where the left hand slopes away as alpine tundra, half meadow, and the right hand is sheer fall, hundreds of feet down to rockscapes ugly as slag, down toward acres of grit-littered, permanent snow, my emblematic marmot at first seemed no different from hundreds. It's just that, to remember what sheer courage looks like, my mind's eye often invokes him.

There, under a sky barely fly-specked with ravens, and atop a jut of flat granite, he suns. Wind ruffles his fur. He blinks, peers around him at nothing. At what there is. His instincts and eyes, his nut-brown pelt, his nose and paws, all seem shapes taken by a design whose true name I don't know—any more than that dim creature knew his. Which I see, now, given his Old World origins, might as well have been Pliny.

Glacier Gorge

L'homme est la vision du monde dans l'amour de
l'instant qui les a créé l'un et l'autre . . . Il veut être l'âme
des circonstances qui l'ont fait ce qu'il est.

—J. BOUSQUET

No clouds, no wind. One of those calms the halcyon bird gave its
name to; a fable—whose floating nests defined seas barely breathing.
But this morning is autumnal, whereas those oceans, leveled to mirror,
marked winter solstice in myth. Fit weather for a radical enterprise: to
spend at least one day of my life as if it were precious.

So, wanting to see what such a day might contain, I follow an October trail with fallen aspen leaves on its breath. Though I call my aiming "Black Lake" I'm hoping further. On the vast stone shelf above it sits
a large tarn named Frozen Lake, which I've seen only from Longs Peak,
three thousand feet higher. Even then, on the summer solstice, June 21,
Frozen Lake was indeed frozen. Its stone shore was grey as lead, only the
vaguest stain of green here and there on its edges, like mold round a
bathtub. Gorse? I suppose. What animals, if any, might live there? I'm
curious to know, but the question's merely a pretext.

Since I've not hiked in months, everything I see juices me. I rise
through aspen groves whose fire-bright yellows dither and stipple. My
pack feels companionable. Among the darker, evergreen thickets, single aspen burn sunlight like flares. A few sheltered trees are still lettuce
green, summer not drained from their leaves, whereas windblown
groves stand half naked. Black muck puddles the trail where the rare,
rock-country life-bits have gone rotten and oozy.

An Easterner could cure homesickness by kneeling, inhaling nostalgias of leafmold; however, with rock the rule in Glacier Gorge, humus the exception, its scarcity recalls the start of our world, when things that weren't human humanized us before we were ourselves. They do so still. This wild gorge bestowing huge insignificance on anything alive and in motion is a good place to feel what we are. So I love hearing its skimpy life-zone of peat thump under my boot; inches beneath lie vertical miles of granite. And from a strange book by a cryptic Frenchman, Joë Bousquet, a line of print comes to mind: "Every event contains the universe." "True enough," I admit, "if you know how to put it there."

Oh, like anyone else, I smell in the leaf-rotten musk of October the fragrance of things drifted off into nowhere. Childhood . . . a grandfather long gone, raking heaps of maple leaves we kids leap into. Yet I'm in granitic Colorado. For all their gold, their autumnal dazzle, this grove's whole season of leaves lie sparse as a poorbox of dead pennies, without body enough to cushion a footfall. Still, the aspen's wan and slender trunks always move me, as if creatures who used to be women.

Above, against clear blue sky, wracks of cumulus stall at an invisible border in the atmosphere, unable to cross the Divide. Peaks such as McHenry's, Mt. Alice, and Chief's Head wear a dusting of new snow on battered faces. A raucous crow draws my eye, which catches sun flashing blue-black off its wingspan. Higher, a hawk glides, gloating hungry—above tremendous cliffwalls where snow-rifted faults show emotions in magma older than rain, older than reasons, and autumns not quite beyond counting.

Geologists tell us when and how this very gorge was ice carven, ploughed by bergs whose violence helps us recall days we weren't anywhere, and that factuality helps our presence here echo. Though the distant crags seem iron-bleak, I pause in my stroll across ballroom-size granite plates matching October: warm browns, tawny oranges, salmon pinks. I kneel to test a smooth passage the Ice Age polished to a glaze, and my right hand—after ten thousand years—is impressed. It rubs lightly to and fro, under inconceivable tonnages.

They remind me what hikes are good for. Lately lost in routine "usefulness," I'd forgotten. Daily, dutiful habit is our way of keeping possibilities small. Not now. Only a few miles from the car and my life takes on the size of gorgeous warnings. Everywhere I look is an adventure. I step uptrail to see how far the world might be true without me.

Second-hand vision is none at all, but aiming the 24-millimeter lens of my Pentax, I'm shameless. I shoot overturned root systems that are already photo-clichés, yet I love their ice-wind and crystal bitten textures, their still squirm of bare bones that have lived out a great-hearted evergreen's story on little but rock, where roots can only spread out, not down. And here their secrets, uprooted at last, contort; flat as a wide open flower, a Gordian blossom.

I focus on a ten-foot root display of hard times and wood. Come winter, as blast-velocities spiked with razorlike crystals roar down off the peaks, they nick an overthrown spruce's root burls into high relief. On such wood the raw Siena tint won't dull to the stone grey of roots exposed in more sheltered places. Won't be allowed to.

Uptrail I pass between twin domes of granite like paleolithic breasts—three-hundred-foot bulges strewn with loose rock, with scraggly limber pine testing crevices for depth. These "knobs," as the map names them, mark the entrance to a six or seven mile trough called—for good reason—Glacier Gorge. From the trailhead's 9,200 feet, the stupendous, crag-serried furrow rises toward Black Lake, but only 1,400 feet higher. From there to Frozen Lake another 1,000, with few steepnesses over the five or six miles.

A hiker's apparent goal is, say, a remote lake or a summit. Really, however, isn't the aim trail-rhythm?—through climbs, windings, dips, and switchbacks we don't want to come to the end of. Munch of broken stone under bootsoles, rhythm of legs and lungs, pleasures of sweat; rhythm of unrepeatable, chaotic forms that recur. As if of some design just up ahead that never appears as itself.

Ever since our world was a circle, hasn't any footpath, long river, road, or caravan route—like this trail—always been a becoming?

For a long while my fascination with Bousquet puzzled me. The last thirty-two years of his life he was paralyzed from the waist down. Most of those he passed in a single, shuttered room in his grandfather's house; Carcassonne, 41 rue de Verdun. Often on difficult hikes I'd imagined him there, immobile. Then I realized a link: we'd each been young infantry officers in combat, he in the France of "the Great War" and I in the so-called "Phoney War" of Korea. He was crippled, whereas I was superficially nicked. Through chance and unconscious pull, probably, Joë Bousquet, long dead—whose odd novels none of my friends and few Frenchmen have ever heard of—grew into one of the people I know. Do I walk partly for him?

When we take a person into our memory his dying doesn't in any way evict him. Often, hiking in mountains, I've seen Bousquet abed in his room, Carcassonne, using written daydreams to explore thirty-two years of never walking again. But he was too frank an ironist for twaddle. I walk for myself.

There's a blizzard-topography you learn by skiing this gorge. Its autumn knobs, gulches, slabs won't be themselves this winter; snowed under, disguised. Thus in summer I've stared upward into the maw of a side canyon explorable on skis, yet felt I'd never been there. Then, if I really concentrated, I could fill it with snow. Whereupon I remembered having skied up it, maybe a half a dozen times. Then too, light is a place. Its rays, tilting toward summer, can make us strangers to our own winter footprints.

Mills Lake and its satellite Jewel Lake are a half-mile of reflection gone blind, mostly iced over, though their span of open water stays darkly alive and breathing. At the far end, boulders with mastodon curves wider than cabins remind me of one wind-bitter day last January, which made sightseeing a bit like sunbathing in Greenland. When I'm miserably cold, I learn little but cold, and what blowing snow does to visibility; a deep lesson yet narrow. So maybe John Masefield was right, "our happiest days make us wise"—by virtue of being more spacious?

Yet I have to taste such weather to know what these trees go through. Their courage can stop me mid-stride, in that way we may admire a profoundly beautiful thing with something like despair.

Take bristlecone pine. Their high-altitude growing season lasts a month or month and a half. They eat, besides light, just granite and rain, but they grow through such limb-and-trunk postures as Prometheus might have writhed into during his chained ages, exposed on the barren Caucasus; as if endurance were its own torture. And they live long. Along Methuselah Walk in California's White Mountains grow bristlecone trees older than four thousand years. I look at one struggling like Laocoön with the python, then realize some bristlecones antedate Rome and Troy; older than myths they remind me of. Tree-ring samples from a living bristlecone in eastern Nevada show it may have begun growing nearly five thousand years ago! So you can stand there, can touch its live body, and know not even the Jewish nation is half such a veteran of sunsets and dawns.

Yet photosynthesis slows as bristlecones age and add more dead wood to their trunks, and this one seems barely alive, with a crown whose green needles I could almost number. Studies suggest that its great age requires adversity; the stone-bare surroundings not only prevent plant competition but keep fire danger low. Then too, a given bristlecone isn't so much one tree as a whole family tree, because its few branches, before dying off, kindle living ones.

Past Mills Lake I come to a soft surprise. After the ramshackle hecatombs of granite corroded by lichen, and pine; after rock-knocking my bootsoles over nothing but stone muted by pinches of dirt, and odd muddles of bog, I reach the one garden moment in this whole gorge. Here a micro-climate cooperates with a rare patch of level terrain to offer marsh. Out of its squish, dry and coppery autumn grasses flourish. Their October hues and the turning blades of kobresia travel a year-cycle whose very colors are motion, throwing themselves away the better to do it again. No end to beginning.

Nothing wasteful in seeds and creatures to burn. The end is quintessential and endless excess, a lavish verve seen equally in nearby thickets of Colorado spruce, which litter the place with cones that will slake nature's thirst for the future. If the aim of coyotes is coyotes, and the aim of trees is more trees, maybe Zeus was a lie, Prometheus. Maybe only the fire is real.

Could Bousquet, as his friends claimed, *really* have forgone all self-deception? By eighteen he had threatened a restless despair with "morphine, cocaine, ether," until—spurred by what he later saw as a strong death wish—he "threw himself" into the French army: Twentieth Corps, 156th Infantry. The numbers march as you say them. In war, a body of men is your address. Mine: Twenty-fifth Division, Fourteenth Infantry Regiment, First Battalion, Company D, . . . the Iron Triangle, the Punchbowl, Heartbreak Ridge, Sandbag Castle—gathering, every blue moon, into one somber wave that wants to be tears; the irrational tide we call sorrow. So maybe Bousquet's useless legs—once young as we all were then—got mixed up with that. Yet, laid low, he spoke of "true joy like the sun itself, lighting my desert island."

Though my boot welts are silicon-sealed and their uppers well-proofed against water, I take advantage of logs offering their accidental bridges over the spongiest places. It's a long hike that begins in wet socks. One of my trail pals swears that the test of a real outdoorsman is feet still dry after three days of rain.

Beyond this mud Eden surrounded by cataclysms of granite, the trail toward Black Lake steepens, obstructive and rugged. Good. My bookish nature delights in doing what I can't do, haven't the energy for. And exertion *creates* energy. "Only begin!"—that's the great secret. Once through the first wave of fatigue, a stronger self comes out the other side. "Only begin." And *up* is a positive value. To ascend in mountains keeps height before your very eyes.

Simplistic till you think about it. As humankind, our first thought in darkness is "don't fall." We speak of "higher" forms, of high life, low life, low language, of hipsters addicted to uppers and downers. Our athletes play over their heads. Wall Street brokers who deal in peaks and troughs of the world-market stay on top of things, watching Third World governments rise and decline, hoping something good will turn up. Merely saying "aspiration" lifts us off the ground, just as "plummet" fills the tongue with heaviness. When the year began to die, our Anglo-Saxon forebears said "fall." As life returned, they said "spring." Clearly, the ascent of humankind, in swapping a quadruped's horizontal spine for the vertical backbone of Homo erectus, altered our moral axis, reversed gravity's tireless pull. Made it a source. Prompt as instinct in a baby trying to hold up its head, the will upward *creates* us.

That's why the upward urge of mountaineers, though simple, isn't prolonged adolescence only. Besides, any rising trail leads beyond moral allegory. It's emblematic. In high mountains it's a year in a day, a climb from summer to winter; or a walk from now up to the world's bare-bones inception. Rising through forest, through the refrigerated soup of marsh, through and past timberline onto tundra, and beyond that onto bare rock scumbled with lichen, I enter a world populated by cairns the height of stone people, entirely outside of my habits, like things standing around in our sleep.

Under summits that can resemble an endless crime, I take pleasure in fear without harm, though there's little daring involved. Yet a lone hiker traveling partly by hand among such rugged fragments feels his or her existence somehow "valorized." Is that adolescent? Somewhat. I'm here now perhaps because as a Midwestern boy I'd have loved it but couldn't. Had no idea. By just hiking here I amaze him.

And the very trees amaze me: a seed-kernel of Douglas fir finds it no trouble to drive this thick trunk a hundred feet up from stone, till the green tree itself takes over; drawn by some desire it returns toward the sun-source. Heady pine-scent from trees leading the hardest of lives makes me wonder why so much of humanity's smell is sorrow. I notice

how a fir's last several inches lift and point like a hand whose aim at the
sky is perfect.

In shade ten feet to my right lies a toppled spruce seedling on a fat
slab, bearing maybe one mossy shovelful of humus far too meager for
even three feet of tree; so the tree lives now on its side, with much of its
root system exposed. "Just resting," it seems to announce, "till I can
think of something." Like a small opinion on what ought to be here.

"Yes, Bousquet, every event contains the universe." And every deep
moment is ancient?

The last few hundred yards to Black Lake are steepest. I do some
boulder hopping, stumble a bit, rattle prickly furze bushes whose blue-
jay stops in midcry, turning wing-smoke and whir. At a shelf lip where
the lake's outlet cascades in ice-heightened glitter, I'm swept by a
steady rush of cold wind wicking away my nimbus of sweat-vapors.

Once on the east shore, however, I've moved from chill into a sort
of pocket meadow with clusters of Douglas fir. The surrounding cirque
that created this lake seems steepsided as a crater. For sheerness and
vertical pitch its hieroglyphic crags take me aback each time. No
matter how often I come, they remain unknowable, utterly "other."
Their very distance seems a completion. We admire wild places because
their forests and mountains meet us as exactly what *they* meant to be;
blessedly forlorn, among many strange ways in which the world keeps
its promise.

The broadest couloir down from Arrowhead, a 12,600-foot summit
to my right, is an avalanche route. In winter you see shattered timbers,
rock trash jumbled with boulders of snow, bush-gobbets; thunderous
disarray fallen silent. Above Thatchtop's westerly ridgelines like amnesiac deities, a layer of light cirrus, backlit, rainbows and fumes but
can't cross the Divide. I've seen that abrupt border between cloud and
clear sky—cold air and warmer—hold firm as a shoreline all day, while
fast as easterly vapors drifted into the wall of warm air, they vanished.
At a confluence in Alaska, I once watched a clear tributary and the silt-
laden Tanana River keep joined waters distinct: to my left, a deep trans-
parence, to my right, an opacity like liquid dirt.

The pocket meadow is softened by marsh grasses, the same coppery
brown blades I saw lower, but wetter. From my pack I draw forth a pad
of blue foam to sit on, unwrap two chicken breasts from sunbursting
aluminum foil that momentarily blinds me, pull forth my canteens—
water and French Colombard wine—and set out my Royal Kona coffee

can in which a square of carrot cake couldn't get squashed. The sun's warm enough for basking, thus for realizing my radical aim of looking into the day for itself, not what's beyond it.

Five or six miles of rough trail seasons food, so there's a double devouring; in chicken breast you're eating proto-rivers and mountains earned. You chew meditatively. Sharp as a blade, distant skyline meets the eye through miles of thin air. I listen. A soundlessness whose smallest effect is awe; hermetically pure; a speaking stillness. Like good composers, mountains never play the same silence twice.

The silence of Bousquet's midnights. "On certain rare evenings," he wrote, "the stillness is an ocean with yet another silence inside it, one no mere noise could end. On those nights, I'm nearest to guessing the man I would've been." I mull that. This profound quiet I've climbed into on sheer luck and strong legs allows me to hear all the way to a Carcassonne evening gone speechless. Deep within Bousquet's past future, I listen to the nothingness everything comes from, and becomes.

Then I hear fellow creatures. Arctic jays—"camp robbers"—begin hustling scraps. Why of all high-country fauna are these birds most brazen? "Bold" doesn't touch it. Yet their wheedling wins pinches of whole-wheat bread, cashews, strings of breast meat. I bait my boot toe with dabs of carrot cake. Camera prefocused, I shoot frames as jay after jay swipes away with a morsel. And overshoot, because through my viewfinder the bird is a grey swerve.

Warm as it is in sunlight, Black Lake's mostly closed but for a loop of open water that, despite high cirque walls, October sun still hits like an eye. "How long till it's shut? A week? Two? Maybe one cold night would do it." Up here summer is weeks, not months. Back of me the shadow-bound foot of a near cliff is already massively iced, sheathed in pale turquoise. But from across the lake I hear waterfalls pouring off wide glacial benches like distant applause. Water's great wheel, still turning.

The arctic jays decide I'm good for more food. One arrives with a floating swerve, wings extended and slightly upcurled, like mouth-corners of a fey smile. He veers and blurts, riding a warp in the air, then brakes in a soft flurry of pearlescent downfeathers—a magician's sudden fan of cards.

"Where's the grub!"

I look at him, try imagining what's in his head. His toes are jet

black, his beak jet black, black as his eyes. On the lens of each dark eye
floats a tiny point of light. And that's the whole sky.

What does he see? I suppose a simple hedonic calculus: hiker =
food = swipe = me. Simpler yet: food = fly. I test him with chicken
skin. Sometimes they do a bit of beak-work a few yards from me. Or
right on my boot toe. As this latest fellow takes bread from my fingers, I
enjoy the prickle of beak-tip and claws. Sometimes they swoop instantly off to a bough and do mysterious numbers, dipping, cramming,
tearing. "How much actual eating goes on?" I wonder. "As for that, do
arctic jays really eat the meat they take?" I've fed them tuna, cashews,
apple, cookie crumbs, raisins, you name it. But maybe only their
swiping's omnivorous. Perhaps their eating discriminates. However
that may be, their habit of hiding food after compacting it into a ball-
like form called a bolus is well known. Given the harsh terrain they call
home, I've an impression that sooner or later they turn any edible scrap
into flight. And into more jays. Five years back I was frying hamburger
when one hustled over the *hot* skillet, beaked up a sizzling curd of
ground beef and flew off in unbroken motion. But there's a limit.

"Damn it," I mutter to a jay making a snatch at chicken headed
toward my mouth, "go find your own!" He could care less. Perched on a
tussock three feet away he watches me chew, as if to ask, "Going to eat
it *all?*"

Facing this mindless creature I forget myself enough to hope he understands tone: "Listen, you've already had plenty. Knock it off! I'm not
Saint Francis!"

By way of supposing I might really arrive at Frozen Lake, I ascend
a flow of shattered granite, the forty-five degree causeway of a summer
waterfall now barely a whisper. I climb in northerly shadow where
drifts deepen, collected by dwarf evergreen called "krummholz," groveling trees that will winter-kill unless buried alive. Soon I'm post-
holing. Not much can keep me out of the mountains, but that can. Two
steps on a drift may hold. Then a third step plunges you in, up to the
hip. In minutes, the required high knee-action fills thigh muscles with
lead, because here, toward eleven thousand feet your lungs aren't
pumping enough oxygen to them. Thighs and lungs flounder.

With snowshoes, no problem. But these October drifts aren't continuous enough to make snowshoes worthwhile. Instead the billows are
local to the lee of a small cliff where wind turbulence builds flow patterns of snow. Knowing it will ease shortly, I stagger upward, laughing

out loud at the figure I cut for no one to see, because at times *both* legs sink me up to my groin. Though my bloodstream has forgotten its four-footed moves, I find I can't heave myself out except by crawling on all fours to lower ground pressure: Charlie Chaplin in the Yukon.

Many large areas on the shelf itself are blown snowless, magnificently bleak. All around me hundreds of boxcar rock chunks sit on granite plates, each wide as a world-turtle, mottled by centuries-slow drizzles of lichen. Down from the sides of Longs Peak three thousand feet above me the chunks have tumbled literally ages ago, and come to rest here. In them time's immense cascade has slowed to a tick. In fact, proud of their strength, which lies in always being found by eyes that so soon won't be, they return my look with disdain: "Do you actually pretend to *exist?*" I feel like a whiff of trained vapor. I look away, toward Frozen Lake. Reaching it would add a round trip two hours of zig-zags.

By now it's almost 2:00 P.M., and hours downhill to the car. Gorge depth will cut off the sun by mid-afternoon. Even if at eleven thousand feet I don't feel the French Colombard at all, Frozen Lake's too heavy to add. Some other time. All day I've been where I wanted to be, astonished. And here, now, on a stone plateau so grand and heartless it's impossible not to sense creation destroying its own beginnings, which endings have long since begun, amid gorgeous upheavals nearly brief as I am, I'm part of a pulse. That pulse is neither benign nor malign. Not "love." A force not a force, nor anything that's a thing. The formless maker of forms, whatever it may be.

Wandering down from the shelf, I sidle toward snowprints left by an earlier hiker, not because he or she knows the way better than I do, but wanting that touch. To follow someone's lead through snow isn't laziness. Alone for a long time, you can find warmth in footprints filled with nothing but a direction in common. One pair of boots making tracks is an opinion; two, a slight tradition.

But I'm soon startled. Though my foot had been stepping into some stranger's footfalls with an affection I'd never show myself, I now see the bootprints are mine—and feel saddened at my own self-distance. We're separated from the world, Bousquet felt, because we are from ourselves. Our destiny? Never to be who we are.

His military career still gives off a certain manic dazzle. He spoke of being "costumed" as a lieutenant, earned a reputation among his own troops as daredevil the devil wouldn't have, won a *Croix de*

Guerre, along with other citations, three battle stars, the *Médaille Militaire*, a *Croix de la Legion d'Honneur*—veteran and hero not yet twenty-one. Then he got a letter from his girl saying she'd be a suicide by the time her words reached him. Though false he believed it, considered himself already killed, and abandoned what little caution he'd exercised: a silent movie. Except, war isn't kind to brave gestures. The German bullet grazing his spinal cord reached it through his chest.

As a farm town boy moving from B-B gun to .22 rifles to the gift of a 20-gauge Browning, I didn't guess hunting might be our male excuse for walking around outdoors. As for Bousquet's considered view of war, I don't know; just know that if enough voices call the other side "enemy," a young man might believe it. I fired at a difference in cloth. Some of our bloodiest notions we've sewn into flags.

Toward Black Lake I'm surprised to spot a man and woman flycasting along the unfrozen shore. Earlier I missed them. They must've been hidden by trees.

"How many times," I wonder, "have I been here without seeing anyone fish?" Despite my floundering, they don't hear me approach. The man, forty-five or fifty, is intent on stripping line from his reel. Nearing the woman, I ask, "Any luck?" expecting a negative shrug.

"Oh yes," she says, "plenty of fish here." Indeed. They've already caught half a dozen beautiful rainbows, laid out on snow. "Spawning," she explains. "They come up toward shore to lay their eggs." I stare into the pebbly shallows, see nothing. Rainbows, I'd thought, spawn only in spring. The caught fish are real enough. I'm half-mesmerized by the wet gleam of trout, liquid silver on snow. Set off by the near-white of their plump bellies, there's an amazing swash of *brilliant* red. Arterial red. And perhaps really blood, a wild flush that goes with spawning. "My god," I think, staring down at their succulence, "all I'd need is salt, pepper, and a fork."

We talk about how close to ice that lake water must be. By this time the man meets my curiosity with trout-lore, though I keep flicking sidelong glances at those silvers and reds on snow. As I move off to try glimpsing live fish in the shallows, an arctic jay swoops down near the trout.

"He's trying to get the eggs," the woman tells me. I note "he," and guess the jay has larger ambitions than roe.

While we're staring at the bird, her husband catches another trout.

Its scales look flashy as mercury—contrasted by its slash of blood-blazed skin. Tossed onto snow, it flops, powdering itself with crystals the cold fish-blood doesn't melt.

The man holds it for me to examine the jaw's forward jut, characteristic of rainbows. He too admires the creature. Then, using both hands, he whaps the very head we've just studied, whacks it hard against a boulder. The trout slithers from him and writhes, flecking the snowcrust with tiny spatters of red. The flycaster scoops it up for another whap. Harder this time. No further motion. He lays it alongside the other trout like a man relishing treasure, both hands agape and sticky with trout goo. The jay hops only a bit to one side. The man studies the bird, which cocks its head to study him, then the fish.

"Well," he says to his wife, "we're going to have to do something with them."

At the lake's outlet where its spill begins so many downhill miles over stones, through bogs, ponds, pools, Jewel Lake, Mills Lake, and back toward the sea, I pause, turning slowly, as if to look at something that will never quite happen again.

Maybe October does that to the blood. The season itself seems to be saying good-bye, but it's we who pass, as this world passes through us. Bousquet was "back there," really, along with World War I uncles: a sepia snapshot, a doughboy grinning, holding up his drilled pocket Bible and the bullet that pierced it.

A grey lodgepole pine catches my eye. Bark-shorn, limb-stripped to bare pole, its dead trunk remains faithful to the slow spiral which some people call "timberline twist," a contortion that its grain learned from past forests, and perhaps—though the causes aren't really known—from wind.

Continuing downtrail I enjoy far more than usual the tumbled postures of granite, the muck-muddles sucking my bootsoles. I stop dozens of times over pools, looking for trout, hoping a few will add themselves to the afternoon. Not one. It's as if the stream had wealth it's withholding. By now it's 4:30, the sun long gone back of lofty walls, creating a gorge of wide open shadow over sky-blue snow whose breath I inhale as high-country chill sharpens the air. At a fan of water falling over stones that have grown nodes of bright ice, I stop to refill my canteen. On stones there are ice lenses, refractions. As water slithers underneath them, icelights sparkle along that sloshing, half-freezing cascade of runnels and freshets. The ice knobs are like armor whose nodules glitter. Or like transparent crustaceans that bleed and congeal.

At Mills Lake the trail acquires an identity crisis, believes it's twins, then triplets. I try first a lower, lake-rim version, soon leave it for a higher path more opinion than trail, and conclude their difference is identical. Again by the lake's edge, I note the floating forest of logs which wind has jammed into a chaotic raft at the outlet. They've been floating there while years of ultraviolet skies dyed them deadwood blue, windfallen blue, as if a dismantled armada. The lapping lake-edge of broken ice tinkles like wind chimes near a couple of young women who lounge on a grey-green platter of mossed granite, and talk. Above them a nuthatch feeding upside down twitters among cones of a Douglas fir.

The women are twenty or so, neither pretty nor plain. The redhead in a yellow windbreaker has her legs propped on a log while discoursing. About friends? Hannah Arendt? Embryology? I try to catch a phrase or so, but don't much care that I can't. It's enough that fellow creatures are enjoying "my" afternoon, in a moment unconfused by males. Males—no matter what—have the women's groins somewhere in mind. I've always resented that tyranny, felt used by it, as if nature's blind urge cared less for my wishes than a carpenter for the feelings of nails.

Despite my almost never daydreaming of women, a sly voice from some locally omniscient tree inquires, "How many women would you want?" Before I can answer in person, that masculine rapacity—mindless as any jaybird—has blurted, "All. I want them *all*." Long after I chanced on Bousquet, long after his useless legs and my sturdy ones fit into one thought, I discovered his mystic-carnal obsession with females, the one illusion he never abandoned.

To "want them all" isn't sex, though it begins there, and rises, unconsciously reinventing Plato's ladder of love. We begin as animals, want things that as animals we can't imagine, and, over evolving eons, become the kind of animal which can imagine them. The gullet and groin "transcended," though vital to the transcending: no dirt, no flower.

Is blind desire the beginning of eyes? If so, what would it see in "all women"? The Great Mother? For me, somehow, every evocative landscape contains something "all women" embody to withhold, and offer. To offer the withholding. An ageless motive, this trail; this journeying outward to one's inner self. Is that what I'm doing here? Walking toward a flawless woman only my faults could create? I sense maybe so, but consider also the kinship in Latin between *mater* and *materia*, mother and matter. Our natal, uterine soil.

About this rockbound Glacier Gorge, I'm not so sure. At the moment its sparse fauna condense to one snowshoe rabbit whose coat shows, amid a suspicion of brown, black hairs turning white for the oncoming winter. Her paws, fluffy as pom-poms, make her *sound* soft to the eye. Even motionless her whole body has a soft sound. She sees me now, but doesn't stir. As if to say, "Listen, with these four or five months of winter I'm facing, you are *no* problem. I've got to sit here and think this thing through. What to eat next, and eat next after that. In fact I should be nibbling something right now."

Again I pass by the indomitable green of bristlecone pine whose gnarls make me for a moment hardy as they. Knobby and strained as a weight lifter's back, their torsos *will* themselves up, out of the rock, while in contrast the bark is sometimes pink-skinned as new potatoes. Nothing can kill them.

I slide my hand over the smooth bark of one bough, just as, coming uptrail, I slid my right palm over glacial polish left on that granite plate—myself touched by its glaze, sensing the ice oceans that rode it. A sip or two could be circulating right now in me. In who knows.

Strange—this nostalgia for ourselves as inanimate matter, of which my brain consists, enlivened for a while by some solar quirk. Yet brain molecules never quite feel that molecules are all they amount to. The brain's neo-cortex stays lunar years ahead of the blood; nonetheless, even blood-wisdom tells us, considering our situation in a world only on loan, our highest reason is a joy not wholly glandular. Glacier Gorge easily knows how to kill me, and may, and doesn't care either way; yet in it I feel less alien than "at home," feel a natural delight so prompt, so animal, it might be encoded. As if we had receptors for it. As if, along with our fang-and-claw survivalisms, we're also coded for wonder.

Gradually the rhythm in hours of walking becomes a true story. Do we turn the world as we walk? From science I remember the proof that an artillery piece, recoiling, budges—however infinitesimally— the planet itself. If there were units of measure called "infinitesimals," Earth's budging under my bootsoles might amount to one ten-millionth of one. But reality itself *is* motion, even in its motionless twig bits and pebbles. On this trail I've followed clear back to my boyhood, I study somebody's recent bootprint in mud, already filled with long, delicate stars of frost. It too moves with the late afternoon.

Anaxagoras, who reasoned—with a certain logic—"*All which now exists, or will*, must have dwelt (implicit) in time's primal atom," might say each of our living moments is—hypothetically—ancient; and has been traveling toward its unfolding called "now."

Thus when I round a bend that reveals some arresting, trivial detail—a root system so contorted you have to be brave to just look, a grey bird that won't take "No!", pine marten shucking a fir cone—I come upon a voice that's been woven of every prior event inside creation, since the primal atom: my own silent cry of surprise. This time it springs from crosslight raking an entire forest. The glacier that furrowed this gorge out of mountains aligned it north and south so that crosslight from the setting sun I can't see now picks out each branch on a thousand ten thousand trees swathing Bierstadt Moraine. The westering sun carries a warmish tint not yet golden; still, the trees aren't so much lit as illuminated. And speaking. To a man who had a day to spend, and spent it—on nothing better than seeing what is.

Once home I'll sip coffee, my head floating inside its own wilderness images as if I were still half here. I'll grin. Anne, my wife, won't be sure what for. I'll be too tired to be analytical, or recall my childhood amazement on first discovering, low to the ground in farm machinery at the end of my grandfather's fresh, Illinois furrows, a curved mirror reflecting the field; a steel mirror, shaped as a ploughshare.

The Magpie Scapular

The main thing: that it go on. The antecedent of "it" being "Things . . . you know, everything." Most of all, though, unspoken, we mean "Let it go on with us inside it." Oh, we *do* know, there'll come a day. The day. The one that doesn't.

When I step out our side door, the U.S. Geological Survey tells me that my foot comes down 5,640 feet above sea level. This morning, strolling upslope through grama grass, gumweed, and long-stemmed kobresia on our backyard mesa, toward my personal shelf and lichened slab of sandstone, I need every lug on my bootsoles. The icy uphill trail is newly powdered with six inches of snow, that snow lightly flecked with blood. Some coyote with a cut paw, most likely. Crystallized by the snow almost instantly, that blood hasn't oxydized to sombre red, but is still a bright scarlet against the white.

"My" shelf? "My" slab? Other mornings, yes; this morning, no. What with the ice, I look up only on arrival—where exactly atop my spot lounges a yearling buck, ruminating. I mean literally ruminating, chewing his cud with that sideways grinding of the back molars that reduces silica-laden browse to mush. Enzymed and twice-chewed roughages thus become stuff a mule deer stomach can dissolve.

It's a free greenbelt (gone late-November brown), so how can I complain? But one of my eccentricities is dawn: my Book of Hours, ascent of the heart. By walking for a full 120 seconds or so, southwest up the mesa footpath near my door, I can enjoy the panoramic sweep of Colorado's high plain—treeless, unbroken—over which the sun will soon rise, nothing between us. I like that. Enormously. To watch the

24

sun rise that way, out of the sleep of matter, from the sea or up out of the ground, is to stand in the middle of the world.

So I wake, drink *caffelatte* by the quart, read a bit, then go out— often puzzled by the emptiness of our streets, their dark houses; as if each person abed were certain dawn would happen again.

"It always has, hasn't it?" Yes. Which may be why I think of dawns that'll happen without me. I think, too, of blind chance, its accidental filaments fine as root hairs that have grown someone named "me" to be part of dawn's moment. So I've dressed and stepped forth into morning twilight: my "self," a movable circuitry of Here, Now, This . . . with those inveterate escapes into Elsewhere that create our true nature.

The view-thief who's taken my place isn't human, probably cares little for panorama, except insofar as openness gives stalking coyotes and mountain lions a tougher assignment. His head wears yearling spikes, two; which will recur, annually augmented till he has the full rack of a mature eight-point buck. Just now, however, his eight-inch antlers look as silly as a boy-man's fuzz moustache.

He heard and saw me coming, but hasn't budged. Typical. Our Boulder deer have grown so domestic they all but eat the cat food, and this yearling "spike" is a mule deer of true Boulder greenbelt breed. I close to within fifteen feet, then twelve, then less than ten, expecting at every step he'll up and leave. Oh no. He ruminates; he looks me straight in the eye—as if saying, "First come, first served. Take it on up the trail, Buster."

On up the trail I take it—another forty feet, and make a stand. While waiting for the sun's glint to break the rim of our vast Colorado plain, I suddenly notice the young buck has a friend. Ten yards south of him, near "my" stunted Ponderosa and some mullein stalks poking up chest high through blue snow, lies a young female, nonchalant as he. Though it irks me a bit not to await dawn from my ritual spot, the usurper is after all a deer. Two deer. Whose lithe and silent kind roved the mesa centuries before Columbus. *I* am grumbling at *them*?

These November mornings, the weedy mesa slope wears its autumnal-tawny look mixed in with winter, all of summer's greens and juices having gone off into the machine of the seasons. Yet summer's designs are most visible seen against snow: the hardy fragility of Indian rice grass, of brome, oat-grass, not yet beaten flat by winter. Each stalk outlined. Dark leaf veins. Husks of the minutest panicles. The slight, finely drawn slash and hachure of tall, ocher stems. Spray after spray of seed heads whose delicacy makes my stepping through them rich with vandalism. They float over snowcrust, each seed a historian carrying the past into the future—and not just one sunrise inside each, but millions, which like that moment we call "the present" have acquired the trick of forever dying into life.

I face eastward. Widespreading and level, or ever-so-vaguely undulant, cougar-colored expanses stretch 180 degrees before me. Their horizon, literally an earth-line. If I'd climbed a bit higher to Dakota Ridge, I could glance one hundred miles south to Pikes Peak. As it is, in the mauve and burgundy sky over Denver's Stapleton Field, the fly-specks of DC-10s float all but motionlessly into their approach patterns. Even thirty-six miles distant any landing lights aimed this way make them mechanical stars. Immediately at my back, mountain foothills tilt enormously: red sandstone's abruptions. Their carnal hunks and faultforms are thick with snow-whitened pines climbing wherever the big stone isn't, right up to 8,200-foot summits. How recent the Pyramids are! Not these. On any one of my given days, their power and height can still put a small pause in my breathing.

It's true. We're gifted with dubious grandeurs of context. Within which, geologically or sidereally seen, we've the knack of hyperevanescence. My particular set of heartbeats, my yard and a half of trained skin, the Gordian Knot evolutionary time has tied in my particular cranium—all hoping not to die out of a life as brief, almost, as that of gluons or mesons.

I was taught to be everlasting. Craftsmen in the art of heaven drilled me on it, as did twelve years of admirable, ivory-linened women, Dominican nuns. How my thought lifted up in the name of unleavened bread: the elevation, the rising over the altar of God's body—a pale, a wafer-thin moon baked by Sister Mary Gertrude in the convent oven. Nowadays, the slow ascent of dawn's solar disc, like a Host escaped from all god franchises, gives truer focus to my origins. Yet bored as I become with St. Augustine's groveling god-blather, I do love the verve and size of those words beginning his *Confessions*: "Great art Thou, Oh Lord, and greatly to be praised; great is Thy power, and Thy wisdom infinite. And Thee would man praise; man, but a particle of Thy creation."

What would dawn be without colors more fugitive, far, than those on a hummingbird's throat? Over the high plain an early rose madder blurs into tangerine, which rises, in turn, toward a midnight blue just dissolving its last dozen stars. Winter, summer, and round again, the full spectrum of dawn is a hummingbird with 365 feathers.

Perhaps my snufflings or boot-shufflings in snowcrust ruin the doe's concentration. Haunches and hind legs first, she stirs, extends her folded forelegs, then eases downslope. The male looks, ruminates. He too gets up, slowly follows his one-girl harem, both rumps bearing the white blaze mark of their species. Wildlife biologists conjecture some survival advantage in that highly conspicuous whiteness. Presumably it facilitates single filing through forest gloom; fawns do indeed spend months traipsing behind mother, long after weaning. Against the advantages, however, I count my own experience in spotting deer—easily, and at considerable distances—by their white rumps. If I can, so can predators. But mule deer, being a most fruitful species compared, say, to grizzlies, can afford losses that would wipe grizzlies from the face of this earth. Do some adaptations simply break even? Any living form is, I guess, still experimental; in this evolving world no form is final.

Thus the least lichen blot or chaffinch is a "transform," to use Gregory Bateson's term; or, to adapt a current buzz word, everything we see is "polysemous"; transforms of messages. So the young buck's annually replaceable antlers send one message to his doe friend, another to male rivals, a still different message to us, but one including those others.

Female deer probably don't think of a buck's antlers as an elaborate spur or rake, but that's how they work on his women. When the buck signals by lowering his head, he coerces now this doe, now that doe. With his array of pointed bone, he needn't touch any female in his seraglio. He herds them before him by gesture, nuanced intimidation. And they obey. It's enough that a doe sees his head dip, senses those antler tines aimed toward her. "OK," she says, "I'm going. See? See? I'm going." All the females do. They trek along so meekly, are so invariably "cowed" that I'm at once humiliated for each, and deeply ashamed to be male.

The sky's clear, fairly cloudless. The presunrise east brightens toward the ripeness which, in my eye, is always a birth and a gift. And the gift of a mystery. In a barn of red brick built on medieval lies and great wisdom, I remember, as a boy, rising to questions posed by a hugely important visitor, our bishop. Sprays of white lace. Aroma of frankincense. Gregorian thrums from the choir loft. Illuminated by stained glass fables, cassocked and caped by the shifting grain of watered silk, the bishop swayed in his episcopal crimsons. He let my lips graze on the gold brand of his ring. Then, as part of my Confirmation, he asked, "Who made you? What for?" And, "Where are you going?" Tongues on all the lit candles quavered. My boyish treble rose half an octave in the sing-song of rote memory. I answered as drilled, parroting verbatim evasions conned from the Baltimore Catechism. They bring a smile now. If they've confirmed anything in me, it's an inquisitive skepticism.

Facing east, my body is a silo of days and other arterial dawns, other horizons whose pinches of fire I look out through: time's reticulations webbed in the synapses of an eyeblink. Cortical neurons, used, abused. Yet poised for adding to my store one more dawn that death is never going to have.

True enough. Still, I don't know how we can honestly say the living are luckier than the dead. We do say it. But honestly? Living things want to go on living, that's all we can say. And admit we honestly don't know which is best. In the nature of things nobody can. At times haven't we envied the unborn? Haven't we even imagined ourselves as one of them, our bodies blissfully asleep, made of and infused with some dark, uninterruptable nothingness. Neither happy nor sad. Thus happy.

Dawn helps us not to envy oblivion made in our image, on whose familiar features the seal might have remained forever unbroken. Antaeus drew strength from being cast down by Hercules, hurled to the maternal dirt, whose invigorating touch made him rebound all the livelier. Greek myth says his mother was Gaia, or Earth; but in that story I'd say his mother was courage. So we phototropic organisms drink the clear, pure waters of dawn and are solaced; because dawn is an enactment of hope, and hope is our healthiest skepticism. My own darkest night-thoughts begin dissolving when the sky brightens, then—as light slowly reopens lakes east of here—my heaviness gives way to the sun's first touch on face and lips.

Maybe that's animal. A couple of sunrises previously as I walked round the southeastern side of this mesa I counted thirty-five mule deer awaiting dawn with me. A few browsed; most lay on the snow, their winter coats rimlit from the expanding radiance of our eastern horizon. In the crisp air each creature exhaled dimly visible wraiths of vapor.

Since half my existence unfolds in a spoken world occurring *within* words as they occur within me, I can't deny that some of the light I go out to meet, morning after morning, derives from luminous filaments leading into and out of a syllable. When we say "dawn," "sunrise," "daybreak," each word is a memory system of implicit motion. Our nouns for dawn are verbs. Yet the luminous movement each distills is one that our memory only imagines, because often the words themselves do the remembering for us. In "dawn," in "daybreak," live moments creating more than there is.

The all but unbelievable complexity of, say, a box elder's root system exemplifies why words can't be transplanted; that is, translated. How could I explain even to a Japanese fluent in English exactly how *dawn, sunrise,* and *daybreak* aren't synonymous? Digging *dawn* up from English involves such wholesale tearing of its special root hairs, that almost all our connotative relation to that syllable has to be left behind in its native soil; the living flesh of speakers born into English.

The transverberations in a word. Just as some forgotten childhood whim can last a lifetime in secret, so all language is filled with lost discoveries. In *dawn,* in that word's imaginary magic, there's archetypal brightness our inner use of its sound builds upon, like a saint's halo and bones encrypted at the bottom of a church.

Twenty years back, with deer herds rarely larger than a dozen or so, Boulder's environs lacked many predators. Now, about two hundred yards away, my binoculars pick up the motionless stance of a coyote; poised, lurking. His pelage warms to fox-red with the warming light, and blends so well into shaggy swatches of fieldweed that only chance backgrounding by snow kept me from overlooking him. Deer having become the bane of all gardeners near Boulder's westerly edges, my wife's hope of ever seeing her plantings unruined by their gourmet habits partly depends on coyotes—and on the occasional mountain lion.

Yet a lone coyote can't be after deer. He glances my way, sees me, but like a trained setter on point doesn't budge. Has he sniffed out a mouse? If so, he's got competition right overhead.

Through the binoculars I track the wide circles of a prairie falcon soaring above the coyote's patch of meadow. Its wing feathers share blond and rust and burnt umbers of fieldweed, pine bark, and red rock, as if Earth's grasses had, over epochs, lofted into the sky a sharp eye with talons.

Unaware, the coyote remains fixed, intent. I've seen a coyote stalk, pounce, scuffle after, then swallow up to seven small rodents within fifteen minutes. I'm about to turn aside from this one when he gives a mighty leap into the air, floats suspended a split instant—back arched, all four legs stretched straight down. What's he pouncing on? Deer mouse? Vole? The second he lands, his forepaws begin shuffling snow, but whether he sorts out a rodent I can't tell. He noses elsewhere; then, with his walk soon breaking into an easy lope, disappears over a rise down into Skunk Creek gulch. Maybe to regurgitate, as wolves and coyotes do, the morning's catch for his pups.

Looking back to the falcon, I'm greatly amused. That lofty raptor excretes a silvery filament of about a meter long, falling, vanishing while still 150 overhead. Though it may be coincidence, the timing seems inescapably an insult to the coyote.

By now undersides of clouds that earlier were berry stained with light's first blush are flooded with hot pink. Our snow mountains, their upper ridges only, go infrared. The east glows, exudes a range of tints that seem liquid, drinkable, pristine. And I realize that in me dawn's root system may include not only hominid atavars, but—far closer—a juvenile pastime using mumbo-jumbo imitations of Latin.

They were part of the kid-liturgy my little sister and brother and I devised. Using cider or Kool-Aid for Mass wine, swamped in the chasuble of a father's old overcoat, I was the celebrant who mugged, who mimed sacerdotal motions. Things blurred; what we mocked was also a threshold of awe, of enigma. To signal the elevation, Paul—who at age five was server and half the congregation—tinkled a little brass bell our mother still has. Whereupon, mumbling false Latin, I gravely raised the Host of a soda cracker.

Looking up, now, toward a westering moon I smile at my occasional memory quirk of making its pale shape Eucharistic, the viaticum. Which in a way sun and moon both are. Partly from years of genuflection before gold-plated, Host-exhibiting vessels of lavish sunburst-design called monstrances, I often see the solar disc rise as the one true, holy, and apostolic elevation.

Metaphor quickly evaporates, however, in the face of a star. Ours, typical, is classed by astronomers as a Gl dwarf. Sweltering at the bottom of the Grand Canyon I've wryly pondered the fact that Earth catches *less than half of one billionth* of that dwarf's outpour: a holocaust of X-rays, of ultraviolet, of rays visible and rays infrared, of radio waves, and, who can say, maybe infra-audible ones we hear without knowing. Oh yes, though the sun rises quietly as a rolled eye, in the mind it can roar. I've always felt that. Whenever I've put a shell to my ear, its distance wasn't the sea's, but the sun's—burning, burning. My inner ear feels that solar force as so instantaneous, so immediate, I find it hard to imagine the truth: that the sun's energies, born of the nuclear fusion at its core, require not minutes, or days, but *millions of years* to reach its surface. Another unreal reality.

Far from the paragon that alchemical ages held the sun to be, it too—as everybody knows now—is mortal. Helium ash builds up at the sun's center like snow falling inside a volcano. Transgalactic otherlings may one day study our daystar's surface by flashlight while walking around on it, provided they're hyper-gravity proof. Meanwhile, solar gold is easy enough to come by, till one day it's there and we aren't.

Of solar hues, however, my favorite is the tinge of green where— like a faint impulse dying at the border between moods—its aura barely differs from brightening yellow, below, and the clear blue just above. Color that pure, though derived from the solar core's ancient history, is nonetheless fresh to us. It asks what we are, and more. It asks what we might be.

How punctual the dawn flights of magpies! Each morning just before sunup they fly down from nests among the back-of-town mountains with gaudy, bird-of-paradise swerves; with dip-and-glide descents making a smooth succession of linked plummets that go beating and falling, cawing past me downhill—like surpliced and cassocked acolytes, or sleek Dominicans rushing to their places. As if without them dawn couldn't happen.

Gorgeous and silly, that's how I see these plump-breasted members of the family *Corvidae*. Fluffing down onto a ponderosa limb, or taking flight, they throw themselves wide open. Up close their neck feathers iridesce black dawns of deep bronze, green, and purple. Perched on a ponderosa limb, their jaunty black tail feathers cocking and winking for balance seem a foot long. Against black velvet bodies the white tibial feathers dazzle, as do the long black-and-white scapular feathers and mainly white primaries. Since North American magpies occur only in the American West, tourists from more eastern states invariably startle and ask, "What on earth kind of bird is *that*?"

"A crow that's swallowed dove," I think but don't say, half regretful that a bird with such breathtaking plumage is cousin to carrion eaters. In recompense, magpies—like crows and ravens—have a high IQ. "Hard to trap or catch," claims my friend Denice Arthur, whose ornithology is of the hands-on variety. "Once you've trapped a magpie," she has told me, "you can just forget about trapping another specimen in the same area. They won't go for it." I recall Denice rubbing her scalp reflectively, soothing old wounds inflicted when magpies once mobbed her. "Hurt? You bet it hurt." Those lovely black beaks can and do kill small mammals. When a magpie chases a squirrel we're amused, but the magpie may not be kidding and the squirrel *knows* it's no joke.

To my left where five deer cluster near the lip of a ravine, two magpies dive into pine boughs. They flicker among evergreen needles a while. Then one swoops onto the back of a grazing doe—who doesn't interrupt feeding. After beaking up a few ticks from the doe's squirrel-colored coat, the magpie then flutters exactly between the ears of a buck—who soberly wears the bird like a hat, or a sudden idea more outlandish than his antlers. The second magpie now flies down onto the vacated doe. Far from trying to shed or shrug off these arrivals, deer seem to welcome their symbiosis. Apparently magpies will even peck maggots from an animal's festering wound.

A cluster of five come flocking overhead and blurt three hundred yards further down past my mesa-shelf, squawking and cawing toward the tall cottonwood. There they suddenly open and close like tropical blossoms reverting to buds, and strike up conversations. Another three choose Peters' honey locust, whose twig-tips they descend upon and cling to like springboards subsiding—as if maybe they enjoy the ride. And maybe they do. Faintly I hear the lot of them chattering, congratulating themselves. They've swapped dark nest sites among evergreens for this better view of the sky's peach-and-magenta tones. So we and the deer and the occasional coyote make up dawn's audience. Us regulars.

In another few minutes the sun will look us directly in the eyes. Its huge, sidereal splurge is about to happen, and that prospect often excites me to the point of trepidation. Even fear.

For many years now, I've often said aloud certain lines of poetry which seem dawn-appropriate. Lately, a short poem by Blake, containing the lines, "O Earth O Earth return / Arise from out the dewy grass . . . " At first I'd say its words only sometimes. They seemed pleasant, fitting. Then doing so began to seem a rite, a requisite. If I were almost late for dawn and huffing uptrail I nonetheless felt the need to say them—however pantingly—*before* the sun actually arose. And I had found thereby how easily a grace note might turn to superstition, a personal quirk harden to cult, obsessive and fixed. What began as one of dawn's effects might easily grow to seem its cause. In saying the poem aloud to myself and to the dumb sun, I had found how a primitive lit-urgy might be born. My misspeaking one word meant I had to begin again. Then again. Till I got it right. But who on earth would know? I would. And "something." If "something" did, then what? Ill luck? Surely the primitive mind would have supposed so. If saying "dewy grass" amid snowdrifts makes me laugh, too bad. "Dewy grass" it must be. No extempore variants allowed.

Thus, over the span of months, not centuries, I observed in myself a curious regression toward archaic thinking. Among traditional Hopi and Navajo, to this day, mistakes nullify the rite. Which must begin again. From the beginning. Otherwise? Bad medicine.

Even so, I enjoy the "liturgy" of a few lines spoken—Blake, Hopkins, Bishop, Dickinson, Shinkichi Takahashi, Shakespeare, the neurotic but forgivable St. Augustine. Words to no one: to November grasses and cactus; to pine cones, boulders. To the lovely dumb deer. To the vast fireball of a nuclear reactor—naked, weightless, ascending.

And to magpies. What does corvine intelligence make of daybreak? Maybe their blurting, breast-stroking descent down over a thousand vertical feet—half glide, half hurtle—tells me, "You fly for as long as you fall." Might as well. From one such swooping creature a wing feather falls, fluttering into bushes nearby.

As if picking up a loose page dropped from some hypothetical treatise, *The Book of Bird-Learning*, I stir myself enough to clamber atop or around huge red boulders to retrieve it; a magpie's scapular feather, as it happens. I've already an assorted bouquet of feathers in the coffee mug on my desk, but certain boyhood habits seem to have a will of their own. So, because even adult life thrives not on Big Deals but just such trifles, my lug soles slip on the rock's lichen-smattered nubble, dustings of snow shock my bare hands. I fetch it from among leafless twigs, descend, brush ice crystals off my jeans.

Being cautious that way, I examine the feather for bird lice. None meet the eye; instead, like sun at midnight, the black end of that feather gives off iridescence. My two fingers stroke its nicks. In the way that a magpie's bill preens, they rezip parted barbules, and sense with how slight a touch the gaps heal. Many hundreds of thousands of bar-bules, millions of barbicels and hooklets: time's web. Indeed, consider-ing its warp and woof of keratin, any bird's feather is almost literally a woven thing. Considering the time gone into it, the feather's a local infinity.

Fascination compounds itself as I observe my own brain examining barbules, barbicels, and hooklets whose weft was once simple as a snake's primordial scale. With its keratin weave, first birds caught and climbed into the atmosphere. They did it so well we often take them for personifications of air. But their rise out of reptile eons still melting to air is yet visible; the reptilian leg skin of birds reminds us they're not entirely clear of the once unanimous mud. Like mind out of mire, while continents surfaced and dissolved, the solid horn of paleozoic scales ramified into the web of a feather.

Downslope from me, that yearling buck now chases the young doe. It puzzles me to see him lower his skimpy prongs—hardly a rack— and pursue her with the quick shifts of direction I'd expect of colts or field dogs, not deer. Yet he dashes and she flees; as quick, as nimble. Their sharp hooves kick spurts of powder over weedy patches of shadowed snow still faintly grey-blue. Nor does the gap between them vary much. She won't let him close it, doesn't try to widen it. He chases her in bursts interrupted by moments of grazing. Then another flurry of either pursuit or high spirits, with the doe content to keep her young buck at a tolerable distance.

In addition to the rutting season, I ask myself, can it be the oncoming of sunrise that stirs these youngsters? I should think it might. Also, the urge to warm chilled muscle, get the blood flowing. Most importantly of course, the parentage encoded in that blood speaks to her: "Let only able-bodied males have you. Test them. Run. You're lively and quick, as were we. The buck fast enough to catch you carries good luck in his sperm."

Women create men in more ways than one. The antlers I see daily on one or another eight-point buck do indeed grow out his head like the antennae of a thought, yes; but a thought implanted there by the very female whom those antler-tines help him herd along so meekly before him. His antlers are gender issues. Hers. And she, in turn, embodies *his* thought, is literally as he would have her. The circle game. Even socially. Aren't we ourselves mainly for others? And those others, themselves for us? "Eve was Adam's dream," said Keats; "He waked and found it true." Sexual evolution in less than a dozen words.

Beyond sex, I think of the coyote seen earlier, helping instill deer with silence, alertness, speed—which in turn beget coyote silence, alertness, and cunning. Two animals, one circle. Sometimes the circle breaks. One of its halves disappears, surviving only as a trait in the other. The North American cheetah, long extinct, bred astonishing speed into Colorado's pronghorn, often called antelope. Coyotes surely collaborated with other predators, however, in perfecting the virtual odorlessness of newly born fawns, an advantage they share with elk newborns.

Recently the *Boulder Camera* reported seven mountain lion sightings—within city limits! These big cats are naturally wide-ranging; and apparently our expanding deer population has drawn lions down out of the high country. But mountain lions are sly, nocturnal. My son Tim was sleeping out at the foot of this very mesa one summer night when he woke to cries of pain: "As if some sort of animal were eating this creature—that was making these awful sounds. Like a human *baby* being eaten." Tim was young, imaginative. We said, "Oh, Tim! A baby? Come, come!" That was the end of it. Only days after, the *Camera* ran an eye-witness report of a mountain lion killing and partly devouring a cocker spaniel.

Apparently the lion—or lioness—trickled out of sight along the dry streambed of Bear Creek into a neighborhood, where she or he studied the prospect from a shadowing culvert: then pounced. Hot housedog! Giving owners of several recently vanished pets something to think about.

We humans, of course, run the risks of predation—accidental and otherwise—just by drawing breath; for example, in the lifetime of near misses we manage while roaring hither and thither at highway speeds, or by adding a new circuit to the house wiring. The barbules, barbicels, and hooklets of our innumerable, mostly unknown reprieves keep getting woven into every sunrise.

Despite the Korean War's exposing my hide to places such as Heartbreak Ridge, the Punchbowl, the Iron Triangle, Sandbag Castle, and White Horse Mountain, my combat duty with the Twenty-fifth Division as an infantry platoon leader left me—by purest accident—with a skin only slightly punctured. At the U.N. graveyard outside—was it Pusan?—I remember wandering among thousands of soldiers my age, tucked under white crosses aligned with the greatest precision. Name, rank, serial number. As I kept looking for one name in particular, I remember feeling, "Him. Him. Him. And him. And not me?"

A small lifetime ago. Still I never mention those men or that place in conversation. Merely to go near its image brings on waves of sorrow that mount like a warning; like waves of nausea telling a seasick person he's about to throw up. The waves in this case—each a bit more intense than the one before—are an incoherence of tears and fury that wants to indict somebody, blame someone, wants to *scream* at someone, make somebody *pay* . . . and can't. So it has to swallow its tears and its rage. It has to subside humiliated by its own irrelevance. It knows, despite the sincere feigning of others, there aren't any listeners. The only ones who could speak with and answer that grief, and be understood by it, are young men living ten thousand miles off, underground; in a dark beyond sympathy or flags; in disturbed earth my spoken words never go near. Occasionally at dawn I think of those men. Their eyes and my eyes look into each other.

Right and left, whispers of mauve appear on clouds that were slate colored. Reefs of nimbostratus closer to the auroral focus have begun reflecting wild orange along their undersides. Behind and high above me I see rust pines on rust ridgelines, the peaks already glowing brick red. The lower slopes, all pink snow, blue snow. And I who have collected innumerable dawns say to myself, "Beautiful, yes. But what's merely another, that its beginning should awe you?"

I'm not sure. In fact I'm surprised that it does. Or am I? After all, the factual never got anybody out of bed early. Only what isn't quite real.

Now standing atop *my* sandstone hunk on *my* repossessed spot I notice that the buck's body heat had begun turning snow he lay upon to packed slush. "They're used to it," I reason. In my nostrils, the early mile-high air is frosty. "All the same, it *is* a bed of snow." On another slope a group of five deer lie also in snow, each pair of forelegs tucked under, each body curled nose to tail like house cats. To winter animals *daybreak* and *warmer* must be the same word.

Then the coincidence of Earth's rim with the edge of the sun's photosphere burns open our horizon, and a bead-fine, red incandescence levels its fireburst straight at my averted eye: a radiant violence too pure to even be naked. Too dazzling, too utterly virginal and deadly to be "dawn." No. Dawn comes before and after. At the split instant of that first direct glint, all epochs built into my eye's design by the sun, and the sun's own birth, fuse to a "now."

Whatever I am, then, feels like a point that time has nothing to do with. I'd say it's like an escape into vision, if my nature were the least bit visionary. But no, the escape is simple as seeing. Seeing what is. An average human maze, who at other times is named me, stands simplified on a mesa and watches the truth, ascending.

A half-moment later, my post-Copernican brain makes the helio-centric adjustment; makes the sun stand still, turns the planet. It skewers Earth on the axle of a geometric line piercing both poles, then extends that line through the now invisible Polaris, and rotates me with the brown continental plate whose mesa I'm standing on; rotates us both with the roll of a fat planet inside its bubble of air, turning my eyes toward the nearest star. A daystar, hanging relatively motionless in black void. Other stars surround it, far too far away to complicate Earth's clocks by creating, each of them, its own dawn as each clears our horizon.

So much for the mind's heliocentrism. Our *bodies* happen to be pre-Ptolemaic. The body says "sunrise," the mind says "earthturn." Even while mind halts the sun's rise by rotating the planet, the body cau-tions itself, "Steady! don't fall off. We're tilting." The mind is lately; the body, poor thing, primeval, retarded. At dawn, each person knows she or he's unusual, and the only one who'll ever know it. At dawn, the mind/body sees that what's true isn't so.

"None there be, can rehearse the whole tale." Thus runs a line from the Dead Sea Scrolls. And I, once letter-perfect in verities of rote memory, ask the mind: "Tell me, you who do the knowing for me. Are you anything beyond fancy twitches inside a skull?" The mind answers, "No, not really. I'm chemistry. Traversed by something that pretends it isn't a thing."

How candid. Therefore, given our situation, any life worth living must—like the mind—contain something of great value it knows isn't there.

Maybe the origin of life is simple as that. Or at least its persistence. Like trying to make yourself come true. Maybe that's what I've climbed this mesa to believe, or rediscover, or to pretend I have. Then, as a fast magpie no different from dozens of others gives a swoop right by me, my surprise—for no reason—makes a human sound of spontaneous de-light that isn't even a word. And suddenly my motive in going out to meet dawn is clear as our desire to be created by what we love.

For that half second, my body truly believes what it knows. By the good light of morning it knows without "reasons" that our highest rea-son is the joy that says, "Yes, let these things be as they are, and me as I am now, within them."

On which subject, merely my looking around freely speaks to win-ter yucca, to fieldweeds, to a coyote now gone, and a falcon. To a young

Wind

It's snowing sideways. My skis leave a trail blown over in minutes. Good.

"Let me get this straight," says the mind's other side. "You like mountains best in December and January? When there's nothing up here but sudden weather and snow?"

"Yes."

"And another thing. Why so keen on skiing alone? The obvious motive is fear, isn't it? Alone you're afraid, a little. You *know* you are. Admit it. Isn't that the attraction?"

The mind's other side has that twentieth century quirk of supposing base motives are truest. Hence its sentences beginning, "Whereas what you *really* . . ." No use replying that a taste for the out-of-doors isn't always juvenile. Against one's own brain, what defense comes to more than a shrug?

"Seems to me," says that brain, "what you're really fond of is bad news."

"You mean the truth? And 'really,' isn't that what we're here for?"

No end to self-skepticism. Out of its duet for one have evolved the power and tediousness of our species, so my in-progress last word to myself on skiing up here alone is only part confession: "Colorado's back country in winter is tricky indeed. No secret." But when we look honestly at this world, maybe the greatest risks take place inside us.

Last week, near timberline, I skied into a high country made of exactly its own black islands of towering fir, exactly its own snow-cornices curled fantastically over thick ledges, exactly its own snowfall of fat flakes. Because the grey sky was stalled, as close to motionless as Colorado wilderness ever comes, its snow floated down almost vertically. Rare. No wind, just air leaning slightly; gentler than breath. Against dark fir trees each flake descended apart from the others, a tuft of clumped crystals, a once-and-for-all of intricate stillness made visible.

Any "This, Here, Now" so entirely taken with being exactly itself can't help arresting a lone skier, just as any mind that arrives there takes one look and stops mumbling. Stops cluttering itself with thoughts. Hasn't a name, isn't anyone. Becomes what it hears: mountain snowfall in which silence ripens.

But today, skiing Glacier Gorge, weather tries to tear off my head. Failing that, wind settles for my knit cap—hurling its burgundy wool like a limp blossom into a naked clump of dwarf willow. Fetching headgear from willow twigs while wearing skis seven feet long will improve anyone's sense of being the Unknown Marx Brother. By the time I get my cap back, snow blown into my hair has already clotted, to go along with the crisp feel of January's edge at the rim of the nostrils. Oh well. I'm out for whatever. Today, whatever is wind wind wind.

Owing to chill factors, mountain wind can seem triple-sinewed, hyperactive, fanatic. Isn't it this minute dilapidating the mountains themselves? Even without ice for an ally, it could do the entire job, and has, on summits ground down to prairie before these mountains first lifted. A chip or sliver here, a grain there. Wind and rain have all the time there is. In the central Sahara are mountains that wind has brought down to the humility of floor tiles. Their "mosaic" remnants stretch as if hand fitted—like wind's anagrams, or a code without messages—level to every horizon. Given air's origins, that seems ironic. When stone invented atmosphere, how could it have guessed the strongest force on our planet would one day turn out to be air?

That air with its weathers now intends to level the Rockies? Oh yes. And shall. Nothing can stop it. Meanwhile, I suspect that our part of North America may not contain upthrusts more naked than these granite faces forming headwalls in Glacier Gorge, whose hierophantic jut rises ahead of me: the cliffs of Longs Peak, of Pagoda, The Spearhead. Against them our life spans have no chance at all, just as their own slab-sided ramparts, against wind, have none. This too is where gods live. Minor deities, it may be; forces dumbly, humbly immortal. But godlike in one thing at least: not knowing how to lie.

Near Mills Lake, tiny white mushrooms of snow pique my curiosity. Some coyote or fox must have trotted past, compacting snow just enough. Now wind undermines those tracks till each paw pad stands pedestaled, two inches above surrounding crust. Amusing. I've heard of wind blowing bark off the trees, blowing chickens into the sea—white chickens, and in the Hebrides, as it happened—but never of this. Yet the likeness between these ice mushrooms and pedestaled stones in New Mexico, Utah, and Arizona bespeaks inanimate nature's versatile monotony: two or three ideas, varied perhaps less than a dozen ways.

Altered states is one. Mills Lake is now a long pool of fluid gone rigid. Over its milky, wind-polished ice there's a skinny line of ski-packed snow that, like the paw prints, managed to stick. All the rest, blown clear. I choose the lake's locked edge, its snow so wind packed you could quarry or saw it—a crust my metal edges barely incise.

Wind wind wind. "Restless" doesn't touch it. The sky, however, has cleared except for rags of fast cloud which quickly veil the sun, quickly strip it naked.

The day that wind slowed Ruth Magnussen till it killed her, I was a few miles east, two thousand feet lower in the same weather. My friend Ron and I were trying to ski up an old mining road to Buchanan Pass. We did OK till the twisting, forested road entered a clearing. There wind had a straight shot at us. We leaned forward, fought with it, tottered comically in it, made headway more and more laboriously against it. I remember how angrily the bee-sting of snow pricked my face; and how, shoulder to shoulder, Ron and I heard each other's torn shouts as noise, not words. In fifteen years of our fairly pedestrian mountaineering together, we hadn't let weather deflect us; nor have we since. That day we did.

Next morning under DIVIDE WINDS CHARGE ULTIMATE PRICE I read how in that big blow, Ruth Magnussen's climbing party had let her lag behind, then on their descent from the summit of Mt. Alice found her "not moving." And I knew it wasn't just any wind. It was *that* wind. Even so, the incident puzzled those of us who knew that her group was not only experienced, but included biologists. They of all people.

We like to believe in the avoidable. We? Not those who describe this world as machinery. The Marquis de Laplace boasted that if he could know for one moment the exact position of each particle in the universe, he could predict everything from there to the edge of infinity. If. A very big word. Needless to say, he lived in the era of Newtonian physics. In any case, it's an omniscience most of us feel blessed in not having.

To see wind purely as a jostle of gas molecules deanimates even its most baroque whims; makes them mere products of solar rays heating Earth, and of our planet's rotation. Which they are. But if our future is physical laws, have we one? We'd prefer weather whose quirkiness is odd as our own minds—random, capricious. Otherwise, strange to say, we can't take ourselves seriously. The world wouldn't be real enough.

If meanwhile the laws of astrophysics have a steely, predictive glint to them, living matter is—happily—a truant to prediction. Our biological past is an unbroken record of the slightly off-center, the slightly imperfect. Praised be imperfection for it! If we owe ourselves to evolution, evolution owes itself to that one continuous, omnipotent glitch. Mere physical laws might have wanted living stuff to repeat itself with cookie-cutter perfection. Nothing doing. Only the flaw, only the glitch in repeatability seems flawless. Its perfection is that nothing repeats, not exactly.

It does so almost. A nudibranch designed to recur without bumps somehow gets one. The bump somehow gets passed on. Imperfectly, though, because that bump gets another—a bump that its encoding hadn't been encoded to ask for, just got. And that bump, another; and so on, till bumps grow ruffles, ruffles grow gills, gills grow brains, and brains blunder their way into eyes. We ourselves are anthologies of birth defects that proved workable—like every creature that is—because life is "error tolerant." Hence "junk DNA," a nucleic acid that neither promotes replication nor deters it, just floats uselessly around in our cells. Through the necessity of chance—and perhaps through oddments like "junk DNA," whose potentialities can as yet only be guessed at—the small, still wind of minutest difference "blows where it pleases to blow." Thus the great ash tree Yggdrasil ramifies. Thus the fruit eaten by Adam and Eve sows within living cells its escape properties, their enabling imperfections.

A fortunate fall, that. It released us from the tyranny of perfect replication to the creatively flawed: nature alive and ever so slightly askew. Whose creatures we are. But why *these* natural quirks become laws, and not others? "Among worlds that never happened," I often ask myself, as the soul of certain chemicals made mortal, "why exactly these limits and mysteries?"

Air, for example, has one-sixtieth the viscosity of water. But mightn't wind have run as rivers now do, in fixed channels? Streamlines. If you didn't live near a wind's flow, you wouldn't get any. Meanwhile, water in its usual state works that way already; a wind too heavy to fly.

On the other hand, wind isn't wholly amnesiac. Lacking fixed channels it shows preferences verging on habits. Winter to winter, my return past particular snowdrifted ledges, boulders, and overhangs reveals air-carved forms I remember because wind remembers how it made them. Each year, it reshapes them so much the same way that I've come to rely on and use for landmarks their mimed turbulence—where otherwise your skis are the trail.

I know too that although I'm now damp with sweat from kicking side-steps up the deep powder of the last steep ascent over a frozen watercourse, there's a most chilly blast expecting me at the lake's lip. No matter how extravagantly the here-there-and-everywhere winds lurch or wheel, one special air torrent, assigned as if by decree, pours down over that lip like the waterfall's winter ghost. Ordinarily I'd be braced for it, but the ascent has so belabored my breath I forget. As Colorado altitudes go, 10,600 feet is nothing; however, what with skis, ski boots, a winter pack, I notice my lungs have lower standards. Over this wind-crusted snow just below the lip of Black Lake, my metal edges barely keep me on the slope; but the sole risk is looking silly, sliding helplessly down about a hundred feet and having to reclimb the same snow.

Then it attacks. Air's avalanche. Like thunder, a wind mightier and older than life itself suddenly lunges past me, hurling, screaming, charged with snow billows like stampeding herds of white bison. My wool headband isn't enough, needs help from my parka hood—which seems entangled by pack straps. I fumble frantically, because the windchill is instantly serious. With that hood finally yanked over my head I watch Niagaras of snow boiling past. Between me and the black-green of fir forest below the lake's glacial shelf I see the frantic writhe of white crystal, as of some creature, spasming. I feel I'm inside a comet, robed with its broken ice and cold gravel. In such wind even granite might wish for life enough to die, to be killed, "Once and for all. To get it *over!*"

No such luck, not for granite. And that may be the sadness of stones. Lives briefly intense as our own can at least expect an oblivion—endless, durable—which the life of granite is far too dim ever to hope for. As the berserk current abates to just weather, I realize it was the wildest turbulence I've ever been out in.

Anyone new to Black Lake might turn back here and now; however, long acquaintance has taught me that by skiing another fifty meters further, apparently into the teeth of it, I'll get clear of the worst. The lake's outlet being a granite gap in high cirque walls, its breach simply funnels cold air falling off the peaks; and, as from a funnel, those currents stream fastest at the spout.

In the great cirque above the lake's own far smaller cirque, it's true, vagrant wind cells lurch around like bullies. Exposed fir grow all twisty, lower to the rock the higher one goes, till—past timberline—their final clumps grovel and surrender completely; wind's abjects.

Roaming our planet, the same wind keeps changing its name to suit place and mood: zephyr, breeze, gale, blue norther, chinook, tramontana, twister, cyclone, tornado, hurricane, williwaw, mistral, sirocco, harmattan, monsoon, typhoon; the trades, the westerlies, the squall lines of easterlies; varied sounds naming air's seasons, its motions, contortions.

Another sort of wind word, *ventifact*, appeals to me especially, not as one of wind's names but as a term given certain of its victims: sandblasted pebbles and small stones on which it imposes polygonal shapes, cleanly sculpted ridges, oddly pyramidal hints. Stone litters thus abraded—whether found on the high barrens of Outer Mongolia, or across central Saharan flats literally paved with miles of the things, or Utah, or West Texas—are ventifacts.

But wind-carved buttes all over Utah, for example, don't count as such. Nor slump-shouldered hills whose once mountainous brows wind has ever so slowly made off with. No, those are "deflations," more remainder than sculpture, despite the ruddy, troglodyte features that look down from their heights everywhere in Monument Valley, and fail to notice us. For just now, though, I stretch *ventifact* to include me, my hair, my nylon hood crackling in wind—though some gusts make me less "ventifact" than "deflation." That latter word is best reserved for phenomena such as Big Hollow, west of Laramie. There one can see absent kilometers and tonnages of soil long since removed by Wyoming winds single-minded enough to be in the business of excavating. If locals sometimes call them "blowouts," who'd argue? They're places wind remembers well, and works on.

But how are we to measure such weather? By the cubic yard of soil blasted into the air? We gauge, for example, morning calm by the way smoke rises straight up out of chimneys. If smoke drifts, but in currents so slight that weather vanes don't react, we say, "Hardly any wind at all." Later we notice breeze on the cheek; maybe weather vanes stir. Leaves and small branches toss lightly. Wind begins picking up dust, swirling loose papers around. Branches thrash. Strollers beside the lake see whitecaps cresting on its waters. The largest branches of big elms sway. Power lines swing back and forth. A woman opening her umbrella feels it go wild, try to yank free. Children walking to school stagger forward squinting, fighting not to lose balance. Whole trees start bucking and plunging like broncos. Limbs tear loose from cottonwood trees and go flinging downstream. Shingles fly through the air above rooftops. A parked car's rear window caves in. Stud walls of houses under construction buckle, as plywood takes to the air.

Each of these stages marks greater velocity, and can occur almost anywhere; in contrast, Wyoming people speak of making your own wind gauge, fit for Wyoming conditions: "You take about twelve foot of as heavy a log chain as a big man can drag, and a dozen or so railroad spikes for fixing it good to an oak stump. Now, if them links only stir a little, expect calm weather to continue. If your chain thrashes around some, there'll be a breeze by afternoon. If it should lift and stand straight out like a flag, the next day will likely be unsettled. But when your log chain gets to where it's whipping and popping and snapping off links, look out. That's a Wyoming storm warning."

Toward the microscopic end of wind's influence there's "saltation," tiny leaps and bounds made by sand granules as they're blown. Oh, I feel a bit of that too, when the wind's blast is loaded with snow crystals. Meanwhile, true saltation occurs constantly on the summits overhead, where sea beaches begin as a speck that ice, wind, and rain pry loose from its cliff and send spinning, tumbling. From there to Mississippi's or Alabama's Gulf Shore is but a question of time and spring runoff.

In southern Colorado, at the Great Sand Dunes National Monument, we've about forty square miles of sand that wind has piled up against a sort of cul-de-sac formed by the Sangre de Cristo mountains. The highest dunes rise seven hundred feet above the valley floor. Far from fossilized or coarse, they're shifty, fine-sifted, pure. Thus a park ranger once startled me by saying that when the National Park Service first built there, and sand was needed for mortar, it was trucked in from outside. I gaped, incredulous. Surely that was carrying the concept of eco-fragility to absurd limits. The dab of mortar used now and then for setting posts and other campground maintenance would hardly violate forty square miles. He was pulling my leg? But no. Those duned and wind-driven granules have endured so many thousands of years of saltation they've tumbled themselves round-shouldered, and thus lack angularity enough to bind really well in mortar. "So," that ranger explained, "when foundations needed pouring, better sand was trucked in."

By now I've reached the half-naked banner trees verging on Black Lake's east shore. Owing to wind they dare not branch out on their west side, so their leeward streaming boughs give an impression, even in calm, of speeding in place. I pass among them, and through, up a steep rise that keeps my skis pretty much out of sight, powder-whelmed; but the cliff I'm intent on comes into view: an icefall whose half acre plates of grey-blue runoff have wept down over tawny bulges of granite and frozen like armor, or like the ever-thickening shards of a beetle. By edging a few meters forward I cause the ice's grey-blues to tinge with five-fathom green, or with zones of turquoise, subtle and eerie. The shifting colors fascinate, as if hinting at a world in which the whole spectrum could be frozen.

The granite wave they embellish so arrestingly is itself the size of intimidation. Megalithic, tremendous, it rises just three or four hundred feet above the white plateau of Black Lake. Gawking from its base, I feel the ice-and-stone presence of numb forces crushing my next thought so completely it becomes a barely inhabited stare.

I decide to boost energy and morale with a few hunks of milk chocolate. As has happened before, however, the cold makes it wholly flavorless. My mouth must be nearly wind temperature. Though I chew and chew till the squares feel like sawdust, they don't melt or release the slightest taste. I tell myself, "Wait, it'll warm," and I do wait—a reasonable while—but to no effect, so I lose patience and swallow. Chocolate incognito, I find, isn't chocolate.

Not having seen another soul for hours, my earlier self-interrogations now recur to mind; I realize that along with good old everyday animal fear, what I love about skiing alone in Glacier Gorge is the abyss between me and its presences. The more distant the nearest things are, the more dubiously I'm tangible. Or even here. Yet I know their "grandeur" is me. Has to be. I who am minuscule. Without my endocrinal secretions, however, and the neural responses they trigger, all blue-black cliff shadows and white sheernesses remain a closed circuit. Poised on skis, finding no signs now of animals—human or otherwise—where my own tracks disappear, I scan panoramically while mulling that over. The feel is of being in the world alone. And not as if.

High in winter mountains our spontaneous awe makes a gift of it-self to what caused it: snowfields whose whitenesses are absolute and untracked emotions—even if spattered with rock-and-ice Gothic. And light that can't make up its mind, shifting all day through cloud, and through the snow-shouldering, sun-starved forests. Gargoyle crags where silence and wind are never home the same time.

But ice-quarried rock, we know—or believe we know—is only the random effect of cold and crustal upheavals. Why should raw bigness summon the deepest, oldest feelings we life forms can have? Perhaps by the very size of indifference. Because mountains scorn the astonishments they give rise to, because they pretend to live entirely within the limits of the visible, because they despise our memories, we respect the hugeness of their refusal to confide. Which awes us. And we say so—inwardly. Meanwhile, snow and rock read our minds perfectly. To show their contempt for our least selfish thoughts, they ignore them. Where-upon we're awed all the more.

And we're grateful. Among fellow humans we're merely super-fluous at best; at worst, part of the competition. But winter mountains enlarge the needle's eye of our tiny brains and their labyrinthine triv-ialities. Thanks to the rude unity of winter's fourteen-thousand-foot peaks, we feel our insignificance expand like a strange prestige—which makes being alive a kind of magic, easy as being not quite real. Small wonder that wherever terrain permits, primitives go around filling their habits with mountain gods. As for such earth spirits, we moderns—we whose houses are built of retired forests, we whose bodies are made of matter everlasting, and who each night before bed may drink a few sips of cloud—never think of them.

My fingers and toes remind me, "Get moving." Yes. Often my pause turns daydream—till, finding myself at a standstill, leaning forward on ski poles, I waken when wind smacks the body heavily as cold water. Other times, as my heart pounds with me uphill, the hours of acceler-ated thump lull my senses into hearing neither its red hammer nor the thump and thud of weather. Suddenly wind stops: I panic, feeling my heart has too. Then wind resumes and so, its seems, does my high-altitude heartbeat. This would be entirely ludicrous if the sudden scare were less chilling. Somehow my years in mountains have tricked me into confusing wind with life-signs in the world's body, including my own. That's nonsense, of course, but something in me doesn't know it.

It's that something which gets ambushed by a sudden confusion, mistaking life and mountain wind for one thing.

Embarrassing, wholly unscientific. Yet where life forms are concerned, atmosphere on a windless planet might indeed feel inert, cadaverous. Columbine pollen would drop right back onto the lip of its bloom. Thistledown would fall at the base of each stem that contrived it; so maybe there'd be only one, a husky stalk clotted with dwarfish progeny. Pine forests, I recall, are among the earliest living exploiters of wind power—without which the gold smoke of their pollen would be a fine needle-sifted rain confined to the tree that released it. Groves just one tree wide. Happily, our actual forests wander like migrant tribes, mile after wind-sown mile.

As it is, spring pools often wear yellow films of wafting pollen; their stones are banded and waterlined with it. I've seen impulsive bursts of April wind huff pollen clouds for twenty, thirty yards still in the shape of its pine, or the shape of whole tree-clusters atop a mesa—the soul of a forest suddenly taking flight. Inland temperatures on a planet lacking convection would depend on solar rays, period. The sea would be glass. Sand wouldn't dune, and lacking saltation, mightn't even be sand. Snow wouldn't drift. Cities would be visible beyond the horizon as puddles of fume. Weather would be predictable as arithmetic, or yesterday. Nobody would run up a flag.

And I'm not sure all this snow would be here. Microscopically fine dust, as things stand, gets blown about the globe, providing nuclei for flakes and raindrops to crystallize around or condense on. And fallen snow often takes to the air again. I look up where Thatchtop Mountain's high ridgelines smoke with vortices of blown crystals that wisp and unravel like unruly root systems changing natures with fronds. Backed by an expanse of clear, blank-blue and half-violet high-country sky, snow's turbine shores feed back into air just now raking Mt. McHenry. Solar explosions prism within crystalline veils, and become sun dogs. Fast updrafts arrest themselves, then plunge, as if terrified of their own intentions. Powdered torrents sweep down like waterfalls, coil upward again like sidereal nebulae whose spiral arms pull themselves limb from limb, or ambitions whose first maneuvers destroy them.

Wind's motions: a mind always deciding, never made up. Why should its habits differ wholly from ours? Beyond the practical aims of food and shelter, we use motion to assure ourselves a future—as if movement kept our possibilities alive. Thus in watching Wagnerian winds rake the summit of Thatchtop, I feel the paradox of wanting to come again—to where I'm this minute standing. Wanting to see again what I'm seeing right now. A roundtrip inside moments of standstill.

Skiing back downtrail I pass the Y-shaped writhe of a particular bristlecone pine I've known for years. If trees can have doting admirers, this one has me. Today, for no reason, I decide it's female, and christen her Yvonne.

As bristlecones go, her few hundreds of years make her a girl, but her figure nonetheless is centuries of violence enacted. I've only to glimpse Yvonne's evergreen torso and limbs to know what wind's sadism feels like. Even the slab her roots knuckle down into wears the wind's name etched into its granite like wood grain, a past still in progress.

All at once I'm ambushed by a snow devil, whose bluster can't stand contradiction. Its spindrift blinds me, makes skiing impossible. I halt, bobbing in it like a middleweight boxer, gasping for breath sucked from my lungs. Slowly my clenched eyes dare to blink open, wet, as the snow devil roars elsewhere. Through clotted lashes I watch its local shambles of powder kick up a ruckus as it goes. Across the gorge, high on the sides of Half Mountain, acres of granitic ruck smoke and howl. Three thousand feet overhead the flat summit of Longs Peak is also getting dismantled one sunlit grain at a time. Air's wildest routines, its iciest ways to catch fire include sudden geysering swirls torn off snowfields on quirks of velocity that spiral high, higher, then explode when cross-currents attack them, just to have something to kill.

Impossible not to remember Ruth Magnussen. And because I'm looking at the flank on Longs Peak where he came to grief, James Duffy III. He and his mountaineering buddy were trying to bag two peaks on the same outing. Though young, they were experienced; but their decision to go light, leaving heavier clothing out of their packs belied that experience. Coming down off the second peak, Longs, in colder wind than they'd bargained for, they began going into hypothermia. Duffy grew cranky, irrational. Should they try somehow to shelter among boulders and wait it out, or descend? They couldn't agree. By this time, Duffy's talk wasn't making good sense. The friend took off downtrail.

Desertion? To have stayed with Duffy up there in such weather might well have finished them both. If Duffy could hold out, the friend would bring help. But they had already spent many thousands of calories climbing a pair of difficult summits. And it's a long, rocky trail down. On such trails the last mile feels like five.

When at the Longs Peak Ranger Station the volunteer men and women of Rocky Mountain Rescue finally began uncrumpling from Jeeps, vans, pickups, and Volvos to head uptrail, in foul weather, hoping to find Duffy still alive, they were not mountaineer novices. Nor are Rocky Mountain Rescue people a gang of beer bellies in four-wheel drives. They are lean, fit, and—unfortunately—well-practiced. And very well equipped. Such persons take outdoor gear seriously. If you trek around much in Colorado's mountains you hear of people who didn't. James Duffy's story was even now being added to the local repertoire.

True, there's a strain of morbidity in rescue work. That day, despite the optimism of their effort, they must've guessed they were likely to find, if anything, a young corpse. What they guessed, however, I do not know. I do know that if "heroic" has meaning, men and women of Rocky Mountain Rescue have often been heroic. And if at thirteen thousand they report running into a snow-charged, eighty-mile blast that forced them back down the mountain, I *believe* in that wind.

But it lifted. Or enough. On reascending, what their search finally turned up was a young man in the prime of life, except for being dead. Deranged by severe hypothermia he'd apparently tumbled some 150 feet. What weather had begun, head injuries ended. Duffy was added to the list of those who've died on Longs, a list over forty names long.

Skiing over the scene of summer, now altered almost beyond recognizing, admiring wind-billowed snow as it streams thinly, beautifully off the highest ridges, admiring the late-afternoon blue of clear sky, I'm aware of watching snow blown around by nuclear fusion. If, as is true, solar energy drives Earth's weather, all winds, strong or gentle, arctic or tropic, arise at the sun's center.

Despite the fact that our planet's energies take millions of years to seep outward from the sun's core to its surface, the very cold that now tries to refreeze my left earlobe, once frostbitten severely, owes its windchill to that frantic solar core, whose fusioning produces temperatures at such astronomical degrees as to leave imagination helpless, empty. Looking around at a seeping cliff's icicle thickets, at creek ravines cargoed with drifts, I'm bemused by knowing that beneath Earth's crust, deep in its inner core, resides heat rivaling that of the sun's surface. Meanwhile its brilliance storms inside Thatchtop Mountain's veils of ripped snow. One cloud remnant opens, surprisingly like lids of an eye filled with the blank blue of the sky behind it.

As afternoon wanes, Glacier Gorge quickly chills. In open shadow its east-facing snow slopes go bluer, while sun on opposite slopes tinges warmer, more golden. My pole-baskets leave wells of aquamarine light, delicate, glacial. Many levels under their lovely, cold omen abide our oceanic progenitors: strata of tropical fossils, stone fish swimming within the currents of Lower Permian time; then Mississippian levels, then Devonian clamshells, brachiopods, and—for all I know—imbedded in the Cambrian strata, trilobites by the billions; whose light was the way we came.

About twenty-five miles under those life-cousins, Earth's crust gives way to the mantle, and that in turn to the so-called outer core, mostly iron in a fluid state. It has always bemused me that people who perish in local storms—such as I'm watching now—freeze while superheated winds of liquid iron stir at snail-slow velocities beneath them. I imagine white hotness, an incandescence that is at the same time thrice-fiery and red; yet black, totally. Its magnetic fields tell the lost traveler's compass needle which way to point. And that needle obeys, reliably, even after the mittened fingers holding the compass may have frozen solid.

What fascinates yet further is to realize that underneath Earth's superheated outer core lies an inner core so compressed that its superheated iron can't budge; is thus, at 7,200 degrees Fahrenheit, frozen. When gravity's avarice grows that intense, its familiar tug seems evil. If wind begins at the sun's center, Earth's inner core is surely wind's antipodes: a white-hot blackness, or so we imagine; yet red as lava. Planet dregs compressed to an anvil.

Though when wind rages the crazy flailing of spruce boughs seems less dance than anguish, maybe forests consider it exercise. Could it toughen their fibers? My reverencing of great-hearted fir and spruce trunks is partly rooted in these atmospheric devastations they defy, and thrive on. But wind is now upping the ante with so much blown powder I find myself skiing downtrail in whiteout. Visibility gone, I stop, wait. The blank air roars, a local blizzard that snuffs thought. A snowy nirvana.

The fact that *nirvana* combines Sanskrit words for "blow" and "out" strikes me as funny. But this cold air isn't fresh from India, and

I'm not liberated, just erased; the weather of the mind is words, and for the moment wind has blown every word out of my head. Asian wisdom might do the same thing, though I suspect any sojourn in either Nirvana—as place—or in the fabled well-being of Eden would feel to us like the Doldrums. Wind is itself a kind of emotion, even when it behaves like a wild breathing no one has mastered. In windless Paradise there'd be no reason to stir, perfection being what and wherever you are, and each moment identical to the moment before. Instead, we postlapsarians are happily animate in a fallen world—which compared to Eden has every disadvantage but one. Ours, at least, never holds still.

That makes for a chaotic existence just now in Glacier Gorge. Would it seem so, I wonder, if I watched by the eon instead of an afternoon? To stand in this snow-smothered creekbed and stare unblinking, tireless as gravity itself through a half-dozen centuries of wind might shake my faith in chance. Snow's identical patternings, the madly rhetorical gestures of fast moving clouds, even the warp in wind-twisted trees—might prove regular as the zodiac.

I arrive at Mills Lake. Winter or summer, its windward shores are log-jammed with grey creatures who, could they but talk, might settle the matter. But they're not trees any more, just carcasses. When alive they met these very winds and won, or stayed evergreen enough to believe they were winning, or believe—if they weren't—winning was possible. Their twisted grain has long since been picked into relief by "ideal particles" and high velocity snows. Icebound now, blank as drained calendars, with the thaws of late May they'll revive their hopes of drowning themselves, of at last rotting away, dissolving downstream. They've been at it for decades, and still wind isn't finished with them.

On one hand, the squalor of mere physics; on the other, something beyond physics, something for which the lowliest snowshoe rabbit munching spruce tips in the gorge is just one of innumerable masks. Though for long stretches this earth goes mute on me, I still expect it to be a speaking world. And because we're made of the same stuff it is, I wonder if certain of its voices—which we humans may never evolve receptors for—aren't there, all the same, just below the threshold of feeling, however inward and still.

Facets of our hidden natures may be less well concealed than we think. At times their secrets seem to stream outward, as if to disguise themselves in this world's often alien promises. Looking up into air's gaudy ways with fast cloud—whose edge sunlight iridesces to a hazed, transhifting rainbow—I half suppose I'm looking up at one of my own interior descriptions. At the same time, I know only too well that cloud-tatter is real, "other," apart; part of the sky's punctually restless mechanics. Of which I'm led by either culture or instinct to say, "Beautiful!" And I do.

But the fact we like it here, often immensely, wholeheartedly—was *that* inevitable? In wondering, "Why these things and not others?" I can easily imagine a rational species whose nature is simple as a two-spoked wheel: "GO / NO GO" or, "NIGHT / DAY", "USEFUL / USELESS", "YES / NO." The luck of imperfection, however, impels us exuberantly beyond so starved a response.

But exuberance won't get us past cold fact. "Face it," says fact; "Those voices you hear in wind aren't there." True, no matter how often I've heard dead trees cry. In thick forest that's a sound the wind makes: a dead trunk gets caught in its topple and is held, supported by living trunks which—for decades, as may happen—won't let that dead one fall, like our habit of taking along those who couldn't make it. When wind tosses the living tree crowns, that grey trunk rubs audibly against them, as if a creature dismayed. It's my voice that makes it a creature. Ours. The kind of voice we humans lend things. Especially whatever sighs as it ends.

Fact: the late afternoon turns colder. Time to go. When weather's calm, the very act of turning to leave seems sad; far less so when it's this windy. For the steepest few miles of descent I want ski boots firmly laced, and must take twelve or more miserable minutes to do what—without windchill—I could manage in 120 seconds. Removing pile mittens, I quickly unsnap my left gaiter, find its zipper-pull with numbing fingers, and unzip. Then I must thrust the bare hands into my knicker pockets to warm. I clench and unclench them, moaning a little. For their next sally forth, my fingers pick at and untie the yellow bootlace's firmly knotted bow. Back into the pockets they dive. Still cold but not frozen, they emerge to partly unlace and relace the boot, till each finger feels like a zombie—though oddly enough not the thumbs. Then more warming. Whereupon they must rezip and resnap the Gortex gaiter—hardest of all. After that I coddle them considerably longer, so that they can repeat the whole process on the other boot. They cower in my pockets like children begging to stay inside.

Before setting off again I look up at the sunset-tinted shambles of granite above me, and startle. As if I'd never been here before, as if I hadn't been glimpsing on and off for hours that long familiar hulk, now its mountain cragged with twelve-story spicules, its colosseum-size flakes, its rude chunks and smithereens seem wholly new; wanting to say something important. But it doesn't. Is itself, no more. Winter stone.

I turn from its crush and look back at the gorge headwall. Iron peaks. Against blue sky deepening nearly to indigo, loose snow spumes from their turrets in the frenzies and onslaughts I've watched all afternoon. Except that now, their distant, slow motion detonations—soundless as dust blowing off the moon—spell out a presence openly hidden.

The lowering sun reddens monolith knobs and snags and minor summits. It sets snow cornices afire till the westernmost ridgelines become one blazing rim. A ski pole in each mittened hand, I lean forward: windburnt, chilled, transfixed. Veils of thrown crystal that plume over high desolations of granite, and over my own whiff of existence, become a "we." We who are. And are being annihilated inside processional volumes, each enclosing the other beyond comprehending. For once in my life I see all that is or can be, felt not as a thing but a power; and that power, a unanimous, self-radiant motion.

I see that we life forms stir, move to and fro a while, then slump down; even while wind grinds our cities to powder. Like everyone's, my birth and extinction always were, there, inside what I'm seeing. So.

Real as a gun muzzle, the eye of my death aims straight into me, and fires. My body is shot with its own blood; its redness is fear at the level of despair. Not one of my personal molecules will ever again take anything personally. The pure animal truth of being wiped utterly *out*. That terrifies me. Yet I feel the rightness in that, as part of what is. So be it. For once in my days, I *know* myself to be completely inside an implacable and luminous power, which, though itself, is also the power of a dark absolutely without edges. Its vastness infuses the delicate force of each particle of each atom. Each echoes it, just as each echoes all others. Tiny globules; pale, spherical, vibrant. Tiny intensities of blue fire, fire-flakes thick as snow. Each tiniest globular intensity hums with a humming *imparted* out of the very dark against which each is made visible; a darkness so encompassing, so total, it isn't there. Against which, all those invisible, particulate energies making up what we call the world's surface now pulse and float; one strange levitation.

I watch the skyline's western rim burn. In the backlit and prisming tatters of snow cloud, in their flash against the sky's high-altitude blue,

I see that I'm to be destroyed more immeasurably than I'd ever dreamed of. The awareness fills me. My neck hair rises. This isn't "death," the thing people talk about, which is a mere mouth-sound, petty, inconsiderable. This is complete annihilation.

But for the only time in my life I feel who and where I am. Truly *within* creation, no escaping. No place to dodge or hide. I was drawn forth. And am being even now scattered, taken back. Into everything. Into something that destroys all it makes. As it must. Otherwise it wouldn't be what it is.

So I can't wish it different. Literally can't want to. I can't both see it and want to do that. All I can be is dumb, scared, fascinated; a "yes."

I've never felt so invaded, never *been* anything this true. Its fading feels like one tremendous presence gone. By comparison, "reality" feels starved. Even its grandeurs, meager; poor, pinched, desolate things. The gorge returns. Rock and snow slip back to be where I am, among fellow ephemera. The grandly stupid stones of Glacier Gorge, their dusk-blue ponderosities. I sympathize with them, with the dear, wind-haggard fir, living or dead, with the wind-flustered ravens, the pine martens. And with myself. I see that each of us will have been the only one of his or her species. Our entire, ingenious planet is a single blown snowflake. Is an eyeblink.

Yet as if admitting there's no place to go more real than here, no terrain that goes farther, even the mind's built-in critic relents: "Well, at least you came, looked around. You spent the energy. I'll give you that much."

The whole glacial trough has by now filled with open shadow. Every drifted ripple and snowfield is a skylit and empty blue. So are the snow-swagged pine boughs. Many thousands of feet higher up, the summit of Longs Peak warms itself at remnants of sundown. With alpenglow fast losing color across wind-bitten escarpment, I watch the final rays go dull, watch the life of all afternoon slowly turning to stone, as the sun's red gold gets sucked into granite.

Sacred Space

⌇

At the dawn tips of lowly creosote twigs in the Mojave Desert there's a stillness I want to hear. Again. Today the eight hundred miles to Joshua Tree National Monument seem worth it, just to listen to the sound made by our most precious of all resources, open space.

Since late May is perhaps its best season, I toss my backpack into the car, check the oil, clean the windshield, adjust my sunglasses, and head out from Boulder—shadowed by one or two doubts. Can my gravel-dinted Volvo handle still more stretches of often unpaved road? Will $250 see me through ten days of gasoline and food? It'll have to. All my nine-year-old car lacks to take me south as a typical American paradox is some sort of banner reading "DESERT SILENCE OR BUST."

"Typical American?" Maybe "Westerner" would be more like it. Every now and again a Coloradan gets into his car for a cruise through the neighborhood: across the Divide, west along I-70 to Utah, south to Arizona, then east through New Mexico and back home to, say, Boulder after 2,500 miles—most with *no* traffic. None. Great highway stretches where you can stop, strip naked in the middle of the road while changing to jogging togs, and give scandal only to crows.

After surreal red walls near Moab, after the evergreen-and-snow oases of Utah's Manti-La Sal summits along on the highway past Monticello, toward Blanding and Bluff; after Mexican Hat's painted desert at the Arizona border—just where the asphalt side road to Sunbonnet Rock has been recaptured by sagebrush—I know the Monument Valley overlook is at hand. Will I have visited its monoliths of red sandstone once too often? Apparently not. As I top that crest, my one-word murmur, aloud, without thinking, is "Oh-h-h!"

Huge buttes everywhere. Some, haze-blue and therefore all the bigger for being so visibly distant, set off nearer butte forms whose purple, as I drive toward them, enlivens to the red of beef hearts. Green with May, with flowering yucca, globe mallow, with clumped rabbitbrush and sage, the valley floor's panoramic span of high desert *feels* wide as a lifetime in which—right, left, and ahead, far as this world goes—great buttes rise like islands.

She sits at their picnic table writing something—postcards? journal?—while he stirs charcoal under foil-wrapped potatoes under grilling chicken. Having noted their license plates, I offer the hospitable gesture and say, "Your German's pretty good—for Californians."

They both smile. Turns out they're Swiss, married two weeks, just over from Zurich. He's a balding twenty-seven already pudgy, she's a plump blonde slightly younger. "You scribble while he cooks," I tease. She explains that as chef in a Zurich hotel he's in his element. I compliment him on his courage. He glances at embers under the chicken. "No," I say, nodding toward their rental camper: "I mean the nerve it takes to drive one of those things." Flattery, yes, in front of his new wife, but sincere. "And," I add, "in a strange country."

But how strange? Later while I'm stirring a pan of chili I watch him switch lenses on an Olympus, choose a filter, frame the shot, squeeze, rewind and frame again, squeeze another . . . until I see a Zurich apartment on a Swiss winter's evening, hear the slide projector's blower-whir, watch a white wall dissolve to Mitten Butte, with foil-clad potatoes and grilled chicken as foreground. "Nice shot," I think. While the Zurich couple's dinner guests stroll homeward along the Hirschen-graben I overhear them mulling, aloud, the feasibility of an Arizona adventure for themselves.

Though Europeans smile wryly at tourist scams puffing "the romance of the Old West" (which comes down to three bullet holes and a rusty ore bucket), they find its actual spaces unique, otherworldly; they find that an evening cloud-show in Monument Valley can make you briefly immense. For example, through altitudes of air in high desert you see that in one or another part of the sky it's always raining. Always raining and never hits. Near my camp chair, an Adidas-togged photographer and his girl crouch for a sunset foreground of yucca blossoms stacked like fresh eggs. She squints through a viewfinder, as does he, framing weather fifteen miles off, while the three-thousand-foot flume of orangeade comes showering downward, curving as it pours "ghost rain," which evaporates just short of the ground. In desert stillness we watch other thunderheads let fall their own Niagaras of pastel: pink, periwinkle, cerise. As the valley darkens we see high burgundy cascades like blown curtains altering ever so slowly. Meanwhile creamy billows of cumulus topping the stratospheric thunderheads have caught fire.

And while we follow sky changes over blue-butte horizons, low ridgeline beyond blue ridgeline, the sand at our feet, ruddy as powdered sundowns, deepens its red, enhancing the greens in rabbitbrush . . . even as sage begins to be half the colors of moonlight. Though the camera couple fuss at "capturing," they know there's no question of capturing. Instead, we feel all the more strange to ourselves because *this* world is primeval. In such moments the psyche becomes almost a soul, and if the distances seem near, it's because they're inside us. That most delicate and powerful human invention—language—falls silent. We breathe the times we might have lived in.

The photographers drift back to their tent site. From my chair on a rim three hundred feet above a great basin stretching to Utah, I watch the last light wane till only the San Juan Mountains in Colorado retain snowy glimmers; then only the cloud banks above them. Twenty miles away, headlights crossing out of Mexican Hat into Arizona twinkle and diffract through warm air rising from the desert floor.

When the Swiss couple invite me into their camper for a glass of wine, I note that such rigs retain a lot of daytime heat, and smile at their surprise when I say I'll sleep on the ground. Under so deep a night sky, why pitch the tent? I drop off drawing story lines star to star.

Shortly before dawn I stir from my sleeping bag to look eastward and grin; eight or nine sleepy-eyed Germans are trickling through sagebrush toward the same advantageous knob, extending tripods or checking f-stops as they go. When the first flare of rising sun first streams into our eyes just left of Mitten Butte it feels a bit like June solstice at Stonehenge.

The half-hewn look of Gray Whiskers Butte and Three Sisters Butte —like roughly sculptured Permian animals—make a local story about an allegedly educated woman almost credible: she insisted that Monument Valley's forms were the work of a lost civilization! True, at the three-mile circumference of Arizona's famous meteor crater I once heard with my own ears a sixty-eight-year-old skeptic insist, "You can't tell me they haven't kind of improved this with bulldozers."

"What," I wondered, "would he say of the Painted Desert, or the Petrified Forest?"

But there is worse. As if to report the outer limits of imbecility, rangers at the Grand Canyon record the perennial reactions of this or that tourist refusing to believe that *such* a canyon could have happened naturally.

By car I low-gear it down a steep dirt road to the valley floor, then cruise a seventeen mile loop of red sand from butte to butte, past herds of goats nibbling sage, past Navajo dwellings. At one hogan a clumsy sign says, "TAKE PICTURE OF NAVAJO WOMAN & HOGAN—ONE DOLLAR," but it's early; whoever collects isn't out yet. Among the scrub and juniper, thousands of yuccas blossom like candles.

Down the road I stop every few hundred yards, get out, look around, breathe deeply. Putting my hand on a warehouse-size flake fallen from Spearhead Butte, I'm ignored. Its "slickrock" towers so monolithically that my life at its base isn't worth squashing. Fragments the size of a pond have spalled away with the cleanness of chipped flint. Have I a soul here, now? Looking at the tremendous losses each butte has so easily been able to spare from its hugeness, I feel the darker side of sacred space. A soul? No, here I'm a pillar of blood and grease, nothing more. As for humankind, forget it. We never existed.

Maybe so, but the blue-purple of lupine blooms does exist, and the orange mariposa calyxes I love, the plumes of Indian ricegrass, sulphur flower, desert paintbrush. And, where I stop to look at an abandoned Navajo stock pen of juniper saplings, a songbird exists—one I've not heard in Colorado. For many minutes I try to catch sight of him, while in the cool, flowering desert his morning trill rinses the mind.

Southward from Monument Valley, I feel that if sagebrush could vote, rain would be president. Then sage thins away, giving in to naked rock, "hardpan," lichen-mottled to snakeskin. Twenty miles north of Kayenta, pulled over for lunch, I watch Navajo wool on the hoof— white sheep, black sheep and brown. Their browsing in a small box canyon gives off the clear, distant tinkle of sheep bells. By noon the rocks are made of solid light—ocher, rust, bright yellow, red—glaring back so hard you hurt your eyes on all colors. Easy to see how naturally Navajo weavers choose plants whose dyes echo this desert, where every hue either touches or alludes to the others.

Contrasted by litter. Still there, is the blown tire somebody's grand-dad appraised, patted once, and set rolling toward greasewood shrubs before I was born. Chucked whiskey bottles, tossed aside back in President Coolidge's day, glitter and soften exactly where they landed.

In the general store at Tuba City, junk food aisles bustle with Navajo women, many of whom wear opulent squash-blossom necklaces in silver and turquoise, turquoise earrings, silver bracelets with "pumpkin seed" motifs in finely worked turquoise. The store's big walk-in vault doubles as office. A Navajo woman sits there, surrounded by lockboxes, putting numbered tags on belts, bracelets, necklaces recently hocked. The swag-bellied Navajo male wearing jeans, gaudy silverwork belt, bright turquoise-colored shirt, and the obligatory black Stetson strolls out with a pawn ticket, and money.

Occasional tumbleweeds blow across the road like fantastic insects or mad animals. Then a deer mouse skitters onto the asphalt. We miss. A prairie dog runs part way, stops, stands bolt upright, gazing straight at my onrushing car. No time to brake or swerve; I zip over but in the mirror see him alive, unbrained. Apparently the prairie dog gene pool can afford even him.

Further south, toward the canyon of the Little Colorado, sacred space fills with emptiness. Across its brush and hardpan, you could set forth, walking steadily, keeping your eye on whatever nubble of sandstone you've decided to call a life's work. Summer dust devils would spiral and die as August heat cooled toward September. Winters would pass, many. Under each spring's renewed nimbostratus the desert scrub would green again. Your pace unslackened, your rhythm unbroken, years would drift across your face quietly as cloud shadows. You would leave less trace than fly tracks on sand, would never arrive, and never stop walking.

It helps some to be passed by "BILL & BETTY / WARNER ROBINS, GA.," who, like others of their tribe, advertise themselves on the spare-tire cover attached to their Winnebago. Health and long life to them! And wisdom increasing with each place-name decal.

Doubtless the most interesting surface on earth is the human face; otherwise, the Grand Canyon's walls would lay claim to that honor.

Near 6 P.M. at Slate Creek, deep in the Inner Canyon, I find myself on a boulder in a creek bed dry as chalk except for a flow of thin glint, wetting pebbles. Four thousand feet above, the ocher band of Coconino sandstone turns gold, as do the South Rim's juniper fringes, casting their last looks at sundown. And eight hundred feet higher than those juniper, a few ravens, whose evening caws don't carry half this far, circle slowly.

Tourists invisible at guardrails along that rim see quite another place: expanses of grandeur, yes, as advertised; ruined color bizarre as sun thunder, vistas hazed or clear or blotted away by seven-league systems of weather. Hour after hour, sightseers uncrumple from cars or tour buses for ganders at a stone postcard.

My years of backpacking in Colorado's highest mountains left me long unable to guess why *anyone* wanted to hike the Inner Canyon. "Too much like eating ashes," I supposed. And to an outdoorsman who—in pre-Giardia years—used to dip his Sierra cup into icy runoff anytime he was thirsty, toting a gallon or two of water seemed masochistic. Besides, going *down* instead of up violated my mountaineering instincts. Just as geologists are astronomers turned inside out, Grand Canyon hiking would be reverse alpinism. No matter that a descent of, say, a thousand feet takes you—in terms of climate—six hundred or so miles further south. No matter that the bottom is Mexico. "I'd as soon visit a slag heap," I thought. "You can have it."

Well, my little camp among mesquite trees on Slate Creek may be only four thousand feet down from the rim, along only eight or nine miles of trail; but it took me six hours hard travel. I'd allowed for my thirty-eight pound pack, knowing water and food get heavy, but hadn't allowed for how heavy, even in early May, the heat gets down here. Rather, in it the body weighs more. And the stone trash means each downward step is unique—each a separate decision, making rhythm impossible.

Along scrabbly footing at times all but a rockslide, sweating past Redwall limestone whose breath is hot as it looks, I suddenly cross warps of perfume put in the air by pale yellow sprays of blossoming cliffrose. Their aroma is delicious, narcotic. Like a vacation from labor.

Far down, out on the Tonto Plateau an agoraphobe might go rigid; an acrophobe would congeal. But after two days of wandering trails in the Canyon's labyrinth, I sit here as if at home in mountains, deliberately at a cliff edge, feeling the speed of its sheer drop for eight hundred feet, safely scared, delighted by fear. Shaded by my wide-brimmed straw hat, I've enjoyed a lunch of home-baked whole wheat and canned tuna. For company, there are agave plants with their ten-foot splurges of yellow blossom like rocket smoke, claret-cup cactus, cushion cactus, and no rattlers I know of. And wind, tottering the extravagant stalk of another agave, also called "century plant." Though "century" is excessive, these do bide their moment for a decade or so, then lavish years of stored energy on blossoms that attract, as foreseen, pollinators: black bees almost too bulgy to fly. Thousands of waxy yellow florets are the will and testament of the agave's last summer. Having bloomed, its stalk and blades turn from avocado green to all the dead colors of straw.

Surprising as the Sonoran plant life . . . the stillness, which I hadn't expected. Between the flora and the hush, I feel no urge to drive 350 miles further, to Joshua Tree. Why spend all those hours in a car when, by descending another two thousand feet, I can dip into Mexico?

Azure cloud shadows slide across the burnt blood of the canyon's pyramidal buttes, like the passage of freighters over underwater reefs sunk in the deepest stillness I've ever heard. Across it, distance signals to distance. If I were on the sea's surface, though, or in Kansas looking into prairie sky, I wouldn't feel vastitudes *enclosed*. But here I do. That sense of huge magnitudes contained, *inside* yet greater magnitudes, gives the eerie depth of an infinite regression in which infinity keeps getting larger, yet is real as rock. Far less solid is the truth that this peculiar universe, having swallowed me alive, isn't quite ready to spit out my bones.

Near my blue pack are cacti offering blossoms red as a lipsticked kiss. Other species bristle like schemes of the insane. Tall teddy-bear chollas sweat needles thick as fur. Some of the beavertail cacti begin green but turn livid as they grow. A larger kind, like prickly pear but four to five feet tall, stands up verdant and truculent except at its base. Down there its colors are stone. Without the consoling slosh of a water supply inside my pack's milk-gallon canteen, the Spanish bayonets, the grizzly bear cactus, the beaver tail cactus would soon burst in the eye like bad dreams and high fever.

What's more, the instinct that *up* is good, *down* ominous, verifies itself when I count the eons it took me to descend through petrified rainbow—Kaibab limestone, Toroweap formation, Coconino sandstone, the redbeds of Hermit Shale, the thousand-foot thick Supai group, Redwall limestone, Temple Butte limestone, and so forth, down to Vishnu schist and its nearly two billion years. Their year-weight now buries me alive. Only up on the rim does the present continue. Down here, I'm time out of mind. My very breathing comes and goes before breath was.

Astronomy and geology deal in multidigit figures so impressive they quickly mean nothing. At the Grand Canyon, however, the abyss between flesh-time and stone-time isn't conceptual; it's a gasp. "*That* wrinkle of water down there did *this?*" In the visible zone between "that" and "this," space and time fuse. Shift in scale becomes shift in kind. We see then that a change of place changes our nature: *where* we are is *what* we are. Canyon space won't let us misread it.

Sound of gravel, scattering. I glance steeply down to see a park ranger trudging uptrail toward me, over a slide of reddish Hermit shale. He's about thirty-two, lean, but with a round Irish face, ruddy and sweating—under not only his forest-green bill cap, but a full pack and a heavy walkie-talkie, hip-holstered in black leather.

He checks my trail permit and asks if I've water enough. I say, "A gallon, plus my canteen," knowing it's plenty. His eyebrows lift. Turns out he's been sidetracked by a hiker with heat prostration, hasn't even a full liter left for himself. "Take some of mine," I insist. He refuses. Ranger pride. "OK, but at least take a swig from my canteen," I say holding it toward him.

He doesn't hesitate long. He drinks. And drinks. "Guess I *was* getting dry," he hands it back, grinning.

We chat about the necessary evil of the Park Service's "wilderness permits." When he says, "Actually, more Germans use the Inner Canyon than Americans," I'm surprised and not. Last summer I camped and hiked among so many Europeans I began hearing foreign accents as "natural" to Southwestern locales.

Morbid fascination turns my curiosity back to asking about the heat case. "Oh, she was heavy, a sort of a fat girl, overweight and all. But the thing is, she had to *know* something was wrong. You may not know what to call it, but you know you're feeling strange. You know you need to sit down. You know you should tell other hikers, 'Hey, I need help.' " He shakes his head. A young woman needlessly dead. "There's a lot of pride on that trail."

"Which one?" I ask.

He nods east. "Over on Bright Angel," and shakes his head again. "A *lot* of pride." It sounds like a Standard Explanation for what he can't really explain. Many such cases.

The one trail nonhikers are apt to try is Bright Angel: a trail you can descend by mule, a trail whose foot traffic speaks French, Japanese, British English, Spanish, Hungarian, American. And many of them arrive with no idea how fast the high desert's invincibly empty winds may wick away body fluids. Extreme dehydration can thicken blood toward red sludge until a heart balks at pumping the stuff, then doesn't.

From Horseshoe Mesa, I look eighteen hundred feet down to see the same Colorado River I followed through so many of its altitudes now running unmuddied, cleared almost to blue-green. Its roar, on the hot wind, is whispers. Its rapids, white flecks.

All around me are distances that allure; they create the impulse to go toward, to cancel their separation by entering them. Many of their buttes and spires have never been climbed; plateaus where no one we know of has ever set foot. So space here often seems a mask hiding what it reveals: red pedestals and pagoda forms that speak, but not to answer.

Names given these forms mean to emphasize mystery, but undercut themselves by nineteenth century addiction to the highfalutin. Within a dozen or so of its two hundred miles the canyon includes Zoroaster Temple, Brahma Temple, Horus Temple, Osiris Temple, Buddha Temple, Buddha Cloister, and Confucius Temple—an overkill of inscrutabilities. These contrast ludicrously with my knowing that toward the bottom of Tanner Trail a ritual pilgrimage, quietly undertaken each year by Hopi priests, still gathers and returns to their reservation the Hopi ceremonial salt.

Well, sacred places often disguise their powers. About me I see nothing deific, just grey-green alluvial fans dustier than elephant toes. Chaos created by ugly, alien, arid laws; by the laws of cactus-bitten, yucca-blotched, scorpion-spiked, lizard-flicked rubble. Like a cloud shape, the "sacral" alters to sheer rock-tinted distance gone mindless. Not even malign.

Despite the quiet that fills it, despite its 2,500 years of almost continual habitation, despite Hopi ritual, I know the Inner Canyon's mystery is the chance intersection of one natural force by another. Temples? Horizontal layers of limestone and shale have been granulated by the verticality of rain, by gravity's plunging and tumbling cliff-bits. Erosion. Reality. An aimless building up to throw down—where a misstep can turn any animal's guts inside out, allowing desert glare to slowly pry open the skull.

Perhaps that's what Grand Canyon sightseers leaning forward from the South Rim feel their lives mixed with. The banded layers speak, but of a sort of marvelous annihilation that the very grandeur won't let tourists turn away from. Oh, it mesmerizes all right. It tricks a man from Eau Claire, Wisconsin, to staring five thousand feet down inside his past futures.

Hours of trekking to and fro across creekbeds dry as aspirin finally bring me to a sand beach alongside the Colorado's torrent. Especially at Granite Rapids where stillness gives way to roar, it's hard to believe not one drop of this wild, animal water reaches its age old destination in the Gulf of California. For a quarter-century now, growers between here and the Gulf have drained it dry. At first the current's forty-five-degree chill delights me, but by 9 A.M. the sky's already too hot. And no shade. I find a boulder casting shadow enough for head and shoulders, while sun scorches my jeans as if they're being ironed.

My mind slows to a doze, perhaps matching the age of the black-collared lizards, and of Vishnu rock—oldest, lowest, darkest, and by far the ugliest in the canyon. Its schist faces hardened at a time when all reds were black. Its v-shaped gorge now creates a solar oven, where every cloud drifting between me and the sun is a small mercy; the bigger the cloud, the wider my gratitude.

How many sunsets and moonrises inhibit the vacuum inside one billion years? I pick up a schist fragment that old, and in hefting its blackness I lift all those dumb suns. The gone moons, too, are inside it, as am I. Down here I've already happened.

Torpid with heat and stream-roar I watch collared lizards slither around, bask on rocks, stare, eat crustacea the size of salt flies off beach sand. Nearby, astride basalt, a lizard pumps now and then, doing push-ups. A male, its throat pouch blazed with cobalt, while the female's throat and torso are touched with crimson, which should mean she's pregnant. To my surprise she slides under him, over him, on top of him—as if to attract interest. Nothing doing. She pauses, blinking. Still nothing. Finally he tops her.

Other lizards behave more traditionally, the male chasing the female through chunky jumbles of black gneiss. "How can he know," I wonder, "which turns she's taken? Scent?" Given their quickness, the ruck they chase in, and all the other lizards—I'm amazed his nostrils could be that keen. Especially with the fishy smell that gives this beach its seashore aroma.

A blue speck has appeared upstream, all but lost against sheer-nesses of Vishnu schist directly above. The speck grows. I hustle toward the manic rapids to watch it shoot by twenty yards from me.

The raft says WILDERNESS RIVER ADVENTURES on its side and floats about fifteen people puffed up in life jackets of bright orange—soon hidden in the wavetrain. The long pontoons wallow, accelerating, bucking like a bronco for less than five seconds of tense shrilling and whooping. Safely past those cold explosions of whitewater, the rafters give themselves a drenched cheer, then their sky-blue inflatable drifts smoothly on, round the bend of this river which Mormons found "too thick to drink and too thin to plough." A gravelly, boulder-rolling, silt-laden flow that's been eroding its way past my boot toes for maybe six million years.

After climbing at a leisurely pace about a thousand feet higher, up the side canyon I'm camped in, I'm almost disappointed to find my tiny tent exactly as I left it, food bag still slung from a branch under the mesquite tree, unmolested by rodents. So, my companions won't even be thieves; just twilight bats flittering above the raucous, goatlike croakings of spadefoot toads. Otherwise, not a soul.

These little toads make racket enough for a jungle. The April torrent that, in spate, begot them now runs narrow as a fire hose, but less deep. Soon it'll dry to pebbles and sand; therefore, the toads must announce themselves, mate, and—as "spadefoot" implies—dig back underground till next spring. Dig so far that random showers won't seep down and break their aestivating; only the return of a wet season. The toad I've caught is full grown—the size of a big English walnut, chocolate brown, in twilight—and doesn't much mind being handled. For his cousins in the Mojave, drought could easily make that self-interment a three-year wait. "One year, three years—whatever it takes," says my spadefoot.

Evening darkens as it began, utterly windless. My mesquite tree with its locustlike foliage doesn't move. Rooted in prehistory's hot suns and scant rains, its tiny leaves economize water; a sort of green nimbus, less foliage than haze. In it not a twig stirs—as if to remind me any motion here will be mine.

The windless dusk in these beautiful badlands makes me hugely aware of being alone, yet unlonely, just as having to depend entirely on what my two legs can or can't do gives twilight monoliths their slight adrenaline charge, which I rather enjoy. Even more, I enjoy the fact that prehistoric loins at the source of our species have granted me the mysterious power to go walking around in it.

Not only around, but out. I waken in the half-light of 4:30 A.M., not an instant too soon for beating the heat, hustle my gear together and begin the long climb up from the past. Yesterday my first step away from the river occurred a billion years ago. Now, at the base of junky mocha-and-cream stuff called Tapeats Sandstone, I've re-juvenated to a mere 500 million years old. Though by the time I reach Kaibab Limestone I'll have been traveling for 375 million year-miles, my decades spent trudging up Colorado's mountains carry me to the rim faster than my pace going down. As if "up" were an energy. Were how our human energies began.

Forty miles northwest of Flagstaff I'm driving straight at the San Francisco mountains, where the gods live. Their forested and snow-covered heights belie volcanic origins so beautifully that it's easy to see why the Hopi hold these peaks to be sacred. But because their pantheon of sky spirits and earth spirits must have been powerfully corroborated by sporadic vulcanism, I realize that before gods were, sacred space was. *Therefore* gods come to inhabit it.

My kachina-belief totters a bit, however, when I approach close enough to see ski runs in clear-cut swathes through the forestation. And see the march of steel towers feeding now motionless chair lifts up toward the snowfields. Imagining Hopi distress at the desecration, I startle myself with a question so obvious I'm surprised never to have asked it until now: "Where are *our* sacred places?"

None natural, I think, none untouched. Instead, all human-centered; a battle, a birthplace, a document. Well and good, as far as humankind goes. But where not one *natural* space is held sacred, what gods will be found?

Beyond the Coconino, on I-40 eastward from Flagstaff, the roadside is once more private property, so Western expanse has to begin past billboards: KACHINA DOLLS 50% OFF / TAX FREE CIGARETTES / NAVAJO SAND PAINTINGS / INDIAN JEWELRY CLOSEOUT / LAND FOR SALE $295 AND UP / JACKRABBIT JEWELRY / MEXICAN GOODS / CHERRY CIDER / MOCCASINS FOR THE WHOLE FAMILY / LADIES PURSES / COWBOY HATS. The profit motive is inexplicably broken by a slogan spray-painted onto basaltic chunk: FREEDOM FOR CROATIA. On another, CROATIA.

Further along, more billboards whet the appetite for what's ahead: FORT COURAGE / BREAKFAST 98 CENTS / RESTAURANT SEATING CAPACITY 104 / TOUR BUSES WELCOME / ARIZONA LOTTERY. These disappear in favor of bold yellow and black ones saying, ICE / U.S. POST OFFICE / GROCERIES / INDIAN JEWELRY / NAVAJO RUGS / KACHINA DOLLS. There are billboards offering DISCOUNTS TO SENIOR CITIZENS, KODAK FILM, COPPER BRACELETS, CACTUS PLANTS, BULLHORNS HALF PRICE. Then the "Old West" theme reappears: TAKE PICTURES / FORT COURAGE / POSTCARDS / KACHINAS. The fort itself turns out to be miserably flimsy; a metal sheet annexed to a palisade of unbarked pine slabs, the thin kind that sawmills discard. Topping them is a watchtower inhabited by plywood cut-outs painted as Indians. Nearing Winslow, Arizona, a nature motif occurs: BURGER KING / FREE PETRIFIED WOOD, followed by INDIAN TEEPEE VILLAGE / FREE PETRIFIED WOOD / ICE / BEER / GAS / TURN LEFT NEXT EXIT, and GAS / FREE PETRIFIED WOOD WITH FILL-UP.

My approach to the Hopi dwellings on First Mesa winds steeply up toward pueblos which, six hundred feet above desert floor, look exactly like Italian hilltowns. Startlingly so. Their ash-blond fieldstone underlines the resemblance, though once I'm actually among structures in the First Mesa villages of Hano, Sichomovi, and Walpi the cruder result of using adobe for mortar becomes evident. On the other hand, innumerable Anasazi walls at Chaco Canyon show finer workmanship than *any* Florentine masonry using freestone.

If the Hopi do indeed continue Anasazi bloodlines, perhaps even speaking the unknown Anasazi language in open secret, they've learned respect for and mastery of the fragile desert ecology. Below First Mesa, fields of blue corn grow in total sand. When, many decades back, the U.S. Department of Agriculture dispatched an agent to teach the Hopi nation methods of dry-land farming, an intelligent trading post owner apprized Washington of its folly: "The Hopi know ten thousand times more about that subject than we ever will."

Stopping to survey a couple of the plots from halfway up First Mesa, I spy a file of black-haired kids heading toward one plot about five hundred yards south and below. The kids' buckets are plastic which the sun makes translucent—pink, blue, red. A boy throws his load of water at a Hopi girl. She shrieks, scolds, pleads. I expect a melee, but none of the other kids follows suit. Apparently the water's for corn, not horseplay. The kids—by now eight in all—work clump to clump, watering corn that grows where nothing can grow, in low green bunches five or six feet apart. An agrarian scene—except that these are token crops, really. Like the rest of us the Hopi live in a money economy, don't depend on farming anymore, and raise their famously drought-resistant blue corn mainly for its ceremonial value.

On First Mesa I park at a sign saying "Visitors Center" and meet the mandatory guide, Maria, a plump, bespectacled woman who—like most such guides I've run across, whether in the United States or abroad—dispenses more chatter than fact. "What's it like to live up here?" is what I'd most like to know. Maria, though high-schooled in Los Angeles, remains Hopi enough to be evasive. My eyes meet those of Hopi kids playing near an adobe bread oven. What's their daydreaming like? I'm none the wiser. A crinkled woman with white eyebrows on skin dark as tobacco offers pots for sale and laughs maliciously over retorts she's been hurling at another old woman, now limping from sight round the corner. But her words are Hopi. Then Maria breaches my idea of her decorum by commenting, "They fight a lot. She says her sister's always stealing her money."

We stroll past adobe and fieldstone hovels, and squalor that is almost a style, to the oldest pueblo, Walpi—whose perch on the mesa's very edges offers a 360-degree panorama, all sky and horizon. Hot wind tugs at my hat's choke strap, wants to puff it overboard, set its broadbrimmed straw tumbling, winking, many hundreds of feet down off the mesa. The astonishing Southwestern openness stretches level as ocean floor. The space up here indeed feels like a shoreless sea.

"Undeveloped"? It takes someone from the cheek-by-jowl crowding of Europe, Aldous Huxley for instance, to know what that's worth. Back in the fifties he made it *brilliantly* simple: "The most wonderful thing about America is that, even in these middle years of the twentieth century, there are so few Americans."

Suddenly I know that space is possibility. That the treeless, unbroken desert horizon is like one vast and outgoing motion of the soul, which expands to become what it sees—an endlessness within which we're both lost and found. At any rate, that's my response. But the Hopi?

Below me on Walpi's mesa ledges lie gleams of beer aluminum, shattered bottles, the smudge of oil containers both plastic and metal, discarded shirts, empty detergent containers, sneakers, old coveralls, broken toys, rusted panels of a washing machine—impossible to overlook. Maria ignores it all. If the Hopi don't see litter, do they see "scenery"?

Seventy-five or eighty miles away, summit snows of the San Francisco mountains remind me where Hopi kachina-spirits dwell and descend from to visit these mesas. That's something I know, but don't really see. How *could* I see what I haven't lived, only learned? Looking at the same peak, my Hopi guide—despite her Los Angeles high-school years—stands at least partly inside a vision and inside cyclical time. An arm's length away, I measure my being by the strictly linear time of our technological culture. For us non-Hopis the line between "self" and "surroundings" is drawn with the illusory neatness of a "yes" and "no" deciding all questions.

That heightens the paradox of these Native Americans whose mythologies are so intricate and wise, yet whose indifference to trash boggles the mind. Nor does paradox end there. Our thirst for Hopi artifacts grows annually, as collecting doll-like kachinas booms; yet we regard the general poverty of the Hopi and their near-certain doom with mild regret, as if tolerable.

"What's to be done?" I ask this young Hopi woman, who has mentioned not only the language differences between First Mesa's trio of pueblos, Hano, Sichomovi, and Walpi, but their drift away from native tongues into English. Maria isn't one for sweeping statements. Instead, she simply explains that Hopi children speak English in school, and furthermore aren't learning their Hopi tongue well. "When they do speak Hopi," she says, "it isn't good Hopi. They don't get it right." What's worse, books can't teach it; since the Hopi have no written language, their "scriptures" are spoken. "Some people are supposed to be working on a dictionary now, so maybe that will help," says Maria. Her voice doesn't think so.

I press folding money into Maria's palm as we shake hands on leaving. Perhaps to transform my dollars from a tip to a fair exchange she insists that I accept some of her fresh-baked piki bread—a Hopi specialty. Thin and crisp as dried leaves, piki bread results from ladling blue corn gruel over a hot cooking stone. Hopi think it quite a delicacy. My first samplings of the stuff note only its brittleness and lack of flavor. More nibbles bring me round to the Hopi view. Piki bread, I decide, could become addictive.

Winding back down the First Mesa road, I pass its burying ground. Here where an ankle-high border of sandstone rubble loops each grave's bump of burnt soil, its sparse pinches of weed, the dead claim nothing—except perhaps, "This is how it is."

No end to the end of the world. As I've said, I too am lost in it, like everyone. Down to $65, I nurse nine-year-old shocks over the roughest of dirt roads toward New Mexico's Chaco Canyon, lying sixty miles from mechanics and car parts. At seven to ten miles per hour over bad patches of washboarding, a full stop doesn't seem much delay, so in the face of boundless sage I give way to a whim that arose long ago as a question: "What if you just walked off into that stuff?"

"What for?" replies my sensible side. "To stand in the middle of nowhere?"

As if answering some mysterious appeal—an irrelevance so perfect, so empty of any conceivable tool-value that its very non-sense guarantees a worthwhile waste of my time—I park, look around, choose an expanse without one notable feature, and stroll off among clumps knee-high or waist-tall, like dwarf forest. Each sage plant's stem has that writhe I so admire in juniper, and each grows, from its underside of twigged shadow, a fat splash of silver green leaf tips.

I pluck one, a typical sage leaf—no wider than an ant's mattress—for examining under my magnifier. Knowing what I'll see doesn't forestall my amazement at the leaf's caked hairs. They glisten like spiders' filaments, and web its surface with air-trapping "fur" that cuts down water lost by evaporation. The least hair among them has been spun by who knows how many million turns of the planet. Can we look anywhere without looking into ourselves? No place I know of. Especially when looking into least things.

Only a couple of miles from the road, glancing back, I can barely see its thin ocher scar: the intrusion I'm part of, and want my Volvo-speck to keep bumping along on. Yet the desert space surrounding my body is all sage leaves and blue sky, cirrus-streaked. Like the Hopi parts of Arizona, this New Mexican plateau is truly an erstwhile sea floor whose oceanic volumes are gone into silence that soaks up everything, absorbing it. Amid shadscale, snakeweed, and lupine, I feel ongoing kinship between desert brush and the branching of my own veins.

Roused from that daydream I discover I've come to a standstill, wholly absorbed in listening to nothing. "Nothing," because sacred space is always a listener, never the speaker my ear seems to think its next moment verges on. Which must be why, unconsciously, I slow, then stop. If I moved I might miss it.

Its quiet is partly my pulse: heart, veins, the aorta, their arterial surges and capillaries. So here I'm a slowly burning bush, waving slightly as if in the weather of its own respiration: a blood tumbleweed, whose species is odd as it is common, blowing itself about the world, and being blown, by winds even the wisest among us scarcely understand.

Back in Boulder I may chance to mention my stroll toward the middle of nowhere. I'll perhaps wish I hadn't. Even a close friend is bound to look quizzical. "And so? . . ." Expectant pause. My friend's eyes not quite veiling impatience: "So what's the point?"

Two, three minutes . . . without the slightest intention. Listening for what? My own body-beat, yes. The stir of Mormon tea bushes. Faint crackle-pop of cicadas whose emerging pupae burst their chitin shells. Sound of all Anasazi voices left alive. Barely audible breeze warping my hat brim. Sound of a planet in motion.

To answer, "Well, the point is . . . there isn't one," differs greatly from saying it was pointless, which would be a flat lie. However, to say, "Oh, it was meaningless I suppose," would be the same lie reworded. So the friend with an inner ear must interpret, maybe even believe, my wordless shrug. "It doesn't have a meaning. You have to go there."

Technically Sweet

> Before the effect, one believes in different causes than
> one does afterward.
>
> —FRIEDRICH NIETZSCHE

Notoriously, it's the simplest things we can't know. In this continuum of beginnings, every effect is a cause whose own cause blurs, fading backward into the headwaters of existence.

For example, among effects about to become causes inside the boys at Camp Koenig, why *that* boy? His father has money; but the camp specializes in rich New York kids summering upstate from the city. If he's a Jew, so are the others. Physically he is indeed an utter twit, throws like a girl, can't hit the slowest baseball with a racquet, much less a bat. Years later his own brother, Frank, who idolizes him, will admit that his poor eye/hand coordination in wood chopping produces the comic illusion of Robert's "chasing the wood down the road."

Any ordinary fourteen-year-old would get the message: "Go straight to the bottom of the pecking order. Stay there!" And that would be that. But his comfy upbringing and egghead pursuits have shut him off from what ordinary kids understand. So he doesn't camouflage his brain power. He lets it show, often, and it costs him. During one of his long evening walks alone, a bunch of the Camp Koenig youngsters lie in wait. They jump him, drag him off to the icehouse, and after sufficient "torturing" strip him naked, paint his rear end "and other parts of his body" green. They then lock him up there, to spend all night in that icehouse.

The immediate cause seems plain. He was asking for it, wasn't he? And could any zone of insult attract pubescent males quite so irresisti-

73

bly as an uppity boy's privates? But if in the distant summer of 1918 a gifted misfit gets worked over, is humiliated indelibly as only a fourteen-year-old can be, . . . so?

"The world will remember my boils," said Karl Marx.

Desert stillness. Piñon and juniper woodlands. Bursts of yucca and agave. Sage-tufted and cactus-prickled aridities. Red canyon sands, adobe roads. Mountains, their indigo distances. New Mexico's license plates say "Land of Enchantment"—and most of it actually is. And more. Alaskan wilderness can feel trackless, untouched: in repeated pauses there I've wondered, "Has any human ever stood just where I'm standing? Quite possibly not." On the other hand, like the entire Pajarito Plateau through which it carves, Frijoles Canyon in New Mexico exudes the feel of ancient habitation.

When Europe was still muddy and medieval, bands immigrating from the overpopulous Chaco area, blighted by drought, built villages here, and kept domestic animals. They potted, they wove. They bartered for goods from places distant as the sea. Long before anyone knew where the New World was, Keres-speaking Anasazi, "the ancient ones," were at home up and down the Frijoles.

In the luminous dusk of their canyon I sit doing nothing: savoring the strange pleasures of tired legs, watching the light go, watching white-bellied swallows catch damselflies, watching sunset fade from the spiderlike limbs of cholla cactus. An evening hush makes the light quiet, makes me want to give up the day as slowly as possible. The canyon's bizarre volcanic stone, a kind of consolidated ash called rhyolitic "tuff," includes bizarre bubblelike holes eroded open by wind. These riddle its four-hundred-foot cliffs, making them look as if rock could be yeasted. Taking advantage of tuff's friable nature, Anasazi peoples scraped room-sized cavities into those walls. "Viga holes" show where they socketed logs into the cliff for building stone pueblos out from, and onto. Vestiges of their dwellings line the canyon. Here and there, till dusk thickens, I can make out the enigmatic spirals, masklike designs of Anasazi petroglyphs.

What had they been pecked onto stone to invoke? What to ward off or record? I don't know. Nobody does. All I know is that in this "Bean Canyon" and all over New Mexico's great Pajarito Plateau, permanent victories were won by a people who built hundreds of summers here, and then, for uncertain reasons, abandoned everything.

The New Mexican twilight almost puts me in that neopastoral

mood we use for sentimentalizing what we've destroyed, leaving me free to make them better than they were—just as we eulogize the lost planet we've improved beyond recognition. But even the rose madder and lavender dusk can't quite do it. Not many miles from where I sit, trying to be Anasazi, lie some outbuildings of Los Alamos. Years earlier, when I first visited Cañon de los Frijoles, I drove past the main laboratories of Los Alamos as contemptuously as possible. Tomorrow I'll hike farther off from their pathetic successes, toward a shrine called the Stone Lions.

In one panel of the Donald Duck comic book a bespectacled scientist duck holds up a tumbler of drinking water. Hitler hasn't yet made his big move. The duck in the lab coat says, "There is enough energy in this glass of water to drive the Queen Mary across the Atlantic." Huey, Louie, and Dewey gape.

Mrs. Ferry's kitchen always impresses me with its electric refrigerator, which wears stacked coils atop like a hat. Our family has an ice box. My mother props a square card in the front window so the iceman will know how many pounds: 25 or 50 or 75 or 100. Many houses lack phones. Some families haven't a radio. Oh, a dim and misty age; nonetheless, we kids sipping Kool-Aid have blind faith in progress. Less credulous than Louie, Dewey, and Huey—or more—we look into our glasses of purpled water and believe. All that energy! In there?

Seven miles from Boulder, my favorite bike route grazes the north edge of the notorious Rocky Flats Plant. On this halcyon day in October, fields and mesa slopes are burnt tawny; the near mountains, hazed but not fully blue. Land gulls gracefully cruise for bugs, like an avian leisure class simply taking the air. In contrast, I'm pedaling hard up a steep stretch called the Wall, along a route locally famous as the Morgul-Bismark. Did I say "pedaling hard"? As I top out over the crest, the pedals slow, and I'm gasping, and glad there's no wind.

Those low, industrially pristine buildings of Rocky Flats house the sole manufacture of our country's plutonium "devices," so I'm grateful for the windless afternoon. Plutonium doesn't have to be in a bomb to kill me. Its toxicity in the human system is almost beyond belief. One half of one hundredth of one millionth of a gram isn't exactly oodles. However, a half-hundredth microgram dose of plutonium 239 per gram of bloodless lung has been shown to produce cancers in 100 percent of dogs used for experiment. And through Rocky Flats pass *tons* of the stuff. Since latent cancer may take twenty years or more to announce itself, plutonium is the perfect industrial murder. Two decades from now, if my lung cells betray some long-hidden, accelerating derangement, there'll be no clue to that cancer's having begun this afternoon, with a given breath.

Four summers after my first visit to Cañon de los Frijoles I find myself once again held by evening light over the Pajarito Plateau's scrub forest and volcanic tuff, by the raucous piñon jays and Clark's nutcrackers. Typical corvids! Though they've pine nuts enough for triple their numbers, their calls nonetheless grate, rasp, insist.

My tent—a superlight of Gortex and two thin fiberglass wands— sits bright green on a panoramic spot many miles from Frijoles Canyon. To have trekked those desert miles with just a gallon of water for two days . . . well, that's not enough to be comfortable—which I knew beforehand—but enough to get by. So I spend the evening telling myself I'm not *very* thirsty, though in desert there's nowhere to look but the truth: that we're made of trained water. Even the panoramic view extending thirty miles eastward across the marvelous Southwestern space of the Rio Grande Valley is centered by that great life-giving river. Above it floats the blue hugeness of Santa Fe Baldy, still snow banded in early June, as are other high peaks of the Sangre de Cristo Range. "Blood of Christ"—who but Spaniards would see sunset-reddened snows that way? On second thought, I realize that in humankind's continuous heart the impulse to sow the landscape with gods may be our one oldest urge.

"As actual objects," I told myself beforehand, "the so-called 'lions' will be weathered to a couple of lumps barely resembling any animal. Hardly worth a twelve- to fourteen-mile hike. Go anyway."

So having come, I've discovered that indeed, as sculpture, they're nothing. I loved them.

The New York kid, the sports nerd, the genius misfit who ticked off his mental inferiors enough to get his body "and other parts" painted green at Camp Koenig spends the summer of 1922, his eighteenth, trail riding out of a dude ranch high in the Sangre de Cristo mountains. More than any single human who ever drew breath, it may be he who did most to speed the advent of another Nature. I say "did most." Within the continuum of cause and effect, it takes the entire galaxy, and local galaxies floating adjacent, to create one foetus.

The ranch for wealthy Eastern dudes, Los Piños, is owned by Katherine Page and her new husband. She is twenty-eight, and not just anybody. Her Indian-fighting grandfather, a Chaves, remains legendary in Sandia County. Her father, Don Amado, claims and receives hidalgo status. The Chaves line is New Mexican aristocracy. "Beautiful, charming, warm, imperious" are just a few of the terms Katherine Page evokes from those who know her.

Later, a biographer will claim that the Jewish stripling saw Katherine Page as "a fascinating and romantic figure." Another biographer will claim the eighteen-year-old was "infatuated" and "adoring" of this comely and—by numerous accounts—undeniably vital woman.

The weak-chested, six-foot, 120 pound, citified bookworm certainly flabbergasts his mentor/chaperone, one Herbert Smith. Though the lad's father has retained Smith to accompany his frail son to New Mexico and help Robert survive its mountain rigors, the boy shows unaccountable endurance. He becomes an adept horseman, with a streak of fatalism that makes him "absolutely intrepid" in dangerous situations. He more than fits in. Looking back on the Los Piños summer, Herbert Smith guesses that there in Western high-country, and "for the first time in his life," the boy found himself "loved, admired, sought after."

It's the seventh of August, 1945. With my cheap canvas bag and my four or five hand-me-down clubs, I'm an insouciant fourteen, strolling the two miles home after a round of golf. That hot afternoon I learn they've dropped a new kind of bomb. Overnight *atomic* becomes *the* buzzword. *Fallout* isn't yet a word. *Acid rain, ozone layer, toxic waste, greenhouse effect*, are far down the road. Nobody knows we've crossed into another Nature.

Camped a half mile away from and above the Stone Lions I finish a rather dry supper. North of me thunderheads sulk darkly, emitting voltages whose grumble arrives twenty-five seconds after the bolt. Safe enough. And though rain-sashes pour from the mass of dark cloud, their storm appears stalled. There's still plenty of light for poking around the overlook I've climbed to. So even if it means exuding a tad more of my precious body water, I decide to stroll among the sparse mix of ponderosa pine, piñon, juniper, and the usual sage clumps, clumps of Apache plume. Do the obsidian chips lying all over the place occur in any pattern?

Wherever paleo-Indians and their descendants once paused to chip

an arrowhead or scraper from a chunk of the stuff, obsidian's black volcanic glass now flecks the blond or blood red of Southwestern dust and
sand. Wandering, staring down past tufts of rice grass or the gnarly
stems of sagebrush, I find thousands of chips, never an arrowhead. Deer
and elk prints abound, along with occasional coyote tracks, but of human animals no trace not my own. Except for glassy black spatters of
obsidian. Fallen from hands that weighed and cherished certain stones,
the chips aren't just curiosities. They're part of my huge past that got
flaked away.

At the soda fountain in Ring's Drug Store, Dick Lonergan, fellow
teen, fills me in: "It doesn't necessarily have to be big. They say it could
be about the size of a golf ball."

"Great!" I say. "They can drop a whole B-29 full of them." Four
years of our war propaganda have utterly brainwashed me. While U.S.
Marines hemorrhage from island to island toward the Japanese main-
land, headlines serve up "Jap" depravity as everyday fare. Political car-
toons draw Japanese soldiers in such fanged, such craven, such ape-
browed, squinty-eyed, chinless, and slavering form that one day my
five-year-old cousin Paul asks, "Are Japanese human?" At first I suppose
he means, "Are they cruel?" Oh no. He hasn't yet learned to read, so
he's not sure. He wants to know, literally: "Are Japanese human?"

In our downstate Illinois farm town I've never *seen* a Japanese, but
if they're human, so what? The atom bomb is just what those Japs
deserve.

When about 150 air miles south of Los Alamos, near dawn on July
16, 1945, the Trinity test fireball bursts with radical candor, it proves
that mathematics can ignite the imaginary. What Fermi does during
and says after the blast, what Groves says to Oppenheimer, what Kistia-
kowsky feels, what sort of spontaneous cheer is sent up by eye witnesses
seven leagues from ground zero—all get recorded, recalled, repeated.

What nobody says, says most. Nobody says "disappointing" or anything like it. Nobody says, "Just what we predicted." Not at all. Each
person there is taken by surprise, stunned witless through long, elliptical seconds of animal fear. Then everybody emerges into language and
the general babble. The firestorm at ground zero has been a triumph of
theory. Simultaneously it has lit up a lethal gap in humans of the highest intelligence: failure to imagine.

Only when the skin cringes from appalling heat, only when the fireblind eyes recover, do the scientists' bodies know what their theories feel like.

Thunderclouds continue rising above the Jemez Mountains northwest of my camp on the Pajarito Plateau. "Jemez," an Indian word for "place of the boiling springs," reminds me how the high ridgelines I'm staring toward go there. For the Stone Age and Nuclear Age to share one site would be irony enough. But that the Bomb should have been developed near the rim of a great volcanic caldera, whose present lip—some four thousand feet above me and a dozen miles west—is the high-country skyline of the Jemez Mountains, seems ironic indeed. For days I've been roving a tiny fraction of what it spewed when it blew, with a force six hundred times greater than that of Mount St. Helens in 1980.

On this planet so rich in disasters, the East Indian eruption of Krakatoa represents the greatest volcanic event humans have been around to know about. It produced a crater four miles wide and ejected about a dozen cubic miles of stuff, a baker's dozen to be exact. In contrast, the Jemez volcano hurled out about 150 cubic miles of detritus! The lovely Pajarito Plateau, alone, represents twenty-five cubic miles of that material. Further, when a volcano blows its innards so thoroughly that it collapses like a wet shirt, what's left is a caldera. Thus the Jemez wasn't just any volcano. Its remnant is a caldera fifty miles in circumference, one of the largest on earth, big enough to be seen from the moon. It encloses nearly two hundred square miles of farm and grazing land. Which, as geologists put it, makes Krakatoa "a firecracker" and Mount St. Helens "a hiccup."

Boots Brennan, drummer, handles the vocals. No so much because he can sing—he can't sing worth two cents—but it's his band, it's August 5, 1945, and since news from the Pacific has the Japs reeling, all of us teenagers who whirl, jitterbug, or slide fast round the pavilion dance floor feel that Boots and his music are great.

Illinoians from other towns say, "You Jacksonville people don't know how lucky you are to have Nichols Park." We don't, we just know that the Nichols Park pavilion is a living, open-air antique. Now it's our turn to have the future before us, to be so young that just dancing close and slow spikes our silences with adrenaline.

An actual moon, rising eastward low over the lake near that pavilion, doesn't alter the fact that Patricia Gleason and I look forward to the band's "moonlight" numbers. Overhead lights rheostat down, dim out. High in the dance hall's four corners, spotlights converge on the big mirrored ball that blazes, revolving. The band plays a slow one. The mirror-mosaic flashes shards and splinters of light gliding slowest on the near walls, fastest nearing corners of the deliciously darkened area, while the band's lone saxophonist tries to be the Glenn Miller reed section on "Blue Rain."

As Pat and I glide over a marvelous maple floor which our courting parents had enjoyed in their turn, our joined hands exude a palm-sweat more interesting than any biblical balm of Gilead. Like a mystic bemused, I gaze into the mirror-sphere's dazzle. On the other side of the world a fireball ignites even the birds in the air, over a city whose streets acquire sudden clots of black jelly. On legs and faces and chests of Japanese exactly our ages, the young skin boils.

Maybe in a lifetime, if we're lucky, there's one summer. In the case of Robert Oppenheimer, the ailing adolescent escorted by Herbert Smith from New York to the West and its high country, we can't *know* there was even one.

We can guess, however, that his sixty-odd summers included few happier than that of his eighteenth year, when, certainly, he fell under the spell of a place, and met Katherine Page. "She referred to us always then and afterward as her slaves. 'Here come my slaves,' " as the mature Paul Horgan put it, reminiscing about his stay at Los Piños with Francis Fergusson and Robert. That season the "slaves" find an unmapped lake high on the east slope of Santa Fe Baldy and name it Lake Katherine.

Three years later, writing to Herbert Smith, Robert uses a revealing allusion: "The other night, after a year or so of lethe I dreamt of Mrs. Page. She was standing at the porch steps, in the sunlight, in the olive riding jacket she used to wear. And the doctor was saying to her 'Don't look at me like that' & I wasn't there, & it was all lovely."

The ranch that Robert soon leases, then buys, then for twenty years keeps going back to lies within walking distance of Los Piños and Katherine Page.

The trail past Yapashi ruins is easy. After a sudden four hundred feet of switchbacks on the east wall of Cañon de los Frijoles, it levels through open forest of ponderosa, descends and reascends several more canyons whose volcanic walls have weathered like billowed curtains. Since the plateau slopes gently eastward, its climate changes through only a few miles. Ponderosas give way to piñon only a third as tall, and to scrubby Utah juniper. Spanish bayonet and cholla cactus replace deciduous undergrowth—except for lovely clumps of Apache plume with its froth of tiny white flowers, and mocha tassels gossamer as down on an ostrich feather.

I could easily die here, but know perfectly well I won't. Despite thirst, falling rock, rattlers, scorpions, I can't really see it as did the Rio Grande Anasazi, can't really imagine its land of little rain as *all there is*. Each day. Forever. I can't really see canyon clay going into hand-built, carefully painted pots. The woman pounding juniper bark for menstrual pads and children's diapers belongs to bones in some archeological tract, though she was once real enough to herself. If her man's night fires drove off the desert chill, if she spent much of her day gathering rice grass, or piñon nuts, and grinding corn beween two stones, their way of life touches me only as a measure of distance.

My support system goes beyond a top-of-the-line internal frame pack full of gear. My brain's acculturation makes wilderness disappear the moment I arrive. At the Stone Lions, however, instead of my changing *it*, the shrine changes me—for an instant or two. For a few seconds I become the simplest of expressions, an "Oh-h-h." Nobody had told me that Indians still visit, still leave vestiges.

In a sort of bleached and horny garland, hundreds of intertangled antlers surround the sculpted lions. An antelope horn, taken while the animal was in velvet. A deer antler with fresh, tufted hide near its base. On one of the lions someone has placed a fat, tightly bound wreath of juniper twigs. Centering that, he has inset a fist-sized chunk of beeswax.

Pajarito stone isn't basalt. The figures themselves have indeed weathered to remote semblances of some animal thing. Mountain lions? A guess. But it's clear that the shrine is still alive. From one of the whitest deer antlers hangs a silver and crystal trinket. From another, two bright blue and scarlet feathers swing ever so slightly by a single strand of red sewing thread, onto which have been strung exactly three cerulean beads smaller than peppercorns. Below them dangles the tiny spiral of a seashell, white as pearl.

I don't know their meaning, don't know who left them, don't know what for. Not believing in gods, I believe only in whatever world this is. Yet I want my presence here to be weightless as that feathered trinket. It turns in the hot afternoon, lightly, lightly.

Weeks before "Little Boy" and "Fat Man" are scheduled to fall through bomber doors toward cities where even a newborn is old enough to die, Kenneth Bainbridge, in charge of the Trinity test, looks at the world's first pillar of lethally radioactive cloud still rolling, ascending, and says to Oppenheimer, "Well, now we're all sons of bitches."

In Cañon de los Frijoles I descend the sapling ladder into an Anasazi kiva. The imperfect circle of its freestone interior seems made of ocher dust, which any image I try to summon partakes of. A tribal male squats, putting a live coal to dust in a pipestone bowl. Arthritic and toothless oldsters half doze in the midst of their own stories, whose tongues are dust. Nobody sits weaving yucca twine into square-toed sandals, or discussing the crescent moon's cue for bean sprout rituals. Over the dusty floor nobody outlines a world with pinches of cornmeal, powdered charcoal, pine pollen.

Through the roof hole come shafts of sunlight made visible by the dust I stir up looking for the kiva's *sipapu*. Surely there once was one: a symbolic, navellike dimple in the dirt floor. I've seen dozens in kivas elsewhere—*sipapuni*, some Hopi call them—because pueblos along the Rio Grande Valley and pueblos of the Hopi in Arizona still use kivas surprisingly like Anasazi versions abandoned in the twelfth and thirteenth centuries. Through that hole all humankind escaped a sin-struck nether cosmos turned chaotic; the so-called Third World. From it they fled upward into a fresh chance—this one we now live in, the Fourth World.

The Third World had fallen into corrupt ways, the Hopi believe, because people forgot "the meaning of life." A faithful few remembered. In their songs they asked, "Who are we? Where do we come from? Why are we here?" Their answers reminded them: they had been created by Tawa, the sun. They had come through many worlds. Evil in the human heart had brought each to ruin. So they rose into the Fourth World, leaving evil behind. They were to roam, seeking other Hopi, seeking the place where all scattered and migrating Hopi would meet again.

Up rungs of peeled juniper I climb from kiva-gloom, emerge blinking at the daylight. Hopi myth suggests I ought to feel the significance of being born again into it. But I don't, not a bit. So much for the spot my topographical map marks "Ceremonial Cave."

Or maybe my kiva reemergence into the hard sunlight of this

Fourth World means, "It's all to do again, everything, every time. Daily you have to pump gods back into the scenery; so you can breathe. You can't breathe just scrub woodlands and yucca and cactus and rock." I'm weary, thirsty. Those last Anasazis who climbed out of this kiva must've taken the gods with them.

I. I. Rabi: "At first I was thrilled. It was a vision. Then a few minutes afterward, I had goose flesh all over me when I realized what this meant for the future of humanity. Up until then, humanity was, after all, a limited factor in the evolution and process of nature. The vast oceans, lakes and rivers, the atmosphere, were not very much affected by the existence of mankind. The new powers represented a threat not only to mankind but to all forms of life: the seas and the air. One could foresee that nothing was immune."

Norris Bradbury, Oppenheimer's successor at Los Alamos: "Some people claim to have wondered at the time about the future of mankind. I didn't. We were at war and the damned thing worked."

Thus, among Trinity witnesses, some saw another Nature being born, some a successful test.

A month after Trinity, the nation celebrates VJ Day. Oppenheimer pays a quick visit to a Los Alamos party. He finds "a usually cool-headed young group leader" throwing up outside in the bushes, and says to himself, "The reaction has begun."

Nobody knows what Katherine Page thought of it, or of her former "slave." To imply that Robert Oppenheimer's decision to accept the scientific directorship of the Manhattan Project turned on "imprinting" from his eighteenth summer, and the smile of a married woman ten years his elder, would be worse than inane. His Los Alamos years turned on everything.

Great effects, however, don't always require great causes. A forest can begin from one pinecone. True, Oppenheimer's known reasons for directing work on the Bomb and General Groves's concurrence in choosing the Pajarito site are backed by a host of highly specific influences; practical, weighty, strategic.

True, too, that the Camp Koenig ordeal suffered by a pubescent misfit locked overnight all those summers ago does come to mind. That textbook case of rejection must've gone deep. The entity whose site Groves and Oppenheimer usurp without discussion is, coincidentally enough, a boys' school that stresses outdoor hardihood. Later, "active" materials for the Trinity blast are stored in—of all buildings left over from that mesa-top school—its icehouse.

Looking those thirty miles eastward across the Rio Grande Valley, I pause in my evening stroll on the Pajarito and can't avoid pondering the hidden affinities in mere coincidence. Through mauve-tinted air I watch sunset color peaks of the Sangre de Cristo, knowing perfectly well that, from Los Alamos, Robert Oppenheimer often watched the same effects. On the other side of those summits lay Los Piños. Lots of things that just happen, we realize, may not have just happened.

Probably Los Piños and Mrs. Page were by then a time quite out of mind. The mature Oppenheimer could have his pick of women, who found him decidedly attractive. On the other hand, it's the psyche's buried folds and abysses that account for certain happenstances we've arranged with closed eyes. The mature Robert casually woos another man's wife, as it happens, and marries her; then, a few years later, brings to Los Alamos the woman everybody calls Kitty—whose given name is Katherine.

Alchemy's wildest dreams. Through nuclear testing and its instant perpetuities, a substance once nowhere because it didn't and couldn't exist, plutonium is now—as one medical researcher puts it—"available for inhalation." Yearly more available, as the Third World progresses into Bomb-love. Thus my breathing, like everyone's, has had to avail itself of the opportunity. If research is to be believed, I've a touch of plutonium in my body right now. If research is to be believed, so has virtually everyone alive. We're a sort of alchemical experiment nobody intended. And nobody on earth has any idea what effects that plutonium will work. Or cause not to.

Among acquaintances who felt that Robert Oppenheimer had a "Messiah complex," as one biographer puts it, is his companion at Camp Koenig, the founder's own son and virtually the camp's only gentile kid, Fred Koenig, who says he doesn't see how the "torture" episode could have been "anything but traumatic." Over and above their green-paint humiliation of young Robert, Koenig says, "They, as it were, crucified him."

Does a "Messiah complex" underlie the odd code name for the blast called "Trinity"? Oppenheimer refers the choice to Christian poems by the Renaissance poet John Donne. If his study of the *Bhagavadgita* suggested a Hindu trinity—Brahma, Vishnu, and Shiva; creator, preserver, destroyer—the allusion remains apt and unsettling.

To my surprise the university's Glenn Miller Ballroom is already packed when I arrive. People keep trickling in though it's nearly 7 P.M. High on a wall to the right of the fancy oak podium with its microphones "live" for Peace Night hangs a huge, Hollywood-era blow-up. From it an airbrushed and brilliantined Glenn Miller glances aside at us, before putting his trombone to his lips. On the opposite wall there's a matching blow-up of his penciled score for "Elmer's Tune."

At dozens of tables people are sipping coffee, soft drinks. I spot long-haired guitarists, conga players—even a keyboards person. Return of the sixties. And tomorrow we'll all cover the seven miles south of Boulder to the Rocky Flats Nuclear Weapons Plant, for the Encirclement. That'll require 17,680 people around its seventeen-mile barbed wire perimeter. We'll join hands, as planned. There'll be a long, unanimous silence. And that'll be that.

The ballroom's array of colored spotlights razzles my eyes, as I speak extempore a few simple facts. Leaning toward the podium's microphones I'm scanning hundreds of faces and saying my say. When I mention 1,200,000 Chinese estimated killed in "my" war, the Korean War, something deep in me overflows. I choke up, can't talk. Then the upwelling subsides. As if giving myself confidential advice, I murmur into the microphones, "That's a minefield. Better stay away from there."

Later, alone, it feels bizarre. I didn't hate the "Chinks" my infantry platoon faced day after day; but their shellfire, machine guns, and snipers worked over my nerves. To anyone predicting that Chinese dead could *ever* get to me, I'd have said, "That'll be the day!"

Next morning I'm pedaling past droves of hikers, alongside other cyclists being passed by loaded cars, by motorbikers riding double, and truck beds full of young hair whipping in the breeze—streaming toward Rocky Flats. Mercedes sedans, BMWs. Harleys and Hondas. Bikes by the many hundreds. VW vans, Volvos. A big old Buick on which everything is loose, beginning with its front license. I overtake a twelve-year-old boy pumping uphill on roller skates! Miles off, along highways from Denver, I see a continuous glitter of windshields converging toward the same area.

Not everyone is with us. Towing a sign low overhead, the engine of a cruising silver-and-red Cessna burrs like a Bronx cheer: UP WITH THE NUKES DOWN WITH THE PUKES. Frat-house humor? Blue collar counter-demonstrators have publicized their intent to burn 269 Russian flags, in token of those who died aboard Korean Air Lines Flight 007. As one of the "PUKES" I recall that nausea goes with radiation sickness. I recall too the young scientist that Oppenheimer saw outside a VJ Day party at Los Alamos, throwing up into the bushes.

Come July 16, 1945, New Mexican weather over desert flats known as Jornada del Muerto isn't right, it's wrong—a virtual reverse of what the scientists have specified. But President Truman, meeting in Potsdam with Stalin, wants a trump card. Word is passed down: "Test by the sixteenth!"

The blast is big. Good. And "inefficient." Bad. So it spreads plutonium-enriched dust particles over thousands of New Mexican acres. No one knows what long-term effect these may have. Meanwhile a radioactive cloud floats across New Mexico and Kansas, Iowa, Indiana, upstate New York, out over the Atlantic. In less than forty-eight hours it circles the globe like a prophecy. Nobody will ever again live in the world which, till Trinity, every human had lived in.

Glimmers of ancient gods have come to us through the Dark Ages and medieval times by way of planets. Toward the close of the eighteenth century, Sir William Herschel discovers Uranus; eight years later a peculiar new element is named uranium. None can know how apt that name will become. Even that most furious heavy metal, plutonium, is a "transuranic."

Back toward the start of the past, Earth Mother (Gaia) and Sky Father (Ouranos, whom *we* call Uranus) disagree over their offspring. Gaia incites her son Cronos to rebel. He castrates his father. From droplets of that "Uranian" blood fallen to earth, monsters spring up, among them the Furies: avenging creatures, "those who walk in darkness," with snakes for hair and eyes that weep blood.

Herbert Smith wonders if Freud's description of the Oedipal complex may not explain young Robert's delight in New Mexico—far from his father's well-meaning but often obtrusive ways. When Robert learns that quite near Mrs. Page's place there's a 160 acre spread for rent, he blurts "Hot dog!"—which he decides to name it. Katherine, however, prefers "hot dog" in Spanish, *perro caliente*. Her "slave" Robert agrees.

Perro Caliente it becomes. One wonders if the astute Herbert Smith noted anything remotely Freudian in that.

Night rain ticks lightly on my tent. Around dawn when I unzip I find puddles held by wrinkles in the groundcloth, water enough to be worth drinking; on all fours I lap at it like any other desert animal. Up and dressed, I use my steel cup to transfer as much as possible to a canteen.

To save water I shortcut, bushwhacking and bouldering steeply down toward the Stone Lions, all the while getting showered by thick, dripping foliage of Gambel oak and New Mexican locust, but the chill of my soused shirt and pants in this desert is a form of savings. Water I won't have to sweat.

At the shrine itself everything remains as it was: the crudely sculpted vestiges of two animals crouched side by side, the bleached antlers, the obsidian bits, the pottery shards within the circle formed by the antlers—like coins tossed into a fountain. Then I note the recent addition. Atop one chunk of rock somebody has left a stack of corn tortillas not there earlier.

In 1925, Robert Oppenheimer is back at Los Piños, eager for the arrival of Katherine Page and Erna Fergusson. Walpi on the Hopi reservation in Arizona will soon be the scene of a snake dance climaxing sixteen days of ritual, and Erna, expert in Indian ceremonies, will make a perfect guide for the Oppenheimer party. Come fall, the twenty-one-year-old Harvard grad will take ship for further study in England and Germany. Will it occur to Robert that the dance is Hopi physics?

On a morning bright with sea haze and vapor still rising from dark ripples near shore, my troop ship eases toward its berth past cargo vessels riding at anchor off Yokohama. I'm still awed by the enemy of Pearl Harbor.

On our ship's port side a picturesque wooden vessel passes, as if out of an earlier century. From its gunwales right down to waterline its timbers show stop-gap repairs far older than the five-thousand-man "general class" transport whose rail I'm leaning over, hearing crewmen call to and fro in a most guttural language. Can that really be Japanese? More like a dog fight.

As we slide toward our pier the harbor's warehouses hold me spellbound with their obvious war damage. They've been just cobbled back together, not rebuilt. The roof on a low, reddish brown warehouse shows lots of patching with slats and tar paper. Our bombs! Unreal. To be here where they landed!

Perhaps I last saw them dropping through belly doors opening on movie screens during four years of flat, scratchy black-and-white images. Fast shrinking in size, they fell away from their own light reflected off our movie house faces . . . toward crewmen and docks my face is now somehow among. Over the placid water of the harbor morning, busy gutturals from bandy-legged little men on an oil tender carry to me, as if I'm *inside* a travelogue. Yokohama! Evil empire of my boyhood. Its quaint wooden vessels delight me, while stirring misgivings.

"Well," I think, "it's too bad. But they started it. And we finished it."

On a hike up Cañon de los Frijoles Niels Bohr stops to look at a creature he's never seen, only heard of, one peculiar to our New World, the skunk. Enrico Fermi meets Maria Martinez, celebrated potter of the neighboring San Ildefonso pueblo. His wife Laura goes hiking in the Frijoles with Genia Peierls, wife of the physicist. Emilio Segrè enthuses over the fishing in streams of the Pajarito, describing them as "full of big trouts. All you have to do is throw in a line and they bite you, even if you are shouting." Europeans take naturally to the hiking and skiing. Trail riding grows popular.

In truth, the mathematicians, physicists, and their mates are young, some twenty-five to twenty-nine, on the average. Anyone forty is an elder. To the brainy immigrants from manicured landscapes of Europe, this New Mexican terrain and wide, vaporlessly clear Rio Grande Valley seem magical, surreal. Phyllis Fisher and her husband are typical: city bred but soon in love with "the rocks and trails and open spaces of New Mexico."

Edward Teller, whose passions are physics, music, and Edward Teller, explores Schubert and Bartok on his Steinway. A foot having been crushed in a streetcar accident, he is—like Hephaistos/Vulcan—no hiker. His Hungarian childhood has imprinted him with an image of Russians as boogeymen. He thinks a fission device is small potatoes. He sulks, connives, schemes to give birth to his thermonuclear dreambaby, the fusion thing, the "Super."

The solace these people take in the beautiful Pajarito Plateau and its setting will help them make areas of the West, and our Earth's northern hemisphere, unnaturally radioactive for the next 24,000 years. Yet they mean well. Hitler's *Wehrmacht* is no figment. Amid leftovers from the Stone Age, they mean to make the world's most intelligent bomb.

Before leaving Bavaria and the Munich area—"Fun City" as our two boys name it—I begin hearing the insistent voice of my friend Reuben Rabinovitz. Back in Colorado I once told him I had no stomach for visiting German death camps. Reuben did not mince words: "You have a moral duty to go."

So I head the Volvo toward Dachau, fifteen or twenty minutes from Munich—whose combination of 133 concert halls, theaters, galleries, botanical gardens, zoos, science museums, and Baroque churches right next door to a death camp sums up human nature.

At the virtual suburb for which the camp is named, I inquire. The twenty-five-year-old German male wearing his university's black sweatshirt with its white lettering and insignia seems puzzled. I try various words for "prison camp." He cannot understand what I'm talking about, either in my German (bad) or his English (not bad) or any mixture thereof. Next I try a city bus driver of about forty-five. Surely a bus driver will know. He shakes his head, can't help me. Can't or won't?

Finally I ask a robust, heavy-set woman with shiny red cheeks, and hard eyes. Scarcely breaking her rhythm while sorting newspapers and magazines on sale at her kiosk, she says the camp is a mile or so outside town; gives directions glibly as a recorded message. Lots of practice. Yet I'm convinced that the twenty-five-year-old was sincere. His bewilderment seemed too spontaneous for faking.

Rocky Flats is, of course, no death camp. Instead there's an eerie potential: of seared faces we don't choose to foresee. Of posterity's face, which may one day ask, incredulously, "They *knew* all that stuff was piling up? They *knew*, and did nothing?"

During arduous summers in the Pecos, at Perro Caliente, Frank Oppenheimer joins his brother, the sports-nerd of Camp Koenig, now a tireless horseman. Together the two of them ride as much as a thousand miles in a summer. "Once," Frank recalls, "all the way to Colorado!"

While teaching theoretical physics as a twenty-five-year-old with concurrent appointments at Berkeley and Cal Tech, Robert studies Sanskrit, begins reading India's great metaphysical poem, the *Bhagavadgita*. Decades before it becomes fashionable, he flouts professorial dress code by often going round in a blue chambray shirt, and jeans belted onto his bony frame with a big buckle of New Mexican silver.

"My two great loves are physics and New Mexico," he writes to a friend. "It's a pity they can't be combined."

Unlike the canyon hideaways at Mesa Verde in Colorado, the Anasazi village whose ruins are called Yapashi had a panoramic view. Its rubble still has. Eastward I look across the valley to the Sangre de Cristo range above the Pecos, where the Oppenheimer place was and is. Forty miles south and to my right, the Rio Grande winds through wide open spaces toward lower New Mexico and the Jornada del Muerto, site of the Trinity test.

By now it's a gorgeous summer morning full of birdsong and bright yellow cactus blooms. Overhead the sweep of high-curving cirrus cloud makes a breathtaking gesture wide as only a Western sky can be. The Yapashi setting fills me with its openness, with the plateau's pygmy juniper, desert grasses. The empty joy of the villagers pours into me and vanishes. I stand on the floor of their sky.

As for the Anasazi's mysterious disappearance, theories abound. The reigning favorite, "ecological catastrophe," sounds too modish, too moralistic. Unless you know the Southwest. Anasazi in Arizona's Chaco Canyon, to choose an exhaustively well-studied instance, seem to have leaned too heavily on nature. Even beyond the threshold of ecological collapse, they somehow held on, temporized, met crisis on crisis. "Then when it really started to get away from them," as an anthropologist working in Chaco told me, "it would have gone fast. Could've really crashed."

The vendor's wares are familiar and strange: Japanese candies like jujube fruits or something between gel and a sort of tapioca. The chocolate's *like* ours, though more crumbly and bitter. From the fruits I choose two red apples.

During our troop train's fifteen-minute stop in Hiroshima, I see no damage whatever—neither in the station's well-laid pairs of rails, nor its platforms crowded with Japanese, half of whom still wear the traditional garments. Nor do I see war scars outside by the vendor's stand whose snacks I've hopped off the train to sample. Anyhow, I prefer not seeing them. And what if radiation levels aren't yet safe? But the Army wouldn't route us through Hiroshima if they weren't, would it?

Hustling back toward the train I pass a three-year-old so cute he slows me to a standstill—a darling, doll-like little fellow in a rich burgundy kimono with cream colored sash. On his feet are white, split-toed socks and wooden "gitas," the elevated sandals I'd supposed long out of use. His brown eyes widen at the sight of me, big, uniformed, and bustling.

Even as I kneel to hand him the apple he hadn't asked for and which his parents probably won't let him eat, I feel foolish but charmed. Cautiously he steps toward me to take it, steps back toward his parents, also wordless, also in kimonos, split-toed socks also chalk white, and "gita" sandals. The more coolly aristocratic their half smiles, the more gauchely presumptive I feel—a barbarian from the south, well aware of my appalling joy that day I first heard the name "Hiroshima." With terse rectitude the father cues his tiny son; a nod, a syllable. Whereupon the boy thanks me in a deep bow, out of centuries.

Through his bullhorn a demonstration marshal warns us not to lean against the wire fence—"U.S. Government property." Word-of-mouth news is that we're waiting for more people to arrive. Rocky Flats' perimeter fenceline isn't quite twenty miles. The 17,680 people it will take to encircle mean 35,360 hands. The autumn afternoon is unbelievably clear. Its sole clouds are two or three iridescent wisps, near high October sun. Still, the girl in blue canvas shorts shivers a bit as the breeze on the shaded backs of her legs raises gooseflesh.

Across sun-gold riffles of field grass, words drift from a distant PA system: there's a stretch of about four miles along the south fence without any people. The voice asks persons in already well-stocked areas to please leave and go *there* if at all possible. Apparently other spots are skimpily peopled too. In places, demonstrators eke out the encirclement by holding garments or blankets stretched between them. Even so, we're an estimated twelve thousand—a triumphant number, considering that, just a few years back, antinuclear types were a caste of untouchables: "Peaceniks" driving rusted VW vans full of unwashed pot smokers and dogs. In an opposite field across the highway, fifty head of Black Angus cattle graze and gaze; stolid, unpoliticized. I wonder what "permissible levels" occur in their milk, their beef.

My left hand holds the hand of a woman in tight, high-fashion pants of black leather, and snug leather jacket; my right hand holds the hand of Fred Denny, the one person here I know. Out of thousands, our clasped hands become a coincidence.

Finally, the moment: to encircle a bomb plant with ourselves and our silence. To let that do the talking. Then leave. Preceding silence, buglers along the perimeter will play "Taps." From about 150 yards off, the familiar notes carry to us; the lucent October afternoon takes that simple, slow tune into its radiance. Evergreens and crags of foothill/mountains seven miles off meet the eye through air absolutely transparent. The bugle's last note hangs, fades. Breeze rustles bunchgrass in front of us, a gust or two hums almost inaudibly past the barbed wire, and I find that twelve thousand people make an incomparable silence, as if humankind's highest good could be right now. Inside each of us, the miles of joined hands are saying a thing that can only be said without words.

When house hunting in Berkeley, Oppenheimer enters one possibility, takes a look round the rooms, and writes out a check for it on the spot. Sly voices hint that its appeal may be the address: "1 Eagle Hill."

The tough-minded Nobel laureate I. I. Rabi doesn't mince words: "I was never in the same class with him . . . I never ran into anyone who was brighter than he was." Rabi sees in Oppenheimer "the best mind of his generation." Others, assessing that mind, often resort to terms like *poet, philosopher, mystic*. Yet on grasping the possibility of fission, Oppenheimer's quick, hypercivilized brain aligns him with our two-handed, primitive past; the Anasazi hand coiling clay into pots, the hand chipping obsidian to an edge that will fly; the life of death and the life of grace. So perhaps his reaction would be Everyman's: "fission . . . energy . . . bomb."

Thus at Trinity, brain was made glare—the brilliance of a species able to desire escape from the deadly side of its nature, helpless to imagine how without ceasing to be itself.

The gravel road climbs, winding steeply upward toward Cowles, up toward the headwaters of the Pecos River, a clear mountain stream whose fast riffles and depths sweeten the valley the road follows. A red pickup rushes past me, the bold MITSUBISHI of its tailgate disappearing in rock dust. Back in my downstate Illinois during the war years, anyone driving a truck named Mitsubishi would've been hauled from the cab and beaten—savagely. For that matter, workers once "Japs" have assembled the very chassis, motor, and wheels of my pre-owned Toyota now bumping along toward Perro Caliente.

Even to a Coloradan, the Pecos valley is unusually beautiful. The higher my 1600 cc engine climbs, the more open the valley's forested slopes become, the swifter the Pecos. By the time I reach Cowles, which amounts to a dinky store and a mailbox, I realize that the rich Eastern dudes knew what they were doing. Back in the early 1920s Cowles and Los Piños would have been well off the beaten path.

They still are. And the Oppenheimer cabin even more so. To reach it I turn right at the sign directing backpackers toward Iron Gate, and, as the road roughens, find myself wishing for a Land Cruiser; find myself thinking, "When it came to picking a hideaway, young Robert didn't mess around. You have to *want* to get there."

"Yes," I think, "but why do *you* want to?"

Oh, . . . because.

So having parked, I foot it up the path to his cabin of mortar-chinked logs, hardly less rustic for its three roof dormers, little altered from long before the Los Alamos years. A child's tire swing dangles by a rope strung to the porch roof, and round back there's another swing. I'm happy to have learned that Robert's son, Peter, and his wife are absent just now. Even to climb the footpath a hundred yards or so up from the road, and be standing here surveying the place feels intrusive enough.

Westward, through a break in tall groves of fir and spruce there's a fine view of Santa Fe Baldy with the ridgelines of companion summits, snowfields and all. No wonder Oppie and brother Frank often slept on the porch, overlooking. No wonder Oppenheimer balked at hiding the Bomb project in a canyon. No wonder he nudged General Groves into approving the openness of the Pajarito. He always liked a view. Back in 1929 writing from Berkeley to brother Frank he mentioned often visiting "some boys who have . . . a beautiful cabin on the hill, with a view and great stone fireplace and balconies and so on." For Oppenheimer there was ever and always the aesthetic dimension.

Though I've climbed camera in hand, intending to photograph the cabin, I decide simply to remember it. The child's swings, the roof dormers, the thick chinking between wolf-colored logs. The bright blue of boards setting off the windows. The front steps and threshold. The meadow, with its wildflowers, sloping eagerly up to the porch. The wonderful westward view of high snowfields. What converged here once, and still radiates from it, is too blessed and cursed for trivializing in a snapshot.

Two nighthawks veer past me about fifteen feet away—nearer than I've ever seen them come—as if supposing nobody's here, as usual, and almost nobody is. Up from Capulin Canyon begins the comic racket of spadefoot toads, small hopes whose loud, primordial croaking goes farther than sound. They're brief creatures, too, and this is their hour.

We humans see ourselves anywhere we look, just as my aims are reflected in chips of black glass, and the occasional painted potsherd. Southwestern mesas are sown with such millions of shattered pots, only the smallest fraction of which will ever be pieced back together; still, I'll leave them to the eventual student archeologist—a young woman, perhaps, who will see in their black and white designs some variant of Rio Grande Anasazi. Or, finding the black and red one I have in my hand right now, may say, "Trade goods. Possibly Mogollon."

For a moment, though, that scrap of hand-painted clay and bit of chipped obsidian chink together in my palm like opposite lobes of the mind, or Rome's enemy twins, because our most backward look into pre-history reveals a comic and dismal sameness: males sharpening oddments of stone in the shape of their own organs, to stab, pierce, jab, cut; women reproducing their wombs in wet clay, to give, receive.

Los Alamos, "the cottonwoods." Los Piños, "the pines." On my way back down from the Oppenheimer place through Cowles, I decide to stop by. My host and hostess of Los Piños are now Bill and Alice McSweeney. The clustered cabins and outbuildings of peeled logs seem to look at me all the way from 1922, when Robert began discovering in himself an outdoorsman and horseman. Trail rides continue, as then, to be the featured activity. Below the large ranch house, a sunlit corral encloses a couple of handsome palomino mares with blond manes, and several chestnut geldings. Bill McSweeney is about sixty-five, lean, affable. "Yes," he tells me, "this is her old place, Katherine Page's. We've had it twenty-three years. They come from all over, New York, Chicago, Massachusetts . . . South America, foreign countries." His own pronunciation hints at Eastern origins. "No, we're not too busy just yet, but any day now. They'll be arriving." And he invites me inside.

It's a time warp. The big screen porch seems furnished with almost antiquarian exactitude to give the feel of a half century that never quite went by, as if some of that 1920s daylight stayed behind to put a slight dinginess on everything. Or maybe it's just the stands of dense evergreens shading Los Piños.

On a wide pine floor sit bulky chairs, rustic divans of varnished pine. There are heavy tables and lamps, Indian blankets covering a kind of glider; a bookcase with titles so oddly assorted they can only have been abandoned to it, book by book over decades, as dudes returned to the city. In the spacious parlor adjoining the screen porch, Alice McSweeney stands ironing linens near a large fireplace built of stream stones. Impossible not to imagine, standing beside it, the teenage Robert Oppenheimer alternately gangling and cosmopolitan, gauche and witty; insecure, erudite.

Through my pocket magnifier I examine shock waves on an obsidian flake—like pond ripples from a tossed pebble. It's as if I'm looking over an Indian's shoulder, looking at his hand with its working chunk of obsidian. With his other hand he strikes a hammer-stone against it, or a piece of antler. And given the predictability of obsidian, a chip spalls cleanly away.

Through centuries the glassy black chips fell to the ground like rain. It's as if the typical Anasazi carried a fragment of the stuff the way I carry a pocket knife. Needing a blade, arrowhead, or scraper he sat down and literally knocked one out. "Well," I think, "maybe not quite on the spur of the moment. But it wouldn't take long." Then it dawns on me—where I've recently seen percussion waves exactly like the ripple marks in these relics of Stone Age technology.

To start a nuclear reaction by implosion, "active material" is encased within a sphere of high explosive carefully shaped. When detonated the sphere sends shock waves inward, imploding the "active material" into "supercriticality." To study this, Los Alamos uses X-ray photos of force-waves in charges actually detonating. Because a few weeks ago I was looking at such photos, it now comes to me—the close kinship between those bomb-triggering waves and the ripples a sudden blow leaves in obsidian. In each case a shock travels through a mineral.

As I'm about to leave Cowles and Los Piños, I thank Bill McSweeney, turn to go, then turn again and mention Katherine Page. "Yes," he says with a half smile that has read my mind, "they do say he was sweet on her. She's dead now. Moved to Santa Fe." McSweeney gives me a look. "You know how she died, don't you?" I shake my head. "Well, some young fellow broke into her place, I guess looking to rob her or something. She was a sort of a feisty lady. Young fella with a knife. She must've talked back to him. He stabbed her—right then and there."

"Remember that Tawa created you out of Endless Space, and try to understand the meaning of things." Tawa, the sun.

With the magical help of Gogyeng Sowuhti, or Spider Grandmother, the Hopi peoples are able to pass through the *sipapu* up into the Fourth World. "In the Upper World," she tells them, "you must learn to be true humans."

Even today, members of the Hopi nation continue to honor a tradition locating the *sipapu* at the Grand Canyon. Annually, certain Hopi priests gather salt at a canyon site near the confluence of the Colorado and the Little Colorado rivers. In addition, stories still current among the Hopi remind listeners: "The older people, however, did not forget the *sipapu* and the meaning of life. In their songs they asked, 'Who are we? Where do we come from? Why are we here?' "

For its first nineteen days the Hopi baby is kept indoors. On the twentieth day it is taken outside by the mother and maternal grandmother, to be introduced to its creator, Tawa, the sun.

It's the biggest bike race in the U.S., and the big story is Greg LeMond versus the Russians; or, as a *Sports Illustrated* reporter puts it, "the Young Man, the Red Menace, and the Mountains." Like professional wrestling: Fourth of July, 1981, on a hilly, closed-circuit of highway that the PA announcer calls "the devastating Morgul-Bismark." And the Russian team, yes, wears red jerseys! Swiftly they pedal chromed sparkles uphill in jerseys gaudy as flags. And like flags they're hotly pursued by squadrons of cameramen shooting from pickups, by support vehicles, TV-adapted motorcycles, Campagnolo vans gaudy as the bikers.

In bike racing, a four-man group should have an enormous advantage over a lone rider with no teammates to help out, and LeMond has none; but the four-man Russian "break" can't get rid of LeMond, who at age eighteen is out there with them, hanging on despite the odds.

Loudspeakers blare all that at hillside spectators, some three thousand of us, getting tanned or burnt, tromping around among yucca and subdesert grasses just east of Boulder. Despite the announcer's blatant hype, it *is* dramatic. Every time the lead group comes round for another lap, LeMond is there, for "us"—young, superlatively fit, American—as against "them," Sergei Sukhoruchenkov, Yuri Barinov, and two red-jerseyed teammates. Like celebrations of life and health and gala color, they stroke powerfully up the Wall and away westerly, along the thirteen-mile loop—which takes them, each lap, right by Rocky Flats and its spooky kilotons of plutonium "devices."

It occurs to me that if I were to walk around a meat mountain heaped up of all war dead from the beginning till now—go entirely around the thing, no matter how long it took—most of their corpses would be even younger than these youthful, beautiful athletes.

Sasebo, Japan. The warehouse gloom seems doubled by its six-tier racks of stored duffle bags, government issue, canvas, olive drab. There are thousands of them, like shelved lives. Before boarding a C-119 air transport for Korea I'm to leave personal stuff here, in a duffle bag which the half-buttoned, gum-chewing corporal will forklift somewhere among these high racks of unpainted lumber.

Except for toiletries, socks, underwear, and an extra pair of fatigues, I cram all other uniforms and personal stuff into the bag. Then I come on a book, and pause: A. E. Housman, *Collected Poems*. Even to me it seems, there, an embarrassment. An affectation? In part I'm afraid so. Literary ignoramus though I am, maybe Housman is too cloyingly "appropriate"? Yet I've brought the book this far. Why? Not so much for its pessimism, which appeals to my youth, as the idea of poetry itself; what people go to poetry for.

The book's sky-blue covers are the one spot of living color in all the windowless warehouse murk. Casualties have been fierce in Korea, highest among infantry, and I'm infantry. Worse yet, I'm a platoon leader. Sure as I bring this along, somebody else is going to end up handing it around: "In his pack the day he got hit. Anybody want it?" No reaction.

Shelved in Japan, the bright blue of that binding, like a secret subversion of the Army's unanimous olive drab, will somehow improve my chances. I've paused between humankind's two modes, predation and an old word for poetry, "making." But that never dawns on me. I simply leave the book so as to come back to it.

Hans Bethe's two passions are mathematics and hiking. His hearty response to the Los Alamos area is that of a young German mountaineer. In the Manhattan Project, he is one of the really big cigars. Among hundreds of scientists he is one of the few. So is Enrico Fermi. On the Pajarito, no one, not even Oppie or Teller, stands above Fermi, whose passions are physics and mountain hiking, skiing; any-

thing strenuous. His summers in the Italian Dolomites give him immediate zest for the New Mexican terrain. He hikes down Frijoles Canyon
to the Rio Grande. Across the valley he enjoys ascending Lake Peak and
high summits in the Sangre de Cristo. Come winter, he skis with much
gusto if little style, quickly deserting the prepared slope of Sawyer Hill
to pioneer cross-country ski routes over the wild mountainsides of the
Jemez Caldera.

Theodore Taylor, that postwar superstar of the Los Alamos bomb
squad, turns anti-nuke and leaves. In retrospect he sees himself as having been "addicted" to nuclear weaponry, admits "it gets very exciting," freely confesses that test shots are fun: "Here are all these fairly
young people running around in baseball caps and short pants, setting
off these huge bombs, like a bunch of kids playing with fireworks." Yet
his admission that such Bomb involvement creates "an altered state of
mind" echoes a realization that Richard Feynman, for example, and
many of the Los Alamos "first team" had arrived at independently, and
much earlier.

Convinced that it's the scientists themselves who spur the nuclear
weapons mania, Taylor says, "It all starts with that devilishly creative
act of imagining something which is infinitely destructive. Then they
go to Franklin Roosevelt or Harry Truman or Ronald Reagan and say,
'Here's this thing, do you want that?' The answer is invariably, 'You bet
we do!' "

In Capulin Canyon, shaded by ponderosa boughs, I discover a
petroglyphed serpent making its meter-long zigger across the blond wall
of tuff. Under the time of trees and the rhythm of broken sunlight, I've
hiked a way up the canyon hoping for better water than I'm able to find.
Every hundred paces or so, one or two stranded puddles appear, sun-
stricken and greenish, aswarm with critters such as millipedes, tiny
enough to crawl through a needle's eye. As for the petroglyph, it doesn't
take much to guess its snake-sign was a response to just such dying water. The Anasazi hand that chipped its outline, less serpentine than
zigzag, meant, "Rain. Send rain." Snakes and streams go together. A
snake is a stream. So they danced to improve the rain. Their gods were
part of the weather.

Several times during my hike back toward the trailhead I hear from
Los Alamos's side canyons the unmistakable "Kerr-r-ackk!" of high explosive. Not faint and far off. Loud.

Emilio Segrè, himself a Los Alamos physicist, lifelong friend of Fermi and finally his austere biographer, relaxes his usual rigor in touching on the plateau's beauty, which "was to have profound influence on many scientists who by inclination and long habit were sensitive to nature and could appreciate the noble country surrounding Los Alamos."

Segrè assesses the Jemez mountains, the cloudscapes, the profusion of wildflowers blooming through long New Mexican summers, the hiking trails and trout streams and ski slopes and Indian ruins and mineral beds. These played "a decisive part in sustaining the great effort made by the personnel." Often, he says, "at the end of a strenuous period of work one felt completely exhausted, but the out-of-doors was always a source of renewed strength."

This general delight is undercut by barrack-style housing, by streets alternately paved with dust or mud, by fence-patrolling guards and military regulations; however, Oppenheimer's hunch about the Pajarito turns out to be valid. The streams, canyons, forests, and peaks will keep morale high, will speed work. The Bomb will get made.

Perhaps it is only the snob appeal of Sanskrit, which, long before the Bomb, impels Oppenheimer to study the *Bhagavadgita*. Inside that poem, however, is a god whom any physicist might find attractive, a god telling how to be, what to do. Krishna's voice speaks to Oppenheimer, surely, in many ways—not least of which is Krishna's authorizing Arjuna to wage war.

Between the two armies poised opposite each other in battle array, Arjuna wants out. He realizes that even if his army is successful thousands of his fellow men will die, many of them his blood relatives. This sickens him. He suddenly sees the pitiful ephemerality of all human existence. He tells the almighty Krishna that he can't bear giving his army the signal to begin such slaughter.

Krishna counters this attitude by agreeing with it: human life is indeed pitiful and brief. In the cosmic perspective, no action can possibly matter—either to wage war or refuse, either to slay or be slain. Each comes to the same thing. "Therefore," the divine Krishna says to Arjuna, "Give the signal. Attack!"

Taking my cross-canyoned way back over the Pajarito to the trailhead leads me through pygmy forest of the sort I've admired for many a year. It's pleasant to share my joy in the sky's paleozoic blue with Anasazis translated to what Hopis call "the cloud people." Right and left of a scarcely discernible trail, trunks of Utah juniper and occasional alligator juniper warp like smoke. In their haggard bark, deep twisted arroyos give the runty trunk boles a time-blasted aspect. Bark-tatters peel away till each juniper mimes a stricken beggar standing so low not even its shade is easily come by; but like Odysseus's disguise, that's only a ploy. Trees that won the West—and keep much of it to this day—haven't risen to be timber; instead they bend to their own desires with the torque of a fine muscularity. From juniper, as from many another life that water takes on in deserts, I learn the trick of surviving even technology: "Be a tree not worth cutting down."

"We scientists have known sin," says Oppenheimer after Hiroshima and Nagasaki. On another occasion he speaks of having done "the devil's work." Introduced to President Truman, he startles the literal-minded Missourian: "There is blood on my hands." "Never mind," says Truman, "it will all come out in the wash." Privately, however, the president is furious at "that idiot." "Who does he think he is? I'm the one who made the decision to drop the bomb!"

Does Truman take the blood-on-my-hands remark for that of a poseur? Stephen White, a science writer and friend, notes Oppenheimer's continuous self-awareness and concern for how others see him. One of his former students feels that Oppenheimer's postwar disgrace merely adds the role of "martyr" to Robert's already large repertoire of selves. Persons less well disposed find the role-playing "insufferable," but I. I. Rabi, another friend, doesn't let it stand in the way. He sees Robert as living "a charade," and accepts all the posing as quite a tolerable price for the stimulation of his company. Not only does he see that there are many Oppenheimers, he sees that Oppie himself doesn't know which one he is. "He is put together of many bright shining splinters," Rabi concludes. "Identity is his problem."

Often after Hiroshima Robert Oppenheimer faces the question, "Why did you scientists build the Bomb?" He varies each sincere answer, like a man trying on honest hats. Like the person each of us knows best, whose very name may be the sum of self-misunderstandings we answer to. Oppenheimer's more obvious motives for directing work on the Bomb certainly include genuine horror at the thought of such a weapon in Hitler's hands. They also include intense patriotism . . . and a reason given so offhandedly it chills: Oppie admits that the Bomb's physics are "technically sweet."

However, if we accept Freeman Dyson's point that at Los Alamos Oppenheimer "made a Faustian bargain" we flatter our species. Working atop Anasazi footprints, Oppie and all the others did what in the long chronology of the heart all humans do. Make pots and paint them, shape weapons and jab. The better to love and prey on each other.

Despite his cultivation of poetry, art, and philosophy, Robert Oppenheimer winces at seeing in himself "traces of beastliness." In a candid letter to his brother, Frank, he admits "it is not easy—at least it is not easy for me—to be quite free of the desire to browbeat somebody or something." In strong contrast, through his postwar lectures and books runs the leitmotif of "the common bond." Our feeling for each other, for all humanity, he argues, both is and ought to be stronger than national allegiance. The humanitarian vein is far from his only mode. For example, there is also the problem of the Super, to which he lends his mind because "as a scientist you cannot stop such a thing." Besides, the solution embodies the elegance a theoretician lives for. In his formal farewell to Los Alamos he glances at many an implicit discrepancy by admitting "what people say of their motives is not always true."

Perhaps we misspeak in referring to the "mystery" of the Anasazi. Their descendants are among us as pueblo dwellers all along the Rio Grande. Drought, the theory goes, simply forced them off the Pajarito Plateau down to the river, and water. If Anasazi seed, ironically, becomes part of the hired help at Los Alamos, it does so to assist a war secret the Pueblos from San Ildefonso and Santa Clara knew nothing of.

As menials they bemuse the wives of Los Alamos with their childlike naiveté, their Pueblo rituals and dances. Phyllis Fisher, a scientist's wife, is startled to learn that "a particularly handsome, middle-aged man with long black braids solemnly ladling out food in our cafeteria" is "an Indian chief."

Her visits to Anasazi ruins in Frijoles Canyon whet the usual curiosity about "the ancient ones" who lived there, then disappeared. Disease, she wonders? Ecological disaster? She who has come to love the "rocks and trails and open spaces of New Mexico" then realizes the potential parallel: "How strange for us, as the residents of another part of the Pajarito Plateau, to ask those questions. Where had we come from and why were we here? . . . We wondered what kind of disaster we were creating on our own mesa, only a few miles away."

During the tense evening before the Trinity shot, Oppie looks to the low range of the Oscuras just as dusk blurs ridgelines with darkening sky. As if even the arid Jornada del Muerto is part of the New Mexico he loves, he says to Cyril Smith, a metallurgist, "Funny how the mountains always inspire our work."

I listen. Between Dakota Ridge and Boulder's foothill/mountains, especially in autumn, hikers' voices carry surprisingly. As if these were the talking hills. From high sandstone crags just westward, the thin cry of hawks; gliding, veering. Far below, the shrill of six or eight kids as they advise each other across a steep backside of the ridge. A crisp November afternoon. Atop my lichened rock hunk I sip the stillness of the season, and a beer brought along in my pack. White as woven snow, a bit of spider fluff floats slowly, settling more gradually than I could've imagined—here, in breezy Colorado, where air is almost always in motion.

As a youthful true believer in progress, I grew up in the faith that science could—sooner or later—erase any mistake. How little I knew of human nature, in which old necessities *known* to be ruinous, now, still operate undiminished as if with a life of their own. Given a biosphere prodigally sown with plutonium, however, it's too late to say, "Oh, science will span that bridge when we come to it." In this post-plutonium era, all bridges to the planet of my childhood are long since burnt.

And not by Martians. Across our handshake I've traded smiles with a cordial, laid-back Stan Ulam, whose mathematical solution to the problem of the "Super" gave Teller the map to his El Dorado. For a while, Ulam lived right here in Boulder. Similarly, when he too resided in Boulder I used to say "Hi!" every now and again to Frank Oppenheimer, who once remarked, apropos of Robert, "My brother made you feel good to be with him"—and was, among other things, according to Frank, "the least lazy guy."

If on this serene afternoon I ask myself about inner distances and outer ones, their causes—like answers that open on questions—keep disappearing into each other. Oppie's wounds and ambitions. Hitler's childhood. The admirable, indomitable persistence of Madame Curie. Allure of the technically sweet. The ruinous pleasures of ego. Indeed, doesn't my own egoism, like all long-range weaponry, depend on the illusion of distance?

Lacking bright blood to push it, our dark blood couldn't circle back to the heart to be brightened. So would an end to our self-oppositions simply leave us half hearted? Sometimes, to adapt words of Joë Bousquet, I'm afraid human nature may be a wound in the world which that same human nature can't heal without wounding itself.

Any thoughtful person is aware that posterity might well pronounce one grand, retroactive curse on our century. I hope so. No matter how long today has been dead, if we love the infinitely delicate power of life on this earth, we ought to welcome that curse as a left-handed blessing. It will signal that an intelligent posterity exists. That the ones who came after us care, and find our self-soilings an abomination. And more. That they find them unforgivable.

If, inaudible as gravity waves, no such maledictions cross our forthcoming nonexistence, that will be bad news indeed. Their very lack will signal the opposite: that our devolving inheritors are so androidal as not to mind a debased and man-blasted planet. That they don't even notice the difference.

Uptrail toward me come chirping preschoolers nudged along by their mother while daddy carries an infant in a blue corduroy sling. The kids poke around a windfallen ponderosa trunk. Their young mother offers her baby some apple juice from a bottle. So it's an effortless afternoon, in which we're content just to be here, making this bit of Dakota Ridge a peaceable kingdom. We never started a war, or took one square inch of land from Indians. Yet each of us is the shadow of something much older. Seven miles east, the clean glitter and sprawl of Rocky Flats combines with perfect weather to complicate our self-definitions. Yes, we must be better than we are. That too is our nature.

Naming Nature

Why do we care to know a plant's or animal's right name? And what do we know when we know it? Syllables?

In the Swiss Alps one July afternoon I was aboard a cog-rail train gearing itself steeply up from the great, green, glacial valley at Lauterbrunnen toward Kleine Scheidegg. There, between the Eiger and the Jungfrau, I overheard a sort of primal phase in naming nature. At a half-open window of the train, and with her dark curls breezing across her eyes, a French toddler squinted into the sun at some grazing cattle, Swiss browns, a whole herd of them. Because she was just learning the world, she pointed her tiny index finger out the window. "Oh-h-h," she said, with the rising note of discovery that toddlers have, "*les chevaux!*"

Five-second pause.

Then, murmuring it almost inaudibly, that toddler's barely older sister said, "*les vaches . . . les vaches.*"

It sounded like both a correction and a memo to herself: "Not all big ones eating the meadow are horses. Some are cows."

Soon her baby sister would also see that. Because she would *want* to. We name this spontaneous desire "coming into language," and we marvel that no grown-up, however ravenous, can match a child's hunger for names; but since a toddler's word-hunger is her gusto for this manifold earth, we might as well call it "coming into the world."

So far as I could tell, though, this particular little one hadn't quite come into the world's bovine phase yet. A shadow of puzzlement crossed her expression. "Not horses? But they are big, they go slow on lots of legs, and they are eating the grass up." She saw, kind of. In the cow/horse blur, distinctions gross enough to us just weren't out there for her. The impulse to say a name, however, was as eager as her openness to language—and therefore to the world—was wide. "*Oh-h-h! Les chevaux!*" So, ever since, that herd of misnomered cows has gone on browsing for me in a child's eye, the most memorable blur I've ever heard spoken.

Several summers later, back in Colorado, I groped for a name out of a frustrated impulse far from any childlike innocence. Wanting to identify roadside stalks whose sky-blue blossoms I'd been jogging past for years, I couldn't. Nobody I asked knew what to call them. Nobody I asked seemed to mind not knowing. I minded a lot. "What *is* the name of that stuff?" Its pithy stalks and blue petals had brushed against my socks and calves by the half mile. "Inconceivable," I said to myself, "that nobody around here can say what it is." Were the blooms any less beautiful for being dirt common?

My botanist friend, William Weber, could have immediately told me the plant's names in English and Latin, and much more. But why bother him, formidable taxonomist, with an identification so easy? After all, I owned a thumb-soiled copy of his field guide, *Rocky Mountain Flora*. He knew I owned it. And in improving on a system of naming begun in the eighteenth century by a young Swede named Carl Linnaeus, hadn't Weber planned every least particular of its nearly five hundred pages—dense with detail—to make the book useful to people like me? He had. Was I going to admit, despite all that tradition and care behind it, his guide resisted my powers? I wasn't, till I did. "Oh," he said, "that's chicory."

Later I looked it up in his *Rocky Mountain Flora*: "*Cichorium intybus*. Introduced and locally established as a roadside weed on the plains and piedmont valleys." In learning its name was I really the wiser? Field guides aren't encyclopedias. What surface had I scratched in gratifying the trivial itch of curiosity? True, ever since, in passing those gawky, angular stalks of cerulean blossom, it has felt good to say "chicory . . . chicory." But why? What had those syllables given me? What did I know now, that I hadn't known, except for their sound? Nothing I knew how to name.

Perhaps a *Field Guide to Human Curiosity* would identify these questions as "roadside weeds of the mind." Nonetheless, with the acquisition of *chicory* my vague sense of what we know when we know a name began to sharpen focus: we know a satisfaction. Though true, perhaps primevally so, it's an answer that at once begets the next question, "Why?" Am I lying to myself when I say I had felt indebted as I ran, had felt I *owed* it to the intense chicory-blue of those petals, often backlit by sunrise, to learn their right name?

We do well to be suspicious of noble motives, especially our own. Our impulses aren't often unalloyed. Mine may have been low as pride, even lower: mere vanity, which, etymologically speaking, means "empty." Had empty conceit that *I* should know, even if no one around me did—had that impelled me to acquire *chicory*? I'd sag a little and confess, "Guilty as charged, as usual," if it hadn't been for the passionate, sunfire blue of those petals. In decency, I did seem to *owe* them their name, however arbitrary I know names to be.

"Come off it," cool reason mutters. "Indebted to petals? Hogwash!" The analytic mind doesn't admit of petals being *owed* anything. They're just bee-bait contrived by scheming vegetation. From reason, of course, there is no appeal. All the same, the day we don't feel we owe this world a grace note of response, we ought to be wrapped in graph paper and mailed fourth class to the Bureau of Statistics.

Without bowing to reason on what we might owe even to "weeds," I do confess that pride has its share in wanting to know plant names. Which of our acquisitions isn't it part of? Nonetheless, before considering that pride might itself be alloyed with urges less trivial, it may be well to face that seamy side of expertise open-eyed and unblinking.

Whether in the woods or a public garden we've all met sharks among the botanicals. These are the people who vent aggressive relish in bandying names of, say, wild grasses which—as they rightly suppose—are to us quite anonymous. Lacking a window into souls, I can't be sure; yet it does seem that anyone tossing off names such as "slough-grass," "brome," "three-awn," "tufted hairgrass," "muhly," "false melic," or "little bluestem," and doing so with nonchalance, may be less a friend of the earth than of the performing arts.

My sister Rose Marie isn't really a shark. She likes flowering plants wholeheartedly. She also likes to be good at things. Long ago our family recognized her as the brainy one. No vote was needed, nor were her straight As and scholarships the least surprising. Once, having driven from St. Louis to visit me for a tour in western Colorado, no sooner had her tires stopped rolling than she was out of the car naming flora all over the place. She was strongest on blossoms, none of which had she ever seen except in her wildflower book.

Pacing ahead of me along a trail leading south from Mesa Verde, she kept scoring well and aloud, her extended index finger indicating

"Fireweed?"—at which cue I would nod, or say "Yes." Then a few meters further, "Broomrape?" Yes, again. Within minutes, my own semi-
native acquaintance with Western plants had thus come into play. And
into question. Under the fragrant shade of cliff rose she would pause,
sniff at its pale yellow blossoms, pleased yet baffled, then defer to my
years in the West: "This must be . . . oh, it's on the tip of my tongue, it
just has to be a . . . " Frustrated shrug. "Help me out here, Reg. *You*
know." Often I did, not always. Her joy in seeing live blooms previously
met only in books kept our stroll from becoming a wildflower *mano-
a-mano*. Then too, aside from liking to be good at things, a sister named
Rose Marie may well have felt that she, especially, owed our flora
its names.

Pride leading to a literal indebtedness revealed itself one desert
morning at Joshua Tree National Monument. There, not much east of
Indio, California, with frond-splashes of date trees dangling clustered
fruit, I inhaled cool dawn while drawing water into canteens. At the
campground spigot another early bird arrived with her water jugs.

"Do you know what that plant is?" I asked her, nodding toward
what looked like a somewhat cousin to tamarisk. It grew languid and
wispy everywhere about us, in bushes up to eight feet high.

She was pretty, about thirty-five, with lively, intelligent eyes. "I
know to my cost, literally. I bet my husband $20 it was cottonwood. But
it's creosote."

"Cottonwood! You were really dumb," I said. And she laughed.

Neither of us would've done well in Eden. There, without resort to
field guides, Adam—perhaps seated on the greensward under the Tree
of Knowledge—casually named all the animals. Did Adam, Eve, and
the Creator speak the same language? Presumably our first parents
uttered a language which, like everything else in Eden, was created
word perfect. A charming implication of the account in Genesis, therefore, is that Adam's prelapsarian intellect required the merest glimpse
of an animal to say not just *a* name. Each oracular guess conferred that
animal's *right* name. This gift even has a fancy name of its own:
onomathesia. With the Fall, however, Adam and Eve lost more than the
Garden's ideal ecology; the right names of everything were effaced
from their sin-dimmed intellects. Those angels who evicted them while
brandishing flames for swords might as well have put a road sign over
the gate leading forever outward from Eden: "Exit Spoken Perfection."

And enter confusion with the Tower of Babel, our planet. In its lin-
guistic history since Eden, how many different bits of shaped air have

human tongues coined for the kind of creature Adam and Eve thought they were? How many names for the moon? How many different moon-names are being spoken over the globe right now?

If our own minds were as rich in right words as Eve's vocabulary unfallen, if we her sons and daughters could speak rightly of each plant, animal, and mineral variant to every species within every genus, how many names would we know? At the threshold of the twenty-first century, those best informed still haven't any idea. The two-volume *Synopsis and Classification of Living Organisms* edited by S. P. Parker draws on the global expertise of other biologists to list some 1.4 million living species already described. To name insects alone would call for half that total. But once we got all those insects by heart, naming known plants would seem easy—a quarter million. Beetle species, for example, if fully inventoried, might number nearly a million, since well over 250,000 kinds have been cataloged. Then there'd be the spineless animals—protozoans, worms, jellyfish, corals, mollusks. We vertebrates amount to a mere 40,000.

But if like our ancestor Adam we're going to name *all* the animals, micro and macro, protozoan to elephant, the known and the yet-to-be-discovered, how many names will we need? Using selected habitats on which extensive field studies have been done, E. O. Wilson, a specialist in social insects, supposes that the full inventory *of insects alone* "is likely to exceed 5 million." Wilson admits to be guessing, admits no one has more than a rough estimate. Recently, at a conference on biodiversity, in underlining the wildness of our present surmise, he claimed that there's really no telling. Earth could have 5, 10, or 30 million different species. "There is no theory," according to Wilson, "that can predict what this number might turn out to be." Despite our expensive itch to colonize the red sterilities of Mars, any child can name every single life form on Mars with closed lips. Earth is far more truly the unexplored planet.

Our Anglo-Saxon forebears, on whose lips Old English evolved, knew nothing of such abundance, of course, nor were they sticklers in nomenclature. "Worm," for example, they applied to whatever crept or looked like it wanted to, whether serpent, tapeworm, nightcrawler, or Northumbria's specialty, dragons. Similarly, the countrymen of Aethelstan and Aelfric might call "fish" any swimming or water-dwelling thing: whale, shark, sea otter, herring, starfish, crayfish, or clam. Anatomically, of course, the gap between mollusk and crab—

both "shellfish" even today—is wider than that separating a trout from Cleopatra.

Obviously, more sharply focused names imply the distinctions of closer knowledge. One assumes the Anglo-Saxon eye could see particulars its vague naming doesn't signal, but how vague can labeling become without betraying fuzziness in our view of the world?

Recently I did a wholly unscientific survey among university students to learn how many of them could name aspects of Colorado's natural environment, including things seen almost daily. My sole "method" was to choose questions as simple and as general as possible; and to choose for subjects students who had said they wanted to write about nature. Next to biology majors, you'd expect such a group to be especially keen on naming things.

My one-sheet questionnaire began with Boulder's celebrated "Flatirons," mountainous rock formations rising abruptly as cliffs just a few minutes west of where my students were gathered, and as distinctive to Boulder as Vesuvius is to Naples. "Do you know what the Flatirons formations are made of?" (The answer is sandstone; more specifically, conglomerate sandstone.) Though each student had scrambled among those rocks, sunning, climbing, or just chatting atop great hunks of the stuff, few had looked closely. Here is a fair sample of their answers: "granite?", "slate!", "Big ones," "I suppose maybe slate," "granite," "granite," "sandstone," "don't know," "granite, slate," "red rock," "?", "sandstone?", "sandstone," "granite?", "sedimentary."

Next I asked each person, "What's the name of that big black-and-white bird with the long black tail?" (Because magpies are omnipresent in Boulder, I was able to point out the window at one.) More than half knew its name, the others groped. Responses like "lark bunting," "I've often wondered," "?", or "not real sure" were typical. Though magpie plumage is an everyday sight, 40 percent of my group were content to let our gaudiest bird fly anonymously through their lives.

So much for ornithology. I then tried mule deer. Boulder's western edges abound in them. They poke around neighborhoods, gourmandize from lawn to lawn, nibble tree bark, browse on expensive bushes, nip our roses in the bud, lounge by the half-dozen in backyards, and savor the best that town and country munching can offer. To use a medieval expression for tame, they've become man-sweet. Did my would-be writers know what *kind* of deer? Not really. Oh, three students correctly said "mule deer," while most said "white tail," and one or two admitted "no idea," "not sure."

In every time and clime, I realize, students have had keener eyes for wildlife in each other than for local fauna. So be it. Aside from sparrows, squirrels, and ambling dogs, however, few Boulder animals could be more common than magpies or mule deer. One would have thought *not* knowing would nag at "I've often wondered" till it felt like privation. Doesn't curiosity aim at a satisfied *feeling*? After all, the moment a girl sees a boy she likes the look of, doesn't she ask, "What's his name?" Every time. Though her conscious motives may feel intensely practical, her question comes of an urge older than she dreams.

While I'm unclear on linkage between feeling, seeing, and naming, clearly there is one. My itch to learn *chicory* was somehow involved in it, to the extent that I took sharper, better informed looks at its structure after each fruitless search in my guidebook. Even learning to distinguish evergreens can involve an interaction between the eye and desire—as I discovered one summer.

When I was a boy, anything but the grossest conifer distinctions summed up that particular vanishing point in my knowledge. To me they were either "evergreens" or "pines." Same difference. Then one day a couple of decades ago while hiking under Avery Peak near Gothic, Colorado, I was determined to see better. Perhaps because the July morning felt as buoyant as its cumulus puffs scudding west to east overhead, and because it felt—at nine thousand feet—just comfortably warm, even in shadow, I had resolved to walk along consulting tall trunk after trunk until I could *see* why "blue spruce," "white spruce," "white fir," "subalpine fir," "Engelmann spruce," "one-seed juniper," and "Rocky Mountain juniper" were needed in the tree lexicon. But to see minor distinctions in conifers takes energy we may not recognize for what it really is: a form of desire.

My way led up a steep mining road built and abandoned in the last century. Its sole traffic that morning were shade-tolerant wildflowers and me. And thistles. On one thistle a little higher than my head I counted, in its opulence of prickled leaves, 103 buds. What ambition! So amid the agreeable evergreen glooms of forest, and blossoms repossessing a rock road whose patches of high-country sunlight made its mica facets dazzle, I stepped slowly along—hoping to note instant difference. I wanted to murmur "white spruce" or "blue spruce," "white fir" or "Douglas fir" at first glance.

Fools do rush in. Little did I realize, then, a trained botanist might well have said, "Good luck." I've since learned that even an adept can't always tell a conifer's species on sight.

Any other morning, the seed-catalog lavishness of July's high-country flowers would have distracted me. There were subalpine Jacob's ladder, lousewort; and marsh marigolds pale as winter butter, growing low in their micro-bogs. And lavender daisies, called—among other things—fleabane. Then too, purple loco weed not quite the blue-purple of Wyeth's lupine in ditches, nor yet the midnight purple of larkspur or monkshood. And of course the incendiary red of Indian paintbrush, the hot magenta of fireweed. All of them consorting to produce the kind of a morning that memory likes to build on. But my tree identifying made blossoms just a fringe benefit.

I'd long since noticed that two fir seedlings, for example, from virtually the same cone may grow so much unlike each other as to seem different species. *Where* it takes root can and does greatly alter a tree's character, which can be virtually disguised by conditions its seed chanced to light among. All that forenoon, therefore, I consulted my botanical guide with its "keys," a garden of printed synapses that fork, fork further, fork again, and keep forking, like the Tree of Life itself. Take one wrong turn looking up a conifer, you may end lost in pages devoted to *umbelliferae*, staring at a drawing of "Alpine parsley." Guidebook? It can be a jungle in there.

Meanwhile I tried very hard to learn every which way a Douglas fir might grow that a white fir couldn't mimic. And vice versa. It was a process teaching me how much of what we call eyesight is *wanting* to see. Small wonder that, cytologically speaking, retinal tissue and brain tissue are cousins. Eyes seem to be the mind leaning forward.

The trees I conversed with and sampled! From spruce twigs I plucked needles for examining under my magnifier, and winced each time like a small brother pulling his sister's hair. Did I really believe those spruce boughs felt pain? Ever so remotely. Being wood didn't mean they were wooden. Their chloroplasts and phloem cells and photosynthetic sugars, their rows of leaf pores fine as dust on a bug, their root-imbibed minerals were alive and breathing, as I was. Same era, same season, same hour. Under the blue sky's wisps of cloud I knew that soon the morning and I would have already happened. Soon "today" would become "long ago." As a spruce cone fell toward the half repossessed road, I knew that soon it would have hit and rotted away in a distant century, which was this one, mine while I lasted. Knee-high fir seedlings whose as yet unhardened needles I stroked for their suppleness would rise to be great-hearted trunks still here three hundred years from the moment I bent to touch them. Impossible not to be touched, in turn, by all the chances any great tree must run, growing toward its long continuance.

How many times did I stuff the guidebook back into my pack "once and for all"—then fifty yards further along pluck it with a resigned sigh back out again? Ever so slowly, however, distinctions began coming clear. Or clearer. *I began to see difference in sameness.*

Wouldn't the earliest language have had to grow its store of thing-words the same way? For example, "that!" in post-Edenic proto-Indo-European must have narrowed through millennia past numbering to something like "tree," which in turn would have split—whatever their actual sounds—into versions of "cone tree" and "tree of no cones," with each of those splitting—again, however crudely—into practicalities simple as "edible" and "not edible" or "good wood" and "wood not so good." It might be a long time before the earliest speakers *needed* to see any difference not related to use. But the word hoard would grow with that need, *as difference got spoken.* It might require 500,000 years for a word like *tree* to beget the syllabic differences needed for naming kinds of trees in a forest; nonetheless, even if the very first vocal noise for tree begot and gave birth to its offspring unimaginably more slowly than an actual forest ramifies from one cone, it would, at last, re-produce that forest in words. The longer our species carefully looked into it, the more our languages would receive in return.

We may weary of hearing that Inuits have lots of names for snow—certainly I myself find it wearisome—but not of realizing how needed those names are. For seeing by. For finding our way. In a whiteout, in level terrain so very near the magnetic pole, snow's texture, direction, granulation, incrustations, may be the only workable compass. Desire to see difference in sameness could hardly be stronger. Similarly, rain-forest dwellers have a wealth of ways to say more than just "tree," but know only one or two sky words.

Thus in trying to coax differences from my generic sense of "ever-green" or "conifer," in trying to see ways "firs" have taken that "pines" haven't, in matching the syllables "white fir" to its distinction from "Douglas fir" and "subalpine fir," I felt myself crudely rehearsing the invention of speech, which is as much as to say the birth of my species. Whatever the truth of that conjecture may be, features under my nose also conspired to make me feel like a tree dunce. "Oh," I kept saying to myself as one or another hitherto invisible variant in cone shape or twig pattern declared itself, "how obvious!" Not all such distinctions were. Some required squinting through a pocket lens. I could just hear my friend Hal asking, "Is it worth all that bother?" To me, yes. But the more interesting question remains. Why?

Beyond utility, beyond the satisfaction of seeing more clearly, the deepest urge may, I suspect, be primeval. Not the urge to dawdle along the gash of a wagon road being healed by forest. Instead, toward naming. I further suspect that our other motives grow like trunk and branches out of that taproot. In saying some names have "charm" we use a syllable derived from chants and spells rooted in magic; so remarking a thing has charm doesn't go far enough. Once upon a time, certain names *were* charms.

In special cases, to name was to cause, to cause to befall, even to create. The history of religion teems with examples of sacral names that contained or conferred real power, power devoutly believed in as real, just as anthropology has yet to discover primitives who consider names arbitrary. Whereas *we* know that a rose by any other word would smell as sweet, it's highly unlikely that humankind's earliest speakers believed it would.

Twentieth-century children of technology reflect traces of that ancient attitude especially when they begin study of a foreign language. Annually, every high school French teacher sees primitive behavior reenacted. Like Sisyphus, he or she must once again struggle uphill against heavy resistance to the idea that English names are somehow true to their objects, whereas French names for the same things are unnatural. Students *know* better. Exchanging students with schools in France, however, leaves untouched their deepest levels, where the primitive feeling that a thing *is* its name still resides. Annually, therefore, that language teacher's more callow students will feel in their bones that the French way of talking goes against reality. No matter how many million French kids call trees and snow "*les arbres*" and "*la neige*," calling those things by those names is worse than effeminate, worse than absurd. It's wrong.

In fact, there is the story of the sixteenth-century Englishman arguing that French and Spanish are less logical than English: "The French call a fish *poisson*, and the Spanish call it *pescado*, whereas we call it what it really is, a *fish*."

The most naive present-day speaker, however, will scarcely feel that naming brings a thing into being. Our talking avatars seem to have felt otherwise. And more. Felt that without its right name a thing couldn't fully exist as itself. An obvious vestige of that feeling appears in the first dozen lines of Genesis: "And God said, Let there be light: and there was light. . . . And God called the light Day, and the darkness he called Night." The sequence of creating and naming then proceeds through the firmament, named "Heaven," dry land called "Earth," the waters called "the Seas," and so forth. This link between word and works pervades the Old Testament. Psalm 30 offers merely one instance among dozens: "By the word of the Lord were the heavens made; and all the host of them by the breath of his mouth. . . . For he spake, and it was done." In the beginning was the name.

On the other hand, though God created the animals, it was Adam who named them: "And out of the ground the Lord God formed every beast of the field, and every fowl of the air; and brought them to Adam to see what he would call them: and whatsoever Adam called every living creature, that was the name thereof. And Adam gave names to all cattle, and to the fowl of the air, and to every beast of the field." Here the relation between creating and naming modulates to naming as charm or empowerment. God's naming of elements in the cosmos implies that He alone controlled those elements; similarly, Adam's naming the animals implies the power humankind was to have over earth's creatures.

Some of our ancestors either misliked or ignored that distinction, and backslid into the more primitive view. Mythic variants preserved in the Midrash, the Cabbala, and in gnostic lore credit Adam the namer of animals with having created the cosmos itself! These underground variants make Adam the source and origin of the universe. Before it existed, he was. And was hugely good looking. His colossal stature filled up the whole world.

Earlier but still within what is now the Near East, passages in the Babylonian poem called the Gilgamesh epic parallel the implication in Genesis that creating the cosmos goes hand in hand with naming sky, earth, and water. Their nebulous existences may precede naming, but they can't be fully present in the world till their right names are assigned. Gods too. One verse in the Gilgamesh poem speaks of a time when "none of the gods were created, and as yet had no names."

Worldwide, in fact, various myths reflect the feeling that a thing can't fully and properly exist without its name. From skies far greyer and chillier than Eden's, the Norse Eddic poem *Völuspa* illustrates this sense of nameless things not yet fully themselves:

> From the south the sun, the moon's mate,
> Passed its right hand along the sky's edges

Not knowing where it should dwell;
Neither did the stars know their own places
Nor the moon, how strong her own light.

Then all the spirits gathered in council
The sacred gods and discussed the matter:
Night they gave a name to, and to the new moon,
Named both the morn and midday, then sundown
And twilight, so the years might be counted.

If names can translate, charm, empower, and create, they may also invoke. The annals of our human past abound with instances. Through a name's invocation, the named reveals its nature. Five years ago I was surprised to find myself at the spoken center of just such an occurrence. It was a snowy evening, late March—the thirty-first in fact—but its twilight was dim and wintery. Stalled snow clouds covered the upper half of Boulder Mountain. Heading home, I had stopped out on a mesa near my house and, squinting through the slant of clumped flakes, had made out ground-feeding birds in unusual numbers. Their dark forms went flitting and hopping low over new snow on winter-beaten field-weed which earlier snows had long since lodged. Maybe it was the murk of that overcast, saying at the very sill of April, "How about another helping of wet snow?" Whatever the cause, my mood was a touch rueful; that is, it was until I came upon those birds. Their blithe darting and pecking so lifted my spirits that I stopped in my tracks, the better to watch.

Sure enough, the dozens that had startled into the air from a cluster of small ponderosa pines began now to reconsider. They twittered a while among stark naked twigs they'd fled to; then, a few at a time, took wing again, back to the much cosier shelter of those pines. Which were but a step or two from me, living statue. By now quite a lot of snow had accumulated in the blue folds of my parka, on my boot tops, my hood. Gradually, by cautious hops a bird came closer, pecking into withered tufts that poked up through snow, beaking insects or seeds, cocking a wary eye at me as if considering; then hopping closer, closer yet, till within inches of my boots. I stayed budgeless. Soon others followed, a few tentative hops at a time. Apparently I was standing amid an especially food-sown patch; but had disappeared. Had become part of the scenery. Up close, despite snowfall and dusk thickened almost to night, I finally could see to name them: "Bluebirds!"

At the word's invocation they at once revealed themselves fully—
through good omens condensed in its syllables. Thus invoked, they became an apparition transforming both the weather and me. My touch
of the sullens vanished. "Snow or no snow, these are bluebirds!"

Rationalizing, we admit that a name's invocatory power comes of
what's already condensed within. Unlike primitives, we know that any
name "reveals" only what our own prior experiences have hidden inside it. Semantically stored knowledge and feelings may, when conditions are right, thereby release like wings fluttering from a magician's
hat the moment we say "white pigeons." But since context alters content, the auspicious revelations that "bluebird" summons—in containing them—may be intensified by an opposite such as "snow." That's
why any particular name, differing from itself, never reveals exactly
the same things twice. What's released depends on where and how that
name occurs.

Altering its context can show an apparently limited syllable like
rose to be encyclopedic. Which is to say that nature's names are both
sounds and living relationships. Even as concept, words like *forest* and
ocean stand for a deep and teeming plenitude whose highly individual
many are one, and, at the same time, less a thing than a spatial experience. Pronounced alone in a low exhalation, *forest* can create what it
names. Can place the pronouncer inside it.

All this is so. Nonetheless, to deny that words both name and fail to
name would be dishonest. If they reveal they also conceal, and we know
it. As far as that goes, don't most truths include their own opposites? On
the level of folk wisdom alone, you could make an anthology of such
marriages, proverbial "truths" paired antithetically, each partner con-
tradicting its mate.

So, having learned to name "magpie," we'd be lazy to let our seeing
stop at the plane of a name, which is to "see" dismissively. We need to
look past language to discover, for example, what rich iridescences a
magpie's "black" feathers can show: dark emeralds, dark azures, hints
of deep burgundy almost not visible—their prismatic wealth refracted
in preen oil. "Black-and-white" doesn't touch it. Here I must plead
guilty again. Because magpies are identifiable at the most distant
glance, I've often watched one after another swoop down from our
foothill mountains, and failed to see past their name. So I was years in
realizing how different from other corvids their wing management is in
dipping and gliding. In the same way, just as we must look past *wing* to
see what a wing truly is, we must look past *bird* to see the strangeness in

our sky's having animals. To name is, yes, to know. But only to know better, far from completely, and never once and for all.

More important perhaps than a name's cover-up of details is its blurring of the fact that each thing is really an *event*, thus a confluence of forces still in motion; forces traceable—if we've time to reflect that far—back toward the time our solar system was fog, the sun not yet resolved to a focus with hydrogen fusion at heart. To see beyond language may be to receive flashes of a luminous whole; to feel an obsidian chip, for example, change into its molten past or vaporized future even as the sperm and egg we once were stoop to pick it up.

Because mystic experiences can't be spoken, only hinted at, and even then only after years of disciplined, humble waiting for glimpses which can neither be willed nor commanded, it's simplistic to say mysticism, too, aims at being where names can't take us. But that is at least an element in Christian as well as Taoist and Zen practice.

Chuang-Tzu, a wise and kooky Taoist of China's fourth century B.C., speaks of "entering the bird cage without making the birds sing." Through wordplay on "cage" and "song" in Chinese, he hints at entering a state beyond the twittering of words. Only then would one have stepped past the plane of language into the actual. Zen Buddhism aims at the same state: getting outside any webwork of names mistaken for how things really are. To exist in the real. There, as in Taoism, one would have gone beyond the spoken ghosts enabling language to be what it is.

Other than these silences of profound meditation, the only remaining escape from illusions built into nomenclature would be to speak names truer to their things than any names those things presently have. Various sane and crazy paths lead that way. One sane version may be poetry: the poem as a single, complex word unique to what it translates, creates, or invokes, and thus names—often a particular moment. Or a feeling for which there's no word till the poem spells it out. The craziest path would be toward a total language. In it, each actual, particular leaf of sorrel, each individual stem of Canadian reed grass, each particular wing feather of every house finch, each toe pad on a gecko, each and every molar in every hippo's maw would have its own name. To make a world you need some of everything, but to make a language you need a whole lot less. Logically, therefore, as this total language grew to become coextensive with every particle of the universe, it would disappear into itself as one vast synonym for god.

Actual taxonomy, the science of classification, is much more a plodder's route to omniscience, yet the founding father of biology's naming seems at times to have felt that he was divinely ordained to that task. As a child in Sweden, Carl Linnaeus fell under the influence of his father's horticultural passion. Though the mother never forgave her son's choosing the life of plants instead of a life in the ministry, the father, himself a minister, proved more indulgent. By the time that son was twenty-three he had devised a taxonomic system whose essentials remain in global use to this day.

The young Linnaeus's method was to name plants in a way that contextualized each within an order of relationships; hence the title of his *Systema Naturae*, which brought to the helter-skelter vocabulary of "natural philosophy" a set of widely acceptable classifying procedures which science had hitherto lacked. The result was a sort of Dewey decimal system of naming. Though many of us may find biology's Latin labels about as exciting as call numbers on library books, we can't deny their usefulness. From its first few printed pages in the edition of 1735, Linnaeus's *Systema Naturae* won quick acceptance. Successive editions expanded as nature became better known. Taxonomy itself became a science.

Prior to Linnaeus, natural history had been seriously encumbered by a sprawling nomenclature with as many "systems" as there were groups of naturalists. How could a botanist, pharmacologist, or zoologist in Strasbourg, for example, know what a naturalist writing in England meant by *pole cat* or *chimney sweepers*? For that matter, how could a Virginian or Carolinian? In Warwickshire a "chimney sweeper" was what Americans call a dandelion, which in France is called a "*pis-en-lit*," or "piss-in-the-bed." And because skunks are unique to North America, an English writer referring to a "pole cat" might be misunderstood in Pennsylvania.

Or take *kinnikinnik*, whose palindromic syllables I have loved from first hearing—before ever seeing what they named. In Colorado, as my friend William Weber has pointed out to me, this originally Algonquin word refers to a type of ground cover whose evergreen leaves are glossy as laurel. Some people, however, call the plant "bearberry," others call it "hog-crawberry," or "mountain box," "rapper dandies," and I don't know what all. Spoken in Canada, *kinnikinnik* names quite another set of leaves, *Amelanchier pumila*, which has in common with our plant only the coincidence that Indians once used it too for tobacco.

Though scientifically needed to avoid confusing the Colorado plant with one up in Canada, both *Arctostaphylos uva-ursi* and *Ame-*

lanchier pumila do indeed stick to the palate compared with *kinnikin-nik*. Nonetheless, Linnaeus's system of binomial naming—akin to a person's family name and given name—stressed a plant's botanical context. Naming a plant in relation to its genus and species, Linnaeus reasoned, would summon facts about it by association. In effect, there-fore, the youthful Swede who was mad about naming gave science an international code, in which names functioned neatly as shorthand.

Even if his "sexual system" of classifying plants by their reproduc-tive organs was so far from perfect that Linnaeus himself didn't always abide by it, such a method was nonetheless perfectible. And as this "prince of plants" emphasized, "The Ariadne thread in botany is classi-fication, without which there is chaos." Lifelong he held names to be the road to a knowledge of things, an enthusiasm going back to his childhood habit of wheedling botanical names from his father, and from reading that father's old herbal books for interesting names. Years later he indulged that passion through books of his own, as for example in his preface to *Hortus Cliffortianus*, the printed catalog of a wealthy Hollander's zoological and botanical garden, where he saw "American falcons, divers kinds of parrots, pheasants, peacocks, guinea-fowl, American capercaillie, Indian hens . . . American crossbills . . . orchids, cruciferae, yams, magnolias, tulip-trees, calabash trees, arrow, cassias, acacias, tamarinds, pepper-plants, Anona, manicinilla, cucurbitaceous trees . . . Hernandia, silver-gleaming species of Protea and camphor-trees." If ever anyone loved naming nature it was Carl Linnaeus.

In Lutheran Sweden, however, there was harrumphing when it came to Linnaeus's choice of plant genitals as the basis for classifica-tion. No sooner had the *Systema Naturae* begun its influence than the high-toned Johann Siegesbeck took exception to its explicitly sexual mode of plant identification: "Such loathesome harlotry as several males to one female would never have been permitted in the vegetable kingdom by the Creator." The scandalized Siegesbeck despaired to know "how anyone could teach without offence so licentious a method to studious youth."

Had Herr Siegesbeck been with me last summer, he might have felt his dismay confirmed. On one side of a seven-passenger van parked out-side the Backcounty Office at the Grand Canyon, studious youth had stuck impromptu lettering in yellow tape: "UNIVERSITY VAN #7, DAY 16" and on the other side, "2 PISTILS, 5 STAMENS." It would seem that even today Linnaeus's system may risk titillating chaste minds.

It was a risk the studious youth of eighteenth-century Sweden were eager to run. Linnaeus's university lectures filled to overflowing. His field trips became festivals. At the height of his career, young men and women flocked by the hundreds to join his botanical outings into summer countryside around Uppsala. Though these excursions lasted from eight in the morning till nine in the long Scandinavian evening, "studious youth" weren't too weary for escorting Linnaeus back home with banners, French horns, and kettledrums—then taking their leave of him amid shouts of "*Vivat Linnaeus!*" several times repeated. Can any professor of botany ever have been so adulated? Will any ever be so again?

Though given to bouts of depression, in his manic phases this workaholic minister's son seems indeed to have seen himself as the Lord's own botanist. In fact, his status as nature's "second Adam" made "Linnaeus" a household word internationally. By the end, however, the man who lifted naming to the level of science, the man who came to be called "God's registrar," had grown literally oblivious to his renown. On good days, when well enough to be led out into the garden, his delight in its green world—which had begun in earliest childhood—was yet alive; but all knowledge of plants had been taken from him. A stroke saw to that. It left his garden's flora nameless as Eden's had been prior to Adam. He knew neither his own books—not so much as the title of his great *Systema Naturae*—nor even who he was. By the end he didn't know his own name.

The Linnaeus I care to think about, however, is the young man mad about plants, the one whose students choired him home after field trips, the one whose boyhood wonder at the rareness, muchness, and strangeness of his father's garden reached to the ends of this earth. In his prime, Carl Linnaeus, believing with Messianic fervor that names both give order to knowledge and summon it, might have grumbled plenty at the idea that any familiar thing may suddenly choose to transcend whatever we call it by, and reveal its unnameable nature. At such moments, nonetheless, reality deepens till the only really apt name is wordless.

Years ago on the Tyrrhenian coast of Italy, for example, I certainly felt that way. It was toward the end of a hot August afternoon, day's end really. The final 10-year-old vendor had traipsed past my beach chair and faded umbrella, crying up his tepid soda and limp ice cream bars. A few at a time the midafternoon crowd had long since left. Out over the becalmed Bay of Lerici a westering sun ruddied as it lowered. Already the trompled sand was cratered with shadows marking each footfall.

We remaining die-hards were about to leave too, though the evening breeze was still August-warm on bare torso and legs. Having gathered up the usual odds and ends, I was shaking out my beach towel when I turned westward.

The edge of an enormous orange-red sphere was just about to kiss the sea's horizon. Everybody else seemed to be watching it also. Their casual babble lessened, fell silent. In that speaking stillness something important was about to happen. Something serious, and very strange. The placid waters had become a burning smear. We all watched a huge orb of fire taking itself away. More than the sun was slipping out of sight.

Before our eyes, it was pulling one of our days down with it. Our most recent history was being transformed from casual and mindless to something terribly precious, at the same rate that it was sinking forever into the sea. Its mystery—the mystery of what the sun really is, and consequently this world and all our days, gone and to come—now fused with one actual day made visible in disappearing. A half-moment before the great red *thing* had taken itself entirely away, a little girl called out to it. Then gone. Then afterglow off cloud banks, their red memory fading from the waters.

And voices resumed, at first only as murmur. We all—American, Italian, French I suppose, and undoubtedly German—must have had different reactions to what we had seen. I doubt that "*tramontana*" or "*coucher du soleil*," for example, or "*sonnenuntergang*" named any of them.

Later, if some of us, recalling that evening, ever tried finding words to express the inadequacy of "sundown," wouldn't we have been reenacting the rise of Homo sapiens? By pressing back against the pressure of what words can't say—isn't that how we made ourselves human? But the paradox of "the sun," "*die Sonne*," "*il sole*," "*le soleil*" both concealing and revealing isn't really a dilemma; or at least not inescapably so. If we can't be Chuang-Tzu and Carl Linnaeus, a circle and a straight line, simultaneously, it's also true that neither one of them was *always* the one and never the other. If that had been the case, neither could have been either.

Taoism never tires of reminding us that the ineffable remains beyond language: "The name you can name is not the name." That's true of more than just "the Tao." Each presence in nature may tend toward our naming, yet in answering to the aptest word we can give it, each thing in creation asks to be seen, thus known, even more truly. Just as we do.

The Ideal Particle and the Great Unconformity

Slowly we accepted the curve of the earth. It dawned on us like a great change of mind, after which Earth's size came easy. Not its age. Evidence was everywhere underfoot, unmistakable. We chose not to see it.

The canyons of the Southwest take one by surprise. A hundred paces or so to the left a provocative cactus flower draws you toward it, over a pocked table of stone that may grow nothing taller than lichen and sand. Then, as if between one step and the next, a canyon decides to make itself visible. The slabs we call northern Arizona are riven by depths unseen from a few hundred yards distance. Nor does even the Grand Canyon give itself away slowly. It's just all at once *there*.

That fact makes entirely believable the story about a nineteenth-century cowhand who'd never heard of it or its alleged grandeurs. He didn't know what a high river can do with nobody to tell it how, nor had symphonic strings or kettledrums told *him* how to feel. He just stumbled onto the thing, gaped dumbfounded, and gave a yelp: "Something has happened here!"

In contrast, photo saturation has deadened us to Grand Canyon vistas. If, however, we'd like to see for ourselves those mineral centuries we pass our lives walking and motoring around and upon, while ignoring them, we must descend. Invited into its own past, then further and deeper, the inner eye becomes visionary. Having seen that world the best way, for ourselves, when at last we reascend to the rim we'll be standing on a terrace opposite the universe.

Oddly, she carries no pack. "Oh, I'll make it," she says. She is tall, stout, with salt-and-pepper hair mannishly short. She looks fifty or so, and her walking staff lends a kind of seniority, except for her dogged, almost apprehensive step—though the trail along this stretch is easy going compared to what lies ahead. But a mere mile and three quarters into her morning, she isn't. Not making it at all.

Only 1,600 vertical feet above her, above this stretch of sun-thumbed cliffs whose red detritus give the trail its brick-dust complexion, motorized tourists intending to whiz on by are, even now, suddenly slowing at one or another scenic vista, getting out and putting cameras to their faces. From up there the trails are mostly hidden by buttes, and hikers all but invisible. The attraction is photo opportunities.

But to the grim-visaged woman poking along behind the tip of her walking staff, what had been, on the rim, expanses of unpeopled gorgeousness is now red shale made of heat waves. Her step is a trudge. "All kinds," I say to myself.

Downtrail a quarter mile or so I meet the husband. He too is tall, greyer than his wife, but lean. He wears a bright blue frame pack and carries by its top bar another just like it. Seeing me, he sets the second pack aside in the shade of an outcrop, then takes off his own. It handles heavy. "Where you headed?" I ask.

"We're spending our first night at Hermit Creek," he says. Clearly he believes it. Or is trying to?

"Um-m-m," I think. Ahead are the so-called Cathedral Stairs down through the Redwall—*very* steep—then miles more of mounting heat over rock trash and switchbacks down through the Supai formation onto the Tonto—which by the time they get there is going to be torrid. The woman is already whipped.

"My wife's still acclimating," the man says without my asking. "We're from Virginia, just getting used to the altitude. We're shuttling the packs downtrail."

The "we" is him. First *his* pack, for two hundred yards or so, then, having shucked it, the return uptrail for hers—and so on, to Hermit Creek. Lean though he is, doing a strenuous seven miles that way would mean twenty-one miles, packs and all. "Unreal," I think but don't say.

Among hikers into this canyon's desert realities, his brand of magical thinking is far from rare. Heading off again, I wince inwardly as he adds, "We've got food for a week."

As words go, *astronomy* and *physics* have been in use for millennia, whereas *geology* in its present sense dates back only a few hundred years. Till then the earth sciences lacked focus enough to warrant a name. But why? Why should the study of light-at-a-distance, astronomy, have produced notable results almost two thousand years before anything like geology got started? For want of equipment? Hardly. A world of geology has been learned by just looking; not even a hammer is needed. And the laboratory everywhere.

True, the ancients didn't lack occasional bright ideas we'd call geological, "the ancients" being, when it comes to ideas that have reached us, not the Hittites or Chaldeans but almost invariably the Greeks. Yet nobody went around systematically looking to see how the earth is made, or what forces cause earth events to happen as they do. Given the accurate scrutiny of sky effects, what explains such long disregard of activity within the earth's crust? Why the indifference?

The answer may be simple as Up and Down. Things in the sky, we "look up to." Perhaps they ordain, control. Even foretell? Whereas Venus and Mars were sky fire, Earth was just dirt. Unlike Babylonian stars, ours don't portend any more, but we still "look down on" things underfoot. Our sci-fi mania for leaving Earth far below to journey up into the heavens is an ancient ambition. Persons knowing little of the history of science will feel that claiming Up and Down as values, not just directions, is childish. Precisely. Which is why our sense of them as values is ageless. And why geology became really possible in the century of Galileo and Newton, when for the first time in the Christian era our everyday terra firma found itself part of the sky. Like a star or any other heavenly object, once Earth's status was promoted to that of a planet, it became considerable. In short, a proper object of study.

Few backpackers I've met bother much with geological labels. It's all rock, the various kinds have names—which you *could* learn. But what, beyond syllables, would you know if you did? Anyhow, enjoyment may be the best form of knowing this canyon.

Further downtrail I pass a slow-moving, hefty type who couldn't care less what these depths are made of. He simply wants them to take the measure of his character. Gabby in a big-city way, self-conscious about his slow pace and his flab, he blurts his reasons for putting himself through what, in his shape and limping on already awesome blisters, must be purgatorial. As apparently in some sense he intends it to be.

"I do this every few years," he says. "To test the spirit, find out if I'm up to it."

Odd, hearing in his Detroit accent that he's a salesman of industrial chemicals. His limp stalls; I halt with him. "I'm a pretty fair doctor," he says, shucking his pack and pulling from it a pint of whiskey. Unlacing a boot, he says, "This may take a while." To lance the worst of the blisters, then sterilize it with bourbon? "You go on ahead. And have a good one."

Five minutes later the trail's switchbacking has put me no more than a hundred feet below his wild, animal yowl. I look up startled. His face contorted, he holds his bourboned foot while rocking to and fro in exquisite pain—but nonetheless calls down to reassure me. "I thought I was ready for that," he says, "but I guess I wasn't."

What's it matter how old the earth is? These days not much, but in former ages it mattered. Earth's age, implicit in the Book of Genesis, wasn't open to question; therefore, incredible as it may seem now, you once could have been put to death for saying "millions of years." In times near as our great-grandfathers' you could've been suspected of heterodoxy merely by being a geologist. Right up to our own century, "millions of years" could give rise to imputations of atheism.

But poor James Ussher, Archbishop of Armagh! One literal-minded gesture now outweighs his seventeenth-century fame as a most learned man. Amused geologists never tire of celebrating his naiveté in dating the Creation overprecisely: 4004 B.C. But how? Well, to figure biblical chronology for his *Annales Veteris et Novi Testamenti* he calculated backward from known Roman history and Old Testament hints to arrive at Creation's very first day: Sunday, October 23. At Cambridge University, Ussher's estimate didn't cut it fine enough for one John Lightfoot, a Hebrew scholar deeply read in rabbinical literature. Like a mathematician adding a few decimal places to the value of pi, Lightfoot worked it down to the very hour. The Holy Trinity had created Adam at nine o'clock in the morning!

Lifted from their historical moment, Ussher and Lightfoot do seem paragons of fatuity, but less so when we recall that the bygone enterprise of wringing chronological precision from Holy Writ occupied Isaac Newton obsessively for over a decade.

Northwest of Yuma Point there's a vest pocket plateau of Wescogame sandstone far below the rim, but so aloof from terrain far below *it* that it seems to float. A campsite in the sky. And this evening, mine.

Backed to the east by a sheer, straw-yellow cliff of Coconino sandstone looming asteroidally high, this tiny plateau-prominence begins as a steep talus slope footing that cliff, then as its steepness eases, it flattens, ending abruptly as butte. Like a ship's prow it sails into Grand Canyon space and seems to cruise there, high above another plateau, the Tonto, 1,400 feet down. Many trail-hours below, I see glimpses of what I've come a long way to look at firsthand, the Great Unconformity.

The canyon's stacked layers include a baker's dozen of gaps called unconformities, whose missing rock adds up to far more depth than what's here, but my personal aim on this outing is the big one. It's the one that John Wesley Powell first saw, then named the Great Unconformity. Though I've descended right past it on previous trips, that was before I quite knew what it was. Maybe no human mind can know. Nonetheless, I want another look, close up. Having seen Denali, the Pacific, Etna, Mt. Fuji, Vesuvius, the Alps—and having flown in one long admiration over the blue/white snowfields of Greenland—I suspect the Great Unconformity may be the most astonishing physical thing I'll ever lay eyes on.

Not in the sense of scenic magnificence; rather, a rift in geological time deeper than human thinking can go, a wound in the world's body, whose absence I can put my hand on—the better to feel what happens. As a sort of erosional Sphinx, the Great Unconformity seems to promise carnal knowledge of time. I want my flesh-and-blood hand to touch exactly that.

After supper I poke around along the cliff rim to find a slab just right for a backrest. Months ago I'd planned to use these sundown hours for wandering among limestone hunks fallen from the Kaibab formation 2,400 feet above, and the Toroweap just below it, their surfaces aboil with fossil brachiopods and sea worms. Instead I laze, doing nothing, while light shifts among canyon ridgelines in rags, among multitiered amphitheaters, terra-cotta buttes too proud to be human, and miles of haze blue with purple at the end of them.

The seethe of invertebrates over great slabs fascinates me. My ignorance of their petrified lives is flawed by so few facts that when, traipsing along the Boucher Trail, I stop at a hulk toppled from high above, I'm too blank to be analytical. All I really know is what the clear light of morning tells me: that this canyon's stacked sea floors were once densely, dramatically, aswarm with such creatures.

They squirmed, slithered, died, and were buried under precipitates of calcium carbonate sifting down fine as time; were fossilized and resurrected as limestone, covered in turn by stratas of sandstone, shale, what have you; were uplifted, as our continent rose above sea level, and felt immemorial winds wear away all strata between them and the sun; whereupon their particular chunk, undermined by rains beyond counting, at last broke off and plunged them crashing down here to take up a new existence as surface attractions on boulders. And attract me they do, partly because their chert nodules resist weathering so much better than their encasing matrix of limestone.

I know their dim lives once included—*in potentia*—this one I'm living, yet filial piety doesn't keep me from wanting to pick up a rock and bash at the bulgiest specimen to see what his insides are like. But that would vandalize him, so I don't. Besides, from fossil hunting in Utah I know the first whack would get nowhere. My brachiopod avatar, silicified now, is harder than any rock I'd find hereabouts to smash him open with. Chips would fly, the brachiopod's rain-weathered bulge would receive only powdered dints, whereas my hammerstones would soon go to pieces. And I'd end little the wiser.

If I were determined enough to try various kinds of hammerstone I would reenact the invention of geology. The earliest geologist, as Henry Faul tersely surmises him, would have been that person who held a stone in his hand, picked up another, then tossed the first stone aside because his second choice seemed likelier. Nothing controversial there. But when geology began asking where stones come from, what forces act on them, how one kind of "stone" (the kind now called fossils) come to be found inside another stone, and—most important—how *old* stones or fossils might conceivably be—then the bishops and ministers began harrumphing. Fossils become controversial inklings.

What a weariness it is to realize how slowly we humans open our eyes! The absurdities that organized religion led itself into while denying that Earth moves around the sun were lessons still unlearnt when, at roughly the same time as the Copernican revolution, geology began asking why the relics of sea creatures occurred far inland, high up on mountains; began therefore asking, "This world, how old is it? What is its history?" Not even the voices raising such questions foresaw what an adventure *that* would become. In the Grand Canyon alone, fossilized life forms outnumber me and my whole species, yet for a shamefully long run of centuries we didn't want to know what fossils were.

In ancient times a fossil was anything dug out of the ground—animal, mineral, artifact, it didn't matter. As usual, the first person to have understood the marine origin of fossils seems to have been Greek, one Xenophanes of Colophon, at around 500 B.C. Like any culture, Hellenic societies had their follies and taboos, but an apparatus of thought-police wasn't among them. Thus neither Xenophanes nor Herodotus nor, much later, Aristotle felt constrained in pondering fossils, or forbidden to consider how wide time might be.

Our own culture's protoscientists have had to tread far more carefully when it came to such questions. The Book of Genesis saw to that—or, more accurately, Christianity's reading of Genesis as a literal description of how the world got made. Will anything else in the annals of credulity ever match such absurdity? Probably. Fear is often the threshold of knowledge, but the rate at which our species dares to know itself seems brachiopodally slow.

Yesterday evening, the evening before hiking down to my sky-island, I watched a most jovial woman turn away from a guard rail on the South Rim and, laughing at herself, admit to friends, "Ah cain't hep thankin' all this should be *Egypt!*" Moments later another woman leaned forward over the same rail on the South Rim. In a European accent of mild surprise, as if to herself, she said, "It is a hole." That too.

Now, an afternoon later, I dawdle away the light falling on terrain those women saw so differently, and notice that however firmly I pull my look elsewhere, the eyes drift back to a trail wisping across the broad Tonto plateau. From an air mile away and 1,400 feet down, the trail is thread-thin, but the eyes see it clearly enough to discover nobody. I *pull* my eyes elsewhere. Almost without my permission, the eyes return, scanning, reporting again and again, "Nobody." Just cliff repetitions, sandstone harmonics.

Meanwhile, the Colorado River's blue-green continues to be equally mesmeric, with its roar arriving in waves—clear, then faint, then clear again. Between troughs of near silence its crests break like the rise and collapse of one ongoing sigh that always reminds me of a distant stadium's crowd noise, the hurrahs and applause of all throngs: the Roman forum, the Colosseum, Athenian audiences, Persian armies, Assyrian ones. Except that the river is a dozen or twenty times older than anything human.

My eyes vary their routine by also scanning for river rafts. I tell them I don't mind being alone, the views are stupendous, the evening serene. Who needs Homo sapiens? For that matter, the ravens and swifts are company, aren't they? And my little plateau's piñon pines, the claret-cup cacti, the broadleafed and narrowleafed yuccas, the low, half-diaphanous clumps of rabbit brush. Shadow engulfs the Colorado, but crag lines east of it still bounce gold off its waters, with the eyes trying to see rafts in minuscule flecks the miles make nearly microscopic. "Is that one?" the eyes ask themselves. "Unh-unh, . . . just a riffle." And the boat that has pulled ashore onto a sandbar turns out to be plausible rock. Though we speak of the mind's eye, the eyes have a mind of their own.

In fact, they turn far-off motes into people often enough to finally learn by heart each human-shaped trail form that, stared at hard, doesn't budge. In their compulsive scanning for signs of life, however, the eyes won't take no. They insist on finding me some. And they want it human. "Dear bipedal creatures," they seem to feel, "how avid we are to take you in at this distance."

In evening's marvelous dilapidations, the lower buttes are now an enshadowed blue, while the loftier ones grow rustier by the minute, but still lift sunstruck pinnacles proud of their resistances. All of it high above the river's running whisper.

Turning westward to check the sun's remaining minutes, I notice a raven gliding in as if to alight. It skims along about twelve inches above the dust-puddled slab of this narrow plateau, then, as it continues out over suddenly nothing—I'm shot with adrenaline. Unconsciously, I'd become that raven, and when its level glide sailed out over the cliff edge, my safe inches of altitude turned to deep air—with me plummeting through it. An eight-hundred-foot drop isn't bottomless but my surprise makes it so.

Twenty minutes later, watching the daredevil feeding of swifts, I notice a variant; how a smaller, incomparably nimbler empathy causes me to fall a long way through one microsecond of panic. You can become a swift, I discover, wholly unaware you've done so. Any number of times, without thinking, just blurting and wheeling, blithely feeding on gnats or what-have-you, my aerobatic gaze drops from the swift I've become down through the space between me and the Tonto Plateau: "But *I* can't fly!"

Anywhere else, even in mountains, birds passing nearby at eye level have at least a slope under them. Here the sheer drops from this floating platform of butte create an illusion that fools me with as little as a yucca moth, flying two inches above a pool of brown sand. The moment its cabbage-white flutter takes it out past the cliff edge, I startle, then plunge.

For many years, certainly ever since my first Inner Canyon trip and initial glances at the Great Unconformity, one of my large admirations has dwelt on a grain of quartz sand so tiny that *ten* laid edge to edge would span only a millimeter. Through a pocket lens I have often marveled at the gemlike purity and luster of such granules among the pink ridgelines and valleys of my fingerprint.

In fact, a sand grain that tiny is the size most easily airborne in wind, thus likeliest to begin the process of saltation: the chain reactions of grains knocked into the air by other windblown grains which, as they land, then strike yet more sand grains a micro-blow, lifting them just enough for wind to get at them. Hence the term "ideal particle"; that is, ideally sized for becoming airborne, thus "eolian." Hence too, Utah for instance—whose weather-carved forms owe much to the ideal particle's love of flight, and changes of scenery. Around Mexican Hat, Utah, people say, "Nothing here but a lot of rocks and sand, and more rocks and more sand, and enough wind to blow every bit of it away." They know.

Allied with water, of course. There isn't anything in the entire Southwest that sand-cargoed water can't erase and take with it, en route to the sea. The ideal particle and its kin—silt, pebble, gravel, or boulder—created the Grand Canyon. Long, long, long before that, though mountains more than two miles high once rose where the canyon now is, the ideal particle abducted them.

Like water, sand is a wheel. Round and round its silicon goes, grain on grain, cycle on cycle. With its auxiliaries, ice and snow, sand has already leveled Colorado. Not once. Often. Quartz granules are made of pure patience. The smaller, the more durable; as little as one-tenth of a millimeter. How delicately, translucently, its quartz encapsulates the many Tetons and Rockies and Appalachians already brought low! It can afford to seem humble, agree to eat anything. Wherever we walk at the seashore, it nibbles dead skin off our footsoles.

Among Inner Canyon hikers "water" is the most spoken word, focusing talk like a bond, while most reasons for being on these trails go unsaid: buttes risen up from red epochs nobody was there to lay eyes on, monoliths astonished to see us—all shaped by rain and gravel and sand. If that gone water, now nowhere to be seen, is never far from our thoughts, it must be an obsession to flora on the Tonto Plateau. The verdigris slopes of Bright Angel shale afford barely enough moisture for omnipresent blackbrush and cacti—each guarding its water with thorns, or with needles thick as rain.

Then there's the Utah agave's wild efflorescence. Its most yellow blossoms begin head-high, on a single fibrous stalk twice taller than a man. How much pollen they offer or nectar they ooze I can't say, but it's enough to allure the biggest, blackest bees I've ever seen. "Grumble bees" I call them, flying so sluggishly it seems they'd rather not be flying at all. I half drowse just watching one back out of a bloom, then sag heavily down onto a fresh set of petals. The agave's flowering—gaudy as Hollywood's idea of Persia—is, on its truculent side, armored water. Its base is a sword-burst of rigid blades that are reputed to have ripped up the guts of many a Spaniard fallen from his saddle while questing for gold and souls. So the Utah agave has to bide its time, taking maybe a dozen to fifteen to as much as twenty-five years to ejaculate that one opulent splurge of water-costly blossoms—then topple. Its husks litter the canyon like dead steers.

Understandably, backpackers are warned to carry at least a gallon per day per person. I remember a puffy guy girdled with fat who came downtrail into the big campsite at Hermit Creek, shirtless, red-faced, and gimpy from unaccustomed exertion. He slumped down, groaning, moaning. Half to himself, half to anyone within earshot, he said, "There was a moment up there," nodding up toward the Tonto, "when I just didn't know." Long pause. "I mean, I just didn't know." Another pause. Then softly, and more than half to himself, "Oh, I knew." Again pausing. "But I knew I was going to have to take my time."

"Did you have enough water?" I asked.

"Drank six quarts coming down," he said. "And only peed twice."

Earth centered the stars. In the cosmos, only Earth had a destiny. It had been expressly created for us. Every celestial body, however superior, revolved around us. Here Eden had been, and here the Fall; thus Earth was both center and sewer, the cynosure of all creation and its sink of iniquity. In that moral universe, "up there" was linked with "down here" by analogies abounding. Divine light was to the cosmos as the sun's was to Earth, and as the human mind is to its body. After the Edenic apple got eaten, however, all below the moon had been corrupted. As one Thomas Burnet, a seventeenth-century divine, put it in his *Sacred Theory of the Earth*, our planet in its days of innocence before the Fall had been smooth, entirely; but postlapsarian Earth was "a ruin" whose "faults" were at once geological and a judgment of God. Though Burnet was a theologian, his views seemed to orthodox critics more mechanistic than scriptural. He held matter to be eternal, held that the world machine needed no Divine Machinist to keep intervening. Time and the properties of matter would of themselves give birth to this world we inhabit. Yet his was a *sacred* theory, a Creator behind it, which made his science too theological for free thinkers and too heretical for their opposites.

Among the latter, Edward Stillingfleet wrung his hands. If the world is eternal, he complained, then "the whole Religion of Moses is overthrown, all his Miracles are but Impostures, all the Hopes which are grounded on the Promises of God, are vain and fruitless."

Our tongue clacking over religion's meddling with or *in* science is immensely satisfying, of course, and very bad for our characters. In relishing images of churchmen making museum pieces of themselves, even as today's "Creationists" do now, we indulge in the sweet illusion of superiority—a particularly insidious form of self-abuse. Be that as it may, seventeenth-century controversy slowly yielded to the incontrovertible, and geology became possible. But the analogical universe faded slowly; for example, sunspots suggested a correspondence with earthly volcanoes. Ingeniously false, but error too can be fruitful. The fake correlation led to observations that took on a life of their own as what we now call the earth sciences. Thus Earth received a sort of promotion via the stars.

Still, medieval figments waned slowly, especially on geology's central question: "How old is the earth?" What theo-geological dust that kicked up! Lots of highly educated people tried hard *not* to let the planet's growth-rings tell their own story.

Inches from my left ear a white-throated swift hustles past as if showing how close it can come—with the aggressive, sibilant hiss I imagine of arrows. One swift blurts suicidally straight at a crag, misses by a hand's breadth of veer and plunges into its next audacity with a swerve equally implausible. Their changes of direction dazzle me! At high velocity they spin on a wingtip. And as always, watching them feed and aware they've been clocked at over seventy miles an hour (with unconfirmed reports of more than double that), I think, "These are the hottest pilots going." They in turn, watching *me* sit quietly on an outcrop, content to let them fire into blue canyon shadows and out again, may be asking each other, "How can he live like that?"

They might well wonder—these birds that never hold still. I've seen them nearly alight at a puddle, but mostly they drink on the wing. In love with speed, they can mate while in flight, gather nesting materials, and apparently—in certain instances anyhow—*may* even sleep flying. What energy they pour out hustling and plunging and rolling away on the air!

Mornings and evenings make this, their canyon home, one maze of flight corridors. And of stillnesss, stirred by just enough wind to set up a hushaby soughing of piñon pines nearby. Much as I want to hit the trail tomorrow long before sun does, I won't get into my sleeping bag till a first two or three stars come through the twilight, as if walking toward Earth.

Where great walls do the talking, where a gibbous moon becomes visible as desert silences happen, those walls, their depths, with tiny birds hurtling under and above them become so real as to stay that way, untranslatable. And swifts, incomparably more so. Yet what do such creatures amount to? A pinch of white and dark fluff, hollow bone. A mature swift weighs only a couple of ounces; but is anything else in creation so entirely, so audaciously alive? "No," I think, "not possible." So for me the swift is not "a lower form," is instead a perfection.

That's a long flight from archaeopteryx, the world's first bird, of about 150 million years back, whose leathery membranes were "wings" fit only for gliding. Lacking muscle enough to flap them, and thus having to climb any tree it launched from, the archaeopteryx looks comic enough to us; nonetheless, like the failed ignition of some defunct star, its clumsy hope of colonizing the air reaches me now, serialized through intervening species, by way of these swifts. They are indeed the definitive bird. Leaving this canyon I'll top out on a rim that was still ocean floor 100 million years before the appearance of archaeopteryx. Reptilian as its skin-flap and tendon contraption may have been, from such cumbersome glides this very sky's first flying animal was born.

As an English observer put it in the early nineteenth century, "It was a mooted question whether geology and Christianity were compatible." To fervid literalists of the Bible it seemed that those men going round the British countryside tapping at rocks with their odd little hammers were bent on chipping away at Genesis.

For one thing, long before the nineteenth century, a strictly literal reading of Genesis made it risky to say too much about fossils. On the third day the Lord separated land and sea. On the fifth day he created fishes and fowl. On the sixth terrestrial creatures. So how could shells found far inland possibly be marine in origin? Relics of Noah's Flood? Some believers invoked that possibility, but doing so was particularly awkward in the case of fossilized species now nowhere alive. Literally interpreted, Genesis doesn't mention animal extinctions—which in any case the Ark was built to prevent.

Sixteenth-century writers on fossils sometimes stepped very gingerly. A common ploy for avoiding imputations of heresy was to discuss fossils and Earth's age in safely hypothetical terms, as the Copernicans had learned to do; that is, to affirm nothing as fact. Even so, when protogeologists began realizing that fossils might prove the calculus stones with which to date various strata, enormously unbiblical time spans with their unbiblical extinctions and sudden appearances of new species began to dawn.

Meanwhile, orthodox thinkers argued that fossils weren't living animals, ever. Couldn't have been. A medieval view held that they were *lusus naturae*, "sports of nature," possibly conceived by Satan to confuse people. A sixteenth-century savant cataloging the Vatican's mineral collection suggested that fossils were neither extinct creatures nor anything else but just odd things God just happened to have made. Da Vinci, of course, had known exactly what they were, but confided only in the mirror script of his notebooks. Geologically minded others in the sixteenth century knew too, even while orthodoxy kept trying to explain them away.

Little did humble crinoids and three-inch trilobites crawling over the Paleozoic ooze dream of one day becoming Gorgons or Medusas, too terrible for gazing on directly. Theirs was a past we didn't want to believe was inside us.

At 7:30 in the morning, the trail down and across Travertine Canyon remains mostly shaded; a sort of glade, so cool and leafy and fragrant—what with the blossoming shrubs of mock orange, the mountain maple, fendlerbush, serviceberry—that rattlers are quite out of mind. Watching the wing blur of hummingbirds float and dart among blooms on a shrub of mock orange, I forget to be wary. By mere chance, turning to photograph a ledge I've just descended, I see it there, tucked in a niche at shoulder height, where I just now passed within inches. Classic.

If this one's typical, maybe I can't hear them. From its tail vibration, surely it must be buzzing; must've buzzed as I passed it. The lower body coiled, its upper portion cocked in an S-curve, it flicks a black tongue, tasting the air, but often putting the forked tip on the ledge before it. To know where its ledge ends? Pick up vibrations? The final few inches of tail twitch, then blur. I hear nothing. Odd to think of its rattling as I walked by, gazing at hummingbirds.

Usually I keep snakes well in mind, scorpions too. I'd have said I keep serpents at the level of a phobia, except that this one, my first canyon rattler, despite fangs and venom, is beautiful. Very. It disquiets me that my hearing, a bit the worse for loud noises in war, may be unable to warn me. It's further bad news to see that this subspecies, Grand Canyon rattler, has evolved to match perfectly the beige sandstone with its beige underbelly and sides. I'm fascinated by the delicate tongue, a glistening flicker, black as obsidian, liquid as oil.

But shoulder height is too near the heart. If it had struck, I'd have tried to smash it to pulp. Since it didn't, I'm free to see time's intricate beauty in even a rattler.

On an Earth only six thousand years old there would still be sand enough in any hourglass to bury us all. And if the cosmos retained only nineteenth-century dimensions, Earth would still be almost infinitely small within it.

Even the medieval cosmos would do. In Dante's universe, if you traveled at what we know is the speed of light, you'd reach the nearest star in five minutes. In ours, you wouldn't quite have arrived four *years* later! By the seventeenth century, cosmic scale hadn't grown much. France's polymath savant Father Mersenne held the universe to be about 110 million miles across—which in our world gets you only a little past the sun. So despite Mersenne's being a Copernican and a booster of Galileo, his cosmos was still surprisingly medieval: a bit less than ten light-minutes wide. The same Father Mersenne, a formidable mathematician, calculated that in 1634 the earth was exactly 5,954 years old. By comparison, in eastern Nevada lives a bristlecone pine whose growth rings span 75 percent of Mersenne's estimate. When it came to this world's actual age and size, our forebears had no idea.

Or chose not to, like everyone. No sooner are certain realities admitted to the brain than something within us secretly dissolves them, just as, by day, the mind takes back what it dreamed.

During my scrambling descent through Mississippian limestone of the early Carboniferous down into Temple Butte limestone, I'm vexed to see that my $3.99 watch—bought expressly for this rough terrain—is again useless. After half an hour on the trail its crystal is once more opaqued with sweat beads glistening inside it like mercury. So much for "Waterproof to 30 meters." Back in Boulder my friend Ron would say, "$3.99? You didn't pay enough." On the contrary, too much. Well, whatever the o'clock, it's between 350 and 400 million years ago, local time.

The leather headband of my wide-brimmed straw rides on a film of saltwater, and swiping at it with a bandanna is token resistance. For five hundred feet down through Redwall limestone, however, the microclimate isn't desert but shaded oasis, and that helps. Apparently runoff takes the same trail, because green sprays of skunkbush and bricklebush alternate with tufts of long-bladed grasses kept alive by their memories of rain. Which doesn't keep my sweat from finding channels of its own.

What a comic figure I make, slithering, clinging to carnal hunks of Toroweap limestone fallen all the way here, lurching deeper into erosions the European woman called "a hole." To do what? To see for myself. If a judge sentenced criminals to this trail, she'd be removed from the bench. Sweat dribbles onto the lens of my sunglasses, yet looking up at the sunlit ocher of cliff walls without them makes the eyes wince.

Except for my presence, no sign of Homo sapiens; and maybe not even then. Aside from the chink of rock chips scattered by my boots, all I hear is an animal's breathing, and the creaking of his pack. After millennia of practice, I suppose our highest flight within that webworks called the mind has been to realize that's who we are: animals. Till lately, we were too backward to make the discovery, thus closer to being what we feared to be, by that very refusal. Like a kid in a retention home, we fantasized stories we truly seemed to believe—about what a big shot our dad was, and how much he loved us, and how he was one day going to come get us, and take us out of this place, to live in a fancy house and have everything.

Childlike too was our refusal to share the ancestry of mammals. The ruckus we kicked up over being blood cousins to apes and monkeys was the strident denial of a six-year-old whose playmates have just told him how babies are *really* made.

With each knee-jolt downward a last quart sloshes inside its canteen to remind me I'm an erstwhile sea creature crawled ashore; the salinity of that amniotic fluid has come along inside my cells—whose survival requires me to tote the anciently mothering element in bottles, jars, bags, what have you; a fish who preferred terra firma while taking his sea with him.

"The total destruction of the land is an idea not easily grasped, though we are the daily witness of its process." This audacious concept in the matter-of-fact style of James Hutton marks a decisive breakthrough in dating the age of the earth. An eighteenth-century Scot with a genius for both the invisible obvious and good fellowship, Hutton has been called "the founder of modern geology" as well as "the man who invented time." Despite the fact that his French contemporary Georges-Louis Leclerc, Comte de Buffon, espoused similar views about everyday causes, while being incomparably the better stylist; despite Lamarck's wider renown outside his own country; nonetheless, Charles Lyell—born the year Hutton died (1797)—followed Hutton's lead and thereby became the enabling eye behind Darwin. Explorers of stone time included no one who uttered thunderbolts so blandly as Hutton. His facts were few as his insights, but those few were profound. And seminal.

Had I accompanied Hutton on one of his outings—for instance to Jedborough, when he spoke of inland stone having once been ocean floor—I'd have boggled mightily. There, some fifty miles south of Edinburgh, where the younger "Old Red" sandstone lies horizontally across nearly vertical "schistus" of far greater age was a big time-gap. The idea of strata once present now missing isn't fantastic. Hutton's close friend John Playfair, however, would've called the gap an "abyss of time." An abyss? One many thousands of times older than the entire earth was then believed to be? I'd have boggled plenty at that.

Whereupon Hutton would have tried to explain. The nearly vertical layers of "schistus," being enormously older than the sandstone on top of it, revealed—if you knew how to read rock's chronicles—the drowning, the metamorphosis, and the resurrection of continents. All of which required, according to Hutton, epochs too vast for human vision to see very far into. Summing up his view of stone's endless cycles, Hutton chose words more shocking, then, and more frequently quoted both then and now, than any in the history of geology: "The result, therefore, of our present enquiry is, that we find no vestige of a beginning—no prospect of an end."

"Hindu nonsense," I'd have thought, "and downright heretical!" Not all his zesty high spirits, nor the charm of his Scots burr would have got me past the impossibility of rain showers and grit dismantling whole continents.

In his own day Hutton knew well that his *Theory of the Earth* would meet minds conventionally, biblically closed. Exactly as mine would've been back then. Anybody looking at mountains, fault lines, or chasms could *see* that apocalyptic events must have caused them. Thus whether you inclined to "catastrophism" and its doctrine of grand, once-and-for-all upheavals in a past that wouldn't happen again, or to "diluvialism" and its image of a global ocean precipitating, forever, the world's supply of stone—granite included—or to both working successively, you subscribed to the idea that it takes big causes to make big effects. That was common sense, bolstered by the ageless appeal of fire and flood in myth; as if it would be a godless world indeed without wrathful cataclysms.

Hutton's *Theory*, on the other hand, was neither apocalyptic nor Wagnerian. Geologically speaking, he argued, nothing happened in the past that hasn't always happened, and that isn't happening right now. Past causes are ongoing and uniform. Hence the label by which his view came to be known: "uniformitarianism." Though he allowed for leaps and upheavals, he emphasized everyday forces. Eminently sensible now, in hindsight; but nonsensical then.

"If that's so," I'd have snapped, "then why can't we see them?"

"We can and do," his answer would have come, "but we don't realize what we're witness to—because the earth is so much older than we've supposed."

There it was in a nutshell: "so much older than we've supposed." Rather than invoke a past in which remote catastrophes gave Earth its present continents and their appearance, Hutton urged people to consider forces daily seen and felt; in short, to consider "little causes, long continued." These, operating over a sort of temporal eternity, were powerful enough to destroy whole continents. "What more can we require?" he asked, then answered, "Nothing but time." Surely that wasn't asking worlds.

Of me it would have been. Back then, where the age of the world was involved, it would've put me on an Earth wholly alien to my vision.

By changing *where*, it would have changed who and *what* I thought I was.

Hutton anticipated my reaction: "It is not any part of the process that will be disputed; but after allowing all the parts, the whole will be denied; and for what?—only because we are not disposed to allow that quantity of time which the ablution of so much wasted mountain might require."

He was right. Like all the top-flight geological minds of Hutton's day, I'd have been a catastrophist—with a splash of diluvialism.

Surely it's no coincidence that, long before Copernicus, Aristarchus of Samos said, "Earth circles the sun," and was ignored for two thousand years. Space and time do tend to interpenetrate each other. As for time, Aristotle hadn't minced words. Earth and the world were eternal. In the beginning, there was no beginning. There would be no end. Christian Europe referred to and deferred to Aristotle on any subject but that. The eternity of matter was pagan: heretical, insidious, atheistical.

Time-timidity prevailed till the era of Galileo and Newton. In eighteenth-century France, for example, Benoît de Maillet actually dared write of millions and *billions* of years. And of the eternity of matter. Even of life arisen spontaneously from "seeds" and marine creatures. But his curious compilation, *Telliamed* (de Maillet backwards), lay unpublished. Then, in 1748, two decades after his death, de Maillet's timorous editor fudged his original numbers downward by replacing big figures with vague phrases, or simply moving de Maillet's decimal points a few or more digits to the left!

Symptomatic, too, was the case of one of de Maillet's cleverest countrymen, Buffon. No editorial tampering undercut his estimates; he did it himself. After devising a series of quite intelligent experiments with the cooling of molten spheres, Buffon arrived at three million years as Earth's real age. But because even in the closing decades of the Age of Reason, he felt readers wouldn't stand for "millions," he downscaled his own estimate to 75,000 years. Then, having it both ways, he admitted to his readers what he had done. Inevitably, France's theologians roused themselves.

His compatriot Lamarck, a generation younger and a celebrated precursor of Darwin, found time-timidity infuriating. The threshold of the nineteenth century was, he felt, no place to keep nattering over the purblind vistas of what came to be called Mosaic geology—and the world's paltry six thousand years, as inferred from Genesis. Impatient with persons who want to go on counting Earth's years on their fingers and toes, he said, snappishly, "For Nature, these time-spans that stagger the mind are but instants."

"Which is," one can imagine him feeling, "simply how things stand. End of discussion." The nineteenth century had dawned, but of course it wasn't the end at all. Scriptural orthodoxy had become a sort of loyalty oath that custodians of the status quo required its members to sign. The young Darwin, hopeful of a country parsonage, professed faith in "the strict and literal truth of every word in the Bible." Then, only a few years later, weighing animal differences such as those between archaeopteryx and pigeons, he could say, "It leads you to believe the world older than geologists think."

Breathing infinite distances can enervate the soul. Once more readjusting my heavy pack's hip belt I look out now over the Tonto Plateau. Amid its Sonoran expanses that foot cliff lines abysmally old, and side canyons filled with departures, a hot gust of wind empties me. "What am I doing here? What point? Why go or be anywhere?"

Dry slabs, dry shale flakes, dry detritus, dry buttes, dry gullies. Dust, dryness. Parched air, terra-cotta rock. My weather bob reads 113 degrees Fahrenheit. Hearing water slosh inside my canteen I know it's as much there to be abstained from as drunk, know my sips must be few and miserly. Soon I've drifted into trail trance, aware only of rubble meeting each footfall. It crunches under hot bootsoles like slag, my bare legs pass among needled hostilities in the shape of beavertail cactus, but neither heat nor the dryness account for my being instantly emptied in midstride, as if between the world's body and mine a void had opened.

Like stepping into a local warping of Earth's magnetic field, all my thought-atoms realign so that I feel "how it really is." Not a trick heat plays on the mind. Instead, the truth: nature as one self-sufficient machine where anything that can die is called "life," and ourselves the losses we agree to live out. It's as if the atmosphere suddenly vanished. Without a vapor of illusion to absorb its lethal radiations, the sun pours down a ruthless clarity denying everything I'd *like* to be true.

Then, perhaps because any truth is only half its story, the moment passes. What the canyon tells us is, yes, *its* truth, inhuman, not ours. *Our* truth is a small mortality centering a labyrinthine strangeness. Is it a strangeness worth the price of existence to know? We can't know, can't even suppose, can only answer, "Well, yes, certainly it's worth it. Except when it isn't." Meanwhile we feel the size of creational powers implacable, astonishing. But "lethal"? Only so to us mortals, and even then only if we're afraid to die. I am. I can also imagine *hoping* to become slightly less so. I might do it by agreeing to be fully within whatever this is, instead of resisting, withholding.

Easy to say. Yet whatever the "really" may be in "How it really is," that's what I'm also hoping to glimpse at least distantly in this canyon. On the other hand, if evolution has wired us to keep moving by keeping at least some illusions alive, how close can—or dare—anyone come to whatever "really" is?

To my right and a hundred feet up where the sloping of Bright Angel shale breaks downward from Muav limestone, three blossoming agave plants flaunt their pollen-yellow banners among tumbled boulders—Coconino hunks, hunks fallen from the Supai group, oddments of Redwall limestone that carried Temple Butte limestone along as it smashed its way down. How placidly their tons lie around, as if permanent residents, not transients just passing through. As they really are. As it all is, all on its way to the Gulf of California. Meanwhile, above Redwall boulders teeming with fossil crinoids, corals, bryozoans, my big black "grumble bees" drowsily carry on lives of social insects, gathering pollen over trilobites whose habits, unknowable, survive only in seas of limestone. And maybe in me.

Wind whispers lightly through miles of blackbrush—knee high, waist high. What with that, and a midafternoon sun too hot for unshaded rattlers, and the steady boot-crunch of shale almost finer than cinders, the mind quietly drifts into itself. Then a stretch of prickly pear cactus thickens till there's more cactus than room to avoid it, and I waken, picking my steps over their needles, and detritus more like industrial dross than geology.

I look closer. "Mosaic floor!" I blurt out loud. Indeed it is. Part geology, part meteorology, "mosaic floor" has nothing to do with the biblical Moses, but instead describes desert leveled by wind and virtually paved with more or less flat rock bits, like chips in mosaics. The Sahara contains oceans of mosaic floor, all the stones "ventifacts"—wind-carved and polished. These Tonto *tesserae* are much smaller than those African ones, and not so evidently wind-worked; but inlaid by canyon winds they most certainly are, and neatly. Rust-red shale the size of half dollars, verdigris shale, bits small and dark as coffee beans, edges still crisp, unrounded as yet by the ideal particle. It delights me to find

Saharan ventifacts by the mile, here in Arizona—a veritable floor indeed; cunningly, fastidiously wind-paved, broken only by the ubiquitous blackbrush and cactus.

If continental drifting and lifting ever stops—as, with the inevitable cooling down of Earth's core and mantle we're told it must—this flatness is what all terrain will come to. A peneplain. Land's highest elevations will be worn down to, say, a few bare tens of meters above the world's oceans. Abrasive winds and rains will see to it.

It was in southern Colorado where I first really saw, felt, and wandered barefoot over a lot of mountain ridgelines now milled into abrasives. There, on a June morning like a festival, I began suspecting that the oldest, most irresistible of immortals was the ideal particle.

The Great Sand Dunes National Monument sits eight thousand feet above sea level, at the westward foot of the Sangre de Cristo range. As usual in the San Luis Valley's high desert, that June sky was an intense blue set off by a few small cloud-blossoms. Their brightnesses drifted, freely distorting in the usual westerly breeze blowing almost constantly, the same breeze that—as usual, for years by the *millions*—has been granulating blue skylines of the San Juan range, haze-blue in the distance, and tumbling their sands fifty miles east over that valley floor, already thick with alluvium.

Given that moving air and Colorado sun on the skin, the desert morning was cool/hot. At first the dunes themselves weren't impressive. Nothing on their smooth surfaces gave scale—till flyspecks high up on them kept turning out to be clusters of people. Across ankle-deep Medano Creek I waded, carrying my shoes, to begin the climb up sand ridges toward the crest of the Monument's officially highest dune, seven hundred feet above the valley floor.

Legging it steeply uphill *in fine sand* at that altitude promotes heavy breathing. So because two-thirds of each step forward slid backwards, I paused now and again, panting, enjoying the phenomenon of gusts curling a tan haze off dune summits above me, like snow smoking from mountain ridges. Stone snow. By 11:00 A.M. the surface granules had grown painfully hot after only a few steps. Quickly digging the feet just under the crust allows the cool, moist sand there to quench footsoles—exactly like dousing a fire—but before long, those feet may rebel. Short of the highest dune's crest, mine certainly did, insisting I put on shoes again.

Sometimes a gust would seep over that crest just inches above its surface, with hordes of minute grains biting my ankles like static. A bit eerie—not just to see but to feel in their prickle on my own skin those "little causes, long continued" which will one day wear all mountains and their continents down to a virtual slab. Grains considerably less than a millimeter wide are harmless as gnats, but given their own sweet time, Huttonian time, are piranha. Lightly they nibbled at me, tasting my possibilities.

And that is where I first *felt* myself completely inside geological time—deep time—on a gala morning when I and the clusters of people like me were never more alive. Those dunes were luminosities of beige, blond, tan, ecru, fawn, dove-brown—their silicon grains taking in the sun's photons, and giving them back as a luster minutely diffracted. By the trillions.

Then too, over the nuances of beige, summer tourists were spattered like a grand beach party or a flags-of-all-nations display. Sand's luminosity made white slacks, shorts, and T-shirts dazzling, just as it saturated the firecracker reds, the bright greens, the citrons. Meanwhile, in the kind of day memory builds on, a high-desert sky and its fast-scudding cloud puffs presided over everything, including fir-and-spruce forestation of the Sangre de Cristo, the unkempt cottonwoods lining Medano Creek, and higher up on evergreen slopes, pale columns of aspen newly leafing out. So the blaze blue of that sky was omnitemporal: a June of 35 million years ago, and another June, 35 million summers up ahead, with my own "now" in between.

It was there, too, that I first saw sands in the act of crossbedding. "Big deal," I'd have said to myself before hiking inside the Grand Canyon, where I saw that crossbedding is really a sort of voice print left by winds that blew here long, long before anything human stood up in them. Paleowinds the geologists call them. That enthralled me.

In such fossil dunes those flowlines show abrupt changes of angle where wind piled new dunes over old ones. The crossbedding I was seeing at the Great Sand Dunes was, instead, that of winds alive, lively, unfossilized; my winds, ours, our weather unhardened, unburied beneath thousands of feet under yet other deposits. And because I had seen the crossbedding of 270 million years ago in Coconino stone of the Grand Canyon, I was therefore seeing two June mornings in one. That Coconino stuff had been desert sand identical to what I was standing on, rounded by endless saltation in the very same wind. But those Grand Canyon paleowinds had sent dunes piling over each other when "here" was Pangaea, the globe's one and only continent. Now "here" is

North America, and Pangaea has broken up, drifted off as shards we call Eurasia, Australia, Antarctica, Africa, South America. "How it really is" can be dizzying.

So atop that highest dune I felt a paleowind gusting sand's migrations straight at my ankles. Under strong sun drenching our summer colors, amid the laughter and sand frolicking of children, we were flesh-events, happy to owe what we could only repay by enjoying it, cavorting or struggling or strolling on grains fated to sink beneath the sea again, and, solidified, to reemerge with an untrodden continent.

While I was what had become of some sea lily's or ammonite's future, I was also ancestral to an eventual something-or-other. So between the twin blacknesses of Before and After, my being alive went "click!" like the open and close of a camera's tripped shutter. My prints in hot sand were already posthumous.

At the popular Hermit Creek campsite, a nexus of Inner Canyon trails, I meet some of everyone. On my way to jump into a plunge-pool of the creek itself I notice Sunfoot under a catclaw tree. Shirtless, he sits on a square of blue flannel blanket, trying to pull a dirty sock over his severely sunburnt instep. The other foot looks equally angry. Though his lean physique and bearded face imply a working man who knows his way around, I'm surprised any hiker would let his feet get that badly burnt. As he eases another half inch of sock onto his right foot I ask, "How'd it happen?"

"Fell asleep over at Granite Rapids," he says, deadpan, changing to sardonic grin when he adds, "for maybe three hours."

Just watching him work that grungy sock over skin needing burn cream and bandages makes me cringe. Both insteps are so scarlet I wonder how he'll get boots on. "Can you walk?"

"I'll be all right once I get going," he says, then tells me he'd planned on another four days in the canyon. "But with this . . ." He gestures at the feet. We stare at epidermal tissue already starting to weep and blister. "I figure maybe second degree," he says. I nod a bit squeamishly, and wish him luck, trying not to guess what the miles up to the rim will do, glad I won't be around when he peels those socks off.

After my dip in the creek, refreshed with sopping clothes that'll dry only too soon, I decide to stroll the rest of the way down Hermit Canyon to the river.

Because the mile and a half of creekbed down to the Colorado is in places a lush tangle of willow limbs, or tamarisk, of rushes thick and tall and green, my lunging and thrashing along the creek feels African as the Congo. While in a phase of that daydream I encounter Lord Tarzan, heading back up to Hermit Creek campsite from the river. He's an Englishman living in Canada, medium-tall and, for a man of fifty, very well muscled. Though he flew jets for the R.A.F.—in Africa, oddly enough—it was as a twelve-year-old in Australia he saw the documentary on the Grand Canyon that left him "very much wanting to see it."

Naturally I wonder what he thinks now that he has. His voice is mellifluous yet deep. "I've been on the Zambeze," he says, "and on the Amazon. The Colorado is by far the most . . . romantic." Like his athletic body the voice is also muscular. That and its British vowels lend his slightest remark a sort of stage presence. Though he's a librarian, he's frank to add, "But you won't find many librarians in Toronto like me, I'm afraid." He hikes the canyon annually, and is by consensus the informal leader of several other Canadians still recovering from heat at their campsite. "Coming down," he says, "that sun off those walls . . . well, it hit us rather hard, I can tell you. Felt a bit woozy myself—as if I'd had, you know, one beer more than I needed." Then with energy, "Two of our lads got thoroughly hammered by it."

When in 1794 a geo-theologian named Richard Kirwan fired off a critical blast at James Hutton's *Theory of the Earth*, he charged that it belies Mosaic history, and—almost worse—hurls the reader into a view of time "from which human reason recoils." How true. Hutton himself predicted as much. Indeed we do recoil. We come from Germany, Japan, Canada, England, France, Switzerland, Hungary, and so forth, to the Grand Canyon to do just that, gaze into the very abysses that make us tremble. In the canyon's "abyss of time" we find ourselves missing from our own planet.

Here too we see ourselves as transitional creatures: body hair once pelt, toenails once claws, vertebral column adapted from our days as quadrupeds, hands that used to be forepaws, brain on its way to being—perhaps—something better than a reservoir of reptilian and mammalian cunning. Had the Grand Canyon been formed in Europe instead of the American West, these awarenesses might've dawned on us several hundred years before human reason stopped recoiling from them quite so convulsively.

"Recoil? How very naive!" says every Grand Canyon pebble. Yes, egoism is indeed a form of naiveté. But for orthodox minds, what was being deciphered from Earth's palimpsest was too much like being told, "You're a foundling."

The prostrate man had apparently started up toward the rim from Monument Creek. As if thinking he might be a goner, he had kept asking these tourists-hikers to look after his wife. "He would say it many times," the young woman insisted. " 'My wife has stopped moving, my wife has stopped moving.' But then he would say he had to go for help."

Again the Swiss couple shrug, as if still baffled. A fishy breeze whiffing off the loud river stirs among nearby tamarisk fronds. She in her white bikini, he in his swim trunks—they've spent much of the day under those fronds, or sunning on stream-polished boulders while watching the river pour past, on its way to put long slow movements in the backs of Mexican farmers. "He kept asking us to take the compass out of his pack," she says, puzzled, shading her eyes the better to look at me. "He kept repeating it. The compass had been his father's. When we asked what we should do with it . . . he didn't tell us."

Having left him at his own insistence, they had found his wife further downtrail. She had got into the shade of a boulder, had even rallied. Thus able to continue upward? My Swiss pair thought maybe yes. "Maybe" seems odd. Are they now embarrassed at having left the Virginia woman to shift for herself?

Then I put myself in their situation. On reaching that stricken man's wife and finding she's not only alive, but somewhat recovered, is apparently able to move—and has water—am I *really* going to shepherd her back up toward the rim?

Perhaps a thirst for longevity explains the blithe way we deal in many hundreds of millions of years. To be enlarged, augmented, if only vicariously? And do our heady references to "the local galaxy cluster" participate in that grandeur? I suspect so. As if we sensed in these magnitudes our chance—our only chance—to be immortal. The Grand Canyon's Redwall, five hundred feet of time precipitated as limestone, does indeed claim I never existed; but my overhearing ocean long-lost in its fossils fills me with all the 350 million years their waves and precipitates invested here for safekeeping.

Perhaps our quasi-godlike habit of tossing around the big figures of space/time is snobbery of scale; but simultaneously our eon-dealing, like the gallows humor of combat veterans, may also camouflage chagrin at our simply enormous loss of prestige. As if in an expanding universe our egos implode to match the expansion.

Though all this may seem a strictly recent dilemma, the paradox of disastrous discovery is anciently evident in Lucretius, whose *De rerum natura* was written expressly to announce a sort of liberating good news: that our world is not controlled by gods. Nature and everything in it derives instead, Lucretius claimed, from chance collisions of atoms; thus fear and trembling before the gods was childish. The only "immortals" in our world, said Lucretius, were atoms. Earth and sun had a beginning, would have an end, but their atoms would not. They alone were eternal. For Lucretius, however, the price of that liberated but evacuated universe was a sort of brave desolation, expressed on almost every page.

Atop the highest of the Great Sand Dunes, with windblown saltations of ideal particles prickling my bare ankles, I had actually thought of Lucretius and his atom-immortals. Much of that blowing sand I knew to be pure quartz, and such a grain is nearly indestructible. Other mineral grains making up sand tend to dissolve, lose their identities, or be powdered to those finenesses we know as silt or clay. Along the valley south of Lauterbrunnen, Switzerland, with snows of the Jungfrau, the Eiger, the Grosshorn, and the Schilthorn feeding its gravity-fattened waters, I've watched the silt of pulverized limestone go rampaging down the Lütschine river as "glacial milk," in a branch appropriately called "Weisse," or white. But a grain of quartz sand has other and longer journeys to go.

In Colorado's San Luis Valley there are now a few particular grains long eroded from their parent granite, long tumbled by water and wind, which—after thousands of centuries—finally arrived at my ankle. But when the dunes eventually sink beneath other, more recent deposits millions of years from now, those few grains will by chemical action and pressure get cemented to fellow grains as sandstone.

Not the end of the story—far from it! Hence the source of my fascination that my ankle had been kissed by some of Lucretius's eternal atoms. Or, as this world goes, by one at least halfway eternal—because every grain at the Dunes is unthinkably more ancient than the name of any god, known or forgotten. The least grain among them will be circulating here undiminished long after the last god is gone.

Provided the sandstone that captured it sinks no deeper than six miles below Earth's surface, thus escaping the heat and pressure of greater depths which would transform its silicon dioxide, each quartz speck hitting my ankle will remain nearly indestructible. And in all probability will rise again, as further crustal upheavals thrust each once more into the sun. The San Juans they came from, the Sangre de Cristo range, the San Luis Valley—these will long since have vanished from the face of the earth. But ice, rain, and sun-driven winds, the old reliables, will be there to get at those particles. Thus resurrected and set again on their travels, each will tumble and swim till recemented as one of the countless trillions making up yet another sandstone. That new layer will in turn be overlaid by sedimentation, will sink from view, will be again thrust into the light, and its particles will again be granulated, set on yet further travels. "Yes, everything goes," says the wind, "nothing is final." *Ad infinitum*? Not quite. But for such a quartz grain to have its angularities tumbled away, softened toward round-ness, does take a very long time. In fact the degree of rounding is a good measure of such a particle's age.

Oddly enough, the finer the grain, the slower the rounding. Parti-cles that bounced off my skin could, conceivably, be washed along hun-dreds of miles of beach and remain little altered. A study of grains along the Mississippi between Cairo, Illinois, and New Orleans showed slight change in them, though they had been sifted, shifted, and nudged a thousand miles! Laboratory agitation mimicking that swash and roll in streams or ocean waves shows that it takes *many* thousands of miles to produce "even moderate rounding." So Lucretius's "eternal" atoms and my ideal particle seem at least cousins.

Certainly an actual, individual quartz grain can be blown away, buried, resurrected, and reeroded good as new through unimaginable chunks of time. The Harvard geologist Raymond Siever offers his "rough guess" of about 200 million years per cycle. And how many cycles might an actual sand grain undergo? Siever thinks a Devonian sand grain, for example, laid down maybe 380 million years back, could conceivably have circled through burial and resurrection *ten times* since first being nicked off its parent granite some 2.4 billion years ago. As Siever points out, "That is a history that encompasses more than half the age of the earth."

If so, out of tennis shoes worn at the Dunes, I'm still shaking grains older than Lord Kelvin's 1897 estimate for the entire planet. Older by sixty times! That's why I've come to think of a tiny quartz granule as the littlest cause, and longest continued. Though its minute translu-cence may contain only half of all the time in the world, my skin thinks that's plenty immortal, and all the more eerie to be kissed by.

In canyon country, the only thing left of Noah's Flood is a rainbow. Not long ago I stood on a nine-thousand-foot summit of Utah's Aquarius Plateau and surveyed distant blue buttes and ten-mile-long, blue-forested mesas. Had an eighteenth-century "Neptunist" stood beside me, he would have explained those erosional terraces as sediment of one global ocean, forms later scarred and carved by the Universal Deluge. At the Grand Canyon, however, my "Neptunist" would have seen that his theory didn't hold water—because it held too much. Instead of relics from catastrophic inundation, he would have begun seeing "fluvialism," the slow, daily, prosaic stripping away of a continent by the rains and winds of common weather. Southwestern Utah is an odd place to think of Edinburgh, Scotland. I kept remembering the ebullience of James Hutton, and thinking what panoramic satisfaction the Aquarius Plateau would have given him and his theories. In the latter nineteenth century the brilliant American geologist Clarence Dutton did stand there, and—in contradistinction to "inundation"—coined a phrase fitting what he saw: the Great Denudation.

Not long ago, atop a "lithified" dune near Hite's Crossing, Utah, I watched an attractive young German woman scan part of that denudation's sun-drenched landscape. Hundreds of feet below us, Lake Powell's blue waters, alive with wind warps, made those sandstone erosions all the more brilliantly "other." She was tall, slender, dark haired, and seemed timid. Her husband stroked her hair, held her hand, murmured reassurances. Evidently she needed coaxing to stand at that overlook. I chatted with them briefly. They were from heavily industrial Stuttgart.

Because in Europe even the Alps have been domesticated for centuries, Germans, Dutch, French, and Italians flocking to our high Southwest see, in its sensualities of extreme destitution, a world both spacious and wholly alien. In coral dunes, painted deserts of pinked blues and red mesas, they tour under skies that throw the mind wide open. A world away from Europe's hand-crafted landscapes, they steer rental cars or campers among Paiute spirits of many distances: past Bryce Canyon's Pink Cliffs, past the Gray Cliffs to Zion's White Cliffs and eastward from there along the Vermillion Cliffs on their way to Page, Arizona, and Lake Powell. Through red epochs laid naked.

Certainly my Stuttgart couple were doing that, even as they stood looking out over an expanse where seven thousand feet of stone had been eaten away before the Grand Canyon was begun. Did they know these details? Highly unlikely. After some touristic chit-chat, I gestured out toward the mist-free, unmuted miles with their hallucinatory clarities of rock and asked the shy young woman, "What do you think of it? What's your reaction?" In a quiet voice she said, "It gives me fear. Oh, it is of course . . . very beautiful. But it makes me frightened."

As geology accrued fact and coherence, many intelligent Christians felt the absurdity of setting Earth's age at six thousand years. Nature's design, they conceded, was simply of more ancient date than had been supposed. But design there was. On all sides that axiom went unexamined. Behind his "little causes, long continued" even Hutton saw a "wise and beneficent design." Agreement on a moral nature, a nature with aims, a nature swayed by providential guidance—which is to say a nature made expressly for *us*—that was bedrock.

Charles Darwin's guardian grudgingly approved his ward's intent to voyage on the *Beagle*, because, as he said, "Natural History . . . is very suitable to a clergyman." Aboard ship, young Darwin was shocked to hear a shipmate admit disbelief in the Flood.

Meanwhile geologists went right on tapping at the world, which provoked John Ruskin's petulance: "If only the geologists would let me alone, I could do very well, but those dreadful hammers! I hear the clink of them at the end of every cadence of the Bible verses."

Soon the vogue of "natural theology" began collapsing under the growing weight of enormous fossil deposits. Evolution, from ancient times a perennial guess, became more and more self-evident. Not only that. As the millennially slow growth of languages became better documented, and archaeological digs went deeper into our human past, Earth aged implicitly in them; aged too by inference drawn from the known speed of light and star-distances. Scriptural geology began seeming odd as, say, Baptist meteorology or statutory mathematics or Mormon physics.

A pair of ravens are grooming themselves near pools in the rock. A third, apart, perches quietly on a slab. Wind ruffles its throat feathers, which show a surprise whiteness under their black—as if its ancestry were that of a dove whose surface plumage got sun blackened.

This afternoon, once more hiking the Tonto Plateau, my mind had shrunk to only a couple of thoughts: water and shade. What an oasis is made of. Small wonder, I thought, that Arab cultures devised almost an art form of water. For the past hour now I've wanted the sun to begin sinking behind Tapeats sandstone ledges shading this part of Slate

Creek's canyon. Finally it does. Once the solar disc is two-thirds oc-
cluded by ridgeline, its lessened intensity eases my anger at being
drilled by it all afternoon.

I had felt too hot for paying much mind to blackbrush, spatters of
agave, or cushion cacti in their fat clouds of thorn; or acres of shale
giving off heat ripples bright as the onslaught of migraine. My thought
had been water: "How much have I got? Is Slate Creek still running?"
For the first time in my life I had seen pools and water ripples I knew
weren't real—but not mirage. Sane hallucinations instead, wishful
ones, the kind that often precede seeing and create it. When, via
switchbacks off the plateau, I at last began descending into Slate
Creek's side canyon, its trickle glinted salvation.

Resupplied, I had followed its broad but mostly dry streambed
down to Crystal Rapids and the river, past pools full of tadpoles, past
spadefoot toads that hopped into fronds of arroyo willow. Often when
my boots scattered gravel, a gaudy-collared lizard or sleek whiptail had
flicked from sight. Soon the creek's rivulet disappeared into its own
sandy bed. Threading a shortcut through mesquite trees so sparse and
twisted you couldn't use such wood for anything, not even admiration,
I had passed colonies of beavertail cactus as my descent took me below
the level of Tapeats sandstone into steep, fire-struck walls of black
Vishnu schist, rising higher the further I descended. From that creekbed
dry as chalk dust—but well before it came into view—I had caught
faintly audible hints of the river's long power. Its whisper quickened my
stride, rising closer to a roar the nearer I drew.

I'd known Crystal Rapids to be among the wildest runs on the Colorado. Soon its wavetrain, white-capped and crested, was pouring by
me in one muscular surge that explained the Grand Canyon as nothing
else could.

It was not some sort of god. It was no more than gravity's way with
water—and water's way with rain. Loaded with silt, sand, gravel, it
pulled tons of the continent past me by the minute. I could *think* of the
Colorado as a sort of band saw, but couldn't feel it was. Not that only.
In the river's roaring lament of descending joy, in its mountains, mesas,
and buttes going back to be sea floor, I had felt a strangeness whose
force we call "nature." It had left nothing to say, nothing to feel
but awe.

By 8:30 P.M., back at my campsite a mile and a half up from the
river, air has finally cooled from the afternoon high of 113 degrees to 85.
Meanwhile the Tapeats ledges above me have dimmed from blond to

cinnamon to burnt sienna to umber . . . then twilight. Bats low overhead flitter between me and first stars. All around me, Cambrian stone
laid down when the moon was much closer to Earth; a paleo-moon,
huge and luminous: unseen by anyone. From nearby Slate Creek, toad
song.

Desert canyons by night are anything but voiceless. Yet peaceful,
supremely. In such canyons your own presence can feel like the human
race down to one person—which is to exist more actually than any
other way I know. Often I've wondered if all the trail sweat and exertion might not be aimed, unconsciously, at sitting quietly while dusk
rises, and at feeling lost in glimpses that add up to the momentary creature called "me." A someone, in a something. A one.

Borrowing the old idea of the human body as "a little world made
cunningly," we can use it as a microcosm of time. Any woman or man,
for example, standing five feet ten inches can be seen in proportion to
Earth's 4,500 million years, with the planet's birth beginning at the
footsoles. Up high as the kneecaps would be equivalent to 3,200 million
years ago: anaerobic bacteria form in Earth's archaeozoic oceans.
Three inches higher would mark 3,000 million years back, and the development of photosynthesis in anaerobic bacteria. With photosynthesis the planet's conversion of carbon dioxide gases to oxygen begins. A
billion years go by, during which oxygen is poison, unless you can
breathe it. As yet nothing can. Then, at the level of the abdomen, oxy-
gen-using bacteria first appear. At the navel, Vishnu schist and gneiss
are metamorphosed from sedimentary rock of unknowable antiquity.
*Thus far, obviously, time has risen waist-high without raising life
much taller than germs.*

Heart-high, 1,150 million years ago, multicellular plants and animals finally form. Another half billion years go by.

Then at the collar bone, around the time Tapeats sandstone begins
to be deposited, invertebrates develop shells. *Voilà!* Onto the world
stage leaps, or slithers, the brachiopod. Trilobites appear, and with
them life acquires the first high-definition eyes. Earth's seas still contain nothing much livelier than they, and sea worms, naked or shelled.
Dry land is still one supercontinent, Pangaea. Some 750,000 centuries
go by, without creatures yet leaving the sea. Nor will they for a longish
while.

By the level of the mouth, fish have evolved. The tip of the nose
marks maximum dispersal of Pangaea's fragments, our present conti-

nents. Then at the cheek bones, conifers and reptiles come on the scene. Yet at the eyebrows—in Permian time—a setback occurs, "the great dying" of almost everything alive. Only 5 percent of living species escape. And when we've risen to a level *one inch from the top of the head*, death strikes again in the famous extinction of dinosaurs—along with three-fourths of all living creatures. Humans still nowhere.

When does dawn become day? There can be no fixed point at which we modulated from Homo erectus to Homo sapiens, but 500,000 years ago is a widely accepted figure. An "ago" that recent leaves us, on the scale we've been using, invisible. On that scale a man's overnight growth of whisker more than equals humankind's stay on this planet. Our presence as a species gets effaced with his morning shave.

We may scratch our heads in disbelief. If in doing so, however, we find there a single windblown speck of sand as little as .2 of a millimeter in diameter, one just visible with the naked eye, its width will equal— compared to a person standing five-ten—the time spanned by our species. We've been human no longer than that granule is wide.

Up in bright morning and once more out on that broad Tonto plateau which hikers must travel to get from one side canyon to the next, I'm heading for Marsh Butte, and from there to my appointment with the Great Unconformity, when I spy—five hundred yards off—a pair of lounging figures. They turn out to be Tom and Nettie.

Their frame packs propped as backrests, taking their ease in late-morning sun, atop litters of Bright Angel shale, they sit catching rays my skin prefers to avoid. Tom's a lean and grizzled fifty, while bottle-blonde Nettie's not much over half that. In swapping the usual oddments of trail chat, I learn they're from L.A., and have been in the canyon sixteen days. "Ye gods!" I gasp. "How much weight does that come to?"

"What's left doesn't weigh much. Enough for dinner tonight," Tom says.

"We're going out tomorrow," says Nettie.

All that food, plus gear! "But seriously, how much does sixteen days of food weigh?"

"Too much," she says, and her smile winces. Plain-pretty, neat figure in shorts and red halter, *strong* looking thighs and calves, Nettie can't be much more than five-two or five-three, and maybe 120 pounds.

"We didn't weigh it," Tom says.

I nod agreement. "Best not to know."

"Yeah," she says, nodding back.

"Where are you headed?" Tom asks.

"Oh, a butte—near the Tapeats ledge between Slate Creek and Topaz. There's a spot I've wanted to get a good look at."

"It's nice down there in Slate," he says, "a lot of water."

"Lots of water," she agrees.

But I'm still thinking weight. "Sixteen days of food!"

"Aw, you'd be surprised," Tom says, implying I could do likewise. "Obviously you had to really plan. Take the lightest stuff possible." I expect to hear freeze-dried this, powdered that.

Nettie seems abashed. "Well, we ate, uh . . . rice and beans."

"Pretty much," Tom says. "For protein," meaning, I presume, the beans. And "pretty much," it turns out, means "rice and beans only."

"Yes," he says, "we talk about food quite a bit."

"But beans take forever to cook," I say. "Doesn't that mean fuel?"

"Well," she says of the rice, "we've got some, uh . . . quick. And we soak the beans overnight. And then you have to simmer 'em about . . . twenty minutes. We brought *small* beans."

"That's still a lot of fuel."

"Yeah," Nettie says. "We brought a lot."

Well, I think but don't say, "If you're happy, then I am." And since this is Tom's fifth year of backpacking the canyon, they knew what they were doing.

No sooner have I headed off again than I turn around, grabbing my shirt-pocket camera for a souvenir snapshot. At once Nettie pulls from her pack an old time Nikon—big, heavy as a paving brick—and asks me to take one of them with it. "We've got five shots left," she says.

"Do you have any sisters?" I ask, hefting the killer Nikon as if ready to marry into genes that can handle such tonnages.

"Two," she says, not getting my joke, "but I'm the only one who does, uh . . . major backpacking."

"Yes," I say, focusing. "I'd call it that. Definitely major."

"Fatal" was Richard Kirwan's word, when in 1797 he published his strident attack on James Hutton's *Theory of the Earth*. Because Kirwan held that the Bible gives a literal account of creation, it followed that encouraging Hutton's view would be fatal not only "to the credit of the Mosaic history" but "to religion and morality" as well. Though Kirwan seems two hundred years out of date, he was right. Gazing through sun-ripened stone into the back of forever can be dangerous.

Is that an unconscious element in my seeing gneiss and schist walls of the river gorge as hyper-ugly? Could it be I've even sought them out to defy? Maybe they're what I think time without light or us or anything living looked like. Other canyon rock has color, linearity, legible order. Vishnu schist and gneiss is a lot of molten crumples, rock vomit, hot messes riven here and there—and thus relieved in its darkness—by intrusions of pink Zoroaster granite. But otherwise Vishnu (which in Sanskrit means "to pervade") is bleak to the point, almost, of malignancy. Often eight hundred feet high, its faces say, "Nature is anything that can happen."

So Kirwan was right. But religion and morality aren't the only things that rock nearly two billion years old can imperil. Scrutinizing Vishnu walls can put a sag in one's shoulders at thinking how much one has mistaken for real.

Kirwan was wrong too, of course. Everyone who reads his attack on Hutton takes a smack at him—which he deserved. In his petty, literal-minded way, however, he reacted as most of us do when the chill of infinity blows through us: "Close that universe, I'm freezing!" Rejecting Hutton's endless ages of hammer-deciphered stones, Kirwan wanted a world that made sense. Who doesn't? We take a smack at him for wanting it to make *his* sense, and only his. An impulse far older than Genesis.

We too peep into the inhuman vastitudes that surround us, begot us, feed us, scare us, allure us into sighing "magnificent!" even as we fade from the scene; and our hearts insist on evoking some shadow-figure behind the whole show. Which is to say, an invisible It ever so remotely like us. With whom—this sovereign Invisibility, this It—we sense some murky relation, some accord so vague we say "the Creator," a sort of here-there-and-everywhere that does all we know and don't know. An impulse old as mythology: blood taking thought, answering itself with a god. And would our greatest poverty be to discover that reality is what it seems? That what we see is all there is? Would that be destitution?

"There are two things the human eye cannot look at for very long," said La Rochefoucauld, "the sun, and death." Vishnu schist is like that, with its nearly two billion years. A sort of black sun.

Not believing for a moment in shadow-figures, however, I usually find "all there is" so unfathomable—however sweaty and occasionally tedious, however occasionally starved and bare—that, when my senses return from deep boredom, I'm convinced nothing more hyper-surreal than being alive inside "all there is" can ever possibly happen. As for that, boredom itself is a mercy, and its illusory longevities, priceless. Through them we can imagine we really do live here.

"Seeing with one's own eyes." Yet it's the mind's eye doing the seeing, or failing to. I now laugh to realize that by dipping into side canyons several times during the last two days I've passed right *through* the Great Unconformity without noticing. What with reacting to glare, mesquite trees, flamboyant lizards, extraterrestrial cactus forms, my roving this shambled terrain which Thomas Burnet's *Sacred Theory of the Earth* would have explained as the wages of sin—well, all of that had lent me eyes for everything else.

Which shows that the Great Unconformity isn't a thing. It's something you know about what you see. Like erosion itself, it's what's missing. As for eyes, any tourist told what to look for can easily see the Unconformity from the rim.

And yet I had wanted a close-up; wanted if possible to put my hand exactly there where the 550-million-year-old Tapeats sandstone, which runs up and down the canyon, sits atop the Vishnu schist "unconformably." Thus the name. And "Great" because where sandstone and schist meet, 1,200 million years of stone once here now isn't. That's 1.2 billion. Swept away.

Gingerly, I step out onto a slab that looks OK, but when with a crockery grind it teeters slightly, I freeze. "Forget it!" For the moment, anyhow.

Downclimbing stacked slabs of Tapeats to reach its interface with the Vishnu could be trickier than I thought. Less well cemented than, say, Wescogame or Coconino, its mocha- or cream- or cinnamon-colored layers vary from solid to rotten. Weathering undercuts many of the protrusions. Eventually each will give way, crashing down toward the river, like everything here; just as eight hundred feet higher up, chunks of Redwall feel Temple Butte limestone melt from under them, feel themselves come to an edge there's no denying, no holding on to. That's gravity's simple plan: one by one.

Under the shade of a narrow overhang I wriggle very cautiously out of my pack, carefully set it away from the edge, then rest awhile and consider.

Opposite my skimpy perch, raven shadows ripple across uneven layers and ledges of Tapeats. High cirrus veils the sun ever so slightly.

The rippling of those wing shadows entrances me. All the same, I remind myself of being scrunched onto an edge where downward glances send mild electroscares through the neural system. Like an undermusic to canyon silence comes the surge and fade of Crystal Rapids' attenuated roar, as if wind through pines. For a long while I'm content simply to let the canyon happen. As bonus, I spot a much safer route through the Tapeats opposite, less like rock climbing than stepping downstairs.

Finally, by edging out onto a safely sizable ledge of Vishnu, I can actually reach up, put my hand on pebbly stuff underlying the Tapeats. Where that conglomerate meets hard black schist, I touch the Great Unconformity. My extended index finger and thumb grasp 1.2 billion years of absentee rock.

Eons, eras, periods, epochs, ages—it's as if rock time were the size of this canyon, and all life the size of my hand.

Like everything born of fire, our planet is cooling. Eventually its "secular cooling" will bring continental drift to a standstill. As convected heat within Earth's mantle and outer core loses its radioactive enthusiasm, the lithosphere under sea and land will thicken. Once continental plates lock in place, volcanoes won't erupt nor will new mountains thrust up to replace old mountains worn down. Thus our planet's flat future; its alps will be molehills low as a hundred feet or so above sea level.

With mountains—which sand comes from—leveled once and for all, sand will find nothing to abrade but itself. Can only tumble itself to silicon dust. If nothing lay on top of Vishnu schist, concealing its upper surfaces, what I'd see would be a thrice-ancient peneplain. Earth's future, sand's end.

Why should a vast desolation inhabit that prospect? It does—as if the planet's two faces, one back in Vishnu time, and the other far up ahead, fused to an unbroken loneliness. But that's mere sentimentalism. Creatureless planets can't "feel." Besides, those 1.2 billion years of absentee rock were all pre-Cambrian, gone long before the planet was ours. Nothing lived then but anaerobic bacteria, and maybe a lot of blue-green algae, "cyanophytes." Still, a world where feelings have no place to go fills me with the very emptiness it denies.

To approach that sort of tremendous absence inhabiting the Great Unconformity's fathomless rift, I've fumbled my way here. And touched it—as if the stuff it's made of were some sort of power: steadfastly evanescent, without judgment, wanting nothing, holy. Which doesn't mean "good." Nor does it need our belief. It's just that, since neither logic nor physics offers ways to think about it, we've no rational way to ask what or why. It's all we do ask. On sandstone right above me, under Arizona sun, the fine quartz grains glint and sparkle.

In Greek "seeing for one's self" is "autopsy."

Crosswinds on U.S. 180 rock my car and stampede herds of tumbleweed over the road in flumes of copper dust. Later, midafternoon on Arizona 160, I reach Cow Springs just as two Navajo males are running around battening hatches of a big souvenir stand. The frayed edges of its gala banners crackle and burn in gusts that have bent many of the metal flagstaffs.

Winds wobbling my steering for hours now hurl dust devils three hundred feet into the air. After spiraling apart they blow across the sky's intense blue like pink cannon smoke. I approach a valley so hazed I at first assume it's industrial, then find it's just desert weather filling the air with sand tumbled almost to the fineness of silt. Its delicate pinks derive from ancestral Rockies brought down while our Southwestern horizons were taking up a new life as permanent desert—in "just a few" million years. Erstwhile summits now sifting around as coral-tinted particles are actively eating at the ruddier hues of eroded mesas, which are indeed all the colors of Egypt. Before my eyes the Great Denudation goes on. I'm driving in it!

Just as I'm supposing only ravens or crows could make a living here, amid mile on unbroken mile famished for vegetation, I whip past a "town"; one building, three burros. Plus an intelligent dog, barking sheep across the road and down a slight gully. The old Navajo woman following after them wears a loose purple gown bathed by the same wind.

Toward evening the gusts have died to light breeze tousling rabbit brush, ruffling sage. Nine miles off the main road I pull into a favorite campsite among juniper and piñon just above Tsegi Canyon. By now the sun is low. I read awhile. In a brand new book never opened before I'm puzzled at finding sand all but too small to see between any pages I turn to. How? Beats me. With my pocket lens I make out several particles, and smile at their tireless ubiquity. Later, to follow what the last of the light is doing, I climb an overlook of Navajo sandstone. The whole place is dunes now petrified.

For more than an hour I enjoy the living wind on my face, just dawdling, watching the henna ravens of sunset, looking miles up Tsegi

Canyon, deciphering on crossbedded formations what that wind's paleo-flow has written. Is writing. On me, on canyon walls, on everywhere. I give up trying to think what cannot be thought: Time's great pressure and strength. The littlest causes, their long continuance. Their cool, patient luster inside each blowing grain.

The Mind of a Forest

Our first forest may not have been the one in a mother's voice reading "Hansel and Gretel." Perhaps instead it was grown-ups seen from below, ones we literally clung to, looked up toward. Because infants begin on all fours among legs thick as tree trunks, subsequent forests, however trackless, may rise out of those.

The power of verticality. Since before we could walk, "up" is where the elders' voices came down from; and, since before anything moved bipedally, the thunder. "Up" is where the gods live, and have, time out of mind.

Otherwise, how can we account for those vaguely theological moods real forests evoke? Near tall timber, doesn't the casual tourist find "awe-inspiring" irresistible? Seen through dense boughs, bits and pieces of blue sky may even add nostalgias of stained glass to his or her cathedral feelings. But one mustn't smile too slyly. When in 1832, near Rio de Janeiro, no less an intellect than the young Charles Darwin entered his first rainforest he too, even he, felt "wonder, astonishment & sublime devotion" that "fill & elevate the mind."

Again, the primal allure of verticality—to which our mountain forests abounding in Colorado add another attraction, the face of beginnings looking like doomsday. And all on a single high-country trail. Thus, despite human brevity, I've often visited the world's end. It's made of grey granite, a jumble; crazed breakage whose smash appears systematic, no two chunks of chaos the same. Just looking at such rocks makes us old as they are, which is why my origins, on the other hand, are made of precisely those stones, tumbled around by tectonic up-thrust. And by so much weather we call it time.

End or beginning? What's seen depends on who's looking. Or per-haps on *how* the same place is looked at. Under what sky.

To see for ourselves, we've only to head north, walking toward Ca-nadian latitudes and boreal forest; then past its tall trees along trail that's a mess of rust needles, to international timberline; and beyond, into alpine tundra, till at last we're bootprinting mica-glittered sand far north of Hudson Bay; above Inuvik, say, on an arctic shore whose only evident growth is ice.

Water, warmth, light. All three are needed for growth, and where roots are concerned ice isn't water. As for light and snowmelt, these occur atop every Colorado peak, but on the high ones long before ar-rival at the summit we've left the final prostrate tree or shrub far below, near a line called the 50-degree Fahrenheit isotherm. Above which, nothing like July ever comes. International timberline being a latitudi-nal version of the same thing, a rough equivalent of stepping north to-ward the end of the evergreen world can be had in the States by hiking up a mountain. Since each meter of altitude equals a mile closer to the Pole, we can travel entirely through those life zones called the mon-tane, the boreal, the alpine, to the Hudsonian in one afternoon.

Today, cinching my packstraps at a high-country trailhead known as East Portal, my aim isn't so much to climb into the Arctic Circle as to rise through Earth's very thin zone of habitability by way of tracing creation backwards. A way of remembering how it happened, and how easily it might not have. Awareness of the latter possibility makes me think, "Even that 'might not have' can be used in a lifetime, can't it?" and set off walking.

From East Portal, across South Boulder Creek and on up through forest to Heart Lake, then up higher to Rogers Pass at nearly twelve thousand feet above sea level will take me barely five miles—but I'll have climbed far higher than the last tree. If from the pass I care to go higher yet and a couple of miles farther, up to James Peak, I can lunch at 13,294, where the hardiest moss gets discouraged, shoved aside by what the planet is really made of: stone. Rock or magma, molten or frozen. But stone.

A friend is someone who says, "Be what you are without trying." Sometimes a day or a place says so too. Right now, inside forestation inside a still summery morning in September, under skies free of trouble, the "cathedral feelings" my rationality pooh-poohs might try to assert themselves if I'd let them. Though it's no Darwinian rainforest, Colorado's Indian Peaks Wilderness does include great evergreens thick as pelt. "Entered into with a wholly innocent eye," I've asked myself, "wouldn't these great needle-feathered wings of Engelmann spruce seem a fantastic idea made visible?" Probably. And might not my first antlered elk emerging from them pass for some rootless first cousin to trees? A sort of branched-out and fur-bearing conifer.

The same eye might well wonder at crowns of lodgepole pine tossing into the air black blossoms like ravens. Or even at this softened log with the red flower in its mouth. But no, that sort of Edenic wonder is lost to us, like a small boy lost in the middle of a man. Happily, though, this actual world is a far queerer place than any boy or man can ever imagine, so true knowledge of it—as contrasted with fact—is never mere. With each subatomic particle newly discovered, eternity widens.

In the early, spruce-scented air, with the creek flashing past boulders big as dwarf clouds, and past me; and alongside broadleaf plants of the forest floor dithering between light and shade, I find young Darwin's astonishment natural as breathing. A great forest is one of the sun's most complex transactions.

Not so much *like* a brain as like our brain's intermediate stage, before the impulses that were one day going to be "mind" wisely invested themselves in the brightness of eyes, the insistence of animals. For all I know of time's way with matter, maybe this forest continues even now to fumble toward thought, using chloroplasts and pollen and root hairs for neurons. Though the lowliest fern here is incomparably older than humans—conifers are too, as far as that goes—they're retarded, unaware that our kind of brain has already invented itself. Wasn't one of its latest phases arboreal? Often I've traipsed through forest when the day-long sounds of wind have seemed an emotion, but one which, in the long throwing forward of the human mind, I cannot have known; like our species's forgotten memories that return only as blood.

At nine thousand feet the sun warms comfortably toward its September zenith, and just ahead of me across a small clearing, spruce seeds backlit against hyperblue sky flutter down on their one wing, right through a shimmer of gnat-buzz. Yet it isn't August any more. Up here light and shade are distinct seasons. Thirty seconds past sundown this very spot will grow nippy, and by starlight, on the coldest side of the sky, its trail puddles glaze over nightly with ice, which at 9 A.M. the sun hasn't melted. But soon will.

So, because autumn's onset hasn't yet quenched them, over humus dark as the Carboniferous Era, the morning's grey-green logs, the moist umbers in logs half rotted, the green trill of fern, the low ambitions of ground cover, the shriveled petals of lavender fleabane—curled back on their bloom's center as if shrinking from cold—all these still traffic with each other. Evidence everywhere.

If our sense of the cosmos is actually a statue of the human intellect, what shape could be truer to it than that of a tree? Or what truer cult than the tree worship which once circled our globe? In our own century, families of India have sold their jewelry, then borrowed more money on top of that, to pay for ceremonies marrying a jasmine tree to a mango. A tree, being the literal marriage of earth with air, water with fire, easily symbolizes too the wedding of the soul to what it inhabits. With good reason the brains of forest-dwelling Norsemen conceived the ash tree Yggdrasil in the shape of creation. Thus rooted in the mind, their night sky branched out into one great arborescence of stars. And thought itself—a kind of root system whose foliage is words. Meanwhile our cosmos of sidereal fire, its galaxies thick as leaf-radiations, does indeed continue to ramify.

From my earthbound grunting over and around windfallen trunks fat as hogs, rotten and lovely, from my straddling some, ducking low under others, I begin feeling that this particular patch of planet I'm in is about as dense as forest can get. To my right a torrent—half stream, half waterfall—roars down out of glacial lakes over a steep granite bed helter-skeltered with rock chunks and timbers. I listen. Its splays of white water drum against boulders till I feel like I'm in a stampede—but weaker, its echo. And love it.

In fact, if this is the day I think it is, I'm going to like everything it contains: the creek mist, enhancing the scent of damp pine duff over humus, aromatic resins in conifers past counting. Then too, there's an occasional whiff of fungus. Spores exuded by mushrooms? Even the wet granite smells ore-bearing, metallic. Amid the mixed pungency of pine sap and the moldering away of old growth I realize a forest's depth is one of its elementary virtues. That's why it can't help being actual and legendary; its loftiest, most needle-drenched spruces or firs are half botanical, half enchantment.

Despite humankind's having seen trees as creatures, I laugh out
loud when I catch myself in the mechanical courtesy of murmuring
"Excuse me" to a couple of Engelmann trunks I'm squeezing between.
That mood turns pensive, however, at the trunk of a windthrown pine
which, as it fell, must have twisted, tearing apart the living trunk with
great violence. Near it an uprooted fir lies low, its exposed roots a great
tangle of clotted mud, writhing wood, and rock. Ways once dark and
personal to it seem the privacy of some house a storm has laid open.

"Blowdown" is common here. Not only because of mountain climate but because root systems of even the tallest conifers tend to be
surprisingly shallow. Many penetrate little more than twelve inches
while spreading five feet wide. Even the most tenacious bristlecone
can't really eat or grasp *solid* stone, however often they seem to. Roots
spreading shallow as sunflowers pressed against a slab do seek crevices
wherever possible, but where they find no cracks to knuckle down into
they're often less anchor than pedestal.

Like an undefined promise I walk toward, living branches open before me, close behind. Surely a forest was the first maze. Here dawns
and sunsets grow into seasons, seasons into years that swallow us up
while revealing us to ourselves; engulfment, self-knowledge. The very
countlessness of its trees when we wander among them creates the secret that forest, like an endless threshold, is forever on the verge of revealing. "Just up ahead." Always there. "Up on that ledge—where the
twin fir trunks are leaning away from the Divide." I arrive, find only
more forest. "But over there, isn't that more sky between tree crowns? A
clearing?"

Revelations that vanish at exactly the pace I approach them become poses struck long ago by fir or pine trunks concealing disclosures
which, arrived at, turn out to be other, half-hidden gestures now revealed as merely more evergreens. In pursuing their offers while scrambling off-trail to one side, I find that my way back to that trail is somehow lost. Left, right, ahead, behind, now suddenly look like exactly the
route I came by, took good note of, and don't recall wandering from.
My well-considered correction becomes a fresh mistake disguised as
one or another stand of young limber pines I was sure I recalled. A
squawbush grows strangely familiar. Unseen till now—yet I'm certain
I've seen it. "Because surely I've been here before, haven't I? The era I
used to inhabit might as well be any era since humans and forests arose.

So I stand scouting my way up, around, or over dead trees, living
spruce trunks, granite slabs. My wool shirt catches on dead twiglets.

My breathing quickens. Miles of evergreen all to myself! All different, identical. In the act of deciding, I exist between the first footfall along the way chosen, and never arriving. Each resin-scented turn leads to any number of others, yet always to more of the same, as if real travel here were impossible—with all the appearance of motion.

Can "civilized" man's deforestations be read—if only metaphorically—as an unconscious erasure of his primitive, even animal, past? Odd logic: "We can't have come from trees if there are none." This would be absurd, if not for millennia of evidence that forest and town are ancient enemies. *Civitas, felicitas,* as the saying once was. Our first parents fell in the Garden; their regenerate offspring hope to ascend to the City of God. Don't we sneer, still, at those who live in the sticks? My Grandfather Rexroat believed he was "moving up" when he moved off the farm into town. This area's very name, Indian Peaks Wilderness, hints at "savagery," a word derived by way of "forest" in Latin: *silva.* Townspeople speaking Old French used "forest" to say "beyond the pale," "out in the boonies."

But Indian Peaks' cavernous glades aren't barbarism's last stand, much less what was once meant by a haunt. They're evergreen machines, water pumps looking like trunks. This morning their tight shocks of capillaries are working with sheaves of needles, synthesizing sugar from water and gas excited by photons. And from trace minerals imbibed by root hairs. Photosynthesis: stuff put together with light. Sun sugar.

All of whose creatures we are. The chemical and electrical energies now thinking so, in me, were once a titillation that sunlight provoked in electrons, in chlorophyll, within a green plant. At a certain level of excitement those electrons leapt from their atom, thus changing the personality of not only the atom they jilted but that of the atom they left it for. And changing, thereby, molecular dispositions. What's impossible to *feel* is our utter dependence on those transactions.

This illusion of self-sufficiency is of course fueled by the very energies alchemized through chlorophyll. If, on reflection, I'm at a loss to say where my thought really begins, or even—considering origins—who's really doing the thinking, chlorophyll's transmutational magic comes close to being the ghost in my machine.

Dead trees *everywhere.* Trunks freshly fallen lie atop trunks already dead a long long time. A century? Many centuries? A really big log may linger for three generations. Five decades isn't uncommon. The "dawn log" near my house that I visit almost daily, waiting for sunrise, has so mummified in Boulder's subdesert aridity that, from all I see, insects will carry it off sooner than snow and rain.

It's as if these conifers take almost as long to disappear as to rise, flourish, and topple. One spruce is still firm at its west end while its east end is a pumpkin-colored mess. Another is a patriarch expired upright, centering the trunk-turn which may have evolved to strengthen trees growing in extreme conditions of wind and snow-loading. Though the causes of spiral grain are disputed, high-country trees are literally in-grained with a gyre which, looked on, feels like struggle; the torsion of a seed's ascending. This one, naked and twisty, reminds me of the em-peror's war-glories ensculpted in scenes spiraling upward on Trajan's Column in Rome. Still another, ghost-grey, has long been tattooed by generations of woodpeckers. Beside it, ghastly as ashes but equally bird-riddled and barkless, is a trunk of dead limbs like a sort of tortive lad-der. Under the weight of my impulse to climb them, I imagine the "rungs" snapping one by one. What are such derelicts waiting for? The next gale?

And some trees died again when they fell. A huge one that toppled across a great hatchet-head of granite is broken just above the stone's crest. Staring, I hear its tremendous "cr-ra-a-ack!" years ago.

After which, insects would've begun relieving the tree of its re-maining bark, if any. Big scablike flakes would have scaled away. Laid bare, the tightly twisted lines of that wind-written grain would have weathered open, as if given to nothing more lasting than misery, while rain and snow widened them. Decade after decade would've passed, with sunlight and ice prying deeper. Then a hand briefly mine comes along, scoops up a portion of shambled log, feels its fingers bray that sapless heartwood to dust. And this sun already gone cold as a fossil.

"How many dead trees to live ones?" In lieu of counting, I settle for an awareness: "How many? A lot." Far more than I'd realized. But why hadn't I ever seen so before? In cross-country ski season, of course, all but the standing dead are either entirely snowed over or made pictur-esque, visible only as winter. Oh, once or twice while skiing through healthy, snow-cargoed specimens I've been so frightened by the loud crack and splitting sound of riven wood that I've hustled clear—in case. Those were January days of bitter cold, with gusts lunging among the tree crowns. Despite years of passing countless trees dead in natural poses, I've never seen one actually topple. In summer, the life-greens of fern, of ground cover, of mosses, and understory shrubs along with their shade-tolerant blossoms attract what's liveliest in me. Especially on a sunny morning, with so much gaiety, so many exuberant greens making the forest one flower, windfallen trunks thick as slaughter thereby escape my notice. In any longstanding city, it would be morbid to dwell on how greatly the dead citizens outnumber those living; so here what's left of summer catches the eye, just as in cities the eye follows motion.

Certainly in both cities and forests a thing plain as faces and trees is that "life" doesn't need anyone. Like wind it rises inside us, drives us, drives through us—then beyond. Even as we say it's ours, we know its promiscuous whim passes through our borrowed bodies like a desire true to only itself.

Besides, the neat polarity of life and death blurs if one looks closely. Using a fallen limb for leverage, I burst open a log crawling with little animals: beetles, larvae, grubs, pillbugs, nearly invisible mites and springtails by the hundreds, carpenter ants glossy as blackberries, a nimble millepede or two escaping across weblike filaments exuded by fungi. There are also the invisible billions of bacteria, protozoa, and other critters equally minuscule. We humans refer to life's "lower forms" with a dismissive wrinkling of the nose because our empathies depend on shape and size. An even greater poverty than seeing "mystery" where there is none might be *not* seeing it where there is. Certainly no one's "cathedral feelings" are stirred by a woodlouse. Trickling ants may indeed be mindless as a silicon chip whose sand has reverted to granules; and grubs pale as a worm's belly do lack allure. Nonetheless, without these "lower forms" a forest can by no means exist; their lives are vital to forest as the trees are to themselves. So biologists speak of "the cryptosphere": the industrious, unseen enterprises of the tiny creatures whose fumblings I've interrupted. Their work composes what wind plays, blowing through these tree crowns.

The earliest land plants whose fossils have been microscoped reveal fungal colonies of mycelia in their tissues—without which, it may be, Earth's plant kingdom could never have left the ocean. If mind isn't so much a thing as a relationship, nothing in a forest is more proto-synaptic than the win/win symbiosis of fungal strands called *hyphae* and tree roots. Fine and white as underground cobweb, *hyphae* extend the conifer's water-gathering enormously. In return, since fungi lack clorophyll for making food on their own, they're fed by the very root sytems they work for.

The unseen intricacy, delicacy, and extent of activities in the forest cryptosphere are simply dumbfounding. Their workings recycle a crestfallen spruce's chemicals, enrich the meager forest humus, and are fed on in turn, making "higher" forms possible. An evergreen's death isn't contagious, except as life's other shapes, in which its dying wood lives. Along with the beetles and mites and grubs, nitrogen-fixing bacteria resort to it like cattle to a silo. "Down but not done" might be a toppled fir's motto.

All the truer when it comes to "nurse logs," on whose dissolution seedlings can get a good start. Before their elderly host has vanished back into its beginnings, and into them, the seedlings' roots will have fully descended from that log and taken good hold.

Meanwhile, like flat flowers various lichens mottle their symbiotic ways over stones which moss also sips at. Vines enlace upended root systems. Fir seedlings gamble their one life-chance on a root or two sipping nutrients from rifts and clefts in granite otherwise barren as the moon. Endless mortality all around me. The great dead fallen everywhere. And the living undiscouraged.

Conifer? "Cone bearing." One of time's luckiest designs. Back when plants were first stepping out of the sea onto dry land, epochs before any had learnt how to flower, and grasses had yet to evolve, conifers existed. Their profiles occur in strata laid down 350 million years ago. And because fully a third of world forests are coniferous, cones and needles are global successes. They've modified into the planet's biggest living creatures, sequoias, and into its oldest, bristlecone pines. True, recent studies of plants in the Mojave Desert suggest that the most elderly creosote bushes there may be ten thousand years old, but certainly bristlecones remain the Methuselahs of trees. Easily. On Mount Evans, about thirty miles to my south, tourists can picnic under any number of hearty specimens older than Charlemagne's bones, many of them having begun growing 1,500 years ago, before the Roman Empire had entirely declined. In Nevada resides a living bristlecone nearly older than Egypt. Its tiny fertilized seed must've germinated somewhere around the time Narmer unified the Upper and Lower kingdoms and set up his capital at Memphis. If ever a scheme was time-tested it's that of the conifer. And versatile? Hot, cold, wet, dry, whatever.

As with the vague, faceless crowd inside the word *people*, our word *forest* summons into its vertical horizons a lot of trees simply repeated. Even today, driving toward the trailhead, along the early morning's washboarded miles, over rough rock that often needs another two or three runs through the crusher, I saw this forest as mountainside swathes of conifer, hundreds of thousands of tree-crowns like identical cusps, all repeating the same dusty, shadowy green. Seen from inside, though, actual forest belies that, with a complexity that places simple views beyond having.

After a few leisurely hours up the trail, I'm still waiting to come across two even remotely identical trees. Each site imposes character which, if looked at up close and slowly, reveals limb and trunk artic-ulations *unlike* any other. To botanists and forestry workers that fact must be old hat. To me it's news fresh as the forest itself.

I look at a seedling crowded by three mature Douglas firs on one side and big rock on the other. "Does it have a choice?" I ask myself. "Its leaning seems forced by terrain, saying, 'Grow *this* way or die.' " So it inclines to a south-facing boulder for warmth, meanwhile deploying roots toward a scrap of northerly shadow, where a snowdrift provides water till late July. "Even the trunk's upper contortion," I realize, "gives it a longer look at the sun." A slight edge. Which could be the difference. Thus I'm inside a world of seedling decisions, viable or des-perately silly when wiser moves were still possible; but showing indi-vidual character even while the mature tree comes to resemble its species. Like those hit-and-miss ways we take or mistake in choosing ourselves, maybe no single Douglas fir comes more than close to what its seed had in mind. Yet the sun draws each version up, up, electro-magnetically.

Expecting resistance, my boot toe kicks at an old log. Instead, the "wood" scatters like sphagnum. Further kicking uncovers a smaller tree lying full-length inside, solid as ever: heartwood in the shape of a sap-ling. Like a sculpture's wire armature. So gradually the elder tree be-came the sarcophagus of its own youthful form. Yet, as with our own characters even in dotage, those earliest years will be last to disappear.

Having once discovered this, I kick at other logs—and find that each pine, spruce, fir, or juniper is a concentricity. The tree's successive versions nest inside each other, selves of which so-called growth rings in sawn logs are but cross-sections. I imagine those selves as pulsing out-ward from their beginnings. Not rings but waves, growth waves like sound; a seed's resonance. Weather's reverberations in wood. Some pri-mal conifer's remote echo.

All the truer because only in its amazingly thin layer of cambium does that echo really stay alive. Whereas inner and outer bark can be many inches thick—a foot or more in the case of giants—the cambium layer may be thin as one cell. Inward from this, new xylem, or sapwood, grows each season, conducting water up out of roots into needles. Outward from it by the same splitting off of daughter cells grows phloem, an inner bark which carries food-enriched water back down to those roots. Like an ongoing birth, cambium is where a tree's ancestry resonates. Lifelong. If its cells stop dividing, the tree dies. From so thin, so delicate a film the whole forest draws its power.

The more I consider that archaic force, however guessingly, the more of its life I receive. And the more carefully I look at specific conifers, the less apt to their individualities become syllables like "spruce" or "pine" or "fir." Not every voice has a name. Anyway, names are just the spoken shadows of things. For all its inclusiveness, the life of language—like that of any map—depends on leaving almost everything out. Thus our word *forest* names a botanical labyrinth so far beyond language we can only imagine it.

The phrase "a highly probable state" never fails to make me smile. Meant seriously, it's science describing inanimate matter: the arrangement *to be expected* of those particular atoms. Hardly an audacious proposition. Yet I'm amused to realize that atoms making up either a fleck of basalt or gold are—like the minds of Russia's pre-Perestroika bureaucrats viewing a May Day parade—in "a highly probable state." On the other hand, knowing that the whole inanimate cosmos—which is to say virtually every gram of it—is by comparison with living things in "a highly probable state" can make me feel precarious. In this universe where "animate" and "mortal" are one and the same, my atoms cluster in that most improbable array called "alive." Nor are any juniper needle's atoms, its chloroplasts and auxin molecules, arranged in ways *to be expected* of a rock in the sky. Though my mental enzymes understand only that their to-and-fro juices trigger intricate effects, they find it likely enough that any brain, even a gecko's, far exceeds the complexity of binary stars, or quasi-stellar radio objects—to name just two hottest globs of inanimate atoms.

As children we wondered, "What am I doing? And why am I doing it here?" We couldn't guess, then, how wide those questions were, or that merely to ask them was to be more than merely ourselves.

Light's body and angle. Among phase-triggering signals, none unites us life forms so widely as photoperiodism, nor does any voice we're built to receive speak more profoundly. Gravity excepted, none is more primeval. What on earth could be older than daylight? For billions of years it was all that was possible.

Since photosynthesis depends on it, so too do more than our moods, our circadian cycles of sleeping and waking; and we imply sun sugar's relation to brain power through figurative terms such as *bright, brilliant, dazzling, luminous, illuminating, scintillating, sparkling, coruscating, incandescent.* Instinctive homage to the nearest blind star.

If, going further, I draw on solar energies, transmuted, to ask, *"Where do sun sugars truly begin?"* I'm sent backtracking along the steps of creation, through each nested event included in "now." Soon any such quizzical mind enters that vanishing point in itself which everyone calls "the primal atom." The atom that invented space. While its encyclopedic speck may be the best improvement radio and X-ray astronomy can offer on "ad infinitum," I don't see that as any quantum leap beyond antiquity. Sun sugar in ancient brains once spoke of the world's "uncaused cause" or its "prime mover."

Maybe "origin" names a mirage. Isn't it possible that "in the beginning" there was no beginning? But here, where light shines in the only way that we know, we do seem to need the idea of it. Similarly, we may need to equate blue sky with "reality" because our night skies seem so deeply unreal—though when it's night, it's everyone—in prospect, anyhow.

At odd intervals along this trail the Forest Service long ago blazed markers into tree bark, then painted the naked wood red. Growth having by now rounded the bark's cut edges, and the red having dimmed or scaled half away, those blazed trunks still seem to bleed the same color we do. More than once here in winter, with thoughts elsewhere, my skier's glance has fallen on a trunk whose red gash, noticed through snow glooms, has made me startle. Though the trunks themselves don't feel the pain I project into them, each blaze is, in point of botanical fact, a significant if venial wound. But blaze marks are nothing compared to the tree slaughter porcupines and beavers leave behind them. This morning, less than a mile from the trailhead, I walked through the carnage of aspen trees attacked by beavers.

It was as if aspen vandals had berserked all over the place, never pausing for breath till the once flourishing, stream-side grove had been utterly trashed out. Not only had its trees been felled; trunks eight inches thick had been chopped into segments, or chopped half way through and then left. Pale bark and boughs littered the banks like battle leavings. Saplings an inch or two thick were slashed at a steep angle as if by scimitar. But a close look showed the "berserkers" were creatures with teeth sharp as chisels; able in one chomp to shear green wood cleanly. Three-inch trunks made the beaver bite only twice, but really stout trunks called for steady application—which sometimes faltered. Rather, the beaver incised halfway, then quit. We're assured that damming compels them to fell and gnaw; however, the look of that grove made me ask if lumberjacking might not be their true passion. Besides, why should animals boggle at eating the scenery?

If, however, root and leaf competition among species for chemicals and for electromagnetic waves is omnipresent here, terms like *war* and *combat* may distort what is more like a cooperative against risk and disaster. Out of decaying wreckage promoting the whole, an attunement is forever happening. It too, along with all micro-critters, is present in wind's roaring hushes over this forest. Sound of an attunement always in motion. Voice of one "highly *im*probable state" where, for all I know, we can hear the whole story, as if catching sight of ourselves by surprise. After all, attunement is what our bodies are made of.

Anthropologists suppose, reasonably enough, that early humans found more safety in grassland than the forest we slowly emerged from. If this were way back then, I'd be a bit jumpy always; would always be wary some lurker might get me, would feel a furred shadow crouched inside my fear, aiming its teeth at my throat.

Well, if the better to glimpse predators, my hominid forebears of Africa began preferring savannas to trees thickly sown, this protective advantage has survived right up to recent times and turned on itself—as prejudice. Through Greek and Roman antiquity, all through medieval times and well into our own country's idea of improvement, the ratio of stumps to trees has measured a culture's level of civilization. To "develop" was to fell. A stump was Progress. How many forests now inhabit *that* ax-blade?

Whereas most of the trees felled in our country's earlier years weren't sawn or milled but just burnt up to get them out of the way, Europe—even in its Dark and Middle Ages—made more of its millennial forests than firewood. If I'd been a swineherd then, I'd have led my pigs out daily to pasture among the still unbroken expanses of oaks, there to fatten on acorns. Beyond obvious uses for timber in buildings, I'd have thought nothing of trees turned into cooperage: barrels, vats, buckets, dippers, all hooped or banded with birch twigs or willow. Lacking cheap ceramic ware, my wife and I would've eaten off and out of beech trenchers, beech bowls. Beech ladles, beech spoons would've served and stirred our chestnut porridge. At a wooden wellhead we'd have drawn water into beech buckets, for drinking from beechen cups. Chicken and pig droppings would've been swept clear of our floor with birch brooms. Night errands to a neighbor would've been lit with pine torches; and bundles carried there, lashed with cordage or rope woven from linden bast. While haying in early July we'd have used rakes with maple tines, then tossed it onto an oak barrow with maple pitchforks. We'd have threshed with willow flails, scooped grain with maplewood shovels. If we were well enough off to own a cart, its carriage, axles, spokes, and wheels would have been oak—like many a mill wheel, olive press, wine press, stock pen, and fence. Even my plough and ploughshares would have been carved from forest, along with ox yokes and the very willow cages in which I'd have carted live geese to market. My ax helves of ash would not have reminded me, illiterate, of ash used in helves and spear shafts way back in Homeric times. But huntsmen and militia men trooping through my village would've carried alder bows, bows of yew, alder arrows and lances; just as the river running past that village would carry all sorts of boats, barges, and dugouts whose masts, rudders, and oars had been hewn from forests upstream. Their very hulls, caulked with pine pitch or resin, would have shared such waterproofing with my wife's resin-caulked buckets and churn, her dippers, brewing tubs, and kneading troughs. If I'd been a tanner or dyer I'd have spent lots of time peeling hemlock bark for use in those trades, just as the village midwife would have come gathering bark for medicinals, while other villagers used bark for fertilizer and fodder.

Given the striking exfoliations from stone perpendiculars which naved thirteenth century worship, for example, at Amiens, Chartres, Rheims, or Rouen, it's hard *not* to see Gothic cathedrals as rational forests, pillars like trunks chiseled into belief. Oh yes, eras earlier than our own have owed nearly everything to trees.

In many Third World countries, of course, a voracity called Progress chomps away unabated. On the other hand, even in ancient times deforestation led to ruin. The fabulous cedars of Lebanon disappeared under axes barely improved from the Bronze Age. Like any other tourist in Rome I've gaped at the stupendous Baths of Caracalla. Their colossal scraps of brick lost some of my awe when I realized that those indoor acreages of pools, hypocausts, and steam rooms were kept comfy with the heat of chopped logs. "Wouldn't there have had to be a stream of wagons," I asked myself, "bringing cordwood into Rome? And wouldn't it have passed a wagon stream of empties, rolling back into the hills for more trees?"

Not only in Italy. Imperial style and prestige called for public baths wherever Romans fought, won, settled in. Their wood-heated amenities were often available twenty-four hours a day, year round. No wonder Rome's hot-water habits eroded miles of present-day Italy into badlands.

Chancing to look upward toward a patch of clear sky, I'm aware of an aerial to-and-fro going on all the time just over my oblivious head. About twenty-five feet above me insects swarm and dither in bright wing-blurs the sunlight makes translucent. A butterfly passes "at speed," disappearing before I can guess at its species. Slender tips of the forest's great firs sway ever so slightly, with a motion that always takes my life into theirs, as, without thinking, my body mimes that slow, lithe sway. About a hundred feet up a bird flits into and out of view—possibly a robin, which surprises. Higher yet, clouds swim face down over evergreens thick as grass; and over the clouds, the blue sky. Over it all—insects, flitting bird wings, fir tips, cloud puffs, atmosphere—floats the motionless, westering sun at midday. Back of the sun, invisible stars populous as Asia. Beyond them, nebulae diaphanous and gaudy as tropical fish. Beyond all, beyond the last quasar, a nowhere and nothing of such absolute vacuity as to be made from one seamlessly impossible thought. What other stuff could a universe be inside of?

Winters, I ski past animal tracks enough to imply a forest in hiding, snowshoe hares behind every third drift. Hardly ever do I *see* one, winter or summer, because their browsing on forbs, twig-bark, and spruce tips is largely nocturnal. Mule deer are considerably more evident. Forest settings helped shape them. Downed trees all over the place have taught mule deer the fluent leaping they do with such nonchalance it seems gravity doesn't fully apply. Instead of forest their white-tailed kin prefer woodlands where the more open terrain has made better runners of them than leapers. With both species, the dapple of brightness and shade explains their mimicked sun-spots in the pelage of fawns.

Perhaps I tread too heavily. At over five pounds the pair, my Swiss boots aren't exactly stealthy. Perhaps moccasins. Along trails that are often rivers of rock, however, heavy boots allow me to glance around instead of forcing my gaze to range no wider than my next step. And animals do well to be shy of the scent given off by us carnivores. Occasionally elks grazing in a high meadow grant me permission to watch them, but always at a respectable distance—some hundred and fifty yards. Which they never permit me to narrow. In a forest's marshy swales whose greens they find so delicious, I find glints of water seeped into their bovine hoof prints, where they themselves have chosen not to be seen. How any animal the height of a horse, angular as a cow, can ease soundlessly off through underbrush and thickset trunks, I do not know.

Understandably, the higher you climb the more animal size dwindles, like the trees. Above timberline, survival depends on keeping out of the weather, so mammalian profiles of bears, elks, and the like give way to ones low as marmots, voles, pikas.

At a loud whir I startle. A blue grouse, unseen under a low-spreading juniper, thrums suddenly up into the air, blurting out of the boyhood where I used to hunt quail. Not much of a flyer—plump, underpowered compared to quail—but colorfully marked, the grouse flashes a scarlet brow and bright purple neck-pouches set off by dusky plumage. As it skims a granite upthrust rimming a ravine, then flaps-whirs out of sight into spruce trees across the way, I chuckle at how each of us spooked the other. Probably it was feeding on juniper berries when I flushed it—and it me. Whether blue grouse eat needles in summer I'm unsure, but in winter that's about all they get. So how would their flesh taste to predators? Like eating a painting? But I quit hunting long, long ago. When people give up their whims of dominion they often begin with the animals, so as to own more of a world.

Bacteria and insects going about their business as part of the forest's cryptosphere don't qualify as "fauna." Lives speaking to ours must be of a certain size. So despite the fact that tree roots depend on their contribution to the food chain, the omnipresence of amoebas, mites, twig borers, pine beetles, weevils busying themselves around me by the billion hardly makes them companionable. The fellow creatures I find myself inaudibly talking to, admiring, consoling, quizzing, are trees. Perfect listeners.

Besides, the more of its bewildering complexity this forest reveals, the more nature's essential unity amasses within me. A lot of my life—and not the worst part—has been spent alone with the planet, trying to know what it is. If nothing else, that would have made being born worth it. In my old age, just realizing one or another distant forest has escaped being sliced into plywood will make its canopy a light-source to all but the eye.

On the high spruces around me, resin-glittered cones hang in clusters so thick their trees seem generous fountains weeping for joy. Some tops are so cone-laden that only their cones' cinnamon shows, not the fathoms-deep, blue-green of needles. Like bounteousness overflowing, on crown after glistening tree crown not a cone could be added. Just to see them fills me with the great on-going desire of their species.

Since squirrels and birds eat them all the time, I decide to munch a seed or two, knowing well they're nothing like the butter-rich piñon nuts of southern Colorado and New Mexican woodlands. The cone I pick up has fallen off a white spruce, with resin oozing between its tightly closed scales exactly like honey. Breaking it open I finger forth a couple of seeds, chew them, and receive a turpentine flavor which persists on my tongue for half an hour. My lips remain sticky with resin. Maybe there's a trick to knowing when a cone's seeds are ready, but if a squirrel eats what I've just swallowed, the squirrel itself would taste awful.

Rarer than needles in haystacks, the unplundered cone. Each resin-free specimen I examine has long since had its pockets picked by bird bills, squirrels, chickarees, what have you. Insect borers leave the seed's tiny husk clean of meat, while squirrels and chickarees will rapidly shuck a cone, scale by scale, like a manic gourmet leafing through an artichoke. Because the chickaree does so in a favored spot, the cone scales build up a midden that can be six human paces wide and a foot deep. If the midden is moist and well-shaded, the chickaree will bury unrifled cones within its cool protection, to keep food in reserve.

Between birds, chipmunks, squirrels, mice, and insects, it would seem that few seeds ever hit the forest floor, much less germinate. Now and then I watch one flutter down like a fleck of brown paper hoping to carry its message forward. And maybe it will. Certainly no spruce seed goes forth uninstructed. Inside are 350 million years of life, whispering directions, because whatever "life" is, it's something that never quits trying. Nonetheless, odds *against* are enormous.

Take a particular seed, where time's pressures meet. While still unpollinated, a female cone's twig can easily be wind-whipped off the tree. If the cone survives to open normally, pollen still may not light on a given seed; and even if fertilized, a dropped seed has about one chance in five of germinating. Not enough water. Bare rock, no soil. Not enough sun. Too much sun. Birds. Chipmunks, mice, squirrels. Insects. Worms. Fungi. Foresters calculate that any given seed off ponderosa pine has one chance in a hundred of becoming a seedling. As for any hope of survival beyond the seedling stage, "slim and none" pretty well cover it.

Yet a forest surrounds me. Like a vacation from realities badly constructed it allows me to voyage among a paleozoic splendor, and designs not made by hands. I gawk upward at a ninety-foot Engelmann and think what a splash its seed made after dropping to earth through hundreds of millions of years. Its least cone, now fallen, is a shell I can listen to. From an imagined memory wider even than light, from the ocean of whatever was when nothing was real—out of which existences rose, and flow, and continue—wave follows wave toward the shore of my inner ear. There our forest origins ask us more than what we are; they ask what we might be.

Winters, when I'm nearing the end of the trees, like a boy excited by the roar of a cataract long before it comes into view, I can usually *hear* timberline. In Switzerland, German-speaking biologists refer to the "*kampfzone*," the zone of struggle. Struggle? That's putting it mildly. Trees up here don't swim in the wind any more. They stream. At timberline's upper limit—which around Heart Lake is over eleven thousand feet above sea level—the final haggard conifers seem like birth defects, compared to what the identical seed would have grown into further down on the mountain. As victims of winds addicted to sadism and furious riptides, small wonder such conifer stands are sometimes called "elfinwood." Another German label, but one we've borrowed into English, comes to much the same thing: "krummholz"; literally, "crooked wood." It certainly is. Trees sunk to shrubbery—whose seed, elsewhere, could've towered. Still another name for such warped disguises is "windwood," which at its lowliest botanists call "prostrate." Apt again. With wind's high-country whims and onslaughts beating it down, the tree can never lift up its head. Yet branches touching ground may take root, cloning into a long line of "trees" that really is one subalpine fir.

Already in warm September the clump of krummholz near me appears to cower at the idea of yet another winter. Accordingly, among the most tortured and dwarfed specimens, even sex life is stunted, producing little seed. Merely by daring to germinate in such a "struggle-zone," species that elsewhere rise like rocket smoke can never, here, grow more than knee high; so a timberline seed finds itself pushing back at the impossible, a few new cells at a time. For all their apparent defeats, their midget successes, such trees surpass even bristlecone pines in the terrible endurance heroism calls for. Scary. No matter how often I pause near such indomitability, I'm more than humbled; any claim I might have to bravery is silenced. Because, after all, this is the edge. The upper limit. Line between what might be, and must be.

I'm reminded of that by my body's response to the altitude. In descending to Heart Lake for water, pumping it into my canteen by way of a Swiss "Katadyne" filter, then reascending the steep slope near the shore, I gasp under the flurry of mild exertion. "Eleven thousand feet is nothing," I carp at myself—as if to say, "C'mon, get tough." But legs aren't wings, and this air's a mile higher than my house, which sits at timberline's *lower* limit, among dwarf ponderosas. Trees too have their troubles. Some upstanding alpine specimens form "islands," little co-operatives where the micro-climate may be a tad more favorable. Fifty yards southeast of the lake there's an island of subalpine fir, shorn trunks huddled together like a sparse palisade, because all the lower limbs have been "high-lined" by elk, as high as their winter hunger could bite.

Yet it's not animals or lack of rain or light or oxygen that slows growth up here. It's the way warmth falls off as you rise. The 50-degree Fahrenheit isotherm. Or as a krummholz spruce might say, "Our summers never warm us enough for new needles—that is, for growing them properly. And *keeping* them." Worldwide, trees of all species seem to agree: "If the hottest month of your year doesn't average even fifty degrees Fahrenheit, forget it." That's as true of tropical mountains and their high "elfin forests" as it is of the international tree line in Scandinavia, North America, Eurasia, wherever. Botanists feel this *may* be because new material can't mature into woody tissue, the sort woody enough to survive abrasive gales, ones laced with crystals. If new shoots don't "harden off" by fully developing a layer of cuticle before cold weather again comes round, winter kills them. Or so it seems.

Having taken my share of snow-barbed gales full in the face, I'm puzzled that any botanist could imply there's room for discussion. Some timberline trees get completely debarked on their windward sides, snow-blasted down to bare wood. A twelve-foot Engelmann spruce to my left stands freakishly tall considering the site, straight as a flagstaff, yet branchless on all sides but one. Its sole limbs grow so directly leeward of the trunk, in a plane so faithful to its thin windbreak as to seem a cruel joke.

Elsewhere the tundra surrounding Heart Lake tells a similar tale; self-evident proof—to me anyhow—that without wind protection more than dwarfish lives can't happen. Streaming away from the lee side of boulders are trees that have taken exactly the form of snowdrifts which, all through winter, keep them alive. Like incautious soldiers poking their heads up out of the trenches—that is, above snow level—twigs too curious get zapped. Their evergreen meets the eye as a winter-killed orange, deader than broom straws. Wind has clippered the dwarf tree's surviving members neatly as any electric shears. What's left is a subalpine fir, say, aerodynamically shaped, streamlined by air in a hurry. On calm summer days their high-velocity quietudes act out what winter's rampaging looks like.

In such held motion, too, I marvel at the hardihood of trees that won't take "No!"—till the iron will that they're unaware of having leaves me doubly abashed. Not even their plucky "Yes!", however, gets me past the fact that after the final stunted conifers come reassertions of "No!" in stone poking through tundra. Then the fellfields, where rocks predominate; junkyards of more or less flat stones, where life becomes mosses cobbled with granite.

Almost for companionship I stop to listen to a couple of ravens, flapping eastward thousands of feet overhead. In notes raspy as a struck match, they caw, and keep cawing. For the pleasure of it? "Probably not," I decide. But who's to say? Their caws seep into distance. At a certain moment I'm aware of just standing here, listening to nothing.

With schist oddments and crag chips strewn underfoot, with life just peeping through crevices and gaps betwixt eon-bitten stones, morale sinks a whit or two as odds against living things rise—and toward the summit grow all but prohibitive. Certainly my spirits have often quit chirping when I've traversed a fellfield alone in cold fog; or when July flurries and windchill made a joke of our calendars. At such times, even the stacked rock of trail cairns can seem sullen, funereal. "Your presence isn't more real," they seem to say, "than a few pinches of air mixing *our* dust with water." As if my future were already inside them.

Today's sky, however, is still mine, even if southeasterly rain clouds amassing, drifting toward James Peak, may want to continue their summer habit of the afternoon storm.

Several paces ahead to my left, a stone's greyish brown now bulges spontaneously, stirs a bit further and turns into a waddling bird. Ptarmigan! Its cryptic coloration matches perfectly with lumps of tundra and lichen-spattered granite. Then another, smaller stone does the same! Followed by a third. And, though by this time I'm looking closely, a fourth. Each bird had been virtually under my nose! I edge closer. Ptarmigans are a sort of grouse, plump as Cornish game hens, and so stupid about *not* fleeing that my benevolence wants to advise them: "Wise up, Fly! I'm human. I might for all you know be a 'sportsman.' " But ptarmigans don't bet their salvation on flight. Slow of wing, they practice invisibility—to perfection, as my hen and three chicks have just shown.

Winter and summer, the ptarmigans pass their lives near timberline and beyond, among its final wind-shuffled sticks, eating juniper berries and spruce needles, eating willow buds, whistling to each other, roosting by night in krummholz. In timberline trees it's their whistles that tip me off to them. A sweet, clear call; and often its answer. From talking to trappers in Alaska, I know that when ptarmigans have fed on just spruce needles and buds not even sled dogs can abide their resinous taste. That doesn't prevent neolithic voices in my genes from hinting how easy they'd be to kill: "A club, a stone, nothing to it."

I ease closer, hoping my bootsoles won't scatter rock. Within eight or nine feet of them I scan intently for yet invisible chicks. I see everything there: rubble of the fellfield scattered like tiles clumsily laid, grouted with moss. No ptarmigans. None. Another appears. Does so on the identical square inches where my keenest, most intent perusal had seen not a feather.

The effect isn't "magical." Stones turning to birds is impossible. Though humbled, the eyes nonetheless insist that no further bits of granite can stir into life. Cannot possibly. The eyes take their oath on it: "Because the show is over. Trust us. That last one was *it*."

Who doesn't want to believe his or her own eyes? Certainly I do—on any object or surface not ptarmigan. So I'm merely confused when another chick appears *exactly* where my incredulous gaze has been staring. In short, I was looking steadily at the chick. Not "close by" or "pretty near." My eyes were *on* it. And none the wiser. But this time the show really is over. While I their audience stand incredulously shaking my head, they waddle toward a clump of dwarf juniper, with "the full strength of the company" now consisting of mother hen and her five offspring, all of whom used to be granite. The eyes admit they've seen invisibility happen.

On second thought, maybe I've seen a short-circuit version of how we came. Us improbables. On a planet begun as naked rock, where else could we—however slowly—have sprung from?

Beyond tundra and fells, despite gathering signs of rain, I decide to go all the way to the summit of James Peak, high above forest, amongst dumb matter whose atoms are in nearly the likeliest of states. *Not* to feel "lord of all I survey." What nonsense! The higher I climb, the smaller I grow; a bipedal animal out to sample the range of its own ephemerality.

Thus on a peak whose shattered granite is indeed blunt as ruin, I clamber around gazing off into all points of the compass, then lunch with no other company than the stones' rude stares—their way of asking, "Why breathe? Why bother? Why come?"

Maybe the forest sent me, to go where it couldn't? Perhaps so, remotely: my life as arboreal offshoot, a sort of restless tree. Maybe out of contrariness I decided to come on up to this summit where even the mosses feel pinched, and altitude pinches my breath, knowing full well only the end of the world can be really at home here. Proud of their mindless immortalities—compared with anything married to oxygen—the massive slabs seem bored with human pretensions.

"So in your view," I ask them, "my body is smoke?" Their inertness sounds willfully smug. Oh yes, I know. If the prophets of exhaustion have it right, one day each particle of matter will be in "a highly probable state," meaning blackness. Every last atom squeezed empty of heat. "Sooner or later," as at least some astrophysicists assure us, "entropy will proceed to maximum." No wonder my sun sugar enjoys clambering among these avant-garde smithereens of that dire prospect. Simply to spit in its nest.

Either in reprisal or accord, a first dozen rain drops flick and darken on the pepper-grey granite around me. My ascent had included sidelong glances to the southeast where, about ten miles off, rain sashes veiled steadily down, slate-blue, drifting a shade nearer between every two glances. Now it's arrived.

Wriggling into a Gortex parka on somewhat precarious rock isn't difficult, but pulling rain pants over big boots can test one's optimism and balance. Above thirteen thousand I find, yet again, even so trivial an exertion causes teetering. Not that any slip would be fatal, but that a toppling body—mine—would find only the oddly angled granite edges of talus to land athwart. By the time I've got one pant leg adjusted, the first spattering of droplets has thickened to drizzle. Cloud is now wrapping around all but the nearest crags, but once I've descended a few hundred feet visibility may improve.

And does. Looking back toward the summit, I'm delighted by the slow-motion vapors coiling among monoliths. Their ever-so-lazy revelations of a crag make that crag seem all the more huge and dreamlike. Then the same graceful currents of mist dim the huge profile till it goes weightless, dissolves. High ridgelines gain heft, come forward like a developing photo in a darkroom tray, only to turn around and disappear quietly, taking their reality with them. Time itself seems apparitional, passing into and through the hardest stones easily as drizzle through fog.

Hypnotic. But I've miles more to descend. On terrain nearer sealevel, descent doesn't seem miraculous; only ways that go up. Well, we may usually get our deepest ideas from the sky, as if somehow we feel life really began there and not in archeozoic ocean—except that here I know better. Among virtually sterile rocks just below the peak, I snug my parka hood and begin further downclimbing, slab to slab, toward the fellfields. Then onto tundra where the trail's already a stream. From there down into and through the most tentative, wind-contested upper reaches of the "kampfzone": beginning of Earth's true habitability. Down where summer comes from.

Past gorse, past islands of subalpine fir tangled thicker than basketry, I splash along a trail that's all loose stone and fast water, down into timberline's first "banner" conifers with their one-sided branchings, and finally back into dense forest broken by steeply sloped clearings. Past their withered meadow-relics, past the frost-slaughtered stalks of cow parsley, past purple husks of larkspur's end-of-summer ruin, past harebells half blue, half gone, I myself go, occasionally slowing stride to take in the full height of one or another great, rain-blackened Engelmann trunk far older than the nation that claims it.

Such "patriarchs," ancestral in more ways than one, arise within a plant-and-animal mazework that can't assemble itself in less than centuries—thirty, even forty human generations. No amount of plantation, reseeding, amounts to a forest. The mind of a forest takes its own sweet time. Before I can know that its labyrinth will evolve into nothing more sentient than surrounds me now, I'd need an eye that can see millions of years up ahead. To our nearest mammalian kin animals like us were, only a short while ago, unthinkable.

At a slab whose wetness is perfectly the color of salmon, I stop to retighten a bootlace. On the granite's water-filmed surface, a grey-green lichen splotch, strikingly wider than any I've seen, looks—despite the crinkled edges—almost perfectly round; round enough to be a photograph of the sun. A self-portrait? And an image of something much larger. Something beyond "origin"; something which, among its makings, has made of the brain a second sun.

Then off again, splashing downtrail, at rest within my own rhythm, in rain that has its rhythm too: steady, finely divided, unanimous. For one long, floating while "reality" seems no truer than I am, nor does my presence inside it feel any less natural than catkins on a wand of dwarf willow. Past miles of water-beaded spruce boughs, my splashing follows a trail become stream. Alone but not really, I'm content that my life and the lives of this forest should be as they are, the impartial, necessary rain falling on us all.

Snow

～

The further I ski into Colorado's snow forests, among great-hearted ponderosa, fir, blue spruce primevally snow-whelmed, the closer I come to entering Russian folk tales my mother read to me as a child. Not that cabin-deep drifts feel magical. I expect them, just as we expect from deep snow the purity of its silences. And more. As if within that tangible soundlessness we feel some presence we remember, though not knowing what it was. To this day, don't certain snows fall all the way from our childhood? In fact, approaching a snow-loaded evergreen nearly as wide at its trunk's base as my ski pole is long, I half feel somebody's about to step from behind and offer three wishes.

"But how is it that the sheer weight of all that snow," I often wonder, "doesn't collapse boughs? Limbs should crack." Surely it happens. Trees are fallible creatures too. Now and then I notice the long, twisting bark-scar where a particular winter has riven a trunk. The fire of lightning can do it; so can the ice of deep cold. Often, in wind, I've heard a dead tree cry. Like humankind, however, despite its terrible wreckage the forest itself is hale.

Today, on a cloudy afternoon in late December, I glide through its pillared world, uptrail toward Roger's Pass, among towers of snow so heaped on boughs that snow seems the tree's main idea and its actual limbs all but dregs. Maybe because I'm in the Indian Peaks Wilderness, I think of the Arapaho and Utes who once roamed the area on snowshoes.

Only a few miles ahead of me lies the Continental Divide, and the pass. This trail I more or less follow can be, in summer, a torrent of rock like a jackhammered staircase, impossible to lose track of; now, snowed over, almost impossible not to. No matter. My skis let me go pretty much wherever the snow goes. To my left the drift-billowed ravine of South Boulder Creek affords peek-a-boo glimpses of the creek's black water, gliding for an open half meter or so through the dimple of a snow hole, then again under. Yet I hear its faint rustle past stones.

Looking at spruce forest palisaded with snow, I feel the lightness and heft of each tree's vertical storm, admire South Seas risen as vapor and fallen here as crystallized silences weighing tons. Out of wind's nagging ruckus and sting, snow's local pacifism caverns me. I ski among trees making their quiet mine; a speaking world fallen silent, in some unanimous hush my speaking would break.

Past our living room's sliding glass door, flurries just begin to blur ridgelines on Bear Peak. Soon boulders in our garden grow hoary. Their pates whiten like old men. The descending flakes thicken.

Inside, on a wall beside our fireplace, two pairs of my wife's skis have retired to souvenir status. The toy skis that baffled her at age four aren't much longer than Tina our cat, whereas the ponderous oaken things with free-heel bindings of the mid-fifties—the pair marked *Kitzbühler schulski*—are just under six feet. Between them, the two pairs span continents, and snows fallen from Anne's fourth to her nine-teenth year. I glance at her kiddie skis, find myself in the middle of grade school, daydreaming out quite another window: late-November overcast, a few meager flurries of ice crystal. Which blur past my ten-year-old gaze like good news.

Even in dense forest, "animal life" is usually tracked snow, chewed bark, shucked cones; rarely the creatures themselves. Without their snow traces, I would say there are none. Apparently this can be true of animals in the remotest terrain, where people rarely go, and thus where fauna should be least wary. I recall one naturalist's admission about a Himalayan area known to host several species as various as blue sheep, snow partridges, and foxes; yet his expedition trekked for days without catching sight of any. At a wooden trail sign put up by the U.S. Forest Service I stop, run a mitten over whiskery edges where rodents have gnawn three-fourths of the sign's plywood away, presumably to get the cow's blood gluing its laminations. A layer of "food" thin as the sign's coat of white paint.

One April, snowshoeing to Buchanan Pass, I was puzzled then

moved by deeply sunken deer and elk prints that led up and over its twelve-thousand-foot saddle between peaks. In spring snow the going gets heavy as slush. Unlike the more bovine-footed elk's, these tiny deer hooves had sunk in so far with each step as to imply a desperate energy-expense; perhaps the animal's last try for food.

More mysterious energy spenders yet are the small brown-grey birds I now see twittering nearby, hovering and pecking at a fir's cone clusters, hung from its crown. Finches? So I presume, judging by the touch of rust on head and throat. The mystery, though, is what keeps them alive in high-country winters cold enough to freeze shallow lakes solid. If my friend Denice Arthur were along she'd explain. Something about brown fat—vital to wintering birds—and puffed feathers, which cover the bird's feet when it perches. "You know how warm your goose-down jacket is, don't you?" Denice would ask almost blithely. "Well, that's what a bird's down feathers are for. No problem."

Indoors, my brain swallows her biological facts dutifully enough. Out in this deep cold, right now, "No problem" fails to persuade. My body plain doesn't get it: I'm moving right along, skiing with wool-and-polypropylene gloves inside pile mittens, which in turn are covered by Gortex, and my fingers are fast losing their senses. On a day like today, with windchill and temperature agreed on Arctic conditions, if you stripped to your shirt and stood still you'd be dead in ten minutes—while your wristwatch that timed them kept going. "Down feathers or not," I ask myself, "how is it those little birds don't turn to stone and fall off the trees?"

But no, there they twitter overhead, the only visible animal life besides mine; fluttering and mixing and faintly cheeping to each other, settling briefly onto pine tops, then spraying aside toward another tree crown . . . till falling snowflakes dissolve them from view. Denice's facts are cerebral, the cold is visceral. It feels simple as force, mindless as the space between stars. Fingers returning from the verge of frostbite hurt as if each had been hit with a hammer. It makes anything my neo-cortex can say a mere fume. Numbly I wonder how many pine nuts or dormant bugs fuel how many minutes of hovering flight, pecking out more pine nuts. How many wing beats in a calorie? Hundreds? Two dozen? In this chill, the metabolic transaction feels hopelessly en-tropic. Yet my eyes see it can't be.

Arctic jays, on the other hand, present no mystery whatever. Their opulent breasts of lovely, pearl-grey down keep each jay fat and sassy. Once when I was winter camping above Montezuma, Colorado, two such jays invited themselves to dinner. One swooped into a just-emptied beef stroganoff pan to scavenge meat bits, tail-feathers bobbing comically above the pan rim. After a few pecks he flew to a nearby juniper bough while the other jay hopped into the pan. Though I hoped they'd get in together, there wasn't room for anything but taking turns, which they did for many minutes.

Ptarmigan seem equally well-adapted for winter. By autumn their stone-colored plumage mottles with white, and though the cock ptarmigan retains his scarlet eye mark, bright as arterial blood, by the season of deep snow both hen and cock waddle around white as clouds, like minds changed by the weather, wearing feathers so apt that sometimes only their blue shadows give them away. Along with buff-brown snowshoe rabbits translated to white, and dark weasels turned ermine, they echo drifts they winter among and live by. Oh, snow's memoirs are written in more than water; in fur, in feathers.

Once, about forty miles north of here on Bighorn Flats, through binoculars I watched a winter-white ptarmigan sit in plain view atop a snowbank, motionless, while a soaring hawk patrolled the area to detect just such prey. The ptarmigan, caught far from cover but probably alert to those cruising wings before I was, held still as death. Except for wind lightly stirring its neck feathers, no motion. Since a hawk's focus is about ten times sharper than mine, I wondered, "Is simple whiteness enough?"

Eerie, watching a raptor circle warm-blooded prey in full view. Meanwhile, the dove-simple ptarmigan was betting its life on feathers exactly like snow. If it should startle into the air the hawk would finish it off in short order. So the ptarmigan was also betting on a stillness more elusive than speed.

What I saw adjusted my definition of "hawk-eyed" to include fallibility. For all its keenness, that hawk's retina, so much more richly supplied than mine with light rods transmitting imagery to the brain, failed to see that easy meal. Whenever its slow glide swept directly above the ptarmigan, reflected brilliance off snow lightened the already blond undersides of the red-tail hawk's wing feathers till I could read their brown speckles like print. Then its circling eased away, over a ridge and finally out of sight, never suspecting.

We grade schoolers knew well that any snow thick enough to land one flake on another, and *stay*, was already too deep for adults—whose grumbling made snow the sweeter. Best of all were snows that began in midafternoon and kept on through supper, through homework, then bedtime. Our foreheads would cool against window glass, watching clumped flakes dive through the halo of the street light; our hopes would rise like prayer. "Tomorrow, no school?"

Abed, we'd hear wind rattle ice off the rain gutters, feel flurries swirling around our house, sense snow's gathering depth overhead on the roof, while our sleep deepened under its silence.

Except for my own heavy breathing I move fairly quietly past snowed-under boulders and deadfall, up the steep sides of stone shelves. A ski whispers forward. Now and then a binding squeaks, or the cold snow croaks under my ski pole. I easily traverse slopes which in summer would be all but impassably helter-skeltered with loose rock, wind-fallen logs. Above on a vast ledge, eaved with drift, I see growing from its creviced rock *my* tree, a bristlecone pine. Which I believe in because it so deeply believes in itself. This one is warped and tortuous as curdled smoke. "How old?" I wonder; and guess, "Only a few hundreds of years. Five, six hundred at most." Thus almost young. Its needles poke their green prickle through clumped snow, like a promise at the bottom of winter.

By now the continuously falling flakes have begun filling tracks left by other skiers, perhaps yesterday; but those tracks still show what they did, and, in a way, what they stopped to look at. To my left South Boulder Creek's dark waters continue brief appearances between snow bridges, openings so sensuously rounded my blood feels their curvatures "womanly." On them the light lies virginal, seductive.

From time to time my pole basket will suddenly sink two feet without hitting anything more solid than powder. That comic swing-and-miss effect makes me laugh at myself, but also makes the uphill going a bit harder. The constant roil of snowcloud opens and sunlight pours through like a surprise. I rest, pant little puffets of vapor. Happening to stare at the base of a wide fir trunk, I look higher, then higher yet—like the runt burglar escaping on hands and knees in comic movies, whose "take" on the tall cop begins at his shoelaces. The tree under my rising gaze seems to soar.

Just when my vertical scan tops out I see an avalanche—shelved and holding its breath exactly till now—let go, pouring straight for my face. Skis and all, I dodge nearly in time.

Having wiped snow from my eyes, fingered snow out of my collar, shaken it out of my hair, and dusted my shoulders, I suddenly realize

I've never felt more startled or dwarfish: a mere irrelevance. Yet even in the adrenalin instant, I saw its backlit cascade, sun-rimmed, as gorgeous. I recall an avalanche victim near Aspen whose last words, overheard by a survivor, were, "Here it comes!" Beautifully? Even for an instant?

Where wind has tossed tree crowns, of course, their evergreen is blown bare; but only the upper third. The rest, sheltered by neighboring trees, holds unstirred great cargoes of snow.

Approaching the wall-dregs of a collapsed cabin, I feel them become, caved-in or not, a touch of company. Surely as a prospector— and maybe his partner—peeled green logs, notched their ends, then hoisted them atop one another, the primal peaceable instinct impelled them: shelter. A single room, maybe nine by twelve. But home. Each time I ski past it, what once lived here decays a grain or two further.

Because not even a lit candle promotes daydreaming so easily as a hearth fire centering a house backed by white mountains, I sit sipping Red Zinger tea, staring at log embers in our wood stove. "In Colorado alone," I ask myself, "how many chimneys, how many $3,000 hearths has snow built?" Without it my own roof would sport nothing but a galvanized "flue" poking up from the basement furnace and its gas-burner's rational array of blue tongues. In weather just chilly or cold, that's good enough. It's snow that calls for a fireplace, even one modi-fied like ours, with cast iron and catalytic element to insure cleaner burning.

Like reflections off lake water, flames bathe the red and black logs. The fireplace's brick arch turns proscenium; licks of fire play shifting roles, evoke scenes unremembered for years. Monotonies of winter amid Illinois flat land. Coal-burning furnace. Basement whose house is long gone. A ten-year-old boy nailing leather skate straps to a board.

That was then. And there. December in our Colorado garden is the season of ice-bearing fruit trees, season of prickly-pear cacti that shrivel to limp bladders, season of suns weakened beyond fertility, their winter arches too low in the south sky for growing anything but ice fronds unfurled across puddles, frosted on windows. And the flakes keep streaming down, thick as memory.

Maybe that's partly why I love living in Colorado, where snow is good news. Here the Midwest's idea of bad weather gives a living not only to people at Vail, Aspen, Snowmass, Copper Mountain, Wolf Creek, Steamboat Springs, Arapahoe Basin, but also to growers and cattle ranchers a thousand miles to the south, where it never snows and where snow is vital; where agriculture and power plants need runoff from our mountains to even exist. Snow-stored energy descending on ridgelines along Colorado's continental divide will, next August, run the air conditioners of Phoenix. Clipped hair will drop to the floor in a Tucson barbershop kept cool because our peaks are a warehouse of ice crystals dropping right now. More locally, and far more important to me, snow keeps Colorado's incomparable high country alive.

Up, then down, our mountainsides, the snowline ebbs and flows with the seasonal rhythm of tides. Unlike a seashore's surf line of plastic bottles, driftwood, syringes, and oil-stained styrofoam, however, the snowline's upward retreat leaves behind in its wake a July "springtime." Early as late June, however, bending over green, pincushion tufts of moss Campion, I can admire once again the pink blossoms barely wide as a shirt button. At a melting drift's ice-laced edge, while collecting droplets into my steel cup, I can expect yellow snow lilies. And when midday sun is two weeks higher in the sky, I'll begin noticing rock aster, bistort, columbine, plus a dozen other blooms. Snow's insulation will keep them alive through winters that split granite. Then too, snow's early return in late August will again shut down trails and meadows before our lug-soled boots can trample their larkspur, lupine, and pipsissewa to straw powder.

No one in that fifth grader's part of Illinois has ever *seen* skis; at least, no one he knows of. Nonetheless, the ten-year-old forearm discovers the hardness of oak while hammering half a barrel stave into place, thereby giving his narrow strip of pine board the curve of a ski tip. That done, he rubs the nail-spliced board-and-stave bottom with a fat candle, then heads up cellar stairs to try his handiwork on two inches of very wet snow. The skis, he understands, want his backyard to be a hill, but his bit of Illinois hasn't any. No hills whatever. In fact, the only rolling terrain he has ever set foot on are slightly mounded stretches where a creek runs through the town's nine-hole golf course.

His homemade things glide. Kind of. That is, can maybe be made to. But because photos of skiers imply an almost self-propelling power in skis themselves, the boy finds the weight and friction of his version a bad surprise. As he shuffles across the meager snow layer, his ski tracks are grass, and elm leaves winter has blackened. Though who knows? If only his world had a hill.

Remembering well the summer shapes of this mountain, I've the pleasure of realizing that what I ski over is not a thin layer of elm leaves, but huge lichened boulders, wild in their brute way as the wild drifts that cover them. And yet the "maya" of the hardest stone will disappear entirely too, over eras our lives find unreal as snow.

Fresh snow doesn't keep many secrets. It often remembers each footfall. I crouch on my skis behind a drifted thicket of dwarf fir, watching a coyote snuffle, circle, loop aside, then return to faint blue rabbit tracks dimpling unbroken white. The coyote's nose, of course, has read those tracks like a newspaper. For nearly a quarter of an hour he cruises belly deep round a pair of grey spruce logs. Is the rabbit burrow beneath them? The coyote is sure, then uncertain. He noses around, tossing snow with his snout, stands, gazes aside as if to ponder. After each sortie to right or left on the mountain, sniffing near the base of undrifted furze, his nose returns him to those mouse-grey logs.

On Roger's Pass last summer I watched a goshawk strike once, twice, then a third time at the same nimbly flying chaffinch, and miss each try. The chaffinch blurted on and northwest, away; the beak and talons went hungry. Like that goshawk, this coyote's winter will be spent hunting, mostly not finding, while hoping to lose less body heat than his rare kills restore.

With marmots and pikas virtually bombproof in their talus-slope hideaways, this timberline coyote's diet will be so pitifully meager as to make "predator" and "prey" meaningless terms. Meanwhile, 2,800 feet above us both, the bleak trapezoidal summit of James Peak looms iron-blind as only winter granite can, while I spy on a fellow animal's failure. The coyote gives up, looks around, trots slowly away through the snow.

Coyote-watching, motionless, gets cold fast, but my bones feel a deeper chill in the life forces at work. As for me, I'm little more than four miles from a trailhead. Nevertheless, I stare at snow-crusted stone, bare patches of wind-burnt tundra, at the few, paralytic fir living like cripples in high-country weather—among which, as if testing, nature has thrust one impulse against another, then stepped back to see what happens. So a coyote pack shoves one of its weaker members to the very edge of the possible and says, "Go off! Live up there! Or try."

In my Uncle Paul's leather jacket, my own corny three-buckle galoshes, I used to love interrupting arithmetic homework to step outside for a walk round the block, then beyond our nighttime neighborhood which snow had monochromed. Ground color was first to go. Then sound. I could sense flake landing on flake, adding silence to silence. When I was snug inside my uncle's fleece lining, the winter air felt soft as eiderdown. Did I understand then how snow's fluff baffled sound waves? Surely not. But snow-silence went deeper than acoustics. Walking atop the embankment of the C.B.&Q. railroad, I'd scan a dozen white roofs while sniffing a faint acridity from coal-smoking chimneys.

And I'd scan for other walkers like me. None. Snow had emptied the few streets I could still see, making every power line and maple limb twice what it was, easing the harsh lines of parked vans, calling ownership into question. Deepening snow reshaped Mr. Kolberer's van as it belonged less and less to him, more and more to the weather.

Below me, occasional headlights would cast long beams made visible by flakes falling through them. Some . . . one. Going some . . . where. Then the car would seep away, replaced by hypersilence. Its stillness would fill me, making fresh night ancient. Before "before." Snow's remote ages, coming down, coming down; each flake a kept promise. "Silent Night, Holy Night" . . . how easily our whole family once entered those words. Small wonder. In them we're still partly the children who walked happily home through snowfall. We'd slow, look around at our street's black-and-white elms. A car would pass. Like a poised echo, we'd listen. For whole moments we were what we wanted.

Gradually the forest thins toward timberline. I begin hearing from wind. The higher, the more. Above timberline this afternoon gale is a blue norther, rocking my body with gusts, tottering me like a boxer. Suddenly it slackens, falls silent. A pause. Then powder leaps up off the crust in swirls that lunge toward me, engulfing my mind momentarily. They fall away, roaring down off the watercourse toward Heart Lake. Even such wind is part of enjoying the Arctic, under tidal waves of magma congealed to geology.

Just below the final approach to Roger's Pass I drink off the last of my orangeade before it freezes. Already its ice crystals are sharp in the mouth. Each swallow is so cold it diffuses intensely painful headache-waves through my frontal lobes.

Nearing the steep mountainside above Roger's Pass Lake, I assess my scheme of ascending further. When a snow slope is ripe for avalanching, any least thing may set it in motion. A skier's weight. Or—recently at Aspen—the weight of dynamite used for preventing snow-slides by causing them. On that occasion, the addition of a few more

pounds tossed onto a snowfield heavy as a small lake began the avalanche even before the dynamite could explode.

I stare at the steep embankment of snow before me. An interesting
moment. I'm solo. Common sense says, "Don't be a fool." But common
sense doesn't ski backcountry trails alone. So I hesitate, considering.
Part of me is afraid the other part will give it a try. The hesitation becomes my adventure.

When sun rose over an Illinois plain of dawn-tinted snow, its pas-
tels soon lost all nuance, dazzled away to blind white. Billions of microscopic mirrors repeated the sun, demanding a child's entire attention,
creating failures of retinal nerve. Icicles grown from Brandon's roof
edge gave off the sharp, hard light of winter's ambitions. Even the
melon-size geode on my Uncle Paul's desk seemed a rock with a heart of
snow. As I hefted its geological past to examine those crystals, ice and
fire burned the same hand.

Toward 11 A.M. under a clear blue sky, wind might kick up, throwing its weight around as if intending to outlive its welcome—and then
some. The words "windchill factor" would drone from my mother's
kitchen radio—a white Emerson—with lunch hour bulletins. Often
she'd send me downtown on errands she worded—perhaps even invented—to flatter me and my sled.

Whereas night's snowfall had said "Hush!" in a way my own motionless lips were delighted to imitate, the daytime sting of whirling
gusts narrowed grown-up eyes to slits. It forced even the gabbiest busi-
nessmen hustling across at East State and Lafayette to keep their
mouths shut. And when the gust traveled elsewhere, left their wet
lashes blinking.

Cold transformed Walter Bellatti, a lawyer, and John Murgatroyd,
an insurance agent my father knew. Gifted with flight, wind-driven
snowflakes would leap suddenly off a parked car to swerve, rise, dart
nearly level—like white flies showing wind where to blow. Agent and
lawyer leaned into it, race-walkers staggering toward Farmer's Bank:
solid citizens snow-changed to motley batches of mismatched clothing.
Yet while windchill stayed near twenty-seven below, anything warm—
even if it came off a nail in the basement—was in style. Anything styl-
ish and cold was just dumb.

Since I'm not headed upward toward the pass, after all, I might as
well ski a while over the bowls beneath it—which are wholly un-

tracked. Our absence is partly what wilderness snow confers: a world cleaner than we are, pure of us, though our minds create the purity we think it has. Snowcloud veils, unveils, cirques and ridges, lifting high peaks even higher when the gloom-line of a cloud edge turns out to be stone—one or another summit I know well, but in this weather feel I've never seen before.

I look around. Amid bewildering hush that takes me out of my life while still in it, I watch snow falling against further whiteness broken only by outcrops of black crag, black islands of evergreen. I like my loneliness here. The dead grandeur, so inhuman, so appalling, so beautifully "other" reminds me of one main thing: "I'm alive." And alive nowhere else so completely, paused on my skis, just looking around, knowing there's nowhere better to go, or be. And incomparably better to be than not be. Yet I say to myself, "If I die here, I die happy."

For an elliptical moment the thought annihilates time, till I'm again compelled by the illusion of futurity in motion. Like those distances between the few people in the world we're deeply fond of, there's a horizon *in* people, and in things. Fast as you close them, new distances open. "Why go?" I ask myself, even while slowly pushing a ski forward. We humans are an elsewhere.

Then a whim overcomes me. I pause again, deciding—since I've the scene to myself—to test its echo. So I shout "Hey! Me!"—and find these mountain walls are fast learners. Then shout the "Io!" of Italian. Good. The echo speaks Italian. I then try it on Spanish, Latin, German. Though the French "Je!" isn't very shoutable, and though my guttural "Ich!" returns as much-muffled German, the whole place agrees to be me, unanimously. But would've agreed to be anyone monosyllabic and quick.

The clouds darken, squeezing the afternoon's last rift of cobalt blue quite shut. Now, under overcast like this, there's no shadow whatever. That makes depth impossible to estimate. To a surprising extent it's shadows we see by. In shadowless white I think I'm staring at snow surfaces twelve feet away—a slight rise, say—but it's five feet, and nearly at my ski tips. Those tips, descending, spew rooster tails hypnotic to watch. And I mustn't, because now I've the balance of a drunk. Balance in skiing depends on anticipation, so when I glide forward over flatness that suddenly doesn't exist, I'm lurched downward through a dip of several feet, which was—under my very nose—*absolutely* invisible. Empty air turns out to be a drift four feet away, while crust I've counted on turns out to be air.

It's eerie, finding my most reliable sense—eyesight—can't tell snowdrifts from nothing there. From nothing whatever. Like skiing the clouds themselves.

Uncertain, I stop often, feel a spell those clouds put on everything. In their surreal light, the snow-plumes that stream leeward back of each boulder seem frantic escapees held motionless, visible energies frozen. Above me, the plumed fell-field just below the summit of James Peak could be stone paratroops by the battalion, whose chutes refused to open.

Flowlines in metamorphic stone can show energy too, but a violence so slow to any human eye it's all but posthumous. Water, itself old as most rocks, gets around so much—even as snow—its fresh arrivals keep it young, whereas boulders are mainly stay-at-homes, making torpor their virtue. No wonder they often look bored. All they can do is sit there letting lichen eat them alive, while sun, wind, and rain worry their faces to puddled sand—which the waters of snowmelt, anciently young, usher downhill. But in snow's ice billows and plumes, the six-sided crystal-designs occurring just once and for all . . . well, they must think boulders eternal.

That's why our relation to snow's memory goes far beyond its silences, beyond its naiveté in believing any junkyard can become an undulant and seamless wonder. Knowing that every falling crystal is unique among billions, we feel snow descend like allegory: Earth's living faces, past and to happen—except that, when it comes to us humans, no two are different.

So maybe the rest of a life typically brief—if its span is even that long—goes around exploring what every child imagines snow ought to lead to. Often I've paused there, totally alone, on skis surrounded by winter forest; and by mountain granite wildly beautiful, beautiful beyond anywhere one child, at least, ever believed he could be. Then— if only to hear how the good life unlooked for might sound—I startle myself by reacting aloud, blurting words like "Oh! Check that, would you! This is it, This is *it!*" Hardly words an adult would admit to. More like some voice out of a boyhood this entire snow forest had remembered, and called for.

Chaco Night

Years ago during a June night in Chaco Canyon I truly believed I had lost any need for the future tense. There, then. My panic, replayed, now seems exaggerated as great dismay in a silent movie, but it hasn't dwindled to merely that. And though it was a night I'd never choose to relive, its effects—perhaps predictably—have become the healthy reverse of morbid.

Therefore the point isn't adventure. In physical terms, the incident was prosaic: I'd been messing around alone in New Mexican desert where nobody was, and got hurt. Nor is the point fear. Yes, I was scared plenty, though "scared" may trivialize what happened inside me. Whatever it was, hours of fear went into it, whereas split-second terror—on highways, for example—is over so fast it hasn't time to dismantle what we prefer to be made of.

It had been a blazing New Mexican afternoon. He was sweating, I was sweating. Backlit by adobe wall, he had stood framed at my car window, politely listening. "I seem to be turned around here. For Chaco Canyon, which road do I want out of Santa Ana?" Given the surroundings, I had supposed his dark skin and black hair were Hispanic; but his accent wasn't. Navajo maybe. Or Pueblo? After all, we were on the Jemez Indian Reservation. My memory of it now is of red dust, red roadcuts—shallow ones—through low rolling hills splotched with desert green; and of the blue cloud shadows moving over them. Beyond simply his badge and neat creases in the beige twill of his shirt, two things have stuck with me ever since; first, that I had liked him on sight; second, that, as he spoke, a subtle amusement in his brown eyes seemed to be answering something in my own look—as if we were sharing the same smile, but differently.

Motor running, my sweaty face looking into his, he answered simply, briefly, politely, said nothing unusual. I listened, thanked him, drove on. We do it all the time.

I fell toward evening. A flake of sandstone came away from cliff that a moment before had been solid rock, and my handhold. When it happened, I had climbed only a little way above the broad shelf that broke my fall. Because I had fallen feet-first, and not far—barely more than twice the height of a man—I needn't have been hurt at all. As it was, I got knocked out, though for how long I'll never know. One moment the sky had been the shady blue/orange of sundown already verging on dusk; then a white flash like round lightning, and the sky I lay looking up at was night.

The reassembly of one's first person singular would be interesting to witness, except that no one who has been hit *hard* awakes with mind enough to preside over such a putting-back-together. As cartoon characters come to, they ask, "What happened?" or "Where am I?" Wordlessly someone not quite "I" groped toward those very things. All I knew was that I was lying twisted, looking up at dark rock I'd never seen before, and a night of stars that wouldn't resolve to a focus. My head ached so tremendously it wasn't a headache but something else. My left side, my left shoulder, my arm, my left hand: hurt. "I fell." Yet it was only some fragmentary "I" who knew that. This partial self also knew the wetness was blood.

The inventory began. Despite hurting, I could untwist, move my body parts. "Nothing broken?" Apparently not, nothing major anyhow, not a hip, not a leg. Then, as I tried to get up, the starry sky and cliff began to veer. The rock was moving, accelerating. I eased back down, the nausea ebbed like a tide going out. So I just lay there, looking up with double vision at stars twinned, yet paying less attention to that aberration than to my own panic. Hair on the left side of my head was sopped with blood. "Jesus!"

I was well off any beaten path or trail. Nobody knew I was even in New Mexico, much less this remote Chaco area. My small pack's one-quart canteen was already half empty. All the first aid stuff which for years I've toted unused—including codeine and other pain pills—was back with my big pack four miles away in my car. Because when simply strolling around I don't carry so much as an aspirin tablet, my resources amounted to that pint of water, some repellent, a much-crumpled bandanna, and—ironically—a small cassette player I'd forgotten to remove from the daypack and leave in the car. Again I tried to rise, again waves of nausea rose with that effort. I lay back down, more frightened than ever. Apparently the exertion produced more bleeding—not profuse, but wet blood added to the panic.

Though my kind of safe adventure can hardly be called "mountaineering," even tromping up and down mountains entails risks clear as arithmetic. Chances of injury may be slim; still, the more time you spend around rock, the likelier. Any rock, big or small, has moved often in its long past and will move again. You want not to be in its way when it does. Perhaps canyons are safer. I don't know. I had slept in Tsegi Canyon one night where another sleeper—who had unrolled his sleeping bag too near the cliff—was drilled through the head by a down-streaking fragment of sandstone. Hardly more than a pebble. From several hundred feet it had reached speed enough that he surely never knew he had died. As an overnight guest I had, in Grand Junction, been offered the bed of a man whose mountain hikes, like mine, had always gone off almost routinely. Then a boulder got him.

That's why, in addition to an assortment of Band-Aids and gauze pads getting more crumpled by the year, with no occasion to use any of them, my homely little kit included pain tablets: for the day I hoped wouldn't happen. Yet I had imagined it, had imagined myself pinned. In some of those fantasies a friend went for help while I swallowed codeine pills and hung on, waiting. In others, there was no friend. I never cross slopes of big talus without imagining how easily, and with how sickening a bone-severing grind, one of those ten-ton slabs could amputate a leg or arm if it suddenly shifted. Unhealthy as that may sound, it had seemed merely a way of remaining alert to possibilities my alertness meant to keep remote.

Toward evening. I had been wandering up by-branches of Chaco, miles from its central complex of restored Anasazi ruins, keeping an eye out for petroglyphs among the many rough ledges of sandstone, with their rust reds and animal forms. Outside its canyons, that part of New Mexico is completely accessible to eyesight. Nothing withheld. Everywhere, an opulence of aridity, tawny sand; a world of solitudes, and their secrecies. The canyon that Chaco Wash has carved there—to fill it again with alluvium—varies from a half mile wide to three-quarters. Compared to Utah's deeper, far narrower canyons which the sun can look into only obliquely, Chaco is both quite shallow and broad. That and its alluvial soil had lent its twenty-mile length to dense settlement by the Anasazi—whose ruined villages are now the sole reason people go there, a past presence making actual cliffs half mythical.

Where runoff from many thousands of years of desert rain has streamed off those cliffs my gaze had poured with them, following their bone-dry streakings, their rain sashes of black. But no petroglyphs.

Instead, I paused to watch hundreds of cliff swallows sip at a water catchment which Anasazi hands had chipped troughlike out of a sandstone bench. Late evening sun coming through their wings had produced a translucence making the swallows even less substantial, more weightless than their own feathers. With a steadily nervous fluttering each bird kept its wings erect, extended upward. Quivering and all but airborne while sipping at that puddle, they danced nervously on tiptoe, never settling entirely. It was as if those trembling, backlit lives were afraid of forgetting their avian natures. At least a hundred swallows sipped there, yet not one had entirely left the sky. And each, after drinking, had blurted up toward clusters of mud nests stuck to the nearby cliff wall; to lumpy, bottle-shaped nests with entry holes just wide enough to slip through. One by one each swallow had alighted almost upside down on the lower lip of its nest, then at a wink disappeared inside.

At several ancient Indian cliff sites in the Southwest I'd seen other, much smaller catchments where, in the black rain-path marked by streakings, prehistoric inhabitants had hollowed small basins in stone shelves. Up cliff walls I'd also seen vertical dimplings where villagers long ago carved footholds for ascending to squash and corn and bean plots above their settlements. The holds had always looked precariously feasible, provided you took your time and used both hands, though Anasazi farmers and their women must've often ascended while encumbered with baskets of corn, water pots, firewood, dead game such as jackrabbits or quail.

In Chaco I had more than once taken long, speculative looks at the "escalade" now called "the Pintada stair"—and let it go at that. In fact, a day or two before my fall, I had stopped at the campsite of a French couple at the mouth of Canyon de Chelly. They were doing a rock climbing tour of the Southwest. Having just come from Joshua Tree National Monument, they would visit buttes at the Arizona/Utah border before going further north for some slickrock climbs outside of Moab. "We tried those stairs at Chaco," the woman told me, "but they were not easy."

Her muscular thighs and calves, and her experience as a technical climber, had made "not easy" hard to believe. On reflection, however, I realized that such steps as we see today must have become—in the nine or more centuries between us and their daily use—eroded enough to make ascent trickier than when Anasazi farmers had first hacked them out. Up Butler Wash, for example, west of Monticello, Utah, when sunlight rakes the sandstone walls at just the right angle, you can spot more than one set of Anasazi footholds—though what they lead to nowadays are further plateaus of sandstone scraggled hither and yon with piñon pine, thorny shocks of blackbrush, yucca clumps, cliff rose; plus the inevitable, ubiquitous juniper. A lot of nothing? Maybe so, from our point of view; but food, firewood, roof traves, hoe handles, digging sticks, baskets, sandals, rope, and twine to the Anasazi, for whom those clifftop plateaus of hardpan were—incredible as it now seems—part of the Fourth World, the land long promised.

My impulse to ascend, to put a hand where so many Anasazi hands had once rested, put my own foot exactly where their sandaled feet by the thousands once poised, had never quite overcome the timidity calling itself "good judgment." Then in Chaco it did.

Chaco sandstone spalls away in natural cleavages that lend themselves to masonry. Five-story chunks can and do break from its cliffs. Though their sheared faces look clean as yesterday, archeologists have proven that—to cite merely an instance—one such monolith at the edge of the spectacular ruin called Pueblo Bonito had separated from its parent rock close to ten centuries ago, but hadn't toppled. Already in prehistoric times its free-standing form had threatened parts of that pueblo, so Anasazi builders tried to check erosion at its base. As metaphysical reinforcement, prayer sticks had been buried there to induce Anasazi spirits to stave off that monolith's grand collapse—which they did, till it finally let go in 1941.

What's more, the foot of every such cliff in the Southwest is littered with reminders that stone can flake away. And if shearing and flaking over time spans geological isn't the same as every ten minutes, those clues should nonetheless have kept my timidity at full strength.

Not so. Having come upon quite a feasible set of Anasazi handholds and footholds that had been there since the end of Europe's Dark Ages, I

actually tried them. And had fallen. But that memory is half recollection, half supposition. It's what "must have happened"—because parts
of "after" are still lost to me, as well as phases of "before." The gaps are
less like page-leaps in a mismade book than a quirkily spliced film. Your
blink says, "They must've cut something there," but you've no idea
what it was, except for theme: life as it almost wasn't.

Even unhurt, climbing back down to Chaco Canyon's floor in pitch
darkness wasn't anything I'd have cared to attempt; dizziness made it
impossible. There I was, eighty miles from a doctor, and the first thirty,
dirt road. Time to time, I watched the twink of a jet's wing lights drawing its whisper across the night sky. If I lasted till morning and still
couldn't move about, dehydration would finish me off in two days,
three at the most. You can't simply *will* to do without water.

The fact is, however, it didn't seem I'd live long enough to dehy-
drate. The next dawn would happen without me.

Wavelike episodes of numbness and tingling were pervading my upper body as far as the lips. Frightened, I had kept clenching and un-
clenching both hands, testing my ability to move feet and toes. The left
leg and side, especially the buttock muscles and thigh, had begun to
spasm. My heart—whose resting pulse earlier that summer had been as
low as forty-one—was now beating arrhythmically and *very* hard, almost like blows with a fist. "You're panicked," I had told myself, "calm
down, breathe deeply." I inhaled deliberately slowly, exhaled slowly. I
tried not to think beyond "air in, air out." It actually helped. But the
leg spasms continued, at intervals of maybe twenty minutes. The way
my pounding heart kept shaking my body terrified me. When one of my
hands chanced to pause on my chest or abdomen, or even my groin, the
jarring felt so alarmingly ominous I at once moved the hand. The heart
no longer beat: it simply whammed. And kept whamming. As if a large
animal were throwing itself again and again at a door.

Out of an almost nil understanding of the neural system, my guess
was "head injury." Brain signals were misfiring. Otherwise, why would
my left side be spasming like a dead frog given galvanic shocks in the
lab? And how long could *such* a heart rate stay well over a hundred
beats a minute? After a certain time wouldn't it just quit? A cracked
skull had thus seemed all the likelier.

Intervals of twenty minutes or so would elapse between episodes.
During the lull, hope crept back. Then the next onset would rape me
with fresh panic. And since nausea attacked every time I tried lifting

my head, I felt real despair. So I just lay helpless. "Maybe I'll feel better after a while." But the realist in me said, "This is the place you've wondered about, wondering where you'd be. The road ends here. Now you know what it looks like."

So I lay that way, looking up at a night sky of stars whose doubleness, over hours, closed by degrees to a blur. Thinking, trying not to think thoughts in which life and death trade places, I'd ask myself "How much of this do I belong to?" and I'd realize, "All of it." The spasms would lessen their intensity, take longer to recur, and I'd say, "I'm better, maybe it's passing." The tingling and numbness would wane. Then my left leg and thigh would start thrashing about, muscles of the left buttock would spasm with them, till my whole body throbbed violently, as if I were being driven fast over rough road. That happened many times. In the longer interims I'd think, "It's better now," while aware how wishful that was. Then the next onslaught. Each new wave of spasming laid morale even lower. Finally I had to face what seemed inevitable: "I'm not going to get out of this. I'm going to die."

Hair on my head's left side was messed with blood half-congealed; the left shoulder and back of my chambray shirt felt sticky, but the bleeding had apparently all but stopped. Yet for a long while I was afraid to let my fingers explore. If . . . but no, the idea sickened me. I wouldn't let my hand touch there; wanted to know, but—especially because I was alone—couldn't bear to know, not yet.

Deep fear carries its adrenaline charge only so long. Then something else sets in—not so much "resignation" as realizing, "No use kidding yourself." My left side felt bunged up, not broken; but my heart kept whamming away. My head hurt more than I had believed anything could. As my mind returned to something like itself, somehow it was aware that it was still more than half stunned. Meanwhile, "I didn't know" recurred, moaning, like a grievance. "I didn't know anybody could be hit that hard." "I didn't know anything could hurt so much. Why doesn't a head spatter open?" My dismay stuck at that same level of unbelief: "I didn't know you could be hit so hard and not be killed." "I didn't know I could hurt this much." Again and again.

For how long? An hour? Two hours? My medical expertise was close to a minus sum. I remembered only that nausea can go with skull fractures, and that people are kept "for observation" because the worst effects may take a while to set in. Finally, despite the headache, I had tried a few tongue twisters aloud. "Peter Piper picked a peck of pickled peppers" should've made me laugh. It did no such thing. The ludicrousness was purely sardonic, and those words simply a tool about which only one thing mattered: could I say them? Was there brain damage? The jaw ached too much to say anything fluently. Mouthing words aloud felt like chewing harness leather. Not only that; I discovered my tongue had been cut, and that I'd chipped a couple of teeth in the left jaw. I tried remembering the English words to one or two short poems by Japanese poets, and found I could mentally say them. I tried remembering each room of the big house I grew up in. I tried naming as many of the NFL's back-up quarterbacks as I could: Kubiak, Tomzchek, Young, Hilger, Kramer, DeBerg, Herrmann, and so forth. That too, OK. Then lost sight of myself.

That's how the night had gone. I'd be staring up at stars, shivering, then nothing. After which, even to close my eyes seemed dangerous. With what felt like physical effort I fought off unconsciousness: to keep the universe *there*. At one point it was as if a spider's filament had been spun from each star to a tumpline round my head, its thinness unbreakably strong. Each star was tied by such a filament to a thousand stars unknown, in cosmic space beyond it, and each of those tied to other thousands, and so on, indefinitely outward. Despite my repeated lapses, the illusion persisted. By willed effort I *had* to pull back, continuously, against every star's inclination to drift away into some high, distant, and final dispersion.

When I came to, the stars would have moved, but not much, so intervals of sleep or unconsciousness must've been short. And the sleep of nervous exhaustion was indeed a possibility, because in the previous several days I had spent a ton of physical energy. From my pack I managed after much grunting and tugging to pull out a Gortex parka, which helped surprisingly to cut down the chill. However, that cost me. Getting it on produced appalling dizziness. At times when my vision seemed to be closing from its periphery inward, my heart rate surged. Runaway cowardice? I didn't care. Even if the cardiac muscles didn't self-destruct, even if their seizures and pounding lasted till morning, lack of water would guarantee the final result. Vertigo would make climbing down to canyon floor or up to the rim out of the question. Under New Mexican summer sun, the last rain-filled hollow would dry up. The shelf that had saved me would become a rock oven. The feel was something like, "Well, this time you've done it. You won't get out of this one."

It had seemed that where I lay, right there, was indeed the spot vaguely named even as we shrug it off in the phrase "sooner or later." Yet most lifetimes do learn what it looks like. Billions of persons have learned it—the ground their steps had all that time been leading them toward. Now I had.

And now, with my life about to end, I could see it wasn't complete at all. It would just stop. More happenstantial than intended, patternless, no real structure, it had filled itself with its own randomness. Its two or three biggest decisions hadn't been rationally made; they had been emotions, impulses. Given a second chance, I'd have done so much differently!—yet with similar results. All the words I had ever spoken now streamed past my inner ear like one long word made of run-together nonsense syllables. Nor was that a judgment, an evaluation. It had seemed a physical fact, as certain as when the fingers let go, a held pebble drops. Not a word I had ever said mattered, *only what I might have said*. Retrospectively, my effort at what I'd thought was a life seemed just oddments that added up to . . . nothing much. Not bad, not good, just me.

The sandstone stratum that had broken my fall had, itself, been laid down countless millions of years ago. Even while its stone warmed my back and the backs of my calves with night radiations giving up the day's heat, the life I contained felt less substantial than smoke. But I had felt substantial, like everyone, having turned away from the dumb truth of stone, the fathomless annals *any* stone implies. From all that time alive in dead matter, I had turned, as one must, in order to live at all. Straight overhead the ghostly, galactic glow of the Milky Way told the same story: "You weren't. Are. Won't be." And that would hold true for longer than even its fires could reach. Cassiopeia's "W," below and to the right of Polaris. The barely visible Pleiades at the sky's zenith. Orion to the south, halfway up the same sky . . . and a hundred hundred thousand others. Their great swarms. Bonfires, fuel dumps. Those nearest and brightest, most personal. Others, fainting at their own distance.

Under their gaze, Chaco's ruined dunes had roved for millions of windblown years, had hardened to stone, been buried, had been thrust again into starlight by crustal collisions; had again been eaten to rejected cathedrals.

That starlight was just now my summer sky, with an immense fragrance of lives not ours, out there beyond the limits of visibility. I thought, "If anyone ever returned from oblivion this would be his first memory." But isn't, because nobody does.

Knowing "each life must die" had brought not the slightest consolation. On the contrary, that was nearly worst of all. Death made of our planet only a holding tank from which, one by one, everyone is effaced. Nor did it bother me that my friends' features would, next morning, be alive when my own had congealed. I wanted everybody alive to go on living. That is, wanted it as much as I could want. My altruism gland had numbed. For family and relatives, for my wife and sons I *should* have wished much that I was empty of. I simply thought, "Well, the world will go on being the world, they'll just have to cope. And they will. People do." My sons would, in part, become me just as I had become my own father, for better and worse, dearer and more recognizably so the longer gone. It had taken twenty years of his death for me to turn and finally see who he was. It didn't matter; nor matter that my sons would need years to see me. I didn't care. Didn't care what they might see or fail to see, good or bad. It had indeed felt strange to realize that both my sons would perhaps live to a great age, and go through this, and die. Surely *that* had mattered? Here, today, I can't be sure it had.

Instead I suspect it had felt like simply the way things are. With our whole species swept over an edge denying even brief continuity, geological and human history had seemed a pathetic flicker compared with the furiously burning stars whose light kept arriving at my upturned face. Though they too were mortal, in the face of their stellar immensities mere planets lacked duration enough to matter. All of it over the edge. It would fall forever.

At the same time, and to my considerable surprise, I saw that despite its fits and seasons of self-contrived turmoil, my life had been blessed. Extraordinarily so. From Chaco's night-long revelations, that had been perhaps the strangest of all. Facing its death, a lifetime had thrown aside its posturing and now stood revealed as what it added up to: fortunate, happy.

But of course, "The Tao you can Tao is not the Tao. The name you can name is not the name." So too the death we can talk about has nothing to do with the death anyone really dies. What I felt myself being drained away into that night bears no relation to anything I'd ever read or heard or thought of. It was neither logical nor self-consistent. Dark, vaporous, without edges. Death was nothing whatever—whose enormousness terrified me.

I saw that poets and novelists maundering or intoning about "death" haven't a clue. Nobody on this side of it has, nor do I; not now. I just know how that one night felt, alone, with *hours* to look straight at the real. I remember enough to know that "death" in literature may be literature, or it may be a writer's cheapest trick, but it isn't remotely like what I saw—which cannot be talked about. Literary death gets talked of on paper, which will put up with anything. Inertness of the body is nothing. That's easily and often eerily described; and is trivial. On the other hand, to feel everything past and to come, the pattern everything makes, the power and delicacy of creation simply vanish as if none of it ever had been—that hit my dumbstruck awareness like a dark comet.

Even so, my feelings had been at odds with themselves, and with logic. In one moment I had felt that "the world would go on being the world"; in another moment I knew it would not be "as if" the universe died when I did. In all its tangibility it would empty, be sucked from time, forward and backwards. Utterly. That filled me with an anger giving way to deep grief at the canceling of all creation retroactively. I had never dreamed anything so hideous could happen. Our cells, senses, suppositions had lied to us. There would be no world to "leave behind." Remembering it now as delusion doesn't produce in me the slightest reaction. Back there it felt real, thus sickening.

At a certain point, during that long night, often as my mind formed the words, "I'll . . ." an irony mocked the futurity in "will." Feeling I had lost any use for the future tense wasn't, as it is now, a point in grammar. Through losing my use for the habitual "I'll," my face got shoved into life's very essence, taken from me. I had discovered how continuously each human moment leans toward the next, preferring to travel rather than arrive. Whenever I doubt my own fear that night at Chaco, I have only to recall how hair stood up on my skin as a thought begun with "I will . . ." or "I'll . . ." whimpered to silence. I lay at the end of possibility. Thus "I will" had left me, and left in its place an awareness: every thought we have implies a presumption we can't do without, the one called "tomorrow." We eat, drink, and clothe ourselves in it. How conceptual it sounds, "losing the future tense." To feel I *had* lost it—that was far and away the very worst single moment I have ever known.

If my heart's serial explosions, I had told myself, were mainly panic or some peculiar sort of anxiety seizure, music might help. Might at least alter the aloneness. I fumbled the tape player and earphones from my pack, pressed the play button, heard Sonny Stitt's alto sax continue, midnote, on "Spanish Harlem." It was welcome yet bizarre, unsettling. I was listening to a roomful of 1975, a reed player, his guitarist, drummer, bassist, his two trumpets, all back there in some New York recording studio, a few years before Stitt himself had died of a heart attack. "The Way We Were," "Funky Interlude," "Never Can Say Goodbye." I tried believing it was music, but in my state it wasn't, just human sounds, recorded ones, barely better than nothing. Also, a shade worse than nothing. Still, I listened. "Too bad Sonny Stitt isn't around any more. Too bad we all . . ."

Too bad? In the context of New Mexico's tremendous space, of the solitude of that canyon, under a sky whose depths sparkled with stars, nobody's living or dying—compared with even silicon grains in the very sandstone I lay on—lasts long enough to have lasted at all, much less "too bad." I heard fellow animals doing peppery Afro-Cuban things with time. It felt weird, dissonant, wasn't really the company I wanted to feel it was.

Maybe the cassette's other side would feel better, a Charlie Byrd album titled *Top Hat*. Battery-fade began distorting Byrd's acoustic guitar to a bass viol. Not good. If the music stopped, that would be the worst sort of omen. In my pack were extra batteries. When they too began to lose energy, I put the tape player aside. Better not to listen than to hear the notes slowly stall, come to a standstill.

Another awareness then stunned me: the JVC player, a favorite possession, wasn't really mine any more. By morning neither it nor my pack, nor my watch, nor my wallet. Nor my boots, nor even my bloody shirt. The body inside them wouldn't be mine.

In imagination he stood over my face. The enormous change in me was invisible to him; he hadn't the slightest recollection of our eyes ever having looked into each other. By the light of midmorning he and his patrolman sidekick were discussing what must've happened. The buddy, an Anglo, pulled my wallet out from under me and was giving it a fast, professional rundown. He slid forth the Colorado driver's license, pinned it under the clip on his board, jotted down its relevant data. He then opened the wallet wide to show its folding money to his dark-haired partner: two twenties, a ten, a few ones. Each drew out a twenty, leaving the rest.

When the dark-haired officer, his chin and jaw freshly shaven, his tan shirt still morning-fresh, bent to pick up the tape player, I could hear his leather gear creak. Hefting the mechanism, he turned it over in his hands, appraising.

His pal's shrug said, "You want it, it's yours."

The other nodded, stuffing the player in his pocket, the earphones inside his shirt. "Yeah," he said, "it's a good one. You can tell just by the feel."

That theft infuriated me. Yet I still liked him. He might as well take it.

My fantasy made no sense. And there he was, the New Mexican cop who'd given me directions way back on the Jemez Reservation. He had tested my right thigh with the toe of his shoe, while the other presided over my face, his own features blocked from view by the clipboard. He was filling in blanks on his report: where found, when found, how found. What found with. But of course state troopers aren't rangers. They never get more than a hundred yards from their patrol cars. My Navajo/Pueblo cop wouldn't be out footing it along trails. That didn't stop me imagining his shoe nudging my body.

My terminal mirage also included ants, desert ravens. Liking an Indian cop hadn't altered my preference: I'd rather be nibbled away by more straightforward animals than my own kind, however small and swarming. Even turkey vultures would be some consolation.

It was then I had decided that if I were going to die I'd at least die looking up at those stars. Clear night, the galaxy in full bloom, no town glow to kill it. And the stars, as usual, "unreal"; yet familiar and fresh, the undiminished constellations of once-upon-a-time. Out of their fire-wealth I made one star mine, no idea of its name, just a bright one; not Altair certainly, not Vega, just one more incandescence among our galaxy's 200 billion suns, among the estimated 100 billion *major* galaxies. All that out there; me, here. Except, where's "here"? Lifelong, it had been the single thing I most wanted to know.

Maybe the thing I'd been truest to was that curiosity. From early boyhood, stars had fascinated me. The telescope I had pieced together of magnifying glass, eyeglass lens, cardboard tubing and black friction tape hadn't been the success of boy geniuses in movies. It had taught me, by way of rainbowing the moon, only that chromatic aberration—avoidable with better lenses—has a beauty of its own. Summer stars had been my furthest-out boyhood adventure. Even hurt and shivering, therefore, I had been able to realize my good luck: What better place than here in Chaco Canyon, among so many thousand Anasazi? The nearness of their own various deaths seemed company worth having. Though I knew they were fossil dust, I felt myself inside what was left of their passage. And what better way to go than looking at stars I had wondered at and loved all my life? "No better way, no better time, no better place. So be it." And that had been my breakthrough.

I no longer felt sorry for myself. I was alone, yes; but that's how dying gets done. I had stopped wallowing in self-pity. This thing would have to be gone through sooner or later. Conditions *then*—would they be more to my liking? Surely not. To die alone, surrounded by Southwestern space, under stars . . . no, what lay down the road wasn't likely to improve on that. I was glad I had collected all those sunrises. Each had been a sort of unrepeatable virtue no life could embody or imitate, beyond watching it happen.

Having learned I could face my extinction without freaking out, I had relaxed my deepest conviction enough to utter a sort of testimony: "Lord of the center and the edge, of the magpie, the springtail, the neuron, the spruce cone, I'm grateful for my life. I'm glad I had it. I was a lucky man."

Had I felt I owed creation some final assent? Obviously, the cosmos doesn't give a damn. But I must've felt, "We're humans, we ought to say *some*thing." It had seemed fitting. Life and consciousness being so exceedingly rare in this cosmos, the least I could do was to acknowledge having been lent them. I knew there was nobody not equally mortal out there. I spoke to it anyway.

But "Lord" had felt vaguely disloyal, sinful. "Lord" isn't a person. Creation doesn't "see," doesn't "hear," doesn't "know." Radiant, inexhaustible, it makes and unmakes; raises up, crushes flat. Woos into existence, then splats. Endless smithereens. Doesn't "care," doesn't "love." Is. Should I therefore have said simply, "Dear Is"? No, not "dear." Is.

If at the time I had felt deeply moved, it was *not* because I verged on "meeting my maker." I verged on a black vacuum. So were my words a small ceremony for my own disappearance? No, they really had been for whatever underlies the design that the whole shebang makes and floats on, or within. Because English lacks a pronoun for which no antecedent is conceivable, "Lord" was the name I had found myself saying. That archaic choice notwithstanding, I had said what I meant.

No longer panicked, I began to feel hope enough to be superstitious about losing the particular star I had made "mine." As Earth turned me toward morning, the cliff overhead had been about to occlude it. I couldn't let it happen. My solution: give that star leave to go, as if its disappearance had my permission; then quickly choose another till it too neared the cliff rim—whereupon I had given it leave, had again chosen, and so forth. Any straw seemed worth grasping toward. As for life, I hadn't known I loved it so hugely, frantically.

Despite desert chill and shivering uncontrollably for long periods, despite headache, bashed up left side, clotted scalp, bitten tongue, I began to take heart a little. Without my noticing, blurred stars had resolved themselves from so many twins to sharp points. Similarly, my heart rate had slowed, the spasms had lessened so gradually I can't say when the last one occurred. I do remember, however, that when it seemed dawn might happen again, my mind had already grown suspicious of its own fears. How could a dying man think so busily about so many sorts of things? I had simply fallen and lacerated my scalp, not broken my skull. Dizziness and nausea were the effects of severe concussion.

As for the muscle spasms, my chronic back trouble might've been thrown into fast forward by the jolting impact of the fall. Any number of lower-spine, pinched-nerve possibilities could have triggered them.

Dawn was too much consolation to entertain more than skeptically—like hardly daring to believe bad weather is finally beginning to lift. When light seemed less than an hour away, I had sat up every now and again without feeling woozy, except for my imagination vaguely mimicking the nausea I was afraid of. Come sunrise, downclimbing might not be so impossible. For the first time I stopped fighting to stay conscious. Till then I seem to have thought death might come if I weren't looking. I fell asleep, neither well nor deeply, and, a half-hour before dawn woke to the barking of coyotes. And to cries of piñon jays. Exhausted, I welcomed daybreak but without joy. Instead I felt dirtied, humiliated by my fear, glad only to be rid of it; like a dog soldier hearing his relief approach after a miserable stint of guard duty.

Retrospect suggests that at Chaco my personal being must have actually touched something like the nothingness we have a word for, but no meaning. Though I don't understand it now, I *thought* I did then. My fear at touching it wasn't physical. Somehow it was worse, far worse than anything that can happen to one's body, which, paradoxically, is our sole receptor for that sort of intuition.

Receptor? No, more. One's body is *it*. At Chaco I had seen that my own should have been better cherished, not treated like a draft animal. So my body/mind had resolved I should take better care of it, out of gratitude for years of good service.

Within three days, however, after minor stitchwork in the emergency room at Farmington, New Mexico, that night's immediacy had already begun to wane. Old turns of mind soon crawled out from their hiding places. Another resolve had been, if I survived, to behave wisely. Having seen what I had seen, henceforth I could not help living with the clarity of a sage, ever after. But that too gradually hazed over. Like hundred-mile-distant ridgelines, my intended reforms grew to be only occasionally visible, and then only if I shaded my eyes and squinted far into my past—as if trying to actually live by what I had seen might not be wise, or for me anyhow, even possible.

At the time, there had been something about both Sonny Stitt's tenor sax and the Charlie Byrd pieces which had felt dangerous, eerie. It puzzles me therefore that to this day I can bear listening to that same cassette almost indifferently. Why haven't I chucked it? Because its music retains a doubleness I want never to lose? Just as the scar from a considerable gash in my scalp isn't visible, just as hair shaved away the better to suture the wound has now regrown, so too has the living tissue of my human complacency regenerated. Once more I'm encoded to fear dying and to sense I never will.

Yet an otherwise banal moment may all at once suffuse me with strangeness when I realize: "This is a day I didn't think I'd have." All the days since have been those. At any odd moment, a room's most prosaic object—a terra-cotta pot, for example—may say: "This light from red clay is light you might not have been around for."

If Chaco gave me that, it also gave me the dark twin to go with it: "nothing matters." In a healthy sense, the latter realization doesn't cancel its sibling. Their two ways of looking differently at the same thing may amount to no more than seeing the evanescence of what's cherishable—except that to leave one's own body out of what went into its deepest knowledge yields a wisdom thin as paper. It takes the actual, that full flood of bodily terror, long continued, to widen the pupil of one's inner eye. Once it has, we forget—though never completely, and rarely for long. Out of the trivial chaos of an afternoon, rain on a manhole cover may suddenly give back the sweetness of existing.

The glossy black tip on a magpie's wingfeather can do it. Checking the body for deer ticks can suddenly bathe one's calves and thighs with gratitude. Iridescence in sun-stricken paint on old cars. Sweetness of the plainest, most everyday faces. Richness of one's boredoms, their motions and textures. Of a bank teller's eyes that, for a half-second, look into mine with normal and therefore intricate brilliance.

Swiss Wilderness

A humble couple from an erstwhile mining town in the Rockies—could such as they find happiness as guests at Villa Serbelloni? Anne and I believed we could.

Not least of what we quickly relished there were the little all-but-invisible touches; the adroit half-turn of wrist, for example, with which—as they refilled our wine glasses—uniformed waiters named Sergio, Natale, Giovanni, and Vittorio kept even one droplet from the table's immaculate linens. But within such an opulent villa's sixty-acre dream of formal and informal gardens, long dinners, witty talk, Renaissance decor, any Coloradan's self-image might begin to blur.

Alain Blayac had laughed. We'd been talking about Chamonix—a French mountain town I can't stand but which he adores. Though a literary scholar, Blayac goes in for macho stuff. He hunts, he climbs. The casually unbuttoned upper half of his shirt offers glimpses of a tanned, hairy chest set off by the obligatory gold chain and medallion. Apropos of Chamonix's namesake animal I had asked, "Are many chamois left in the mountains around there?"

For the benefit of my regret, he laughed maliciously. "Ah, no! None. We have shot them." I asked about bears. He laughed again. "We killed them as well, long ago." Insofar as his laughter expressed a low tolerance for American sentimentality, it seemed understandable. I too cringe from people who wear save-the-whales pieties like a halo. Yet his French cynicism struck me. When it came to the extermination

of bears, Blayac's only chagrin was that France had none left for him
to shoot.

Across a broad river valley from the curiously named Swiss town
of S-Chanf I leave my rental car at the mandatory spot, and through
May forest half tame, half wild, leg it uptrail toward the border of the
Parc Naziunal, still a mile or more from the paved trailhead. Amid conifer slopes I don't at once notice tameness. Instead, I splash along in
soggy weather, amused by day-glo avalanche warnings in four languages, thankful for good rain gear, and boots recently siliconed.
Pleased with European drizzle after so many years in our arid Colorado,
I find omniwetness fascinating.

In Switzerland, the last bear was shot on September 1, 1904. At a
spot, as it happens, right around here. It's not that I am searching out
some blood-tainted handsbreadth of alp. It's just that, on leaving Italy,
Anne and I have come north to visit the Parc Naziunal, within whose
present confines—but a decade before they became the wildlife sanctu-
ary they are today—that last bear was colonized by bullets.

The Parc Naziunal, as it's called in Romansch, was inspired by but
explicitly *not* modeled on our American example. Sixty-five square
miles may seem dinky compared to Yellowstone's nearly thirty-five
hundred, yet considering that our national parks add up to only a bit
more than half of one percent of our land, those sixty-five square miles
make the Parc Naziunal proportionately comparable: a half percent of
all Switzerland. Not bad. What did it matter that the Swiss have only
one, or that its terrain isn't state-owned but *leased?* By the time they got
round to it—a mere decade after the ultimate bear was blown away—
that's how it had to be: rented or nothing. Which is how it still is, every
square meter leased, long-range, through public and private funding.

Rented, leased, or what-have-you, the ecology here is so new to me
that my glances through rainy mist seem half to create what they dwell
on. Larch trees grow in North America, but never near me, so at last to
walk among thousands of them is an occasion. No other conifer is deciduous, nor would even larches be, had they been native to mountain
soils, where meager nutrients make growing a fresh set of needles every
year expensive. Like remnants of a losing tribe, they were once a tree of
the plains, till competition from other species forced them higher and
higher, and finally into mountains. Their green needles, markedly
lighter in hue than the green-blue of other conifers, turn color in fall to

an ambered gold, but my ascent takes me past larches whose May needles, like tiny asterisks, have only begun to leaf out.

Up close, mosses of a lush and emerald wetness make the drenched mountainside feel buxom, upholstered. Yellow-green mosses billow near the roots of fir. They pedestal the thick boles of larches in ways I've not walked among before; nor have I ever seen lichen completely cover living tree boughs. A ghostly silver, this species hangs like hoar frost on larch limbs, setting off their rain-blackened bark with its pale encrustings. Only after an uphill half hour of ambling and pausing, however, do I notice what isn't anywhere.

Not a single dead tree on the ground. None. Nor even trees half toppled. No standing dead. My years in American wilderness forests where each day is ancient make that feel very strange.

Then the instant I step from private land into the Parc Naziunal, the trail changes character. Its mud is now laced with larch needles the color of rust; and, like friends from home, fallen trees immediately appear. For number and size they can't equal the blown-down and windfallen timber in, say, our Indian Peaks wilderness of Colorado, because—given its beginning in 1914—the Parc Naziunal isn't yet a hundred years old. Prior to 1914, every dead tree here had become "useful" the moment it hit the ground.

In Colorado's gold rush days, many a mine swallowed a forest. Even today more than one stump-stubbled mountainside recalls a West when the big idea was to "get and get out." Though such greed now euphemizes itself by speaking of "an extractive economy," the West, like the world, still includes men eager to kill beautiful animals they're seeing alive for the first time; and to fell Douglas fir older than Milan's cathedral.

As for Europe, my Mozartian associations may flow into and out of the name "Salzburg," but in my great-grandfather's time, much Swiss forestation had flowed with the Inn River clean out of Switzerland—for timbering salt mines of the Tyrol. Thus from its inception the Parc Naziunal lacked old growth because its trees of longest standing had already been literally sold down the river. Which helps explain why none of the fallen trees I come across are either very big or beautifully rotten.

Nonetheless, middling as they are, I bless every moldering trunk for helping to return living trees to the fullness of their being, and me to mine; which is to say I now feel myself at last in almost a forest. At the same time I smile to think how uneasy those same decaying trunks must make Swiss visitors to the Parc Naziunal. In this nation of carpenters, carvers, cabinet makers, woodworkers, and of woodburning stoves, any fallen tree allowed to rot, just rot, must look wasteful, sinfully.

So upwards I find myself hiking, along a trail called the Höhenweg, happy in a rain of late May; a fine, all-morning rain that sizzles on my parka hood as I head higher in the Val Trupchun. Maybe to see a chamois, who can say? Maybe even a steinbok, also known as the ibex, whose long, curving horns make it unmistakable. But, of course, never a bear.

Back in Italy, Villa Serbelloni's private "forest," overlooking Lake Como, had been a civilized joy to stroll within. Often I walked for two hours there, uphill and down, under a dithering canopy of May's greenest leaves and the mewing of gulls, not once retracing my steps along its quiet paths; wide, easy, cone-strewn. The forest effect, so casually manicured, had seemed almost natural. Great beech trunks rose ninety feet without effort, each bole a smooth yet muscular rectitude, bearing branches that floated forth their foliage as if weightlessly, like green levitations. The umbrella pines had risen just as high, maybe higher; yet on the ground underneath there was no scruff of dead twigs such as litter our woodlands of ponderosa pines back home. No windfallen trees. No rotting logs. No shattered branches. Each turn of the path set off a picturesque grove, as if brushed onto canvas by Corot. Even the romantic grottoes and caverns, man-made, had welcomed me into plausible rusticities.

Where not one crippled tree marred the graceful verticalities with birth defects, or hints of mortality, and where every massive trunk, every beech sapling grew exemplarily well, my admiration had deferred asking, "Without death how can a forest live?" Which is as much as to ask, "When is a forest a garden? Indeed, when is it an artifact?"

"So what if it isn't 'natural'?" I had scolded myself. "Would you have one twig of it otherwise?"

That final Swiss bear had come to live in my head, emerging from his mindcave whenever, in the Bernese Oberland for example, I noticed a hotel boasting a handsomely savage black bear on its scutcheon. In the lake town of Thun, ursine images sanction every other hotel. Praising what's lost makes the remembrance even dearer, so the Swiss now pay homage to shot wildlife with pelts, antlered heads, bear-sim-ulacrums hung above ski shops, inside or outside any tavern; just as within or without town halls I'd found sheetmetal bears in brass glaring down at me, frescoed bears, bears sculpted of granite. Fronting the Bären restaurant at Trubschachen, for instance. From dozens of win-dowsill boxes red geraniums cascaded right and left, while—over the door—a life-sized bear welcomed me with jaws carved into more than a hint of a smile.

"In the Upper or Lower Engadine," I had asked myself, "is there a single Swiss village without its teddy?" I haven't visited all of them; pos-sibly there is. One. Two is not possible.

Certainly Switzerland's capital, Berne—whose very name refers to the creatures—hasn't for a moment lost sight of them. Not only do its civic buildings fly heraldic bears on the canton's official flags. Not only do its various scutcheons repeat the animal ubiquitously. Berne's loft-iest fountain rises from a base circled by marching bears. Armed with muskets, dressed in Renaissance garb of days when such animals shared the environment with that town's first inhabitants and defenders, they hint that ursine courage comes with the territory.

Naturally enough, Berne's souvenir shops offer bears in every man-ner of craft: whittled, cast, welded, embroidered, enameled, water col-ored, incised, sculpted, or stuffed. As further reminder of its most gloriously bygone animal, the city maintains a *bärengraben* where young and old can enjoy live examples of their town's totemic creature; and for enticing antics from this large open-air bear pit—stocked with *Ursus arctos* as it happens—people can buy a small, bear-healthful cor-nucopia of *barfuten*. On days I tossed them down to a half dozen com-ically posturing bears, *barfuten* had been carrots.

"What do I see here in five hundred years?" Alice Goldstein had repeated, as if trying to *will* her eyebeams through Lake Como's agree-able evening haze, and beyond, into the mists of futurity. Not only had Alice been one of the most radiantly friendly persons we had relished being among at the villa; she was highly qualified to hazard an answer.

We two had been sharing a teak bench overlooking the lake, where sun, the same sun, glinting off those same wind-warps on its waters had once attracted ancient Greeks and Romans to its incomparable setting. Panoramas that long ago dictated the siting and layout of summer homes built by the wealthier subjects of emperors like Nerva and Trajan had survived, even though the villas themselves had sunk back into earth. Two thousand years have left Lake Como's mountain profiles unchanged, despite shorelines that have since filled with vacation hotels and palatial second homes for Italy's affluent few, who are many.

Alice and I had felt our evening complicated by the realization that both Plinys, Elder and Younger, uncle and nephew, had once known by heart the lake's same twilight reflections, the same forested mountainsides rising steeply above us. Not only had those Roman celebrities been born in Como—little more than two hours south by lake boat—but Pliny the Younger had built and occupied a pleasure villa on precisely the site where Villa Serbelloni now stood. Our evening twilight there was both ancient and modern, which is to say contemporaneous, because, in the fusion of now and to come, its ancients and moderns were us.

In fact, earlier that afternoon I had strolled for hours reimagining Lake Como exactly as those imperial-age Romans had seen it. The problem had been easy as subtraction. Take away almost all buildings crowding the shoreline. Erase the highest up farmhouses, those light flecks of stonework set off by green mountainsides. Take the twelve-foot-tall but almost invisible cross off a subpeak of Monte Tremezzo, opposite. Let weed overrun the auto routes. Fill in the train tunnels. Diminish both the speed of the lake boats, and their numbers. Think sails. Behold! Lake Como again perfectly Roman—or so I imagined.

My next trick came up against the limits of possibility: "How would these same shores, their villages, their forested mountainsides, look two thousand years in the future?"

That had stumped me. Peering backward, we've some idea. After all, Roman history is massively documented. But the future two thousand years hence? Any guess would be sci-fi. So I downsized to five hundred. Equally impossible, of course. Star Trek stuff. Nonetheless, because Alice and her husband Sidney are professional demographers, distinguished ones from Brown University, with an international reputation in population studies, I had thought, "Why not at least *ask* them?" Isn't one aim of demography to guess how many may be coming to dinner?

So I had indeed posed that question to Alice. "What do I see?" she had repeated. "Either a lot more or a lot less."

Epigrammatically shrewd, that. Five centuries down the road technology will either have permitted global growth, Lake Como included,

or the whole thing will have crashed. Because we had been sharing evening drinks on the same terrace, I had then asked Alice's husband and
professional partner, "What do you think, Sidney? What's the prospect?
Is Paul Ehrlich's 'population bomb' real?" After all, however unworthy
one might feel, the wine we'd been sipping, the villa, its gardens and
sixty-acre grounds, its palatial decor, had been made available by the
Rockefeller Foundation for the posing of just such questions.

Given Sidney's background, I was thus turning to somebody who
should know. Not only are the Goldsteins demographers; they have
spent decades studying Asian trends, especially in China, whose 250
million *unemployed* equal our entire U.S. population. A friendly, quiet
man who never dramatizes, Sidney had said, "I looked at updates of the
evidence not long ago. I'm afraid I have to come down on the 'real' side.
The numbers may be worse than we thought." He didn't elaborate, nor
did he need to—beyond adding, "You know, in China, 'one percent
growth' means 10 million more people."

That little throwaway fact of Sidney's haunted me for days. As if
the fuse on a population bomb were already shorter than the skin of our
teeth is thin. But we hear such warnings, then shrug. We let catastrophe
happen. Only when it happens does catastrophe get our attention.

Unsurprisingly, after Europe's he-men had pumped slugs into the
last steinbok alive in Switzerland, that country took thought. "What's
to be said," the Swiss national conscience began asking itself, "of a people who permit the *extermination* of their own national animals?" Lest
anyone say it, the steinbok, at least, was "reintroduced."

Indeed, it has been. In an alpine meadow opposite me on the rainy
Höhenweg trail, and across a roaring stream milky with glacial silt, my
binoculars pick out no fewer than thirty-one steinboks! Some hundred
meters upslope from me they nibble away at alpine turf, sharing their
May meadow with several chamois. A closer view would be nice, except that in the Parc Naziunal to leave the trail *ist streng verboten*, and
when it comes to insisting that a rule is a rule, the Swiss don't mess
around. The park's "rangers"—and I was chatting with one just minutes ago in Italian—can fine you on the spot. Frequent reminders in
German and Romansch say: VERLASSEN DES WEGES IST VERBOTEN / ID ES
SCUMANDA DA BANDUNAR LA SENDA. "Leaving the trail is forbidden."

Forbidden? To an American that admonition had at first seemed
quaintly absurd—as if the Swiss, imitating Yellowstone, had bungled

and lost an important part in translation. But of course I was overlooking Europe's people density. As far as the Swiss are concerned, we showed them how, and how not to. Explicitly unlike ours, the Parc Naziunal puts recreation a distant second to flora and fauna. Recreation has been massively provided for elsewhere.

After all, a nation proud of its 1,800 ski lifts has already gone some way toward trading its evergreens for steel pylons. Not only trees. Swiss ski runs often descend slopes "corrected" by bulldozer. At Davos, for instance, even the once-wild peaks. High over town they still loom, but have been taught better behavior through the disfiguring use of snow fences, dozens per summit.

Thus, even if the Naziunal's terrain has been set aside, nominally at least, "for scientific purposes," science in this case may be mere pretext. Deep in their collective psyche, the Swiss may actually have felt a primeval qualm. Had they feared some vague reprisal from their old mountain spirits and bear-gods, the ones their forefathers had invoked before Christianity, long ages before Romulus slew Remus? Had they feared those bear-gods would not forever be mocked?

If the opposite of forestation is a ski lift, and it is, Switzerland may really have said, "This last, least space must be held. Must be held for nature to do as she chooses. Not we but she will decide. For as long as forever is. Untouchably." Yes. If no space is kept sacred, where is a people to keep its lost soul? Where on earth can we go to regret those days when we had one?

For the Swiss, that has to be here, where trailhead notices greet visitors with more "shalt nots" than even Moses brought down from Mount Sinai—like a forefinger poked repeatedly into the chest. Yet with a few exceptions our American parks forbid the same things. It's those exceptions. Under pressure from population densities matching Europe's, will similar areas in the United States have to be put off limits? No leaving the trail? No camping? No skiing? No solo juveniles? No dogs, leashed or otherwise. Otherwise, no wilderness?

Also, if biologists have it right, no further evolution. Not for large vertebrate mammals. Without space abounding, space untrampled by humans, space free of hunters with gun or camera, spaces free of well-meaning folks—meaning people like me—just wanting to *see* them, large vertebrate mammals can't evolve. We've known for long that our human way-of-being, by quenching thousands of species, has reversed evolution's direction, which *had* been toward ever greater diversity. But evolution squelched, ended entirely? "Devolution" does take a while to sink in. Meanwhile the planet loses forest at an acre per second.

Prior to our heading out of Italy for the Swiss Alps, week had followed week on Lake Como with every conceivable amenity. Its setting had been from the first enthralling, literally. Anne and I had been given rooms whose views . . . but no. It's best not to dwell on bliss retrospectively. Suffice it to say that we'd been there a full six days before I could pass our tall and generous windows. Any glance out over the lake surrounded by mountain abruptions had transfixed me, as if a hypnotist had said, "Freeze!" Onstage, his puzzled victims want to move and can't. I couldn't move either, but didn't want to. Had stood gaping. At the center of satisfaction, desire disappears. So do we. That is, if what we were seeing was real—and I could *see* it was—I couldn't really be there. So that first week had been weightless, free-floating.

As time passed a different puzzlement had crossed my mind ever so briefly, almost furtively. I would find myself daydreaming of Utah, New Mexico, or perhaps Arizona. Flashes only. But in their implication, traitorous, ungrateful. How could I have dreamed of being anywhere other than there where—till our actual arrival—I'd never dreamed I could be?

As for missing Colorado's mountains, the summits immediately around us had made that absurd. The Rockies are, yes, higher above sea level, but these mountains rose far higher overhead than all but a very few peaks in the West. "Maybe it's this sea level altitude," I had told myself, "the lake haze." Or maybe the soft skies, their slow, all but motionless weather. Whose moisture I welcomed, after years in subdesert Boulder.

"Well, then, perhaps it's these hillsides spattered with buildings, the towns strung and clustered along the shorelines." In theory, yes, I *ought* to have preferred Lake Como untouched. Fact is, however, the houses and lake boats had given scale, had made the shores more agreeable, the mountainsides even grander. As had church bells floating across the water from Menaggio, Cadenabbia. Pale yellow houses, houses of rooster red. Pinks and hot umbers and burnt Sienas in roof tiles. The occasional maverick façade in moon blue. Those had met the eye as more than just tolerable. I had liked them well, so help me. Hadn't they added rather than detracted? Of course they had. To me, bumpkin, it was a waking dream. Only a color-blind grump could've felt otherwise. Or Italians who'd known Lake Como before the postwar building boom? Which I had not. Instead that postwar scene had been my *only* Lake Como—just as, a half-century from now, a grossly over-populated Durango or a high-rise Estes Park are the only ones posterity will ever know. Adios, Colorado.

So when I, *as somebody else's posterity*, had stood enjoying views from the villa's promontory, I had gazed across the lake at the town of Varenna and felt, "How Italian! A painting." As it all was. Each village, "poetic." The whole place like that, all either "magnificently scenic" or "picturesque" or "romantic."

But despite the densely forested slopes, the towering cliffs, the sum-mits higher above their towns than any in the U.S., and by far; despite my hiking all day on nearby Monte Tremezzo and meeting only two other hikers; despite the broken limestone of its mule trails being rugged as any trail up Gray's Peak, say, in the Rockies; despite the lovely buttercups, crocuses, Bavarian gentians I'd seen along my climb up Monte Tremezzo; despite dozens of ways you can get killed on any mountain around there . . . Euronature isn't nature anymore.

Odd to think that our "conquests" have exiled us from our own planet. Odder yet when we realize that, in our evolving, it was what wasn't human that humanized us. Now, helpless against our own locust-plague populations and power, Earth's very weakness threatens our strength. Nor does the paradox of reversal end there.

Our separation from nature has become our connection to it. After that last Swiss bear was shot, the mountains he was killed among be-came a national park. In it, his kind would now be safe, if there were any. Old-growth trees, safe too. Except, does all Europe have even *one* left? I doubt it.

Oh, in far less than five hundred years our species may contrive various housebroken utopias: their creatures genetically engineered, flora hybridized, local ocean floors farmed, air and sea currents har-nessed, their virulent bacteria rehabilitated—all of which may pour into posterity's lap every conceivable advantage. Except one. When science has laundered their eventual bloodstreams beyond recognition, won't those rearranged psyches, however bizarre *we* might consider them, consider themselves and their world improvements?

Atop a subpeak of Monte Tremezzo, nicknamed "Crocione" for its tall but eroding cross of reinforced concrete, I had stood looking 4,600 feet down on the baked clay house tops of Cadenabbia, surprised by

how clearly I'd heard its delivery trucks and whizzing Fiats honk or suddenly brake. The peevish whine of motorbikes. Scything arrivals of the
hydrofoil, riding its underwater wing. The affable "too-o-t" puffing up
from the steam whistles of ferry boats—all of it had been clearly audible. I'd never climbed a mountain you could hear traffic from.

Westward I had looked down on clustered "development" strung
along the busy road to Lugano, an hour's drive from Menaggio, across
the Italian/Swiss border. There the northeasterly horizon was snow
peaked, rugged as any Coloradan could wish. So what had been my
problem?

It was, to use a grammatical analogy, that nature's speaking had
long ago been shifted from active to passive voice. It still spoke, but as
setting, as backdrop. "Nature." Its very name, thus set off and apart,
called for a condescension similar to quotation marks. Great destinal
powers had either become "scenic," or dumb bulk that nothing as yet
had been done with. The picturesque villages all those thousands of feet
below had indeed charmed me—their pastel walls, straw yellow or
rouge, their ruddy tiles. But the ant-race of buses, manic cars, the
motorbike blat, the vast lake's graceful flow of big boats and little ones
weaving their mazework of wakes, the forty sails of vacationers whose
regatta I had surveyed with binoculars up near the lake's hazy, northerly end toward Colico and Gera Lario—all were presence, human presence. Bulk loomed, mountainously; still, our presence dominated.
Every manner of flood, fire, rock slide, and storm would go on taking
lives; even so, the struggle with nature was over. We humans had won.

Idyllic in April and May, by high summer—we'd been told—the
lake becomes impossible. Every boat owner within a day's drive wants
to carve up its waters. The inboard and outboard blat of its August
weekends motorize the air, creating decibel levels said to frazzle the
nerves. Then too, young windsurfers alone can turn the lake's southern
expanse into an extravanganza of nylon and fiberglass. Being young,
they don't know any other Lake Como. But one mustn't exaggerate.
Even with the postwar boom in people and tourism, the lake shores are
remarkably free of ballyhoo, billboards, neon.

All the same, "nature" there does as it's told. The "densely forested" mountainsides lack conifers and lack old growth. Fires are set to
kill conifer seedlings lest they crowd out the understory browse which
goats, sheep, and cows now wander nibbling among. Well and good.
Our species isn't yet ready to turn vegetarian, nor must trees be of great
antiquity to give a thirsty hiker welcome shade. My stride has many a

day been lightened on a steep European trail by the music of goat bells, cow bells. A herd of Swiss browns, for instance. I love their out-of-sync tinkling—like a marimba band that can't agree on the beat.

Though the teeming human outlay below me had been—in terms of sheer mass—"outwhelmed" by alpine rugosities and peaks, even so slight a reminder as the pontoon plane flying tourists to and fro, day long, low over the lake had made unavoidable the fact of human dominance. Instead of nature tolerating *us*, our species now gives it permission. From my lookout atop that Italian summit I couldn't have helped seeing Colorado's populous future. But in that future, what's missing, however "indispensable," will, once dispensed with, never be missed.

We mustn't kid ourselves. When wilderness was all there was, there wasn't any. Our glances that way are necessarily retrospective. Created by its own absence, wilderness could only have come into existence by disappearing. In a technological century, there is no "away." The goddess *Natura*, the nature of ancient times, "great creating nature," the nature of fateful powers unopposable . . . is beaten, defeated. Technology has it jumping through hoops. We got what we wanted. Real wilderness can be seen only in the rearview mirror; our nostalgia for what in the future nobody's going to have.

Nine-thirty P.M. The May twilight is cloudless, but chilly. For spending a couple of nights deep in the heart of Swiss wilds, Anne and I have chosen a spot called Il Fuorn, which sits exactly high as our house back in Colorado, 5,600 feet above sea level. Because "It is forbidden to camp or spend the night in any way, also on parking lots," we're "camping out" inside: Hotel Parc Naziunal Il Fuorn.

To our north, conifered ridgelines—with snow Alps beyond: Piz Zuort, Piz Minger, Piz Sampuoir, Piz Murters, as they're called in Romansch. Above and beyond them, and everything, the evening's earliest stars shine auspiciously clear. The darkening air is too crisp for mosquitoes, so we open both windows wide for enjoying their constellations from under our goosedown *duvets*. Such, in the heart of those sixty-five square miles, are the wilderness rigors.

Having climbed Munt la Schera that afternoon, I brought down from its flat summit an appetite equal to the hotel's evening meal: bean soup, pumpernickel, the delicious house wine, Swiss-grown, the big portions of beef fillet, the browned potatoes and carrots, and the chocolate sundae—with, suitably, its Matterhorn of whipped cream. Our

Swiss high country meal included, too, a Portuguese waiter teaching us Portugal's word for "fox," as, through the dining room's glass walls, we watched a lone fox crossing the meadow right outside. There, each evening of our stay, a herd of red deer has, by ones and twos, seeped down from the forest of lodgepole pines to browse on the twilight meadow's lush grasses. "Just like back home," Anne remarked.

The chamois wasn't. From forelegs that knelt for better nibbling, it had glanced up toward the trotting fox, stared a moment, then had gone back to its feeding. By the highway along that meadow's edge, cars slowed to a stop as tourists got out—despite the oncoming dusk—to try a snapshot or two, while big sisters or brothers pointed out yearling deer to their littler siblings.

During all this the American Westerner in us tried not to feel smug that our own sons had grown up where deer, black bear, and mountain lions were part of their hometown's mixed feelings: how to make safe from, yet have; how to discourage, not quell.

To drive from the Parc Naziunal through Zernez, then Zuoz and S-Chanf and St. Moritz, over pass after pass on roundabout, mountainously up-and-down roads to Grindelwald—is to drive from nature's last stand toward the wonderful worst that can happen. Where Swiss wilderness begins at a railway ticket window.

More than just nature tamed, Grindelwald's world of glacier-shagged peaks is marvelous, appalling. Anyone who cares about mountaineering must go there. For the full effect, however, he must pay $190 to ride eleven highly unusual miles! Such are the rigors.

So, wanting two seats (second class) on the cog-rail train that winds upward to the celebrated Jungfraujoch, Anne and I fork over two hundred Swiss francs and climb aboard. The U.S. dollar may someday go further, but that'll be in our next lives at the soonest. Meanwhile this morning's weather around Grindelwald is a sparkling contrast to our visit years earlier, in whiteout. Never before has Switzerland seen fit to give us sunny skies so pristine and cloudless.

From the Grindelwald station we ride 3,400 feet higher to a pass called Kleine Scheidegg. It's early June, with muddy heaps of leftover snow still melting near the big, blocky, hyper-conspicuous hotel, ugly as its surroundings are magnificent; but nonetheless a haven for "serious" climbers who dare attempt the famed Eigernordwand.

Our Rockies offer nothing remotely like its vertical difference: the Eiger's thirteen-thousand-foot summit looks ten thousand feet *down* on

Grindelwald; like a shape risen from the darkest past of creation. In fact, the English for its name is "ogre." Thus the Eiger's north face feels so awesome, so savage, so holy that none but the Swiss would have blasted and drilled a railway through it. That upwardly curving route through the mountain's innards is proof: if a hotel or restaurant can be built on one or another Swiss height, it probably will be, unless—even more probably—it already has. No matter how many words Eskimos use or don't use for "snow," the Swiss must have plenty of ways to say "engineering." And if they lack ways to say "sacrilege," it's that they simply don't grasp the concept. Or long ago decided, "no such thing." An official tourist brochure, the *Jungfrau Magazin*, helps foreigners digest this by way of a food simile: "The Swiss treat their mountains like their famous cheese, the Emmental; they put holes in them."

Up from Kleine Scheidegg's tundra pass, our train climbs, out of its switchyard where three separate train lines keep the rails clacking, and where the newly opened SPORTS BAZAAR sits beside the newly opened RESTAURANT EIGERNORDWAND, just below the improved SESSELBAHN. Then somebody turns off the sky, and we're enstoned. Inches from my face, rough rock blurs past our windows. We're more than encrypted. Within those mega-million years of a planet's oceanic and calcareous past, we've become lively fossils immured by sedimentation called the Eiger. Because there's nothing to see, the intercom wafts elevator music into our carriage, interrupting it for tour facts in German, Japanese, French, Italian and English.

Equally bizarre, at several stations *inside* that mountain, we creep past illuminated ads for Patek watches, Rolex and Omega—as if it were the London underground—then unload, moblike, with everybody else to peer through glass walls set high in the face of that famous Eigernordwand's snow and rock. While I stare seven thousand feet down on Grindelwald's summer-green valley, dozens and dozens of climbers who had been killed or frozen by the Eiger's north face gaze down alongside me. The corpse of one young climber had, years back, dangled unreachably within less than a rope's length of the gallery where Anne and I were standing. Then that rope had been cut from above, allowing his now famous cadaver to fall. Comfy, entunneled, I snap a photograph of glacial snow just the other side of the glass.

At the Jungfraujoch proper, a multifloor complex caters to every touristic whim, both within and without the mountain. Punctual trains disgorge and absorb great surging loads of sightseers all day long,

so wilderness rigors there include my waiting briefly in line at the official "Jungfraujoch Post Office" to buy stamps for our cards.

Further rigors: automatic glass doors opening onto the crisp, high-
altitude air of terraces—where we are instantly blinded. Without
cloud to mute it, and at 11,334 feet, the morning's June sun fires into our
irises like a flashbulb. Off the Aletch Glacier it bounces into our
squinched eyes as we look down at a stiff river in motionless flow,
streaming south from just below our feet—more miles of ice than I've
seen since Black Rapids Glacier up in Alaska. Sun glares left and right
off baroque snow-billows piled every which way atop the Jungfrau
proper. Sun blazes off similar snows whelming a neighbor peak called
the Monk.

From our terrace, after swapping photo opportunities with fellow
tourists not invariably Japanese, we look down on a near plateau of
glacier where the much-advertised dog sled rides may be had. There too
is the layout of a minuscule ski area, with rental outfits allowing a person to say, back in Osaka or Nîmes, "You're not the only one who has
skied the Jungfraujoch in June!"

Tame nature is a great convenience.

And hugely enjoyable. For the price of a train ride, some of the
most feared peaks in all alpinism will pose close up for your photos.
Such is the Jungfraujoch. With its "Ice Palace," a blue-green catacomb
of rooms and corridors carved into the living glacier, with its "snow
plateau" for sunning and snowballing, with its multilevel cafeterias,
with its souvenir shops, with its video monitors, with its museums of
engineering history and scientific exhibits, there are roadside attractions for every taste. Also, inevitably, the Berghaus Hotel.

Swiss mountains aren't the only ones that Europeans have housebroken. Southwest of where we stand lies the Italian ski town of Cervinia on the southern slopes of the Matterhorn. Eight hundred people
live there year round, but during ski season Cervinia is a polyester and
nylon anthill: beds for sixteen thousand tourists, half a hundred restau-
rants to feed them, and twenty-seven lifts to pull them uphill. Which is
nothing. Whereas a *major* ski resort in Colorado might have ten or
twelve lifts, or—as at Vail—a couple of dozen, skiers further west at
the French resort of L'Alpe d'Huez can choose from no fewer than
eighty-five! There the high-rise condos violate their alpine setting so
aggressively, with such stark-naked venality, that on first sight I could
only laugh and shake my head in disbelief: "People actually *pay* to
come here?"

Aesthetically, France's L'Alpe d'Huez doesn't even try. To an American it can only be a sick joke, a landscape in ruins—but for tens of thousands, a *très chic* aspiration. At the height of ski season the town's sewage system can't treat three-fourths of the waste. *Que faire?* The town's owners, being French, solve that problem by passing it on. They simply pour the untreated sewage downhill for "nature" to deal with. Winters at L'Alpe d'Huez, the big import is money, the big export is *merde*.

Is nature thus tamed what, in less than a century, our Rocky Mountains must come to? The answer may be another question: Can anything stop procreation? No? Then yes. That indeed is what we must come to: mechanized mountains.

In this age of mass tourism, with the lure of mountain terrain now drawing a combined 100 million visitors each year into alpine areas of France, Germany, Italy, Switzerland, Austria, and Yugoslavia, over-development has already produced backlash. Increasingly, therefore, people of the deutschmark, the pound sterling, the franc, the krone, and the yen, are finding the grand expanses of our American West freer and easier. We offer cheap car rentals, cheap rentals on campers. We offer good roads, good motels, good campgrounds. Food of all kinds is a bargain. Compared to Europe our gasoline sells at give-away prices. During my last Bryce Canyon visit, three-fourths of the persons I spoke with on trails were European. Any cursory inspection of the guest register at Navajo National Monument near Tonalea, Arizona, shows that at least a third of its signees are European also.

Increasingly, they and the Japanese flee their own gridlocked mountains, where—compared to the American West—communing with nature can feel like an industrial experience. More pylons than trees? Switzerland already has 1,800 ski lifts and expects to add another two or three hundred in the next couple of decades, whereas Colorado—though five times bigger—hasn't anything like three hundred in the whole state. So, drawn by a U.S. National Park system which for decades has been the envy of visitors whose countries include nothing remotely like it, either for extent or, yes, for *intelligence*, it's not surprising that more and more Europeans and Japanese fly toward a land whose legendary space and nature are still briefly real; nor surprising that America's unique wealth in those things is being loved to death less and less slowly.

It would be fatuous to blame foreign visitors for that overuse. The problem is nature itself; the nature in us. Living things are encoded to propagate their kind. In my own lifetime, males and females in the U.S. have doubled their numbers. But if begetting thrives as it has, can anyone? Will our progeny? Which of us now alive is prepared to deny offspring to others? Which of us would deny that the main learning device of our species—thus far, anyhow—has been letting itself get hit on the skull by an apocalypse? "Any catastrophe that hasn't happened to *me* is not a catastrophe."

Unfortunately, the very adaptability that made us human may be our most lethal gift. Our shifty species is supple enough to call anything "home sweet home," no matter how befouled. Thus adaptability, having made Homo sapiens boss of all vertebrates, may undo us. What blight can't we get used to, project ourselves into, and love? Our progeny will call desolation "nature" if that's all they've known.

Fog and rain are predicted for Grindelwald tomorrow. By then, however, Anne and I will be well on the road toward Montreux—so the prospect of driving off into soupy weather hasn't dampened our final evening. On the contrary, it has made those briefly untypical skies of clear blue the luckier. At our hotel, *Die Alte Post*, on a far warmer terrace than the "snow plateau" up at the Jungfraujoch, we dawdle over a supper *al fresco*, the better to enjoy a superb view of the still unclouded Eiger. Just to the left of its summit—which sundown isn't quite done with—hangs a half moon of early June. And thanks to the mother of invention, our budget, we've discovered how to make mustard sandwiches.

Off a mountain just east of town, the Mettenberg, paragliders keep us entertained, impressing us with their skill at catching thermals. Green chute, yellow chute, red chute—it seems they can dip and soar, then rise sky high again whenever they want. Forty-five floating minutes are as nothing for the yellow chute, though the red chute seems to be more adept in lateral maneuvers. Once upon an olden time, that mountain surely must've been the throne of some primeval spirit; but now, with its Fingstegg cablelift, it's merely a handy launching device, a limestone accessory those paragliders haven't needed to buy.

Adios, Colorado. As their floating colors and blithe levitations sweeten the evening—and they do—I realize that, as usual, the future has already happened.

The Four-Cornered Falcon

 ∽

By mid-April Villa Serbelloni's wisteria vines had already blos-
somed. Acacia trees and passionate clouds of bougainvillea had
reached their peak before May could begin. Unusual. As if the year had
gone straight into summer. Along with other famous gardens of the
Lake Como shore, the villa's sixty-acre grounds had bloomed so unseasonably soon that guests—though wary of such clichés as "greenhouse effect" and "global warming"—couldn't avoid them. Even the
villa's waiters took such phrases for granted. After all, hadn't winter
featured storms whose violence sent meteorologists rummaging among
Europe's oldest weather records? No climate is normal. But maybe
something really had happened, was happening.

Yet for Anne and me, summer in April had made our garden strolls
all the more delightful. I was about to join friends on the east terrace
for an aperitif prior to our one o'clock lunch, when Elena Ongani, a
secretary, brought me a telegram newly arrived: UNSURE YOU RECEIVED
LETTER ON PEREGRINE TRIP JUNE 9 THROUGH 17. NEED CONFIRMATION ASAP
INFO PACKET SENT COLORADO. REPLY FCS EAST ROUTE MONTICELLO UT.

Elena had just closed her office for lunch, but reopened it long
enough to send my answer: RECEIVED PACKET WILL BE THERE STOP ACCEPT
STIPULATED CONDITIONS THANKS.

Though I then returned toward the terrace's conviviality, with its
play of sunlight and shade under towering cypress trees, I felt less like a
man who had crossed the Rubicon than someone who might have been
carried away in its flow. Even as the waiter named Sergio poured my
double tot of tomato juice onto ice, "WILL BE THERE" was giving rise to

second thoughts. Absentmindedly, I reached toward that glass, backed off while he laced it with bitters, leaned forward again, again bided my thirst while he dropped in a lemon twist, once more reached forward as he stirred the mixture. Hardly the aplomb Sergio's deft style seemed to deserve.

No sooner had the recombination of talk clusters brought Anne and me within range of low tones than she asked, "Who was the telegram from?"

"The Utah people needed an answer. I told them yes."

Anne had shaken her head sadly, wisely, hopelessly. After our two-month stay we would arrive back in Boulder on the evening of June 7. But my "WILL BE THERE" had promised I'd show up for a strenuous outing in southeastern Utah, a *long* day's drive away, less than forty-eight hours later. Foreign travel, the way we do it anyhow, can be frazzling. A realist might even say exhausting—and women are realists by nature. Wives doubly so. Anne had given me her look that said, "You're crazy."

Hours after lifting off over Swiss Alps, I drive westward fascinated by Colorado seen afresh from that European perspective. Thus I give no thought to the Four Corners School. Dark Canyon's the attraction— and has been, ever since my friend Kay Cook told me, "It's the best-kept secret in Utah"—but reachable only over rough roads likely to be the death of my thirteen-year-old Volvo wagon. As for peregrine falcons, it suits my purposes that they find canyonland cliff walls an ideal habitat.

Or maybe they don't. Southeastern Utah's population of breeding peregrines is imperfectly known. Numbers, locations of eyries—these the Four Corners School outing hopes to help clarify. To that end we'll be joined by "interagency personnel" working for the State of Utah Wildlife Division; and by U.S. Forest Service people, even one or two Bureau of Land Management types. If it seems like a lot of fuss over a bird, love of nature isn't the only spur. Utah's mining industry is interested to know whether the falcon can be "downlisted" from its twenty-year status as an endangered species, provided enough breeding peregrines are discovered. On the other hand, could I want peregrines to remain truly endangered?

Turning south onto Utah 128, I'm still seeing the seven-league breadth of Grand Valley by way of Europe's fences, villages, walls. The fact that I know absolutely nothing about Janet Ross and her school has barely entered my thought. With the naiveté of which Brooklyn Bridge buyers are made, I've assumed that any woman leading float trips and backpacks throughout the Southwest must be okay.

Besides, unlike other "participants" with the school, I won't be paying the $835. For oddly assorted reasons I'm invited free. Nor is the Volvo going to be at risk. "Transportation furnished." When I read that, it was "*Alea iacta est.*" Fate's dice practically leapt from my hand. However, the red eddies running alongside just south of the highway aren't those of the Rubicon, but the Colorado.

Anything anywhere. A helter skelter of log cabins—bunkhouse, cookhouse, lean-to, privy, tool shed, another privy—all sagging, aslant, pieced together so long ago by some Utah homesteader that everything has since gone weather-beaten and decrepit. Less so, the main structure, whose second story may seem an afterthought, but which at least sits up straight. At the edges of outbuildings thickets of Gambel oak have encroached here and there, when not fenced off by the miles of upland wheat fields surrounding the place on all sides. Though my information packet on the peregrine falcon trip mentioned a limit of eighteen participants, there isn't a soul to be seen. So this is the Four Corners School of Outdoor Education? Anne was right. I'm crazy.

Also stupid. Before accepting any such invitation, even a dolt would've asked, "Who are these people?" As to actual people, there aren't any. Then from the two-story cabin a pleasant, plausibly serious-looking woman in her thirties comes toward me.

"Hello," she says as we shake hands, "I'm Hildy. I handle the paperwork for Janet. We're really glad you could come." My return smile is rich with misgivings.

Hildy shows me the bunkhouse, a dim affair with nobody in it. Almost no one. Sue Rechen, thirtysomething, with long honey-colored hair, rises on one elbow. Hesitantly she explains that her flight from Maryland has left her jet-lagged and wanting a nap. As Hildy and I step outside she sinks back onto her bunk.

Already it's 4:30. Where's everyone else? For that matter, where is Janet Ross, alleged director of the Four Corners School? Hildy claims others will be arriving in time for the evening meal. We'll eat, then Clayton White, a zoologist from Brigham Young University, will give us an orientation on the peregrine. As for Janet, she's leading a float trip on the San Juan River, but will join us in a couple of days. Meanwhile would I like to meet Rick Ryan, her next-in-command?

The main cabin's interior continues themes established outside. Its

furniture odds and ends look permanently temporary, while the parti-
tions, shelving, stairsteps, and floor plan imply a handyman who made
it all up as he went along. At the open door of the kitchen fridge, a
short, balding, well-muscled man in T-shirt, trunks, and Teva sandals is
busy checking off food items crammed into it. Over a handshake that
feels provisionally hearty Rick's eyes meet mine with that steady look
that male strangers give each other, delving.

We'll be in terrain where character could be important. Or will we?
I'm not so sure. A small voice keeps saying, "The auspices—not good.
Cut your losses. You haven't two weeks to just throw away. Leave now."
As Hildy and Rick go back to their trip preparations I take off on a long
walk, the better to know my own mind.

Whatever the FCS might be or might not, its upland setting is
breathtakingly spacious to someone who forty-eight hours earlier has
been in Switzerland. Though the sky is overcast, its expanse opens high
and wide. Even the dirt road flows with an undulance like that of southeastern Utah's steady breeze. Brown furrows exude shoots of early
wheat, while along the road's shoulders low, silken plumes of cheat
grass nod, as do tiny purple florets of alfalfa. A dove startles from its
nest, flops along on the ground ahead of me, pretending to have a hurt
wing; then having led me far enough astray, as it supposes, flies westward where—thirty miles distant—rise the green summits of the
Abajo Mountains. On my left, ninety miles east, the much taller, snow-
clotted peaks of Colorado's San Juans are still visible. Another fifty
miles south, straight ahead of me and all by itself, a mountain called
the Sleeping Ute says, "You're home. This is your territory"—a wide,
wide West whose "four corners" region feels all the more incomparable
after recent months of being hemmed in amid Europe's throngs and
strictures.

Returning toward the main cabin, I pause at the school's emblematic signboard—a big, colorful wood carving that shows the beneficence of Blue Corn Mother, central to Hopi tradition. Her body curved
like a rainbow, she blesses a large cornstalk with rain. My skepticism
lowers its guard a whit. Anyone who invokes the Blue Corn Mother so
handsomely must lean in the right direction.

Favorable omens continue past the evening meal with the arrival
of a tall, slim, fifty-five-year-old Clayton White, a BYU zoologist who
has brought John Crawley, one of his grad students. John is a husky
sort, taller than White and half his age—yet from Clayton's readiness
in deferring to John's knowledge of raptors it's not only evident that

White is no egoist; it's clear that Crawley has a world of field experience for someone in his late twenties.

With them is Chuck Beebe, an outgoing man ten or twelve years older than Crawley. His amused, likable smile counterpoints the gaping alligator on his T-shirt. He and Crawley razz each other like old buddies, having met last year during a Four Corners School float trip on the San Juan River. Despite Beebe's Naugatuck address listed on my info-sheet, his accent of broadest Clevelandese adds to the comic spin he puts on his joking with Crawley, a born Westerner.

The pert, curvy-legged woman in short shorts and tight blonde curls is Connie Blaine, from Moab, just up the road a piece. The small and spritely Jean Perata, whose legs and "BAY-TO-BREAKERS / 10K" T-shirt imply she too is a runner, lives in San Francisco. Despite the Peter Pan cut of her auburn hair, she holds a responsible job with the U.S. Department of Labor. That fact, along with Beebe's status as an engineer for Sikorsky Aircraft, and Sue's as an employee at the Smithsonian, suggests that the Four Corners School comes to more than its outbuildings.

During the promised orientation my skepticism abates even further. Clayton White has spent thirty years studying the peregrine—in Alaska, South America, Greenland, Russia, you name it. His quick-spoken words come in blurts and flurries. Though he downplays his professional standing, I now realize that he is the "C. White" whose work with the dean of American peregrine specialists, Tom Cade, is so frequently cited by authorities on raptors. To allay any doubts we have about distinguishing peregrines from their falcon cousins, White slips out to his car and returns carrying three stuffed examples. These he hangs from beams of the low, homesteader's ceiling.

Instant relief. Those female and male peregrines, alongside their nearest look-alike in Utah, the prairie falcon, make an immense improvement on pictures in bird books. Burnt umber and tan dominate the peregrine's upper sides, while its underside is blonde as a palomino's mane, with grey-black speckles parallel to the small, compact body and powerful pectorals. Stuffed animals are never beautiful. What's missing here is celerity; or, as one falconer has put it, the peregrine's "almost unbelievable" flying skills.

White then shows two videos which illustrate his remarks about the peregrine's identifiable wingbeat and glide. "It's not quite like needles in a haystack," he adds. "There'll almost always be whitewash on the cliff right below the eyrie. That's what you look for. Raven whitewash won't show the long streaking that goes with falcon eyries. Peregrines are incubating now, so the female will be on the nest. During incubation both birds stay pretty close to the eyrie—which makes this the best time to find them. Females may leave the eggs for a while, depending on weather. Or males may take a turn incubating, but they always return to the eyrie—so it's eyries we'll be looking for. Peregrines are what's called 'philopatric': they reuse eyries. In some cases—Great Britain for instance—there are dozens of nest sites that have been used going way back to the nineteenth century, some even longer. 'Historical' eyries. Once we find an eyrie it's possible to recheck it year to year. That way you get some idea on stability of your breeding population."

Connie Blaine, admittedly not a birder, asks, "Do peregrines mate for life?" White hesitates, touches his moustache, falls silent.

Finally he says, "I don't know."

But if he doesn't, who does? And if nobody knows, what does that say about our world's present knowledge of wild creatures generally?

"It's as if they're more attached to a specific breeding spot than to any one mate. Some pairs return year after year. Take Alaskan peregrines. The male and female may both migrate as far south as Argentina, and yet return to last year's eyrie. If the male shows up first—which he's likely to do—he'll wait there for the female to join him. But let's say his last year's mate doesn't return, you don't know whether she died, or what. Even if both birds have been banded, you might not know. Once the site of an eyrie's been located and recorded, keeping tabs on the breeding population is a whole lot easier. As I mentioned earlier, any breeding pairs will be incubating now, so this is the time for discovering nest sites. That's where we come in, checking on known or suspected eyries and—just maybe—locating new ones."

Jean and Connie aren't sure how we'll be shifting from lookout to lookout once we get to the canyon, which is extensive. Rick Ryan shuffles his clipboard of papers, uncertain, frankly admitting he knows only as much about helicopter support as he can glean from notes Janet has given him. My skepticism stirs again, fluttering. A moth flutters near the stuffed prairie hawk. "Get that moth, will you somebody," asks Clayton. "If it lays in one of my falcons I'm in for no end of trouble." Everyone laughs, Chuck Beebe too, as he claps the dithering thing to a smudge on both palms. Clayton looks around, "Any more questions?"

Our silence isn't disinterest. If my drive from Boulder was fascinating, it was also on the long side. Jean Perata's heavy-lidded smile reminds me she has driven even longer stretches from the West Coast. Chuck's wisecracking has flagged only somewhat, but he has flown from the opposite coast. So has Sue Rechen, and both do look wan. We break up, satisfied if sleepy. Outside we find the night sky has cleared: stars by the thousands. The chance that our helicopter hours could be scrubbed by bad weather now seems lessened.

As the others drift chattering and laughing toward the bunkhouse I dawdle outside, inhaling the scent of alfalfa and sage. That fragrance mixes with the great throw of stars overhead to seem like a homecoming. Their energies sweep through me. I feel ravenously happy. Even the tumbledown style of cabin, I realize now, is perfect, a movie set for some hunks-on-horseback western. However, that doesn't keep me from preferring Utah's night sky to the bunkhouse. Within my eiderdown bag I find myself using details of the Jungfraujoch and the Eiger as a sleep mantra.

While the drive toward Dark Canyon winds us high and higher through reaches of Colorado Plateau gorgeous as any as I've seen, Heather Musclow ignores it almost entirely. She has to. Over a narrow shelf of red dirt and rock that's almost a road, the sudden dips, rises, and switchbacks don't permit much glancing aside. So as Heather tools our beefy State of Utah vehicle with alternate caution and vigor, Jean Perata and I emit exclamations that imply what she's missing. Ahead are more than a half dozen vehicles, all 4×4s, jouncing and lurching enough to churn butter. Since leaving the Four Corners School homestead we've been joined by several Utah wildlife officials and U.S. Forest Service personnel.

Behind us Dave Beatty, the helicopter mechanic, drives the chopper's fuel truck. By now, owing to a sort of Dark Canyon exponential-growth-factor, we're a small convoy. "When it got out where we were going," Clayton says, "quite a few people discovered they had official reasons for coming along."

Climbing, we jolt past cuts in pale Cedar Mesa sandstone. Often the road's shoulder is simply a brink. Rubbled slopes scruffed with juniper and piñon fall away more and more steeply, sometimes a precipice. Youngish, plain-pretty, the delicate Heather shifts gears with the authority of an old hand. Canyon walls a mile opposite show pink strata that deepen to carmine. Just above them lie blade-thin levels of saffron stone, with more cliff-hunks topping those. Elsewhere, two-hundred-foot monoliths and pinnacles of fantastically shaped sandstone rise below us like totems. "I think we'll find birds," Clayton says, meaning falcons. "Plenty of habitat."

Jean Perata, a longtime birder—as are Sue Rechen and Chuck Beebe—asks whether the peregrine will indeed be downlisted from endangered to threatened. Clayton supposes it may. The Peregrine Recovery Team is *the* national group whose recommendation will probably be decisive; it has five members, and White is one of the five. In part, that "endangered" listing is what our convoy's about—to learn how far Utah's peregrine population has, or has not, returned from the edge of disaster. Near Salt Lake, mountains of the Wasatch Front—in which twenty known pairs once nested—soon had none. In the eastern United States, the peregrine population had simply vanished. Across the Atlantic, a similar story. Whereas Sweden once hosted over a thousand breeding pairs, by 1965 only a third that number survived. Ten years later, the known pairs of breeding peregrines in Sweden had dwindled to four. Meanwhile, in Britain the falcon's plight was worse than "regrettable," it was eerie. Species had been wiped out before, but never in recorded history had an animal population crashed so suddenly. Spookier still, its remnants were failing to breed.

Their former omnipresence made that doubly alarming. As a so-called "weed species" which had nested and bred globally, a species whose very name, "peregrine," meant "wanderer," one whose numbers included arctic populations migrating as much as six thousand miles into South America and Africa, *Falco peregrinus* had overcome natural adversities all over the globe. Its sudden crisis, therefore, was surely a portent. Some sort of ecological malaise? But of what kind?

Because no similar crash had ever happened before, ornithologists offered hunches, not answers. Decline of the peregrine's prey-base? Unlikely. Far from specializing, this falcon's known diet includes hundreds—literally hundreds—of avian species. But what of hunters who shoot falcons? And what of nest robbers? Though over the years egg collectors often robbed the same eyrie two or even three times in one season, Britain's peregrines had nonetheless flourished. Then, during World War II when it was feared they would kill messenger pigeons carrying war information, their nests, nestlings, and eggs were destroyed wholesale. As part of that ornithocide, some six hundred peregrines were shot. The fact that this truly resilient creature soon bred replacements for those losses only made its abrupt decline in the early sixties the more baffling.

The answer, of course, is now famous: DDT. Or more accurately, DDE, a decay product of DDT. Other organochlorides, it was soon found, contributed to the poisoning too: dieldrin, heptachlor, PCBs. We had been dosing our ecosphere with them by the thousand ten thousands of tons. So the answer was us.

Overnight the peregrine became a symbol, a celebrity, a virtual media darling. People who couldn't care less about falcons took an interest in aberrations of peregrine courtship ritual; in eggshell thinning, leading to breakage; in refusals to incubate eggs once they were laid; in embryo mortality; in peregrine females eating their own eggs. Sentiment played a role, of course, but the vital factor was enlightened self-interest. Feeding as it did at the top of the same food chain that nourishes us humans, breeding as it normally had all over this planet, susceptible as it was to pollutants, the peregrine had become—suddenly, and on a global scale—the ecological counterpart of a miner's canary. For all but pesticide manufacturers the writing on the wall was clear: "If it's in trouble, we are." By 1970 *Falco peregrinus* was officially recognized as "endangered."

Response was unparalleled. From symbol the peregrine was elevated to talisman. If it could be recovered to anything like its former numbers, our ecological crimes might have some hope of redress, our polluted planet some chance of reprieve. Britain banned DDT, the U.S. soon followed. In our country alone, the volunteer hours and dollars poured into saving the peregrine are unmatched by help given any other wild animal in history.

That it was the only sharp-winged falcon found *everywhere* made it, of course, a natural focus. Like our own species, it had radiated to every continent but Antarctica. Then a shadow cast by us humans threatened it with total eclipse. Our motley little expedition jouncing along over red dirt and rock had been set in motion by a bad conscience.

Gooseberry Guard Station is two cabins sitting clapboarded and white at the edge of an alpine meadow 8,500 feet up. On my U.S. Geological Survey map, a blank spot the size of a fat ladybug had made it simply the absence of forest. Now, as our vehicles ease among the tall aspen trunks circling its clearing, Gooseberry turns out to be the loveliest high-country meadow I've ever seen. Following Rick Ryan in an FCS truck considerably dinged and rock-scarred, we roll to a stop at the main cabin. Despite thirty-three miles of great views, slow winding upward over rough road leaves us glad to move around, helping Rick unload kitchen stuff. The high sun's direct rays are intensely hot, while shaded skin is almost too cool, so activity feels like the best of both worlds.

Tanya Kincaid, a waiflike teenage girl too shy, literally, for more than one or two words at a time, has come along ostensibly to give kitchen help. She hands things down to us: aluminum folding chairs, small coolers, iron pipe threaded as legs for the knockdown tables, pieces of field stove, pots, pans, cases containing enamel plates, cups, and cutlery. John Crawley and Chuck Beebe, whose avuncular affection for Tanya disguises itself as teasing, now climb up to manhandle two huge ice chests nearer the tailgate. From there Jean, short but solid, and Sue Rechen, tall but not robust, help the well-muscled Rick and me stagger away with them, one odd couple at each end. Then the fire-blackened field stoves, the iron kettles, the two big dutch ovens of iron, the nine ammo boxes repainted white for their opposite career as food carriers. The many five-gallon water jugs of red plastic, nearly fifty pounds each. Cases of Pepsi, orange soda, Coke. A six-pack or two of canned beer. A five-liter box of Chablis.

Having been distracted in their grazing, two horses—a chestnut and a sorrel—walk over to check out us newcomers. The sorrel sniffs at Chuck's animal-shirt-of-the-day, which shows a vigorous looking wolverine. Because the cabin's one-rail fence makes it a corral in reverse, the horses halt, nickering at that rail. Leaning against its peeled sapling, they twitch nostrils toward our carton of apples while, naked to the waist, Rick bustles about, putting the kitchen array in order for lunch. Abruptly he stops, cocks an ear. To Linda Seibert, who represents the Bureau of Land Management's interest in wildlife, he says, "Hear it?"

Her loquacity stems its usual flow. She listens, for a moment hears nothing. "Now I do," she says. Faint and far off the sound gathers volume. Low over the aspens a yellow helicopter rushes into view, dips roaring toward our meadow, hovers, settling down. Lush grasses splay furiously, like waves toward the edge of a pond—then go calm again as the rotors come to a standstill.

Our peregrine search calls for flying three-person teams to various lookouts atop the rim of Dark Canyon. Sue Rechen, Clayton White, and I are scheduled to take off right after lunch. Seeing the assemblage—the chopper, the eight 4 × 4s drawn up round the cabin, the field kitchen with fifteen of us lining up for lunch—on a whim I ask Clayton, "How much would an average peregrine weigh?"

"Oh, the male could weigh somewhere around a pound and a half. That's an Aleutian male. Northern peregrines tend to be bigger. Why?"

"Quite an entourage for so small a creature."

Jim Hicks gives us a quick rundown. "I've flown helicopters since 1965 and 95 percent of that flying was safe. This Bell 47 we'll be taking you out in," he says nodding toward the machine at his back, "is one of the most reliable in the business." He shows us the fire-resistant jumpsuits we'll wear, how to lash backpacks and gear in cargo pods, how to chinstrap the helmet, how to unharness from the shoulder and seat straps. Fire runs like a theme through his comment, as to say, "If you crash don't burn."

Our takeoff is deafening. Though my ears are muffed tight by a helmet's radio headset, the roar is considerable. Right, left, up ahead, and straight down, the chopper's plastic nose bubble affords almost total visibility of sun-drenched stone gorgeously disastrous for landing. What's more, the rotors and engine don't give off any comforting drone. Their thrashing, racketing pandemonium makes our craft feel homemade, and with nothing beneath us to set down on, all you could do is smithereen. Prior to takeoff I'd seen Hicks as a sort of good old boy whom high-country sun had incised with sixty years' worth of eye crinkles. All the spires and sandstone fins rushing past two hundred feet below change my thinking. Via helmet intercom I say, "Jim, back on the ground I thought you were just the pilot. I see now you're a *very* brave man."

"But surely a peregrine couldn't catch canyon swallows, could it?" Clayton smiles, "You bet!"

I then invoke my idea of the nimblest bird alive. "You're not going to tell me they also take *swifts*?"

"In the Grand Canyon," Clayton says, "swifts and swallows are pretty much what they feed on, though they'll eat bats too. I've watched a peregrine stoop at swallows as much as four, five, even seven times—and miss. Then on the next dive, wham! he nails one. A swift at full speed can outmaneuver him, but what the peregrine does is dive into a flock of swifts, not necessarily at any particular bird. If he misses he may get one on the pull up."

After scanning sandstone walls till six in the evening, neither his nor Sue's nor my binoculars have picked up even whitewash, much less any sign of live falcons.

Sue trains our spotting scope toward something opposite Deadman Point, at the base of cliffs in Poison Canyon. Sure enough, an Anasazi ruin. A one-room thing of freestone and adobe, with the characteristic keyhole door. On a ledge fifteen feet above it lie building timbers which—given the cliff's overhang—couldn't simply be fallen trees. Though canyons of the Colorado Plateau abound in ancient remnants of the Anasazi, Sue's discovery adds interest to our view of mute spires and cliff lines. Its adobe might easily retain thumbprints from nine hundred years ago. I ask myself whether those Anasazi saw any peregrines. From piñon pines rimming a neighbor canyon we hear a blue jay.

Sue wonders if *she* will ever see a peregrine, much less see one diving on prey. "How fast do they go when they do that?" she asks. "I've heard people say they're the fastest animal alive."

Clayton touches his moustache and grins, "Falling maybe, not flying. A fellow named Orton calculated a maximum speed of around 230 miles an hour—but that would be terminal velocity. It'd take a stoop of five thousand feet straight down! Peregrines don't go in for mile-long dives, but there was a European peregrine actually timed in stooping on pigeons. It used to winter in the tower of a cathedral—Cologne, as I recall. It *lived* on those pigeons, so it could be timed over known distances. Naturally, speeds varied, depending on angle of descent, and depth of the stoop—anywhere from 150 to 200 miles an hour, but those were short stoops, so that probably isn't maximum speed. In level flight the maximum might be 60, 65, even faster, but they can't sustain that for long. Cruising speed is somewhere around forty-five miles an hour, which isn't too much faster than the pigeons they catch."

But Clayton doesn't sell the bird short. "In a really steep dive they can exceed terminal velocity," and here he stands, elbows tucked to his sides—elbows now falcon wings—"because a peregrine will give little pumps like this," he says, grinning, letting the elbows stroke a time or two before tucking back in. "Oh, they can rocket. Deadly!" he says, his blue eyes sparkling enthusiasm as he warms to his subject. "And efficient! You'll see a peregrine dozing on a perch high up on a cliff; you think he's not paying attention to anything out there, then—all of a sudden—it's as if he looks at his watch and says, 'Hey, it's that time again,' and he'll take off. Ten minutes later he's back with a bird. I'd call that efficient, wouldn't you? And any raptor flying too near the eyrie, they'll go after it. Up in Alaska I watched an eagle pass an eyrie. That eagle must've been a mile away, but the male peregrine took off after it whs-s-st!—like a shot. Chased it out of sight."

"On the other hand," Clayton adds, "where prey are plentiful, you might find falcons nesting close to eagles. Apparently it's a question of food supply."

By now the sun is almost touching our western horizon, yet that piñon jay's call is only the second or third I've noticed. "Come to think of it," I ask, "have we seen even so much as a raven?" Sue, diffident and guarded, is also an acute listener. She recalls hearing one—and the nearly ultrasonic calling of swifts. As Clayton dismounts the scope and its tripod, he mentions seeing a couple of "violet-greens," a species of swallow. "Otherwise, this canyon looks pretty sterile," he says, summing up its scant birdlife, "but that's field work—99 percent patience." If his tone isn't exactly glum, "sterile" doesn't promise much for tomorrow. Dark Canyon, Deadman Point, Poison Canyon. Names to make you wonder. Yet Poison Canyon is beautiful too. Over whose cliff walls our binoculars have poured, on and off, much of the later afternoon; in stillness allowing notes of the smallest bird to carry.

Back at our little camp we pitch tents, eat supper, chat. Sundown smears ponderosa pines with red gold. It puts a blush on the cloudlike junipers. Manzanita clumps glisten with it. I'm nowhere so at home as right here, right now, utterly happy.

When asked about her work at the Smithsonian, Sue says, "I classify specimens, really tiny ones." Perhaps it's too specialized for easy explanation. Apparently the specimens are microscopically small, but whether recent or fossil is still unclear when she changes the subject to her saddle horse back in Maryland.

Clayton asks Sue if she's married. "No," she says. "I guess I've come close," but doesn't explain.

Perhaps by way of commenting, Clayton and I, with a frankness that surprises both of us, find ourselves sharing the inevitable problems in raising offspring. Sue isn't one for disclosures. Instead she says something about people "baring their souls." Talk lags after that. In long, contented silences we listen to the canyon's quietude, watching dusk give way to dark. Then a sudden onset of rain laced with hail chases us like startled prairie dogs into our tents.

A half hour before dawn, under the sky's grey-blue, and in damp sand cool under my own footsoles, I find lion tracks. Booted, I follow them to our yesterday's lookout—then back to camp, all round the tents. Clayton agrees, "Had to be after the rain. He—or *she*," glancing toward Sue, "seems to have had us covered." Sue says "Hm-n-n."

For our dawn falcon patrol Clayton suggests we spread out, increasing our chances. With the female peregrines incubating eggs in the eyrie (assuming there is one), and with the male doing her hunting for her, he's likeliest to be on the wing around dawn or sunset—when the insectivorous birds that peregrines prey on are feeding.

No sooner have Sue and I settled down atop the rim than we hear Clayton's yells. Is he hurt? Running toward his hullabaloo I remember the lion tracks, but know that loose rock or snakebite is far likelier. Sue runs too, binoculars in hand.

"A peregrine!" he shouts, "a male . . . headed your way . . . going lickety-split! I think maybe it came from my left, out of that side canyon." Clayton is excited. "You see it, either of you?" Abashed, we shake our heads. "Well," he says, "it's not surprising. They're really hard to spot this way from above. Pure luck I saw that one." His almost boyish enthusiasm is a surprise. Thirty years studying falcons, yet it's as if he'd just seen a peregrine for the first time. That too, I remind myself, is science. You have to give a damn.

On the strength of Clayton's guess that the peregrine flew from the box canyon south of us, I volunteer to hike toward its rim and take a look. Chances are the eyrie, if any, won't be visible from the rim, but who knows. Besides, it's an excuse to poke about, use my legs.

The route twists and turns among piñon pines, manzanita clumps, deadfall, bushes of curl-leaf mahogany. In clusters of ten or a dozen per colony, blossoming claret-cup cacti light up the juniper glooms they seem to harbor among, with a redness less like wine than hot blood. Elk and deer tracks are all over the place—so I'm unsurprised by lion prints a mile and a half from our camp. Nor by the strewn elk ribs picked clean as chalk, marking an old kill. No matter how often I happen on bones scattered like that, pelvic basin pried in two, skull bitten open and emptied, they give me pause. A past that's a presence. Saying, "This is how it is."

Reaching that box canyon rim takes a while. From it I see lots of erosional statuary, more cliff faces, but no telltale whitewash on walls opposite. As I'd guessed, clambering around doesn't give much of a look at cliffs immediately beneath, and to explore further risks missing our helicopter pick up. If Clayton was right about the peregrine having emerged from here, its eyrie could still be somewhere below.

Sue stands pointing, "There it is again!" Clayton scans, soon picks up the bird, raises his binoculars. On the verge of rejoining them I stop in my tracks, can't see anything but blue sky. Then sure enough a falcon! The sight triggers an adrenaline rush. I'm a tenderfoot prospector staring at his first flake of gold.

Winging along just above and level with canyon junipers opposite, the peregrine now veers steeply upward in a fast climb. "Hey-y-y!" I exclaim to no one, "look at him go!" The long, spiraling circles gain altitude quickly, especially when into the wind—a good two thousand feet, and still climbing—but not much higher. There its full wingspan begins a series of wide-gliding and lazy-like ellipses, yet even at that height the underside is visibly blonde. And its wing tips are indeed sharply pointed—unlike the broad, almost square-ended wing tips of buteos and hawks. In its soaring mode, the flared tail should make it easy to tell whether this peregrine's male or female, but I can't. Despite distance its cries are clear, sharp, insistent. Clearly it is calling *to*. Is declaring or announcing—and in repeated cries whose note is shrill, even strident. Their insistence is unmistakable, and seems amplified by canyon walls.

Now Clayton is shouting and pointing. Another peregrine has appeared, climbing toward the gliding falcon, rising on quick wing strokes that carry well above its body and sweep down deeply below it. Clayton calls out to Sue, "We may see a food exchange here!"

Soon both birds are cruising together. As their glide takes them between my binoculars and the morning sun, the trailing edges of their wing feathers go translucent. The second bird's longer tail suggests that it's a female, though of our group only Clayton—and maybe John Crawley—can tell at a glance. Then the other falcon folds its wings and dives—in the high speed "stoop" of the peregrine. At about a fifty-degree angle it plummets some eight hundred feet before "throwing up" into an abrupt pullout nearly grazing canyon wall. Like a stunt pilot it now flips into a roll that begins another steep climb—broken off when the second bird dives to meet it. The two of them continue the air show —rolling, veering, swerving aside from canyon walls in pull-ups that take them out of sight over the far ridge.

Amid tons of canyon stone setting off such wing work, my own body envies their fire. "And they don't even know they can do it!" Yet if this pair is already mated, what I've seen is far from the famous courtship display of the male peregrine, in which his aerobatic mastery of snap rolls, loop-the-loops, and daredevil power dives prove his fitness to the uncommitted female. Instead these flourishes are likelier to be just exercise for an incubating female, who, even when sitting eggs, will take to the air every so often. As for the male, it seems possible that his high-velocity conniptions were both a lingering splurge of courtship energy and sheer joy, radiant and weightless as the daylight.

For all Clayton's experience, maybe he felt so too. While the second falcon climbed fast to join the first, he shouted, "I like it! I like it!"

Insofar as he, Sue, and I were in awe of a creature unable—in any way we understand—to know what it was, our three lives were life admiring itself as "life." High overhead we too went dipping, soaring—suddenly blurting past cliff walls, swerving. Merely to watch its stunt show felt dangerous.

But the show isn't over. Those peregrines reappear, sweeping through the cirrus-wisped, ultraviolet blue of Utah sky, using the earlier elliptical glides that had surprised me. Knowing that sharp-winged falcons are built for speed and agility, I'd supposed they probably couldn't soar really well, but these two ride the air like sailplanes. Backlit by sun, their edges burn. Then one dips past the horizon again and the other pursues. I wait. Once more they come rolling and diving well below the rim of the canyon—and once more veer out of sight. Again I wait. This time nothing.

Sue and Clayton are now doubly eager to know if my reconnaissance turned up anything, but aren't surprised that the rim gives too poor a view. "Somebody ought to pack down *in* the canyon," Clayton says; "check it out from below."

Sue looks at her bright turquoise Swatch. "Chopper's due in thirty minutes."

Because the little Bell 47 is only a three seater, Hicks will fly Sue back to Gooseberry meadow first, then pick up Clayton and me. Even idling, the landed contraption is a dust-kicking ruckus Sue runs toward, crouching, her long blondish hair whipping furiously. Still crouching she fumbles quickly into the one-piece firesuit, while Clayton and I hurriedly lash her gear into a carrier pod. At around $400 per helicopter hour, taking one's own sweet time won't do. Then as a whirlwind mixing bark with pine duff and desert grit blows against my tightly squinting eyelids, I hear the machine lift away on its own uproar.

A picnic table at Gooseberry Guard Station has become an all-purpose, open-air HQ: message center, map room, data bank. Jean Perata and Chuck Beebe sit amid boxes of Corn Flakes and granola, and juice cans left over from breakfast, puzzling out notes from a peregrine sighting elsewhere on the canyon rim. Beside them Linda Seibert pores over topographical maps, conferring with Clayton White on next moves, speaking her intelligent, free-flowing thought with a sort of factual unsmilingness. Perhaps she has long since wearied of being dismissed as merely a fine-figured, good-looking woman holding a job which—in this Mormon state—ought by rights go to a man.

Among peregrines it's the female who is bigger, has dibs on the best perch, decides whether and when copulation will happen, shoves the incubating male off the eggs when she pleases (though he dare not do the same to her), and makes the male bring her food. Owing to her superior size she can more than shove him around; she can also kill him.

However that may be, if Linda's sober tone is poles apart from Heather Musclow's lilting, often mischievous wit, her discourses do abound with insights, practicalities of all sorts. She reminds Clayton that, this being a designated Primitive Area, the helicopter isn't permitted to fly below the rim. How much of a hassle would it be, he wonders, for a team to pack down into the canyon, then hike north toward Deadman Point? She examines her list of people, estimating abilities.

Though Linda is a wildlife person for the Bureau of Land Management, ours is indeed an interagency quest. Bill Bates, of Utah's Wildlife Division, has just pulled in from way up north to join our survey. His easy-going temperament seems ideal for a father of seven—the last two of which, Heather murmurs to me, are newborn twins.

The form onto which Chuck and Jean, inured to bureaucratic ways, are entering data is a Raptor Observation Record Card. If any of our expedition prove lucky enough to locate an eyrie, that data will go on a Raptor Nest/Eyrie Record Card. All this—and more—is specified in a document known as the Utah Peregrine Falcon Survey Protocol, whose procedures are also being field tested by the National Park Service, U.S. Forest Service, U.S. Bureau of Land Management, and the Utah Division of Wildlife Resources. Our eventual data will form part of the Utah Peregrine Falcon Standardized Survey.

As for the Raptor Observation Record Cards, I cringe at the sight of them. Their boxes and check-lists ask me to translate an aerobatic magician into library science; but it's blood given in a good cause, so I do—in respect of the big difference between observing wildlife and just seeing it. What's more, the truly massive human effort behind peregrine recovery hasn't been glamorous. Main ingredients have been patience, footsweat, field miseries. Among many hundreds of others, volunteers like Chuck, Sue, and Jean—birders all—have been willing to spend hard cash and vacation time toward that recovery.

Sounds from our incoming helicopter interrupt Linda. Clayton grimaces, saying, "I hate those whirlybirds. Two months ago up in Alaska that's all I did for ten days, eight hours a day. They've wrecked my hearing for one thing. And don't think you can't get airsick in them. Just whiffing that Jet-A fuel makes me queasy."

Each returning of the bright yellow Bell 47 begins a scramble. No sooner does Jim Hicks come swooping in over Gooseberry's dithers of aspen foliage than people in the outgoing team snap to attention. Tim Toula and Connie Blaine climb from the chopper's bubble, shuck their jumpsuits, then hustle to unlash backpacks and gear from the outboard carriers. As they clear the chopper's idling rotors in the crouching run-walk which Hicks insists on, they're passed by Bill Bates and the copper-haired Jean Perata. Nimble as Peter Pan she quickly lashes her own packs aboard before pulling on and being swamped by Tim's doffed jumpsuit, then helmet, while Bill is doing likewise. Each exchange goes briskly as military drill, with a takeoff roar climaxing all that hustle.

At the picnic table Tim and Connie are accosted from every side: "Where were you guys stationed? How was it out there last night? Did you guys get lightning? Man, did *we* . . . all kinds of it! You see any birds? Heather's team found an eyrie!—just below Steamboat Point. Male or female? Incubating?" Connie mentions whitewash near a spot "that seemed peregrine-ish," but adds a familiar, "You couldn't really tell from the rim." Laughing, she admits that after hours of no falcons the mind can wander: "I'd begun daydreaming when Tim goes, 'There's one!' and I jump, like, 'Oh yeah, we're looking for peregrines.' " As people hear of this or that group's spotting a falcon, excitement rises.

Rick Ryan tells John and me that by bushwhacking off trail we can shortcut a few miles from our descent into Horse Pasture Canyon. Though skeptical I say nothing. Because Rick earns his livelihood leading backpacks, float trips, climbing parties, John Crawley and I defer to him. John is our team's peregrine expert, while I'm certainly no outdoor professional. What's more, Rick has recently led an extended backpack through similar canyon lands; he can't help knowing that what looks okay on a map may be impossible. We spend hot and very strenuous hours finding his shortcut won't go.

Our attempts take us wriggling past scrub oak thick as basketry, sliding down red chutes littered with shale, getting switched at and scratched up by piñon branches. Repeatedly, however, we're balked: "Cliffed out" is Rick's phrase; a pitch of wall too sheer or dangerous to descend. So we tighten pack straps for hauling ourselves and our loads back up the same steepnesses we've just slithered down. Crawley and I should by now be teed off as well as "cliffed out"; however, for all John's bulk and muscularity, his often dour look, he is kind, considerate. I'm hot, sweaty, frustrated, worried about John's skimpy water supply, but am enjoying the flora, the sandstone forms, even the occasional bear scat. Each minor side canyon is its own cloistered and shady remoteness, a world.

Though the shortcut scheme has lost us two hours, Rick proposes yet another try. With firm deference I indicate a traverse we can make, following ledges to a four-story outcrop of russet stone. From there, I argue, angling down toward the floor of Horse Pasture Canyon should be guaranteed. And it is. After hard, thirsty labor we can now begin. As our youngest, biggest, and strongest, John Crawley doesn't in the least mind admitting he's already tired; but with our goal still five miles away in Dark Canyon, getting there by sundown means moving right along.

As indeed we do. From the rim 1,800 feet up, the lush floor of Horse Pasture Canyon had seemed level, thus easy. It's grassy all right, but in big hummocky clumps that make footing tricky. Occasional stretches of trail which, from the rim, might've been packed clay now turn out to be sand. The dried-up stream's few pools are dregs seething with larvae. Stream banks which, up there, were knee-high turn out, as we dip into and across them, eight or more feet overhead.

There's a point at which fatigue narrows the eyes. All three of us near that point well before sunset. The sun goes down, we keep going. Our packs creak, our talk grows monosyllabic. We plod along through sand. We come to and pass a natural bridge Clayton had indicated, but "almost there" is a thought it's best not to think. Then, at last, we are: the box canyon below Deadman, the one Clayton believes *might* contain an eyrie.

The twilight sky is clear. As dusk gives way to nightfall, air chills down. Good. Mosquitoes, if any, can't fly. In a weariness strangely euphoric, I'm too tired for fussing with supper, yet more than content with our day. Rick's a good guy, John's a good guy. Tomorrow we'll see about falcons.

"They'll go for hurt prey," John says. "It's encoded. That's one reason DDT hit peregrines especially. Their diet is almost entirely avian, which meant the birds they ate were loaded with those chemicals—because, what do birds eat? Insects, right? And the insects had been eating DDT along with plants it was sprayed on. Birds were *concentrating* pesticides in their tissues, so you can imagine the levels in falcons eating those birds. Like all predators, peregrines are genetically encoded to pick off weakened prey. They see a jay slowed by chemicals—or maybe they see a dove fluttering on the ground half-paralyzed, and they'll go for it. Old-time falconers trapped them that way, using live pigeons for bait."

John is a complex man, saturnine and ebullient by turns. If the subject is falcons he can be almost loquacious. From our ledge fifty feet or so higher than our camp we can't quite see the floor of the niche he thinks may be an eyrie. Meanwhile, Rick has gone further up the canyon, looking for whitewash. The early light is pristine, delicious. My night's sleep has altered the canyon's feel, has freshened its evergreens. The stream of damp sand whose bed Rick disappeared along begins to look interesting and cool. It'll be hours before the sun's high enough to hit it directly.

"That's the only thing about this cliff," says John, "no whitewash at all." Yet the niche is big, a virtual cave in the cliff wall; birdlime could be thick on its floor, with us none the wiser. Certainly the escarpment is plenty high enough, eight hundred maybe nine hundred feet, and sheer. Classic peregrine habitat.

From the first evening and without wanting to be, John has been our group's star. He is biggest, tallest, youngest except for Tanya, has the most direct experience of wildlife, and is, in Chuck Beebe's vicinity, our most tireless jokester. Up there, not here.

With Rick and me his water pistol side doesn't come into play. I ask how he got interested in raptors. "I started on snakes," he says, ."then when I was twelve I had four ferrets and this other kid had a red tail hawk. I traded him a ferret for it, and I guess that did it. By the time I was sixteen I was taking care of Clayton's birds for him."

The heavy sweater I shivered into at 5 A.M. has grown overwarm. Junipers atop the eastern rim high above us begin to glow at their edges. Soon the sun will hit our ledge. We wait. If there is an eyrie, at this hour its male would be out hunting, while his female waits to be fed. Toward that end his courtship flight would have been an audition, proof to her that he can deliver the goods.

No matter how briefly the smallest bird whips into and out of sight down near the creek bed, John identifies it almost without looking. "Couple of violet-greens," he'll say, or "hermit thrush," or "vireo." On our hike yesterday he never once stopped at a plant but never once passed signs of animal life without pausing: fieldmouse, wolf spider, whipsnake. He'll go twenty minutes without a word, then make a remark so terse and shrewdly relevant that I, daydreamer, am shamed by his alertness.

"You can't tell," he says, "there could be an eyrie right at the back." And I can't tell whether he actually believes that. He looks around at ledges near us. A higher vantage point might allow us to see further back into the niche.

"We'd really have to climb," I say. "In fact, no way, really."

"There could be a female sitting eggs right now, it's deep enough— but you just can't tell."

If only peregrines were nest builders that might help. A falcon sitting a nest of twigs and detritus might be just visible. But peregrines don't build nests. They may take over one ready-made by ravens; more often use none. Instead they scratch out a shallow "scrape" with their talons and lay eggs on bare ground—which is one reason eggshell thinning brought disaster. A peregrine's scrape isn't at all cushy, so eggs need full thickness to survive the jostlings of incubation. Even then, many don't.

John has picked up something in his binoculars. A peregrine—or is it two? "Could be kestrels," he says. To me it's just specks. Then the lead bird's flight, its style of wing beat, begin to look—as Connie might say—"peregrinish." But John's the expert. "Yeah, it's a peregrine all right," says John. "An immature."

Almost more surprising than the falcon, the second bird is a raven —chasing it! They pass in level flight below the east rim, about a hundred feet above canyon floor. Peregrines are legendarily fleet of wing, yet if the raven isn't closing on the falcon neither is it being outdistanced. I'm flabbergasted. Crows chasing hawks I've seen often, but that was always many against one; and hawks aren't half so agile as falcons. "But a peregrine can easily kill a raven, can't it?"

"Sure, they can. In fact they do. You've got to realize, though, an immature is still learning. This one isn't the flier he'll be in another couple of years. Besides, you noticed the gap in his wing—two missing primaries?" John asks—then at once discounts it: "Except, really, it shouldn't make that much difference. Could be there were other ravens involved. When they mob a falcon they can't kill it, but those raven beaks are *big*. They can do damage."

Especially in a young peregrine, a hurt wing means starvation. Though moulted primaries will be replaced, even healthy fledglings have at best only a fifty-fifty chance to reach maturity. Their parents foster survival by bringing live prey to the eyrie, letting the young falcons practice the neck-biting by which falcons—unlike hawks—instinctively kill. Whereas hawks use their talons for killing, peregrines sever the prey-bird's spinal cord or head with their beaks, which are notched with the falcon's characteristic "tomial tooth"—something hawks don't have. But if certain hunting instincts are innate, hunting *well* isn't. So because skills take two or three years to develop, slow learners die.

Obviously our raven-chased peregrine isn't yet ready to mate. A breeding male must be hunter enough to feed not only himself but also his incubating female—a third larger than he. Then when the eggs hatch he must, with some help now from his mate, kill for those hatchlings as well. Twice a day, usually around dawn and sunset, he needs to bring fresh prey either to the eyrie or a cache point, from which his mate will retrieve it. The red of that meat triggers feeding responses of nestlings, and since peregrines specialize in live birds, virtually every calorie must be taken out of the sky. No wonder breeding males lose weight!

It's surprising worse doesn't happen, considering the impact when a falcon strikes prey, often—and literally—knocking birds out of the air. But unless the struck bird is quite small the falcon doesn't "bind" to its prey as do hawks. I've seen a grosbeak come apart in midair, its body falling into a snowbank while tufts of plumage were floating and sifting where the falcon's hurtle had zapped it. Nature is nothing if not an ironist, however, so a peregrine finishing off stunned or wounded prey on the ground may itself be surprised—which is how eagles and great horned owls kill peregrines, floating soundlessly down from behind.

Like human predators, some falcons are mediocre hunters, others superb. Their success rates aren't easy to know accurately, because a falcon that harries prey it doesn't kill may only be practicing. Cornell University biologists believe that one of their fostered, then released, peregrines—whom they nicknamed the Red Baron—might be the all-time champ. His 73 percent success rate in hunts during 1978 may also imply the growing skill of maturation, because his capture ratio for the next year rose to an astonishing 93 percent. No more efficient peregrine is known. That spring of 1979, during a forty-four-day period in May and June, the Red Baron took advantage of the season's numerous migrating land birds to fly sixty-eight sorties without a single miss!

True, he was a tiercel, a male; true too that the smaller size of males enables them to capture more birds than females. But if males are indeed the more agile, females, being a third larger, can kill bigger prey. Thus a female can miss two out of three times and still produce more meat than a male succeeding twice as often. Her greater size has the survival advantage of lessening competition between mates—and the encoded responses in raptors can make them dangerous to each other. It also spreads the pair's hunting over a wider range of prey.

But an immature isn't the male John and I were hoping for. Nor does one come along. "Maybe Rick will have spotted something," I say. John knows I don't really think so. Neither does he. The likeliest cliff for an eyrie is right here, and field work has taught him waiting. Again he says, "You can't really tell. There *could* be an eyrie."

Despite his forty-seven years, Rick Ryan has the muscular definition of a gymnast. He needs it. As we saddle up, I help him on with his pack. Its weight appalls me. I insist on carrying our two-way radio, which is readier to his hand in a pocket on my pack.

Heather is to meet us at the trailhead with a vehicle at 1 P.M. By way of confirming, Rick tries a radio check, though all we've received so far has been static. "This is Rick Ryan to Gooseberry base camp. John, Reg, and I are a mile north of Peavine Canyon, heading up. Do you read me?" More static. Rick repeats, no answer. We've seven miles and 1,800 feet of "up" to go in less than five hours. As for John's suspected eyrie, it'll be reported as a likely spot for observation from the opposite rim.

If our descent was tiring, at least it was *down*, and, given the lowering sun, mostly in shadow. By 8:30 the canyon begins to be torrid with no shade whatever. John is smart, alert, insightful; but his mere two quarts didn't last out even yesterday. Between us Rick and I have about that much left. In this sun a gallon wouldn't go far among three people, but our half gallon will just have to do.

With John on his long legs striding well ahead of us, Rick and I lag a bit, chatting. "I lifeguarded ten years," says Rick, as if his mind too were on water, "and in the Navy before that." His Louisiana softness of speech recalls southern voices I enjoyed in the army. "My major was P.E. and outdoor recreation. That's what my daughter's going into— outdoor recreation. She's eighteen now. In 1976 we bicycled coast to coast across America. She was four years old. For the Bicentennial. She rode in a bike trailer, little helmet and all. It was a large group. We'd camp along the way or sometimes in people's yards who'd invite us. Nebraska, Iowa—people were fantastic. They'd say, 'We think what you-all're doing is great!' My daughter loved it, she'll go on about it to this day. In fact it's probably her biggest memory."

I ask if that bike trip influenced her choice of major. "Most likely it did," Rick says. "She was a counselor at sixteen—youngest one at her camp; they had to waive a rule for her. She's doing that this summer too, a camp in North Carolina. Oh, I've worked for Outward Bound, I've led float trips. When I finish this job I go back to Durango; then later I'll have two float trips yet to take out. This is only my second trip for Janet. I'd like to find something more regular, but, hey, not just anything. It isn't as if I'm a beginner. I have my degree, I have over fifteen years professional experience leading groups, I've published two articles in journals on outdoor education, I can teach different courses. I don't think $32,000 a year is too much to ask."

Where the real verticality sets in we pause under the shade of a box elder. Our radio has been receiving Forest Service transmissions out of Moab—but to equipment crews converging on a big fire in the Manti-la Sal Forest. Still no contact with Gooseberry base camp, nor with the helicopter.

We head upward, Rick's Louisiana accent keeping me in thrall, taking the mind off desert sun, off water we don't have. And off pack weight. After five miles, we've fallen into the terse mode. Our way now is nothing but switchbacks that rise, rise, keep rising, with each pair of legs asking, "When will the up end?" It doesn't. Again, as youngest and strongest John doesn't mind saying, "I can't believe this trail." He says it many times. Words no one says are *hot*, *steep*, *thirsty*. Those are understood.

On at last meeting Janet Ross at Gooseberry, I'm surprised to find that despite her competence in directing dozens of outdoor trips every year, and personally leading many of them, she's shy. Also pleasantly pretty, a brown-haired and tanned woman of thirty-five or so; enterprising, intelligent—though obviously her Four Corners School could scarcely thrive otherwise. The shyness may even work to advantage. Janet's soft-spoken manner has a way of getting things done quietly. That suits the kind of group we are. Best of all, Janet spares us the artificial zest and enthusiasm of a resort's "activities director." She wears well—which may in part explain the presence of repeaters like Chuck and Jean, who did the San Juan River trip with Janet last year.

Her mettle is tested when Jim Hicks radios from the helicopter: rotor trouble. If his mechanic can fix it, Jim can retrieve groups from their outposts. If not, then what? Each team has been set down with food and water for a day. Food they can do without, but water? In desert air dehydration doesn't take *days*.

No sooner has Hicks landed his chopper just across the fence from the horses than Dave Beatty sets to work. A field fix can't be done. "Swivel link bearing," Dave says, holding up a gunked mechanism the size of a fist; "it's shot."

Within minutes Hicks has raised Moab dispatch on his radio. The message is long and complicated, but its effect is that Moab will now try calling one of Hicks's competitors in Montrose, Colorado. A half hour goes by, then we hear the intermittent, metallic burr of Moab's answer: a new swivel link bearing will be flown from Colorado to Monticello, Utah. Hicks turns to me and says, "He bid on this very job. But out here," meaning great distances, "in a business like this, we have to stick together. You have to help the other fellow. He knows I'd do as much for him." Then chuckles at the irony, "All the same I did out-bid him."

Janet pulls up in her well-used truck, hand-signaling to Hicks, "Get in. Now." Monticello and back, down that primitive road, could take six hours. Then Dave needs an hour to do the replacement. By that time sun will be low, with lots of flying needed before teams are retrieved. Landing sites around the rim—twice in my own case anyhow—have been "clearings" barely wide enough for Jim to spot and get into by broad daylight. Worse yet, the two-way radios haven't worked any better for others than for Rick, John, and me. Teams expecting the chopper don't know it's down, may not arrive. So, in a truck whose rear bumper bears a sticker reading THIS VEHICLE EQUIPPED WITH WINNEBAGO-SEEKING MISSILES, off Janet hustles with Jim, raising red dust all the way.

Idyllic. Late afternoon sun begins withdrawing from the grasses of Gooseberry meadow. Under tall, pale trunks whose groves make a random palisade, sun-spattered aspen rustle at the lightest current, their sap-green foliages swiveling, splashing like water. A Forest Service man has taken the sorrel horse off in a trailer; now the chestnut grazes alone to my right, in deep shade. On the cabin porch near my camp chair, lanky Tim Toula practices banjo chords from sheet music. Luckily, he's well past the beginner stage—between "not bad" and "pretty good." Earlier he had surprised me with his matter-of-fact remark that one of his climbing buddies was the first American to solo the Eiger. Though a "seasonal" employee, his own rock-climbing skill enhances his value to Utah's Wildlife Division, whose work on raptors can require banding young falcons while still in the eyrie.

In fact, peregrine recovery owes much to rock climbers like Tim. During years when eggshell thinning put the falcon at greatest risk, thin-shelled eggs were removed from eyries, incubated artificially, and the viable hatchlings returned to their natal cliff.

"People think the parent birds will reject them—human smell and all that," John Crawley tells me. "But it isn't true. They have practically no sense of smell. That's not the problem in fostering. The problem is, . . . well, there are more problems than you can believe, but a big one is imprinting. The newly hatched bird can imprint on humans. People doing that work have to stay hidden. Once the young have imprinted on a human, that's it—they'll never make it in the wild. Guaranteed."

Like the rest of us, Dave Beatty loafs near the cabin. Nothing to do till the part comes. He's a stocky five ten, a square-jawed and roughly handsome man of about Crawley's age.

I ask him, "How much would a thing like this swivel link bearing run—just roughly." The red flannel shirt, jeans, heavy boots, and western-style straw hat belie his job as aviation mechanic.

"I can tell you exactly," Dave says. "The bearing costs maybe twenty-five bucks. But out here in the field, no way can you put in just the bearing. You have to have it already housed. That'll run . . . swivel link bearing with housing I'm talking about . . . it could run $1,000, $1,200, even $1,400."

He pauses, verges on telling me that whoever did the last service on that part hadn't done it properly, but thinks better of it. "I'm still working toward my mechanic's license. It takes a while to get fully accredited. Sure, I'd like to be a pilot someday, but first I want to get accredited. My father's a high ranking pilot for United Air Lines. When I was fourteen we built a stunt plane together. Took us four years. Of course I never flew it, my dad did. It wasn't a kit, we made all the parts ourselves—except the engine, naturally. You know, you could put a landing strip right out in this meadow, easy—nothing to it. Make a pass or two with a bulldozer—in a few years nobody would know it was there. I have weird dreams that I've written up, even sent some out to magazines—but of course they didn't publish any. There was one, though, that got made into a movie. They ripped it off. A lot was changed, which you'd expect, but basically that was my story. Before I do a repair, I read the procedure on that repair four times. Then when I'm doing the work I have the manual right there. I read the procedure step by step, and check off each step as I do it. Jim doesn't like that. Jim Hicks is probably one of the maybe five best helicopter pilots in the country. I've seen him do things . . . you wouldn't believe what he can do. He knows every single part in that machine—a hundred times better than me—so he's always at me to work faster. He says, 'There are things your normal book-procedure calls for. Out in the field you can't always go by the book.' But hey, how much longer do I take? Two minutes? I'm not the fastest. In fact . . . I know I'm not. I don't care what he says, that's the only way I'll do it."

During the lull created by helicopter problems, John plays Westerner to Chuck's Easterner, kidding him about being startled by last night's pack of coyotes. Today Chuck's T-shirt depicts a big-horned sheep. "That was the *weirdest* thing I ever heard in my life." For John's benefit he exaggerates his Cleveland accent. "I couldn't believe it. I could not believe it." More derision from John on the timorousness of Easterners, though we know how Chuck's badly scarred right leg got that way. Because he and I have Asian wars in common, he had earlier shown me where the bullet entered, ploughed the length of his leg, and came out near the groin.

As co-jokesters he and John now revive their game of squirting Tanya Kincaid with water guns, little dime store pistols of red day-glo plastic. Though she retaliates with a squirtgun of her own, she does it as she does everything, shyly, cautiously. At forty-two, Chuck is old enough to be her father. Both sense that. And Tanya hasn't a father. She should have graduated from Monticello High last year, but skipped more days than she went. She owes two hundred hours of community service. Chuck and John know well that this pretty, dark-haired, and slender girl may live with an inwardness no amount of joking will open; they nonetheless draw her into their horseplay, their banter.

"They carried on with those same water pistols last year," Jean sighs, tossing her short auburn hair, "during the river trip. By now, I guess it's a tradition."

Has Janet Ross's own shyness drawn her to Tanya? Among our gathering, this girl of the large brown eyes and tiny, heart-shaped mouth is indeed a sort of protégée in the root sense of "protected." She is cared about, and tactfully; and paid attention to—by people with whom she isn't on trial, people who make no demands. A sort of fostering.

From Linda Seibert, often first to notice things, a cry goes up: "Janet's back!"

With sunset only a few hours off, much depends on Dave Beatty's installing the new swivel link bearing and housing quickly. Heather Musclow hurries across the meadow with him. To read "the procedure" aloud? The chopper's at the other end of the clearing, so it's hard to tell, but that's what it looks like. Meanwhile two fire fighters have arrived, an ebullient young Forest Service seasonal named Joe, and his Navajo colleague. Joe—loquacious, gregarious—is delighted to find his guard station a high-country social event. The Navajo pal seems friendly too, but when I ask his name, Joe answers, "Lawrence"—and that's as close as he comes to speech.

Of Joe I ask, "What're chances you two will be called on to help with the fire?"

He laughs, "Darned good." Lawrence nods. They go round back of the cabin and are soon driving stakes for pitching horseshoes. By this time Rick has the butane grill lit for supper. While helping Tanya prep salad veggies, Janet glances across at the grounded helicopter. When the dutch ovens are warm enough she pours gingerbread batter into one, cornbread mix into the second. Soon the clink of horseshoes adds its note to an already beautiful evening.

Then an even more welcome sound. The helicopter's engine turns over, catches, revs. Dave Beatty has made the one-hour repair in thirty-five minutes. Hicks waggles his Bell 47 just above the meadow, maneuvering in quick swerves left and right, testing. Then roars off over the aspen tops to begin bringing in our peregrine teams.

Days pass, State of Utah visitors drift into and out of our Four Corners School nucleus. To me, our sightings seem few, only twelve so far, and only two new eyries confirmed; yet the professionals don't feel let down. "About what you can expect," says John Crawley. "That's the nature of the work." His remark brings to mind advice given visitors to the Parc Naziunal in Switzerland: "Don't anticipate spectacular displays. Wildlife doesn't put on shows for people."

Dutifully, we have noted map coordinates of probable eyries on the Raptor Nest/Eyrie Record Cards. Owing to human predators, however, and an illegal market in live peregrines—bird of choice among falconers—specific locations of eyries remain confidential. Happily, the maze of Utah's canyon cliffs gives the birds excellent and remote protection. Historically, of course, even a city's high places have too; cathedral towers in olden times, New York's bridges and skyscrapers in ours. These are interesting token existences, but a wild creature's true realm is the wild.

Tonight is our last at Gooseberry. Tomorrow we convoy south to Grand Gulch, but, the helicopter budget now having been spent, without Jim Hicks and his Bell 47, or Dave and the fuel truck. From the ongoing jollity around our field kitchen, I slip away, the better to sit on a log by my tent and let dusk take over the meadow.

Tim Toula's banjo twangs into "Bill Bailey," clear if distant. Then someone's harmonica—surely Rick's. And Sue Rechen's slide whistle. And singers, joining in on the classic golden oldies. Any outing with free-floating males and females might've been, I had supposed, a pretext for "meeting someone." Why not? No law against it. For all our easy gaiety, however, this FCS bunch is no singles bar, nor is surveying falcons amid Utah wilderness a pretext. The values implied are values each person here partly embodies, however differently, and came looking for. Being among like-minded others—and in *such* terrain—makes camaraderie natural as breathing.

Nearer, on my left, animal-shadows that have seeped from the aspened dusk into the meadow turn out to be five or six browsing mule deer—growing barely discernible. They remind me of recent evenings in Switzerland's national park, when red deer, obeying a similar periodicity, had sidled out of conifer forest into a clearing—always at this very time of light. However, any strong hiker could cross that Swiss "wilderness" at its widest point in a long morning, whereas Utah's southernmost wilderness, alone, could hold Switzerland and to spare. At that Swiss clearing the red deer had come down into, I had watched how Belgian, Italian, French, Swiss, and Dutch tourists stood whispering, pointing, photographing, wondering at—and feeling awed by the presence of—what passed, there, for nature untouched. Their hunger for Europe's fauna and habitat now destroyed had spoken worlds.

Yesterday Joe said to me in his ebullient way, gesturing at the aspen-circled meadow, "Why else do you think I'm a fire fighter?—so I can come to places like this."

Amen. In this country where we still have such places to come to.

If our FCS group had been falcons winging straight from Gooseberry to Kane Gulch, we'd have flown about thirty miles. A peregrine could make that in forty minutes, just cruising. Either on the wing or by roundabout roads, however, going from Gooseberry's 8,500 feet to Kane Gulch, 3,000 feet lower, means descent—into desert with rainfall exactly that of Saudi Arabia. So instead of aspen groves, sagebrush. Instead of grasses, sand. And barrel cacti like Mexican revolutionaries.

Because the only usable shade occurs inside a rock's shadow, we set up the kitchen beneath a sandstone overhang. Clayton and John, both balding in front, already nurse sunburnt heads. John's nose is peeling badly; Clayton is grateful I had a spare hat to lend him back at Deadman Point. He returns it now as we shake hands and say "So long." Janet's driving him and Tanya back to the FCS homestead. He's needed for summer teaching at BYU, while Janet must prepare to lead a group of fifty into New Mexico, and Chaco Canyon's wealth of Anasazi villages. I liked both, would have liked more of them, but it sounds too formulaic to say. For Tanya the choice was hard: stay with Chuck, John, Rick, and the rest of us? Or head back with Janet? Having noticed her alone out by the vehicles, not stirring, resting her head against a sidewall of Janet's truck for five, then ten full minutes, I had walked over to ask if she were feeling okay.

Her voice trembled. "I'm trying to decide."

Now off the three go into early afternoon glare, while we wave at a truck equipped with Winnebago-seeking missiles, then at ocher billows whose dust hangs above the Kane Gulch road.

"Has to be," says Connie, looking from my pencil's point on the map and the seven-hundred-foot walls looming on all sides. Just now Grand Gulch's stream is sand with damp patches every three-fourths of a mile; yet over the rain-years and cloudbursting eons, runoff has carved among its cranky meanders two bends so bizarre their map position is easy to find.

"Got to be," says Laura Romin, a Division of Wildlife newcomer. "So where's this eyrie they told us about?" Collins Canyon had begun as arroyo. Then the deeper we walked the higher its walls had risen above us. Soon the light was sky. Collins had led into Grand Gulch. Our glances kept prospecting for whitewash. None. Nor, poring over the richly sunburnt umbers and cougar tans of Grand Gulch's cliffstone, do we see any now. It's nearly 7:00 P.M. Sun is already fading from the highest, west-facing rims, but this isn't a canyon we're yet ready to leave. Not only are walls here higher and more striking than I'd expected; we're disinclined to return to Kane Gulch base camp without seeing at least a transient peregrine.

Certainly there's habitat enough, as Clayton might say. Despite its being the evening feeding hour for peregrines, we see no birdlife to support them. Nor insects to support birds. We're in T-shirts and shorts, yet haven't rubbed on one drop of repellent. Still, Connie chooses a lookout atop a cross-bedded peninsula of sandstone while Laura and I poke among tamarisk fronds looking for access to what the map shows to be an unusual box canyon. It's where the south-flowing stream—*when* there is one—almost does a full loop, curving sharply north, then again carving south, but not quite. More eons are needed. When the last bit of loop is carved through, a half-mile island of stone will center it like the middle of an *o*. But because our foresight is short and human we can't imagine, in this land where it rains next to never, how long that will take.

Could walls of such a curving and narrow box canyon be "peregrinish"? Then too, Grand Gulch is known to contain any number of small Anasazi ruins, scattered relics, rock art unrecorded. Might those walls bear ancient signs pecked into their rock?

Laura, laid-back and skeptical, is disinclined to search further. She joins Connie on her peninsula while I have a look. Even that takes some traversing, clinging. Knowing well that peregrines prefer cliffs affording wide views, with plenty of room for hunting, I think wishfully, "But a tendency isn't a law, is it?" And arrive at nothing, just strangeness—a shut world whose curved walls enclose a vast amphitheater. Its sand floor is clotted with sagebrush and weed so dry that when—wondering about rattlers—I force my way through them they crackle like fire. No petroglyphs. Yet the smooth walls would seem to have invited them—or would the Anasazi have found this shut silence as faintly spooky as I do? On my traverse back out again, however, I come upon not just petroglyphs, but something much rarer: painted ones, the kind called pictographs.

Maybe they find me? Either way, my grope for handholds and footholds brings us eye to eye. Like a family lined up for a snapshot there are white silhouettes of seven human-looking figures painted onto red rock. Six of them are about fifteen inches tall; and on their right, a god, it would seem, or some sort of deity. Though it's as if he's one of the family, he stands much taller, is broader in the shoulders, and wears deer antlers on his head. A deer god? "How could an animal the Anasazi killed and ate be a deity?" A few generations ago this seemed credulity fit only for primitives; and seemed especially so to high-toned Christian people who killed their god every year on Good Friday, then ate him.

As for what these pictographs are, I read them to mean: "We too knew the canyon. When we painted ourselves onto this stone with Deer-God, we were the people. We said to him, 'Stand by us.' "

Our lunchtime line-up for Rick's pasta and tuna salad puts us against sandstone wall, a comic version of the pictograph from yesterday. To avoid sun, many of us stand and eat shoulder to shoulder, the better to hug the narrowing shade of kitchen rock. Yet it isn't even mid-June. August at Kane Gulch must offer considerable Fahrenheits.

John Crawley and Chuck have nonetheless poked around in sagebrush and come back with a toad and some sort of horned lizard. John says to Chuck, "Now here's how you work with a field guide. I don't really know what kind of toad we've got, but I know how to find out." Linda Seibert looks interested. Before long she and John are swapping toad possibilities, inspecting the olive-colored creature in John's left hand while his right hand pages through the book Linda has lent them. She rummages in her pack and pulls out a mimeo supplement on southeastern Utah, to which her many handwritten notes have added details.

Rick Ryan sits apart in the shade of the overhang with a paperback by Edgar Rice Burroughs, who, he tells me in that Louisiana accent, is his favorite author. "He's easy to read, he gets everything moving, he gives you lots of action. He must've written fifty books. I've just come across him recently, but I really like his style."

Sue Rechen shares the shade, bringing her notebook up to date. We're loafing, waiting for the sun to lower a bit before taking off again. Hummingbirds busy themselves at fragrant bush/trees of cliffrose. I pull out a bandanna to clean my sunglasses, and the emerald iridescence of a hummingbird blurts over, hovering at its swatch of red cotton.

Dark Canyon, Poison Canyon, Horse Pasture Canyon, Peavine Canyon, Kane Gulch, Collins Canyon, Grand Gulch—from their names it would appear that our questing after that skymaster the peregrine has been largely subterranean, or at least subhorizonal. For altitude Deadman Point would seem to be the sole high spot. About each place, however, I've told myself the same two things: "I don't want to leave" and "Okay, I'll leave. But someday I'm coming back."

Now, for our final search Linda Seibert and Bill Bates put their heads together over maps where erosions warp and furl, in contour lines like smoke or earth dragons. Finally they choose. Rick, ever busy with stoves, propane, and water supply, will be looking after base camp; John and Chuck have bivouacked at another spot, while the rest of us will see what Bullet Canyon may offer. Into Linda's van I squeeze my daypack and myself, though the van already has more people and gear than it can hold. Bill Bates shows the self-amused good humor I've grown to marvel at, as if he asked nothing better than to ride crumpled in back among gear and spare tire.

Once more the land's flatness belies what's carved out below it. Driving south through midafternoon brilliance, we see the low blue bump of Navajo Mountain straddling the Arizona border a hundred miles ahead. To the west there's the nearer indigo of a table-top butte. And that's it. The green juniper/piñon horizon stretches level toward every other elsewhere. When finally we park I check the area for some terrain feature usable in getting back to the vehicles, but see none. Because our hike from the trailhead involves toting spotter scopes, tripods, radios through dwarf forest for a good forty-five minutes, wind doesn't really hit us till we hit the Bullet Canyon rim.

There it quickly makes the spotting scopes worthless. We can neither keep a scope on its target, nor take our hands off its tripod lest the apparatus be blown down hard on rimrock. In gusts that rake us for hours we fight to keep binoculars trained, but can't do even that except during lulls—which last about two and a half seconds. Linda's trick of steadying binoculars by means of extended thumbs against cheekbones helps a bit. Luckily for eyes and lenses, the wind isn't blowing much grit. Just whiffs, not sandblasts. We soon find, however, that although the radios transmit and receive perfectly, all we can hear from other teams along the rim is a phrase between gusts. Often an entire transmission is blown away. With heads right at the receiver we hear its noise but not what it says. This is a wind hard not to get mad at.

"It'll keep ya cool," says Bill Bates, who seems never to have been mad at anything in his life. But he's right. Otherwise, under sky blown clear, and with us on bare rimrock, we'd bake.

Even standing still, we can't stand still, so we're cautious about getting close to the edge. Though Bullet's walls shelve down, thus don't drop sheer to the bottom, that first shelf would do it. Bird life? So far our team of Linda, Jean Perata, and I have seen three ravens. And a few buttes, purpled by the usual astonishing distances. We have examined ledges, crevices, nicks in rock wall after wall for whitewash not there; have displaced further south to examine different ledges, and have found, admittedly, a number of whitish flecks that *could* signal eyries. Jean calls them our "just maybe's," meaning "maybe just ravens."

Then a sudden peregrine comes winging along right overhead: at once unmistakable and gone. Linda grabs the radio, alerts Sue Rechen and Bill Bates, a mile and a half north. "It's at about seven hundred feet and heading your way in a hurry."

Bill answers, "Okay Linda, gotcha." The minutes add up. Finally he radios. They haven't seen it. We scan with new interest, find nothing. We stretch, wander the rim a little.

We also, as always, keep an eye out for Anasazi ruins on shelves below. Jean finds one, a circular room barely protected by the almost invariable overhang. It sits on a shelf so exposed the adobe holding its masonry in place has blown and rained away. What's left are flat shards of sandstone slumped in loose order, as if for work just beginning. "Like a kiva-kit," Jean says to me. "You know, the kind 'requiring some assembly.' " We decide it's not worth descending to, but later, Linda and I spot a ruin not much below the rim, so we downclimb to the crudest Anasazi dwelling I've ever visited. Its one room is hardly six feet across in either direction, and its ill-matched slabs seem never to have had much adobe between. The chest-high roof of skinny juniper traves is still clotted with red mud. Smoke has blackened the inner walls—and curds of grey fire-ash with bits of embedded charcoal suggest cookery. An outpost perhaps? We'd prefer that this hovel hadn't been any life's sole habitation and warmth; but if it was, we're grateful those lives hadn't been ours. Climbing back to the rim seems a reprieve.

Vaguely we sense that those ruins are related not only to us but also to what we're doing here, and have been doing for days: trying to see the life now passing through us, as it has through those who once lived. Trying to see its permanent ephemerality, so as to be what we are more completely. And, insofar as power in us lies, however insignificantly, wanting to help keep its plenitude as full as possible; not wanting it diminished by so much as one small, aerial brilliance called *Falco peregrinus*.

Up on the rim again we find that Bill and Sue have transferred to our sector. "I'm pretty sure that falcon you guys saw never came as far as where we were," Bill says. "We were ready, we should have seen it." Knowing Sue Rechen's vigilance I tend to agree. Bill has a hunch there may be an eyrie nearby. Wind has slackened enough for Jean to use a scope; with it she shows Bill our few flicks of suspected whitewash. Jean says, "Probably ravens," shrugging. Bill, the party's Wildlife Division expert, isn't so sure. He examines our likeliest cliff face in great and careful detail.

"If you get one in your binoculars," he reminds us, "stay on him and stay on him. Don't take 'em off for a second. Stay on him as long as you can."

More vigilance, broken by stretching. Bill spots the restored ruin our maps call Perfect Kiva. Up through the kiva's entry hole pokes a ladder of peeled saplings. Behind the kiva stands a masonry structure with door and windows. We're tempted to downclimb, explore, but it's pretty far below the rim. Not only would the route be slow going, by now it's 7:45 in the evening. If falcons really do have an eyrie around here, the male could be on the wing for prey.

And is—appearing just as suddenly as the previous one, in fact might well be the same bird, flying level a few hundred feet above the opposite rim with the powerful wing stroke of peregrines. "A male all right," says Bill. Big excitement.

Again I learn the emotional rush that prospectors must feel. Just as lots of not finding makes gold far more than gold, we've invested peregrines with long, sun-bitten, wearying if gorgeous days of ourselves. And with much we're unaware of. This one flies grasping prey in its talons, or something. Or does it? As wind jostles my stance, and sets the falcon's flight dipping and wobbling all around inside my binoculars, I hear the same shrill insistence in its cries that I first heard at Deadman Point—clear then distant, then clear again, depending on wind. Then I lose it.

So does Linda. Jean calls out, "It's heading toward that long east wall! I think there's an eyrie there for sure!" Sue Rechen gets excited, thinks she too sees "for sure" where the falcon has gone—the exact, ledge. A scope is focused there. False alarm. Then the bird reappears fast from our extreme left, where we'd no idea. Again we track its wide, swift curving gyre, hear the insistent cries; and again lose it.

This time it's Bill who thinks it flew to a ledge on that same east-facing wall. Once more the scope is adjusted. "Can't tell. It could be in there right now." Unfortunately the ledge is a shade too distant for the scope to resolve detail sharply. We take turns, each hand barely refining focus, each right eye squinting at a brownish mote on the ledge our peregrine may have flown to. I myself see or imagine I see a falcon's upper outline at the very back of a niche, dipping now and then to beak at something. Low sun, big, red, and level with the western horizon, is fast leaving that wall in ever deeper shadow. Bill takes another turn at the scope while Sue steadies its tripod. "Hard to say for certain," Bill admits, sighting on the same spot, "but I'll tell you what—I think we've got one. An eyrie, right over there on that ledge."

We keep checking the sky. The only birds, a pair of violet-green swallows dipping into the canyon. And a high raven, the underside of its wings rusted by sundown. Before packing up scopes, tripods, radios, we sit a few moments longer on that Cedar Mesa sandstone, watching light's late changes over rimrock. Sue, Linda, and Bill sit dwarfed on a toppled hunk of it nearby, its stone now a reddish umber so intense the hunk seems one boxcar pastel. Bullet Canyon's upper strata are now pure, saturated color. With mortar and pestle, it seems, you could bray it to powdered chroma. But that's the high Southwest. Colored distances like nowhere else I know, unbroken by any made thing. And skies that change you to a person worth being there.

Once again, in the luminous evening, its gold modulations over Utah's green-junipered plateau, and with its desert light falling on faces I had come to like more than I'd ever tell them, I gaze miles out over what many people would call "nothing there." I hear my inner self say, surprised, "This is the most beautiful place in the world."

At exactly 8:15 we start back. With a forty-minute walk to the van, it'll be dark by the time we've returned to Kane Gulch. We brought only light snacks for lunch, so no one's had an evening meal. Then too, the sun, wind, the hours have wearied everyone. Our hushed talk includes stretches of silence; of putting one foot in front of the other, sweating along a jeep track with more uphill than we'd remembered. But we did find what we were looking for.

Counting today, in fact, our group has managed fourteen sightings, located two, possibly three eyries not known before. Each glimpse or discovery had been set in motion by like-minded people decades ago, whose exertions had made their concern ours. In the mid-seventies, peregrine numbers in the United States had ebbed to around three hundred nesting pairs. Ten years later, an effort unparalleled in the history of any wild species had almost quadrupled them. Each moment we scanned for falcons was a product of not only ourselves but of that unique effort. The aim was to say to a winged particle flown toward us out of life's unknowable past, the most generous thing sayable to anyone. In the phrase of St. Augustine, "*volo ut sis.*" Literally, "I want you to be." Want you to be as you are.

Peregrine continuance isn't yet guaranteed. So-called developing nations feel they can't afford nature. They pour on the organochlorides, DDT conspicuous among them. That's why our U.S. ban on such pesticides doesn't fully protect Alaskan peregrines, for example, because annual migrations take them to South America where such chemicals are used freely.

So at best, our days here have been a practical form of hope. We have hoped that the peregrine, as a particle of life's continuous departure for its next perfection, will go on diving and killing, wheeling and stooping and gliding. If so, peregrine males will flash with dazzling verve through their courtship flights. They will mate; their females will incubate eggs, will tear the sweet red breast meat from new-killed prey, and feed it dripping to their young, half of whom won't live to maturity. But unless we crowd away too much peregrine habitat—and that grows likelier every year—these falcons will go on answering all the genetic promptings that make them one of time's miracles, and also the face of nature.

Each of us trudging through the early twilight toward a rather drab State of Utah van will soon granulate into dust fine as the dust of this jeep track. Even when—in this world without end without us—the slightest trace of our having been here is no longer discoverable, our lives will nonetheless have made themselves fully present at that miracle; not thinking it such perhaps, but sensing, however unconsciously, that if it were important, we were important too.

Goodbyes aren't my strong point. No sooner had we unloaded Janet's truck into an FCS shed than I shook hands and drove away. The tumbledown bunkhouse, cookhouse, corral—returned to—now seemed funky and warm. Even the oddments fronting one cabin (a wheelbarrow half rust, a child's sled, the deer antlers, the milk can, the two dinette chairs) were exactly as I'd have them. Under a ponderosa pine near the two-story cabin, the last few of our group—Rick, Sue, John, Jean, Chuck—had stood making the small talk that never really says what it wants to; so my way of dodging the sadness in leaving people I liked was simply to leave almost abruptly.

Too, counting Europe, I'd been on one sort of road or another a long while. It was time to go home—and if I had a dozen lives to live but could live them in only one place, that place would be Colorado.

Past Moab, cruising eastward on I-70, I'm still possessed by the reds and golds of canyon walls, by a precious few glimpses of *Falco peregrinus*, which, like humans—but millions of years earlier—had spread to the world's four corners.

I cross the Utah line. For quite a stretch the highway runs alongside the Colorado River, yet the mind keeps running on where it has been;

and what done, and with whom. It dwells especially on that last evening at Bullet Canyon. All I could want was there: "this light, on this rock, with these people." A hundred miles into Colorado, it still feels I'm driving away from, not toward.

EPILOGUE
What's to Become?

⌣

Clearly the gods, whose nonexistence doesn't stop them meddling in my affairs, had spoken: "Como. Go there." Which I had done.
All because of . . . but no; our least whim proceeds from prior conditions which, looked into, fork and divide more finely, more labyrin-
thinely than a sapling's root system. Ultimately, then, I had gone to
Como because of "because."

But also because of a Roman whose absence my admiration crossed
paths with once, in the literal shadow of Vesuvius; and because of a
sunbathing marmot I had met years earlier high up in Colorado. While
watching breeze tousle the marmot's pelt, I had shuddered to think of
his winters. At twelve thousand feet, in fact, the odds against his survival simply didn't seem fair. Yet there he was, tundra-fattened and
basking. He blinked, he twitched his inquisitive whiskers at my version
of a marmot's alarm signal—whose "Tweet! Tweet!" sounds like a fur-
bearing bird call.

Over the years, my glimpse of that small plump body hugging his
mountain-surrounded slab, sunning so as to save every possible calorie
for his forthcoming hibernation, gradually became emblematic. Often,
thinking of hardihood, I had pictured Pliny-the-Marmot. Occasionally
when my life horizons looked somber, I had remembered him. His
spunky persistence embodied all life on this planet. Its long courage
was his.

So for the trivial reason that Pliny the Elder had been a corpulent
man, and that his *Natural History* contains an amusing squib on marmots, I had somehow associated my brave, dumpling-plump little *Mar-*

mota flaviventris with that most passionately inquisitive of Romans. I had even written a few words about them, choosing to do so simply out of affection for both extraordinary creatures: a marmot and the only ancient author who had ever bothered to mention such animals. Some whimsical synapse caused me to see in that Indian Peaks critter a reincarnation of Pliny. Then, years later, when I visited Lake Como, Pliny's birthplace, and I learned that Villa Serbelloni now stands on the very site where his nephew and adoptive son had once built a villa . . . well, happenstance became too weak a word. Clearly, the gods of coincidence, whether above or under the earth, or lurking deep in the gene pool, were pulling my strings.

It was a warm morning in May. Everything but my hay fever rejoiced, as, from our rooms at the villa, Anne and I descended toward the tiny town below. Our sunlit way took us along garden paths, down the stairlike walks and further paths whose hedges, despite being daily clippered back into formality, effervesced tiny white florets and tinier buds, like bubbles off sparkling wine. Through the great iron gates we continued downward, often steeply, along the cypress-shaded, cobbled passageways of Bellagio.

In the "because" is always an antecedent because. So because—beyond Roman brick-bits and scraps of roof tile excavated on the Villa Serbelloni site—no relics of Pliny the Younger or Pliny the Elder survive, Anne and I were on our way to visit the two of them. Within ten minutes we had caught a southbound lake steamer for Como.

Two hours later, we disembarked at the promenade called "Lungo Lario." From there we inquired our way to Como's cathedral, where many centuries before our arrival the town had done the right thing. Flanking the west portal of the *duomo*, we found both Plinys stiffly carved from clay-colored stone: filial nephew and his uncle, two local lads who had left for the big city, Rome, and made good. What with the erosions of acid rain and birdlime, their time-bitten faces had seen better days; but not very artfully carved to begin with. Nonetheless, they offered a focus for my respects. Both Plinys had been decent men during imperial regimes notably short on decency in high places, though it was to the Elder my silence spoke most.

Not very eloquently, I admit. Pliny hadn't been there or anywhere for ages. Then too, his *Natural History* hasn't much to say about the nature we know. Instead, the fabulous "facts" of its *omnium gatherum* make us gasp at Pliny's credulity. Yet even they imply his keen sense that nature's strangest quirks may defy our powers of belief. The *Natural History* is itself one of those quirks; and is an enduring wonder. So instead of just gazing at Pliny's stiffly chiseled figure, I *might* have thought, "You were rich, you were more than one emperor's favorite, you drove yourself like a dog. You said: 'to assist man is to be a god.' To you and not your bad statue I pay my reverence. You tried to know what this world was."

I wish my thoughts had indeed struck such noble poses. Instead they had daydreamed from where I was standing to an August sky of A.D. 79 and Vesuvius erupting; the hail of firestones, then ashfalls like snow. Then Anne took our picture.

Russet dusk. Waters giving up their brightness—but slower than the darkening mountains all around them. Westward out over Lake Como's twilight, I once more tried imagining "then": Pliny himself standing where I stood, looking across Lake Como and two thousand years. I inhabited his absent-minded stare at the widening, watery V made by prows sailing northward toward Colico, and his pleasure at window-glimmer, when oil lamps were lit in shoreline houses. Peasant huts where even illiterates speak to each other in Latin.

All of which set my mind wandering further—to Pliny in orbit. His global curiosity about our planet must've put him there, as if without my assistance. In a way, that's what his *Natural History* had offered: a planetary view. So in the outer space of the mind's eye, Pliny's round figure hurtled along at many hundreds of stadia per second, through interstellar void, with its blizzards of fire specks. In that near-perfect vacuity, parchment sheets on his writing table lay flat, unruffled. Yet his Roman garb jumped and fluttered as if in a gale, making him seem for all the world like a toga-clad dumpling or most secular angel. Indeed, it was "all the world" that he looked down at.

"Always have," he said to no one, which in that case was me, imagining myself not there.

Whenever he peered over the edge of his table to admire Earth's rondure, its cloud-swirls and tawny continents, or dunked the nib of his quill into an inkwell of carved horn, there would be a pause while he rummaged among his notes. Between each dip and its scribble he consulted them. From a small leather bucket, furled scrolls poked up; his data-base of "authorities," his other eyes.

The writing desk was a mess: vellum strips with notes on them, a welter of papyrus scraps, wax tablets, styluses. Several withered apple

cores. A stuffed vampire bat whose blood he had lately drained for testing the properties of lodestone. A dried whale penis he had long intended to "do something with." A fossilized shark's tooth, which he
thought might be a geode ungerminated. A mandrake root shaped like a
horseman, astride an actual lump of cinnabar. They whizzed right
along, orbiting with him.

To my unspoken "What's he think of those galactic bonfires at his
back?" his tacit answer was scorn. Keeping his gaze on his authorities—
with only momentary glances Earthward—he ignored all star clutter
as if deliberately.

"Of no use to us humans," said Pliny the Elder. "Asiatic musings
and star-chartings? Worthless. Babylonian eyestrain! To claim that we
humans can pace off distances beyond the beyond is ridiculous. Beyond
the beyond is . . . something. Call it 'sacred,' 'eternal,' 'boundless,'
whatever you like. Not a syllable written about it is worth a cracked
drachma. Earth's the thing. Poking and prying into the nature of the
gods, if gods exist—which seems too misty for dwelling on—well, such
'soaring' lifts its devotees merely to the loftier realms of lunacy. If anything is god it's the sun. But Earth for my money."

By way of emphasis, Pliny's hand thumped his writing table,
soundlessly of course. Given the vacuum of outer space his woolen toga
shouldn't, on the other hand, have continued whiffling and flapping
like an aviator's scarf, yet it did. Perhaps his hair would have too, except
his pate was smooth as an ostrich egg. Just as central Africa began
sliding hundreds of miles straight down under his sandals, he squinted
into its rainforest greens, paused, consulted his notes; then, as in life,
surmised the most fantastic details about inner African flora and
fauna. For describing its coastlines he elicited further "facts" from
among his bucket of scrolls.

Fathomless, weightless, the violet-black of outer space will turn
heavy as lake water if a boat, northbound, shimmers past as simply the
red-green of its running lights.

Promenades on the Lake Como shore opposite my balcony had also
doubled themselves in long shivers, as had lights from the half-dozen
hotels of Cadenabbia, and the wet headlights of traffic moving north or
south, toward or away from the dimmer illuminations of Menaggio.
When a metallic note crossed the lake ever so faintly, as some driver
leaned on his horn, the orbital image had dissolved. I woke to myself;
and to Pliny, doornail-dead these two thousand years.

Thirty-seven thousand feet down, curds of apparently stalled cumulus float their shadows on the Atlantic, a bright grey-blue, motionless as hammered lead. Galloping along high over an ocean ought to be exciting. After economy-class hours of it, however, I'm less than enthralled. As pastime I look about me, wondering how much of *even the fittings* in a Boeing 747 would have been within an ancient Roman's experience. Not its ambient engine drone. Not the plastic-clad bulkheads in noncommittal beige. Not the molded plastic doors on overhead compartments. Not the nylon or Naugahyde luggage within them. Not the aisle's acrylic carpet. Not the clay-coated paper of the glossy magazine I've been flipping through. Though Romans had glass, even the pane above my right leg is acrylic.

In short, nothing but us—our bodies, their sneezes, grunts, and facial ways. We ancients, us living antiquities. Two rows ahead of me a baby begins crying again. Its father coos, dandles, intones comforting tones. Sounds going back how far? Ten thousand years? Twenty? Fifty? Hearing them, Pliny might feel nothing had changed after all.

The numbers certainly have: of speed, of people. By A.D. 2100, say the demographers, there'll be a planetary population of 11.3 billions—over double what we are now. In just one hundred years! Maybe it won't be a plague of locusts, but it sounds apocalyptic enough. One mouth. One more. Always room for one more. Odd to think of catastrophe arriving a child at a time.

"In any case," people tell themselves with a shrug, "things as they are will probably last till I'm gone. After that . . ." Which is to love and belong to this Earth only so long as it's ours. On the contrary, I think by now even the dead ought to be worried.

November 29, the warmest on record. The light windbreaker over my cotton shirt is still warm enough long after sundown. Boulder's radio voices are ablaze with bulletins of burnt homes, flaming ponderosa pines, roof shingles starting to smoke. Just north of town in a development called Olde Stage Road ten homes are already char and ash, but the fire isn't yet under control. "Volunteers" are asked to please stay away, motorists to keep off certain roads. It's a forest fire the dry wind has made tricky.

Though anxious for those whose homes are now smoke, this fire—some five line-of-sight miles from my own house—might as well be on the other side of the world. I've never visited Olde Stage Road, know none of the residents, and am not aware of knowing anyone who does.

From the high point on my night stroll, I'll probably be able to see flames or embered ridgelines in the distance. But that's not what I'm after. Since there's nothing I can do about the fire, I'm out just to be out, poking around on a night unseasonably warm, wanting simply to take a walk in the weather.

The mesa slopes, the boulders, the low pine boughs which in winter our deer often huddle under while more snow comes down, the black jut of near crags—all start me thinking, "Who knows, a coyote maybe? Maybe a mountain lion?" But of course I know better. In this dark that has me stumbling at rock and pine roots, or tussocks of grass, any coyote would have to be deaf as a stone not to stay clear of the ruckus my boots make. As for lions, I'd rather see than feel one. Besides, everybody knows mountain cats make a living out of not being glimpsed, whereas my present stealth and night vision couldn't sneak up on so much as a boulder undetected. Still, no one ever leaves the inner adolescent behind. Recently an eighteen-year-old jogger was attacked, killed, and partly eaten by a mountain lion over near Idaho Springs, Colorado; so to this tame nocturnal stroll, my inner kid now feels "lion" lending every shadow a dash of paprika.

Certain Colorado nights, since coming back from Lake Como, I've found myself continuing to confer on Pliny an odd stellification; not quite the kind that promoted various mythic heroes to being star-patterns; Orion the Hunter, for instance. My version is more terrestrial, suiting Pliny's love of our natal soil. Following the smooth, pinprick flare of a satellite across the sky, I occasionally find myself imagining it not as some solar-paneled contraption but as a corpulent Roman, our first globally curious author. My Lake Como stay seems to have imprinted me. Having first "met" him where he died two thousand years earlier, having lived for weeks where he'd been born, and having admired his concern for the planet that circles between Venus and Mars, I seem to have made Pliny a sort of Earth-star.

Tonight, however, pausing near Bear Creek to track one such orbital gleam, I picture him not at his desk with its paraphernalia of scrolls, but lounging in flight as if on a triclinium, his fat face and toga giving off effulgence. Or maybe it's Earth giving back his regard. As proto-environmentalist he was tens of centuries ahead of his time.

Any first glance into Pliny's sole surviving book provokes instant condescension. Even among the learned his magnum opus is known mainly as a curiosity shop, one stocked with all he saw or heard or read.

So his *Natural History*, dipped into, amused me too with its oft-cited, classic credulities: fogs that arrive from the stars, elephants that exact oaths of their keepers, sea-dragons using their heads for sails, a tree so old it was planted by Hercules, people whose mouths and eyes are found in their breasts because they lack craniums; people with the heads of dogs; natives who, to fend off hot sun, lie on their backs under a single huge foot wide as a parasol; effect of coitus in improving weak eyesight; power of a menstruating woman to kill parasites in crops by just walking naked all around the wheat field—and so on, and on. And on every other page.

Yet on pages between, Pliny's better judgment redeems him. Far less credulous, for example, than was Herodotus, he debunks more nonsense than he vouches for; and in setting down a world of actual fact, his *Natural History* gave Europe its first—and for a long time its only—encyclopaedic view of nature, a view that pretty much endured up to the seventeenth century.

Thus our initial smugness on glancing through its voluminous pages must turn to admiration if we remember what Roman science was at that time: nonexistent. In lieu of science Pliny the Elder offers lore, fact, hearsay, legend; but he does offer fact, often drawn from remote outposts of Rome's expanding empire. And his remarkable reverence for this actual and only Earth, his keen interest in nature, his dogged ambition of bringing together a world of knowledge useful to his species were as heroic as his book's closing words were reverential: "Hail, mother of all things, O Nature, and deign to favor me, who—alone among Romans—have made known your admirable and various ways." But it didn't work. When Vesuvius blew, Nature zapped him.

Maybe she was getting even. Early on in his *Natural History* he had offered more qualified praise, which—given his Vesuvian demise—was to prove ironically shrewd: "Though Nature seems to have created everything for the sake of man," he wrote, "her blessings are so often mixed with disasters that it's hard to tell whether she's a loving parent or a cruel stepmother." A searching mind, physical courage—both are gifts of nature. Both were his, and they did him in. As commander of the Roman fleet at Misenum across the bay from the eruption he ordered boats forth in aid of its victims, and set sail with them; out of altruism, duty, curiosity. The naturalist in him craved a nearer view of that mountain which had revealed itself to be a volcano.

Boulders of molten stone lost glassy transparency in midair, ruddying and darkening as they fell. Fiery pumice drizzled down, hot ash gusted and swirled. With thick smoke benighting the daylight sky, Pliny's courage and fascination drew him toward that Vesuvian firefall. Born by water, he would die by fire.

Surely it's not possible to exaggerate what would be his amazement, if Pliny really were to have arrived overhead just after orbiting nighttime Europe. What would he have said, for example, on sighting all those to-him-inexplicable brightnesses where Magna Grecia used to be, Cisalpine Gaul, Rhaetia, Gaul, Narbonensis, Germania, and the rest?

For that matter, what would he say of night Rome? Its 3 million moderns make quite a nocturnal display, as do lights defining the heavy industries in and around Milano, Torino; lights of populous Lausanne and the whole Lake Geneva shore, of staid Berne's sprawling periphery, the peripheries of bustling Stuttgart; the boom cities of the Rhine Valley, of central France; the densely lit cities of the bursting-at-the-seams Netherlands—the thickets of dockside cranes in Rotterdam harbor alone. Then the terrestrial galaxies sprawled or clotted across cheek-by-jowl England, and from there, after orbiting over the Irish Sea, lights of Dublin, its suburbs and outliers. In short, while crossing Europe by satellite Pliny could experience the incandescences given off by copulations now become the needs and ambitions of some 250 million human souls!

Once across the Atlantic, he'd be again looking down on virtually continuous networks of sperm-and-egg sequels, electrified. As he floated westward over our East Coast, then over our rust-belt mills and Motown factories, the Great Lakes region alone ought to bedazzle him; especially so, lacking any idea of their urban squalor. In effect, he'd have been staring down, all that time, at what Roman law—his culture's most durable gift to posterity—had done much to make possible. "O!" he could not help exclaiming; which even in Latin is "O!"

"O!" indeed. But what think? As he finally orbited high over electrified Hong Kong, Taiwan, China, Japan, I think I know: "So *this*," he would realize, "is the future."

To appreciate American breathing room, I sometimes recall shopping in an Italian supermart; at one of the SuperEsse stores in Florence, for example, whose aisles—despite small carts—imitate the narrowness of medieval streets. Because an incautious move might topple display cans of tuna or beans, I soon learned to keep both elbows tucked close to the body. After negotiating cart right-of-way, after enduring the glare of shoppers bumped into while trying to avoid others, my Marx Brothers impulses often wanted to vent themselves, but settled for a mute scream: "Outtahere!" Stifled cries are themselves a congestion.

In the Third World there are millions in China or India for whom "alone" never happens even once in a lifetime. For them those Italian aisles might feel half-deserted.

Italy's density is far from Asiatic, yet its latest body count shows that for every square mile there are 486 Italians. By comparison, a Colorado square mile averages less than 30 persons, with Arizona averaging nearly the same, and Utah even fewer—around 20. New Mexico's 12 seems populous compared to the bare 5 of Wyoming.

Today, even in Switzerland, with an average of over 400 Swiss per square mile, cheek-by-jowl is the only mode possible. Yet that's spacious compared to Germany, where the average passes 500; but Germans, in turn, aren't half so jammed together as persons in England, whose square-mile average comes to well over 900. Placid as we used to imagine them, Hollanders now get on each other's nerves increasingly, because—again, on the average—1,029 of them must try to squeeze lives into every Dutch mile squared. That's scarcely any Utahan's idea of tolerable living.

Come to think of it, Capitol Reef National Park in Utah was where I met a retired couple who were fairly reveling in American space. Less and less fond of what he called "living elbow to elbow in England," they'd even weighed immigrating. "Taking the rough with the smooth," he had said, "you Americans are unbelievably lucky. You can go a thousand miles in any direction exploring your country, and never come to the end of it, never see it all."

"Yes, absolutely incredible!" his wife had said. "We began up in British Columbia."

"Flew there to visit her cousins," he had said, chuckling.

"In Seattle we rented this van. Been touring now for two months—and jolly good roads they are too."

Again her husband interrupted. "As for traffic, there's nobody on them! Even the camp grounds. Compared to Europe? Tell me, how would you fancy your tent ropes tangled in with ropes of the chap next to you?"

Only in topping the crest of Dakota Ridge, with the lights of Boulder six hundred feet below, does it occur to me that I've now a ter-

restrial version of Pliny's satellite view; local, yes, but perhaps planetary as well. The ridge's heights of crumbly and pine-strewn sandstone
invest me with sudden clairvoyance: I can see what's to become. Seeing
that it already has.

Whether out of love or habit, man/woman coupling, begetting, has
lit up all Boulder Valley below me: thousands and thousands of city
lights, lights of smaller towns around Boulder—myriads more than
when, from the overlook of Davidson Mesa, Anne and I first admired a
nocturnal Boulder that still nestled, not sprawled.

In those days Table Mesa Drive was gravel. Across its "street" from
our house, some fifty head of Black Angus cattle grazed and ruminated
on mesa slopes. If a fence were left carelessly open, cattle or horses
might drift into our back yard, whereupon literal cowboys on horseback
might ride past swinging lariats to round up those strays.

Slowly houses took over. Much that was yucca, red rock, and cactus got paved, sewered, sidewalked, and streetlit. Real estate prices
rose, the rancher quit bothering with cattle. When Emil Bonness, one
of the cowboys, ended up working behind the counter in the meat
department of our supermart, his days of herding beef on the hoof
seemed—illogically—to share a fate with those red steaks he laid out
in refrigerated displays.

Now, from this same Dakota Ridge where an ownerless burro or
two used to wander, unconsidered by any but small boys, I'm seeing all
the people not here a generation ago. *Generation* is the word. I scan
their thousands and thousands of lights panoramically, exactly 180 degrees, south to north. To my right stretches the impressive flat dazzle of
metropolitan Denver, thirty-five miles south. Nearer, cresting over
Davidson Mesa five or six miles away, beads of all-but-continuous incandescence slide downhill and into the valley toward Boulder. Their
descent fascinates me—as if the ridgeline were spawning them, endlessly, while their distance makes highway speeds slow as molasses. In
opposite lanes along the same turnpike, red taillights ooze uphill, top
out, disappear.

From little Louisville seven miles off, a slightly less continuous
stream of headlights flows over that rim, along the South Boulder Road
and slowly westward, down into town. North or south, however, house
lights twinkle everywhere, scattered or clustered, as far as the eye can
look. By day, that's as far as Pikes Peak, some one hundred miles south.
Even by night, one sees well beyond Denver; and eastward from Boulder
the finely divided blips of glow called Erie and Brighton; then rowdy,

expansive Longmont; and, to the north, dinky Lyons; and distant, ambitious Fort Collins. Everywhere between those neighbor towns and Boulder, scattered lights shine, some star-blue, some faintly green: houses, street lights, headlights twinkling along county roads. From a distant sheriff's patrol or ambulance come sharp flashes.

The rare totally dark patches aren't "undeveloped" land, or land at all; they're mostly the valley's numerous reservoirs. Incandescences now completely fill Boulder Valley and well beyond. Compared to the Boulder I first knew, a "dry" town of 56,000, with one cloth-napkin restaurant and few eating places of any kind, Boulder has "grown." Its present luminosity betokens 90,000 people in the city alone. Because those outlying scatters of habitation give our town and its environs a population of over 150,000, their nighttime display tells me I can't kid myself any more. The small Great Plains/Front Range town we moved to is now part of the new metropolitan West.

Back then in the early sixties, WATCH US GROW! was a billboarded wish following WELCOME at the entrance to every aspiring village. "Growth." In a nation whose allegiance has always been to a material future, the smaller the town, the more it ached to swallow the grenade of fast expansion. In those years, Boulder Valley by night was mostly blackness unbroken. The mere word *developer* was an optimism. It now seems dire as a cat spitting feathers. With my own eyes I can see the hundred-mile stretch—from suburbs south of Denver to those north of Fort Collins—has turned itself into a virtual strip city, exuding big-time pollution to prove it. When Anne and I had stood on the terrace of "the Sphinx" at 11,334 feet up on the Jungfraujoch, we had clear blue overhead; but level across all Switzerland to the north and below us hung a thick brown cloud. We looked at each other in dismay. "Exactly like Denver's," Anne had said. In my lifetime the U.S. has indeed doubled its population; but in far less than that Boulder has nearly doubled its size. I think of Switzerland, Austria, Germany, whose forests are dying of human-induced pollution. Henceforth, will futures built on "growth" consist of new ruins?

We don't so much speak with the dead as overhear them. What they say now and then may help us see virginally. At Villa Serbelloni, when one or another bit from the *Natural History* strayed into my silence, it hadn't seemed a recollection of print, but a voice. Green sunlight through the high crowns of the beech trees must have made some of those opinions—there, in such a place—inevitable.

"Nature can be benign or malign by turns," Pliny had said rather testily, "but Earth—ah, Earth's a different matter. Nature tosses us into existence, naked and crying on the bare ground. Earth is far from any such indifference. Instead, she receives us at birth, feeds us, nourishes and supports us through all our days. Then at the end, when Nature wants no more to do with us, Earth receives us again, this time into her bosom; and with loving care she covers our bones."

West of my spot on Dakota Ridge red smoke billows up and away, wind-driven, from the fire still roaring in the Olde Stage Road area. A few years ago, an even bigger fire on Sugarloaf Mountain devoured forty-five homes, to say nothing of numerous outbuildings—all in terrain inhabited solely by ponderosa pines when we first came to Colorado. The "nothing there" which developers saw only long enough to bulldoze it aside was home, then, to rain-shadow ecologies not "rugged" at all, but extremely fragile. As in the canyons north of Los Angeles, there's no way to prevent fires amid Boulder's foothills of red rock and ponderosa pines—which I call "firebug trees." They've evolved the habit of dropping copious tinder and pine duff apt for combustion. But in killing off plant competition while leaving the ponderosas pretty much unscathed, such fires serve them well. Will they continue to, as houses make fire more and more common?

That "firebug" adaptation helps explain how quickly this present catastrophe spread. When a resident tossed his burning mattress outside, wind took it from there. Human carelessness started the Sugarloaf fire too. Some Olde Stage Road residents, in fact, had contingency plans based on that earlier blaze, but didn't have time to put them in action. Instead, they had to leap into vehicles and barrel through smoke, hoping. On TV coverage thus far, their common reaction at the speed of wind-driven flames has been a widening of the eyes, and the word *unbelievable*.

Pliny's illogical distinction between nature's fickle disregard and Earth's unfailing concern has often made me smile. Elsewhere in the *Natural History* he credits nature with having created everything, Earth included; yet he says that only Earth deserves the name of mother. It's as if Earth and nature were Homeric deities who variously abet or connive against humans. Like Athene aiding Odysseus while her brother Poseidon tries to drown him, Earth, in Pliny's view, never wavers in her beneficence to our species. Doubtless, however, Pliny wasn't aware of thus mythologizing our planet. Yet while pooh-poohing all talk of the gods—beings too vague and uncertain for words—Pliny rises on tiptoe long enough to call Earth a goddess; ever benign, ever faithful to us. He reminds Romans who gather a certain medicinal herb to fill the hole with grain; "a sort of expiation, as it were, to Earth." Hopi and Navajo gatherers often practice natural pieties of a similar kind.

Certainly there at the villa, of all benign places, in the terrestrial paradise of its gardens, Pliny's voice had quivered with righteous anger. "Not to know Earth, to be ignorant of her blessings toward man—that is one of the evil signs of an ingrate!" To Native Americans for whom "White man" has meant an ax and a gun, it would seem that Pliny was a man speaking their language.

This afternoon everybody in Boulder was breathing smoke. Now, despite an all-day drone of slurry bombers, despite round-the-clock brigades working with shovels and pick-axes, tonight's continuing winds make the fire impossible to contain. The northwesterly sky is red smoke blowing eastward from homes that should never have been built. Boulder's mountain hills are filled with them. Literal inroads have made a webwork of what was once largely unbroken forest. The houses they service are carpentered paradoxes, helping destroy what the occupants moved there to love.

A further irony is that "mountain living" forces its devotees to live in a car. Because jobs, doctors, stores, and services are all down in Boulder, our hills teem with nature lovers whose lives are tied to internal combustion. Yet as "colorful Colorado" adds population 40 percent faster than most states, "mountain living" suburbanizes what used to be forest.

Pliny's view of Earth is still way ahead of our time. For example, in describing gold mining in Spain he tells how miners undercut a hillside to provoke a slide; then laments "the victorious poses" those miners strike "in gazing upon this downfall of nature." Nor is that dismay at all atypical of him. Throughout his *Natural History*, greed raises his hackles. Consistently he repudiates the mindless pillage of Earth, the abuse of her gifts—merely to feed artificial cravings and supply luxuries having nothing to do with what we really need to live. "How many fingers have been worn away, and mountains ransacked," he asks ruefully, "just to bejewel somebody's hand?"

Yet in passage after passage he doesn't so much deplore luxuries as the needless techniques devised for changing the face of Earth. In his imperial Rome such old-fashioned views were hopelessly outmoded. Did he know that? He must have. Nonetheless, in the entire ancient world, no voice with anything like comparable vigor had called on humans to behave more responsibly toward Earth. Much Roman history *is* advice; and the future, our refusal to take it.

But since my stay on Lake Como, that was only partly why Pliny had so often come along on my walks. It wasn't my bemusement at how little he really knew about what we call nature. Instead I was struck by his passionate curiosity. I was struck by his caring to know. If his dogged, eighteen-hour work days produced hundreds and hundreds of pages ludicrously misinformed, the passion that amassed them was itself a wonder of the very world they sought to describe. A world in which the least droplet defines itself by such light as it gathers. And if his reverence for Earth wears a religious tinge, as indeed it does, that may be because the etymological opposite of *religion* is *negligence*, just as the etymological root of *pollution* is *power*.

The question every victim asks of its destroyer is "Why?" The answer varies endlessly yet is always the same, "Because I can." Pollution: a display of power. Negligence: disregard of what's sacred; refusal to connect one thing with another. Or as Pliny would put it, ignoring our debt to what made us.

The quasarlike intensities below me are shopping centers: Crossroads, Table Mesa, Arapahoe Village, Thunderbird Square, Gunbarrel, BaseMar, the Meadows—all doing well, what with new lights winking on nightly in Boulder Valley. Far-flung and glittering, their electric horizons of firefall offer a pyrotechnic delight, as spectacle; but as omen, appalling. Despite lip-service paid everywhere in this waning twentieth century to "nature," pollution continues to be the sign of our power, and negligence our truest religion.

Thus what has brought Pliny again and again into my thought isn't what he got wrong, nor his distance in time. Compared with the temporal depth of the monoliths less than a bow-shot west of me, a paltry two millennia are but an instant holding us both. As to "growth," no ancient thinker supposed there could ever be too many people. Yet we know Pliny didn't see the future through rose-colored hourglasses; and from his views on other subjects, we can infer that even he—staunch Roman—didn't equate bigger with better. "We marvel at the turret-shouldering elephant," he had said, "at the strong-necked bull, at the fell onslaught of the tiger; but Nature's masterworks aren't found in mere bulk. Her surpassing intelligence is best seen in her very smallest of creatures. A gnat is barely the shadow of an animal, but in it she has created perfection. And in the commonest bee, a marvel beyond all comparison."

On the Lake Como promontory where I had spent so many pleasant weeks roaming, certain vestiges date from between 1,200 and 1,000 B.C.: pottery shards of broken burial urns; Iron Age swords all but rusted away; Celtic "ritual stones" in pairs roughly circular as millstones, except that their shapes would've made milling impossible. Moss-clad, granitic, they survive as riddles. The lake's town-names, however, aren't so cryptic. On its west shore, Colonna was dubbed "Kolonos" by ancient Greek settlers. The town now called Dervio began as "Delphi" but drifted from those earlier syllables; and, on the lake's northeastern shore, Corena is the distantly recognizable echo of its original "Corinth." Proto-Greeks and Indo-European races far earlier than they now wander backward in time's museums of blackness. Slow as a tongue taken over by another tongue, that's history for you; and is the Old World, which, in once upon a time almost our own, was the future.

In the American West, on the other hand, we look out across great stretches where nothing we know of has happened. Oh, near Rough Rocks, Arizona, the rouge and blonde sandstone focuses human events remembered by Navajos. And up at the Acoma Pueblo atop its New Mexican mesa, the same. But how many of us are Navajo, Acoman, or Zuñi? For us the West is air-and-water soluble rock steeped mainly in sunlight and wind. Going "way back" in *our* history here we find nothing more ancient than bullet holes. Earlier than those, Western landscapes contain only a word, generic and mistaken, for the sum total of human passage: *Indians*.

That's not a lament but an observation. If our mountains, mesas, washes, forests, and deserts don't resonate with Lake Como's three thousand years of more or less civilized presence, maybe they're filled with something incomparably deeper. Even in Switzerland it's not easy to see the world. Attention drifts instead to what people have made of it; taming, carving, tunneling, paving. The rare "unimproved" patches are left almost by oversight, for selling to tourists as scenery.

Not so, "the middle of nowhere." Our grand Western spaces are, instead, an empty plenitude. On the thoughtful person they confer depths beyond any *thing* humans can ever put there. The middle of nowhere is a power, a moving unity of spirit in us, one that habitation can only break up, never enhance. In such a midst, we've our best chance of sensing what this world is, and ourselves. In such a midst, the silence is pure, austere, and—for me, anyhow—addictive. Its eloquence has often held me spellbound for long intervals where there was nothing to hear but stillness. And inside that, a life listening to itself; becoming a question different from any I'd ever learned how to ask.

It's as if such a stillness contains the universe and all. "And why not?" that wide open quietude seems to say. "Where else could it go?"

If our thought waves, smug in their hindsight, ever *could* reach an atom or so of Pliny's orbiting dust, they would doubtless continue the custom of invoking him dismissively: "O indefatigably erroneous Roman, during the interim since Vesuvian fire quenched your inquiries, we've discovered how wrong about nearly everything you were; have learned, for example, a world more about tonight's starry skies than you dreamed of knowing, or cared to know. And about galaxies well beyond this one."

To the writer who took continuous notes on a terrestrial phenomenon even while sailing toward his last breath, knowledge of vastitudes so remote and useless to humanity wouldn't seem much of a conquest. Pliny's implicit answer, as it happens, is already written, and has been, these two thousand years. "Ah yes, very impressive. Meanwhile Earth, the Earth of my lifelong concern, goes on disappearing under your feet."

"We admit it," I hear myself confessing, abashed and complicit; but I'll be admitting it to the next high-country marmot I meet whose butter-plumpness hints at his having been born on the shores of Lake Como.

Oh, I'd never actually say, "*Ave atque vale*" to him. Yet if there were no other creature than he within earshot, who knows what caprice might come to mind? Maybe someday when I'm decrepit, hobbling along on my last trail toward the ever-youthful nothingness of eternity, my overhearing could—out of the fullness of time—mix what's past with what's actual; could warp a small animal's squeaky, whistlelike calls to a sort of a kinship, a reception. "Come with me," I can imagine him saying, "I know a hole in the Earth, the dear Earth, where nothing can get you."

ABOUT THE AUTHOR

By now a longtime Coloradan, Reg Saner was born in 1931 in a farm town on the Illinois prairie. During military service he was sent to Big Delta, Alaska, for mountaineering and arctic survival training, where he saw his first mountain. After service as an infantry platoon leader in the Twenty-fifth Infantry Division during the Korean War, he studied literature at the University of Illinois and, as a Fulbright Scholar, at the Università degli Studi, Florence, Italy. After honeymooning in Colorado he and his wife, Anne, moved there for good. Among other honors, his previous writings set in the American West have won the Walt Whitman Award, a National Endowment for the Arts fellowship, the Creede Repertory Theatre Award, the State of Colorado Governor's Award, and the *Quarterly Review of Literature* Forty-fifth Anniversary Award.

BOOKS IN THE SERIES

The Four-Cornered Falcon

Designed by Ann Walston

Composed by Brushwood Graphics, Inc.
in Pilgrim with Gill Sans Light display

Printed by R. R. Donnelley & Sons Company
on 50-lb. Cream White Sebago
and bound in ICG Kennett